PROMISES TO KEEP

PROMISES TO KEEP

Daily Devotions for Men Seeking Integrity

NICK HARRISON

HarperSanFrancisco
An Imprint of HarperCollins*Publishers*

All Scripture references are New International Version (NIV) unless otherwise indicated.

Permissions appear on page 444 and constitute a continuation of this copyright page.

HarperCollins Web Site: http://www.harpercollins.com
HarperCollins®, ♛ ®, and HarperSanFrancisco™ are trademarks of HarperCollins Publishers Inc.

FIRST EDITION

ISBN 0–06–063885–0 (pbk.)

96 97 98 99 00 ❖ RRD/H 10 9 8 7 6 5 4 3 2 1

Promises to Keep
is dedicated to
my father, Henry Houston Harrison,
to my future sons-in-law,
and to men seeking integrity everywhere

Contents

Acknowledgments

There are some important people to be thanked for their support in the preparation of *Promises to Keep: Daily Devotions for Men Seeking Integrity*:

Mike and Judy Phillips and Mark and Timmy Schoepke for their generosity in allowing me access to their books.

My wife, Beverly, and my daughters, Rachel, Rebecca, and Bethany for their unfailing patience.

My parents and in-laws for many years of kindness and support.

Patricia Klein, an editor by divine appointment.

My church fellowship group for their love and prayers.

North Coast Writer's Group for their camaraderie and insight over the years.

The many permissions editors who were so efficient and helpful. Many thanks.

Friends old and new, thank you for the many small favors.

Introduction

There is, in most men, the desire to build, to create, to be successful. The farmer wants the best possible farm, the most crops he can raise; the entrepreneur wants to build the best business and earn the most profit possible, the attorney wants to win as many cases as he can, the doctor wants to see his patients cured, the athlete wants to win all his games.

Most men search for, and settle on something meaningful to build or to do with their lives. Some succeed greatly. Some fail miserably. But even among those who accomplish much, if you talk to them for a while you often hear stories of regret. Sure, they made a lot of money, peers admire their feats, but their personal lives may be in shambles; their children hunger for a father, their wives for intimacy, their churches for leadership.

With our focus on outer success, so often we men become spiritually impoverished, without perhaps realizing it. We've done all we know to do, and yet there's a sense of incompletion about it all. Something we can't quite put our finger on. We watch Clint Eastwood portray a fictional character we admire and wonder, Why can't we be more like him? Or John Wayne? Or Denzel Washington?

Many men, at forty, are still trying to grow up (just ask their wives...or ex-wives), trying to decide what kind of man they are supposed to be. They may, without words, be wondering, What makes a man? Simple question—complex answer.

A generation ago, the French author Antoine de Saint-Exupery said, "To be a man is to be responsible." Responsibility, yes, that sounds good—that's part of it. But responsible for what? For whom? How?

Many men who would be responsible seem to have lost their footing. They've lost the idea of what it means to be a man, and their lack of direction causes them to wander farther away from whatever traditional notions of manhood remain, in favor of role models who are "terminators," "Rambos" or other fictional supermen.

Others have stumbled into the destruction of addictions to drugs, drink, sex, or workaholism at the expense of their self-esteem, their careers, and worst of all, their families. Even among men of religious faith, there's a hunger for something deeper, something lost in our era of fast lifestyles, sink-or-swim success, and often impersonal megachurches.

Men are indeed hungry. They want a meaningful faith, they want to be good fathers and husbands, they want solid friendships with other men, they want to excel at their jobs, and finally, they want to know how to simply be good men . . . how to be responsible.

For many men the praise of those we love, for a job well done as father, husband, son, brother, employee, or employer would lift a great weight from us. But to hear those words requires something from us for which we don't feel quite adequate. We grew up in a world where men seem to have gradually lost the talent, privilege, and often the will to exercise the leadership required of us. And our world is the worse for it.

Planet Earth is in desperate need of solid, confident *men* who aren't afraid to lead boldly. Aren't afraid to make a mistake. Men whose leadership inspires others to follow. Men who lead out of love, compassion, and respect for others and who lead because they have a vision of some meaningful place to take those who follow.

Each man, in a real sense, is meant to be that kind of leader: in his home, his church, his community, amongst his peers, in his job. The need is there, but where are the men?

Well, many are responding to the need. Men are waking up to the notion that they have a purpose in life . . . a role to play that no one else can. They have sons and daughters to lead into adulthood, wives to love and cherish, and important work to do.

Evidence of this awakening is seen in such groups as Promise Keepers, where Christian men are encouraged to commit to seven specific promises that require action on their part.

Other men's groups are also rallying members to shake off the lethargy of the past and get about the business of being men. Those who do are finding a new fulfillment. The bad PR about manhood was wrong. Real men *can* be strong—and tender, can be leaders—without tyranny; can be authoritative—without arrogance. Men can have deep friendships with other men. Men can grieve when sad—can even cry and maintain their masculinity.

What God seems to be calling us to is the realization that our best source of manhood is rooted in God, revealed through Jesus Christ. When we abandon our own faulty ideas and the world's deceptive concept of masculinity, and replace it with a total abandonment to be the man God formed us to be, we find a great sense of fulfillment, of coming home. Is it any wonder that the result is a fresh wave of evangelism—inviting others to experience the freedom of manhood in Christ?

In Proverbs 27:17 Solomon wrote, "As iron sharpens iron, so one man sharpens another." The following pages of "iron" from some notable Christian men, past and present, many of whom have "been there," are offered with the hope of sharpening the iron in each reader.

Some of the daily entries are devotional readings, others are brief testimonies; a few are poems or hymns, and there is even a comic strip—all designed to begin each day with a fresh perspective.

The writers are men from varying traditions within the Christian church—from Roman Catholic to Pentecostal. Some of the insight is decidedly practical, some is motivational, and some is relational—but all of it is good food for men hungry for manhood.

A word of caution—all men aren't alike. Not all are sports lovers, not all are married, not all are fathers. If you begin to read a day's entry that doesn't seem to fit your circumstances, read it anyway. I believe each entry carries a truth that, in spirit, is universal among men, and each man reading this book can gain from that truth. In fact, more than likely, many of the readings will be right on target, uncannily so.

Finally, if you're not used to the daily routine of reading a short devotional piece, it might take a few days for the habit to stick. If you keep the book in a prominent place—by the side of the bed, on your desk, in your car, in your briefcase, or some other appropriate place, you'll soon be hooked.

January

JANUARY 1
A Clean Slate

And we know that in all things God works for the good of those who love him, who have been called according to his purpose.

ROMANS 8:28

As a Christian I believe my past is forgiven; I can start over with a clean slate. The mistakes of the past need not hold me back. Neither does my fear of failure—because as a Christian I believe God is in ultimate control of my life. While that doesn't mean I'll always win the championship or never get fired, it means I can believe the promise of Romans 8:28, which says God can bring good out of every experience for those who trust in him. So I don't need to worry about failing.

Without the burden of past mistakes or anxiety about failing in the future, I'm free to concentrate on doing my very best in the present. And I believe that's how a real, personal Christian faith can make it easier for anyone to reach his or her highest potential.

Having said that, I realize a lot of people think the idea of a "personal relationship" with God sounds disturbingly exclusive, somehow presumptive, and more than a little pious. I thought the same thing before I read what the Bible said and decided to become a Christian.

According to the Bible, this idea of having a personal relationship with God isn't at all presumptive. It was God's idea. And it's not at all exclusive. It's available to anyone who accepts God's offer.

As far as sounding pious, or giving the idea that a personal relationship with God makes a person better than everyone else—just the opposite is true. Because the first step in establishing that relationship is admitting you're as much a sinner as the worst human being and you need forgiveness.

In fact, the most important lesson I've learned in my life is that God is so gracious that he accepts me, my failures, my personality quirks, my shortcomings and all.

It's hard for a perfectionist like me, but I have to admit I can never be good enough. No matter how sound my strategy, how much I study, how hard I work—I'll always be a failure when it comes to being perfect. Yet God loves me anyway. And believing that gives me the greatest sense of peace, calm, and security in the world.

Tom Landry, *Tom Landry: An Autobiography*

JANUARY 2

A New Day

But the fruit of the Spirit is love, joy, peace, patience, kindness, goodness, faithfulness, gentleness and self-control. Against such things there is no law.

GALATIANS 5:22–23

It's quiet. It's early. My coffee is hot. The sky is still black. The world is still asleep. The day is coming.

In a few moments the day will arrive. It will roar down the track with the rising of the sun. The stillness of the dawn will be exchanged for the noise of the day. The calm of solitude will be replaced by the pounding pace of the human race. The refuge of the early morning will be invaded by decisions to be made and deadlines to be met.

For the next twelve hours I will be exposed to the day's demands. It is now that I must make a choice. Because of Calvary, I'm free to choose. And so I choose.

I choose love . . .

No occasion justifies hatred; no injustice warrants bitterness. I choose love. Today I will love God and what God loves.

I choose joy . . .

I will invite my God to be the God of circumstances. I will refuse the temptation to be cynical . . . the tool of the lazy thinker. I will refuse to see people as anything less than human beings, created by God. I will refuse to see any problem as anything less than an opportunity to see God.

I choose peace . . .

I will live forgiven. I will forgive so that I may live.

I choose patience . . .

I will overlook the inconveniences of the world. Instead of cursing the one who takes my place, I'll invite him to do so. Rather than complain that the wait is too long, I will thank God for a moment to pray. Instead of clinching my fist at new assignments, I will face them with joy and courage.

I choose kindness . . .

I will be kind to the poor, for they are alone. Kind to the rich, for they are afraid. And kind to the unkind, for such is how God has treated me.

I choose goodness . . .

I will go without a dollar before I take a dishonest one. I will be overlooked before I will boast. I will confess before I will accuse. I choose goodness.

I choose faithfulness . . .

Today I will keep my promises. My debtors will not regret their trust. My associates will not question my word. My wife will not question my love. And my children will never fear that their father will not come home.

I choose gentleness . . .

Nothing is won by force. I choose to be gentle. If I raise my voice may it be only in praise. If I clench my fist, may it be only in prayer. If I make a demand, may it be only of myself.

I choose self-control . . .

I am a spiritual being. After this body is dead, my spirit will soar. I refuse to let what will rot rule the eternal. I choose self-control. I will be drunk only by joy. I will be impassioned only by my faith. I will be influenced only by God. I will be taught only by Christ. I choose self-control.

Love, joy, peace, patience, kindness, goodness, faithfulness, gentleness, and self-control. To these I commit my day. If I succeed, I will give thanks. If I fail, I will seek his grace. And then, when this day is done, I will place my head on my pillow and rest.

Max Lucado, *When God Whispers Your Name*

January 3

Challenge

Then Jesus said to his disciples, "If anyone would come after me, he must deny himself and take up his cross and follow me."

Matthew 16:24

We make an egregious blunder when we try to persuade men that the way to heaven is easy. The statement is false to fact in the first place; and, in the second, there is no responsive chord in human nature which will vibrate to that ignoble note. Hardship has a strange fascination for men. Pizarro knew what he was doing when he traced his line on the sands of Panama, and cried: 'Comrades, on that side of the line are toil, hunger, nakedness, the drenching storm, desertion, and death; on this side ease and pleasure. Choose, every man! For my part, I go to the south.' Garibaldi knew what he was doing when he exclaimed: 'Soldiers, what I offer you is fatigue, danger, struggle, and death; the chill of the cold night in the free air; the intolerable heat beneath the blazing sun; no lodgings, no munitions, no provisions, but forced marches, perilous watch-posts, and the continual struggle with the bayonet against strong batteries. Those who love freedom and their country may follow me.'

Men love to be challenged and taunted and dared. Six thousand men eagerly volunteered to join Captain Scott's expedition to the South Pole. Some holding high and remunerative positions craved to be permitted to swab the decks of the *Terra Nova*. A captain in a crack cavalry regiment, with five clasps on his uniform, a hero of the South African war, counted it an honor to perform the most menial duties at a salary of a shilling a month. Yes, Pizarro and Garibaldi, Peary and Scott knew what they were doing. They were obeying the surest instinct in the genius of leadership; for they were following Him who said: 'If any man will come after Me, let him deny himself, and take up his cross daily, and follow Me; for whosoever shall save his life shall lose it, but whosoever shall lose his life for My sake, the same shall save it.' On the road to Golgotha, the Saviour challenged the daring among men, and the heroes of all the ages have in consequence trooped to His standard.

Frank Boreham, *The Luggage of Life*

JANUARY 4

Masculinity

The glory of young men is their strength,
gray hair the splendor of the old.

PROVERBS 20:29

The feeling of being masculine is one of the most pleasant sensations a man can experience. It makes him feel like a man and thus sets him apart from women. This is one reason men strive so valiantly for high honors—not so much for the honor itself as for the realization of his powers exerted in attaining the goal. If he were given an undeserved honor, he would be denied the feeling of manly accomplishment. It is not being a champion a man glories in so much as the realization of his manly ability required to become one.

All men strive for fulfillment, but few realize just what it is or how it is gained. There is a mistaken idea that it comes as a result of money or acclaim. If these goals do bring fulfillment, it is because a man used his masculine abilities to attain them. Inherited wealth brings nothing in the way of fulfillment, nor does undeserved fame. This is a common reason why so many men of wealth and fame become desperately unhappy and commit suicide. Money and fame can, of course, bring fulfillment, but only as a man is a true man in attaining either. *Real fulfillment is a result of a man's growth as a man and his development of a noble character.*

Aubrey C. Andelin, *Man of Steel and Velvet*

JANUARY 5

Endurance

Do you not know that in a race all the runners run, but only one gets the prize? Run in such a way as to get the prize.

I CORINTHIANS 9:24

If you've ever been in a workout gym during the first week of January you've noticed that the place is packed. Ninety percent of the people there have made New Year's resolutions and they're making good on that.

But come back a week later. You may just have the place to yourself. Each week throughout the month, there are fewer and fewer people in the gym. By

February you no longer have to wait in line to use a machine or get a spot on the bench press. The average New Year's resolution lasts less than a week.

Are you trying to get by as a New Year's Resolution Christian?

We need to be men who aren't that fickle with our commitment to God. The Christian life is not a 100-yard dash, but a marathon. It's the race of the tortoise, not the hare. It takes consistency and resolve to build a life of faith one day at a time.

But it takes something else, too. Gutting it up rarely works. You need stamina *and* the Holy Spirit to help you make real changes. That's the difference between the race of substance and the sporadic sprint.

It's not how you start that's vital, but how you finish. Even many of the Bible characters we admire stumbled. But we have to ask: Did they get back up and continue? Were they seeking God until the end?

Are you?

Ken Ruettgers, *Home Field Advantage*

January 6

Choices

The good man brings good things out of the good stored up in his heart, and the evil man brings evil things out of the evil stored up in him.

Matthew 12:35

It's easy to blame the government, society, family, or events for the way we are today. Most people will agree with you when you begin to complain about the things around you that you think are controlling your life. Whether it's the traffic that made you mad, the government that took your money, the boss that did you wrong, or the spouse that keeps you upset. In reality, you are making choices about all these things. Your involvement with them, and how you deal with them is determined by you. While there are accidents, and situations that we don't choose or want, the fact is, we decide how to deal with them.

When my close friends lost a two-month-old baby to Sudden Infant Death Syndrome, they had to decide how to deal with it. It devastated their lives (and mine) for a time, but then they rose up with faith, and love, and went on to minister to others, and live their destiny in God. The negative thing could not control them and throw them into a life of bitterness, anger, or doubt. It is easy to let the negatives of life become the controlling factors, but we don't have to. We can rise up, take control of our thoughts and feelings, and go on with life. . . . It's not what is around you that controls your future, it's what's in you. In fact, your future is in your heart.

Casey Treat, *Renewing The Mind*

JANUARY 7
Facing Our Fears

I sought the Lord and he answered me;
he delivered me from all my fears.

PSALM 34:4

I used to have a terrible fear of being bitten by a rattlesnake. I'm pretty sure I know where this idea came from: When I was a boy, I was a voracious reader, and I once read a western novel in which there was a scene which stirred up a horrible fear of snakebites that stuck with me well into adulthood. But God never intended for us to be ruled by fear.

One night, while I was attending college by day and driving on the test track at night, the company put me on what we called a "ranch test." The idea was to put the tires to the same kind of use they would undergo on a ranch or farm—a combination of highway driving, dirt roads, and crushed gravel roads. They put me in a pickup, and I would run that truck over a variety of paved and dirt surfaces from 4:00 to 11:00 at night. I'd be driving along, praying in the Spirit, while putting hard miles on those tires.

On one occasion, as I drove and prayed, I saw what appeared to be a huge diamondback rattlesnake lying along the road. Even in the safety of the truck, my flesh began to crawl and I felt a surge of fear. Coming up closer, I saw that the "snake" was really just a big stick. Immense shame washed over me. "God," I prayed, "will I never be free of this fear?" At that instant, I felt an irresistible urge to stop. Let me tell you, one thing you're not supposed to do out there at night is stop. In fact, there was a specific company policy forbidding it. I wasn't on the regular test track, where another driver would come along shortly. I was all alone out on the ranch track, right in the middle of snake country, and no one else would be out that way till morning. But I just had this overpowering urge to stop, so I stopped. Then I had an urge to open the door, so I opened the door.

I'm not saying God said, "Get out of the truck, Ben," but I felt sure I knew where this compulsion came from. So I gingerly stepped out of the pickup, and—horror of horrors!—I felt an urge to go walking through this pasture in the dark, praying in the Spirit. I thought, "Whoa! This can't be real!" I walked out a little ways, praying and trembling and wondering how many snakes might be surging toward me through the darkness. I had this impression that I was going to run right upon one of those big Texas diamondbacks, but I kept right on walking and praying the more earnestly in the Spirit.

About that time, I felt something come over me, like the blanket of God's presence settling over me. Up to that moment, I had been stepping very carefully, but suddenly I no longer felt a need to be careful. I just began tromping around, praying and praising Jesus! I had a sense that if the snakes were out there, they were all trying like mad to get out of my way! And not only did I *not* step on any snakes, I also didn't stumble over any of the cactus, catclaws, or mesquite bushes that were all around me! (For the record, I don't recommend that anyone else do such a thing!)

Now, I can't prove that there were snakes out there in the darkness, scrambling to get out of my way. All I can prove is that my irrational fear of snakes completely fell away that night—I have no more terror of snakes, just a healthy respect. . . .

I believe that God often has to bring us to the thing we are afraid of and make us face it. Once we face it, we can move beyond it. But if we never face it, we'll always have to come back to some variation of the thing we fear until we get over it. God is saying to us, "I want to move you beyond your fears. You are one of My own children, and you have no need to fear. I plan to put you in charge of something *big*, and I can't put you in charge of anything if you don't know how to be in charge, if you lack confidence in Me and in your own abilities and decisionability, which I have given you."

Ben Kinchlow, *You Don't Have To If You Don't Want To*

January 8

Restoration

He will turn the hearts of the fathers to their children, and the hearts of the children to their fathers . . .

MALACHI 4:6

It was a cold, rainy night. My son Gordon, now thirty-eight years old but then twenty-one, finally came home around 1:00 A.M. after a long night of smoking marijuana with his friends. I was livid, embarrassed, distraught, and afraid. How could this young man whom we loved so much do this to his mother and me? It wasn't fair; it wasn't right. It was happening to other parents, but who would have ever thought it would have reared its ugly head in the Engstrom family.

We couldn't understand why. But this particular evening I held my peace, even though I had a mind to give Gordon a tongue lashing he would never forget. I listened to him as he shouted that most Christians were phonies, the church was filled with hypocrites, and there were at least a hundred ways to God. On and on he went.

The more I listened, the more something began to happen inside me. After a while, I no longer saw a son whose head was clouded from the effects of pot. Instead, I began to hear him. Even though I didn't—and don't—approve of anyone's ingesting drugs for recreational purposes, I knew that much of what Gordon had to say was true. There is a tremendous absence of love for each other within the body of Christ. Too often our lifestyles do bear little resemblance to that of the Man from Galilee. And yes, Christians are not perfect, and no, they don't all know how to be friends.

I can remember a hot tear falling on my cheek, then another and another as Gordon spoke. I knew in my heart of hearts he was also talking about me. I only tell you this story to say this. Although that . . . evening . . . was difficult, humiliating, and upsetting, I think it may have been the first night I really listened to Gordon. In a fresh, new way, I was establishing a real relationship with my son. It was something that changed my life—our lives. It was the beginning of what has now become a beautiful friendship.

Ted Engstrom, The Fine Art of Friendship

Tearing Down Strongholds

Asa did what was good and right in the eyes of the LORD his God. He removed the foreign altars and the high places, smashed the sacred stones and cut down the Asherah poles.

II CHRONICLES 14:2-3

Physical habits find their root in mental traits. How a man thinks, what his secret thought patterns may be, is basic to behavior. Remember, actions follow beliefs and emotions follow actions.

Change a mind, change a habit, change a life.

When Israel entered the Promised Land the people were told to destroy the idols and images of the nations that occupied the land so that idolatry would not become a snare to them. Their leaders led them in tearing down the great idols in the cities, but winked at the "high places" of the land and allowed the people to worship at them. The "high places" represented places they retreated to in secrecy to worship false gods. Eventually the high places led to the official reinstitution of idolatry.

The "high places" in men's minds are those secret thoughts: strongholds of nostalgia, sentiment, and fantasy into which men can retreat on occasion to satisfy their natural desire. Creative mental habit patterns are constructive, but indulging in compulsions and obsessions is destructive. Fantasizing in lust through pornography seems at first to be a nonhazardous occupation—merely going up to some "high place" for a few moments of recreational worship to an image created in the mind.

God's "scorched earth policy" regarding idolatry is to tear down idols, "high places" and all.

Sons who are unwilling to forgive their fathers their sins, who hold grudges against them, actually find pleasure in thinking of ways to hurt their dads. "High place" imaginations that worship the idols of hatred and vengeance hold sway over such worshipers.

Such habits of the mind are practices that should not be tolerated in any man's life. They can lead to despicable actions.

Habitually washing the mind with the water of the Word of God, practicing positive prayers, repetitively quoting Scripture, methodically and systematically reading the Bible, routinely worshiping, all develop godly traits, build character, and give quality to life.

We are creatures of habit. *Habits can be developed by default or determination.* It has been my privilege in the past to work with some great men, but perhaps the greatest of all I had known (who, because of humility, won't permit me to use his name) arrived at his stature as a world leader by choosing to read at least one great book every week of his life. Over the last thirty years he has read more than two thousand of the greatest books ever written. And people wonder why he is where he is? Books, not dogs, are a man's best friend.

Ed Cole, Real Accomplishments

JANUARY 10

Constraint

For Christ's love [constrains] us, because we are convinced that one died for all . . .

II CORINTHIANS 5:14

The center of Christian discipline is this: "The love of Christ constrains me," or "narrows me." The difference between a swamp and a river is that a river has banks, and a swamp has none—it spreads over everything. Civilizations have organized themselves around rivers, not swamps. Some people are rivers: they know where they want to go, and they confine themselves to the banks that lead to that goal. But some people are swamps: they spread over everything; their minds are so open they cannot hold a conviction; they are everything and nothing. They are not only Mr. Facing-Both-Ways, but they are Mr. Facing-Many-Ways; and they wring their own necks in the process. Paul could say: "This one thing I do." They can say, "These forty things I dabble in." Paul left a mark; they leave a blur.

So I decided, since I belonged to Christ, I would let the love of Christ constrain me. I would do everything for the love of Christ, if the love of Christ would constrain me, narrow me. A Hindu said one day in a public meeting: "Stanley Jones is so broad a liberal." I replied: "My brother, I am perhaps the narrowest man you have ever seen. I am a man of one book, one Person, one message, and one intention—to give that message." In marginal things I can afford to be liberal; in central things I'm narrow. A man happily married can afford to treat all women with respect, since he treats one woman with devotion.

But if this discipline of being constrained by the love of Christ seems mystical and vague, I must hasten to say that this love of Christ constraining one precipitates itself into definite habits that fit in with that constraining. Jesus did three things by habit: "He stood up to read as his custom was"—he read the Word of God by habit; "he went into the mountain to pray as his custom was"—he prayed by habit; "he taught them again as he was wont"—as his custom was. He passed on to others, he shared what he had, what he had gained through the Scriptures and prayer. Long before I had discovered these three things in the Scriptures, I saw this instinctively (or was I led by the Spirit, or both?): the deep ingrained necessity of these three simple habits. So I fixed them deep into habit; they became a part of me.

E. Stanley Jones, *A Song of Ascents*

JANUARY 11
Staying in the Pocket
I am the Alpha and the Omega, the First and the Last,
the Beginning and the End.

REVELATION 22:13

What we men need to see is that winning and losing are not all that important in the end. The crucial issue is who we are, what we are, and what we were called to do on this earth. Is a missionary who has worked for decades in a hard-scrabble desert with one or two converts a loser? Is he a success or failure? It depends on who's keeping score.

That's why it's vital not to react too quickly to circumstances in life, to have the patience to look at a tough circumstance long enough to see how it is going to affect us in God's long-range plan for our lives.

[Consider this sports analogy:] It's hard for a pro quarterback to stay in the pocket—like all the great coaches want their field leaders to do—when the blocking has broken down and a 280-pound bruiser is charging right at him. The occasional young, athletic quarterback can scramble, but the majority of your Hall of Famers hang in there and take it. They don't panic; they stay in the pocket.

That example has been helpful to me over the years. There have been times when I have done what I felt God told me to do, and yet life came charging at me in a 280-pound package, ready to cream me. I wanted to scramble for the sidelines. When I stayed in the pocket and kept doing what I was supposed to be doing, the day eventually came when I saw the whys and wherefores. And even if I haven't seen them yet, I know I will someday. Every time we think we come to the end of something, we may be at the beginning of something else without knowing it. That's why Jesus talks in terms of comparing Himself to the Alpha and Omega, the beginning and the end. What did He mean? He meant both. We don't know the difference. What we think is the end may be the beginning, and vice versa.

Staying in the pocket characterizes any man who lasts in spite of the uncertainties of life. Not knowing whether that half-minute play will result in success or failure should make us want to get the pass off, take the hit, and see what God has in mind for the game as a whole.

If our identity is wrapped up in winning and losing, we're going to be up and down many times in our lives. When we are in one of those slumps, we are the most vulnerable doing something we'll regret.

God is looking for men He can trust, men who have real integrity, men who will prioritize their lives in such a way that loving "the Lord your God with all your heart" is number one and that loving their wives, children and neighbors is next.

A man can't buy a reputation like that.

Bill Gaither, I Almost Missed the Sunset

JANUARY 12
Resolutions

In your unfailing love, silence my enemies;
destroy all my foes,
for I am your servant.

PSALM 143:12

[Editor's note: In 1722, on this day, a nineteen-year-old Jonathan Edwards began to formulate some of his life's goals in the form of resolutions. He would add to this list throughout his life, culminating in a total of 70 resolutions.]

Being sensible that I am unable to do any thing without God's help, I do humbly intreat Him by His grace to enable me to keep these resolutions, so far as they are agreeable to His will, for Christ's sake:

Resolved, That I will do whatsoever I think to be most to God's glory, and my own good, profit and pleasure, in the whole of my duration.

Resolved, To do whatever I think to be my duty, and most for the good and advantage of mankind in general. Resolved to do this, whatever difficulties I meet with, how many and how great soever.

Resolved, Never to lose one moment of time, but improve it the most profitable way I possibly can.

Resolved, Never to do anything, which I should be afraid to do, if it were the last hour of my life.

Resolved, To be endeavoring to find out fit objects of charity and liberality.

Resolved, Never to do anything out of revenge.

Resolved, To maintain the strictest temperance in eating and drinking.

Resolved, Never to do any thing, which if I should see in another, I should count a just occasion to despise him for, or to think any way the more meanly of him.

Resolved, To study the Scriptures so steadily, constantly and frequently, as that I may find, and plainly perceive myself to grow in the knowledge of the same.

Resolved, To strive to my utmost every week to be brought higher in religion and to a higher exercise of grace, that I was the week before.

Resolved, To ask myself at the end of every day, week, month and year, wherein I could possibly in any respect have done better.

Resolved, Frequently to renew the dedication of myself to God, which was made at my baptism, which I solemnly renewed, when I was received into the communion of the church; and which I have solemnly re-made this twelfth day of January, 1722–3.

Resolved, Never hence-forward, till I die, to act as if I were any way my own, but entirely and altogether God's.

Resolved, I will act so as I think I shall judge would have been best, and most prudent when I come into the future world.

Resolved, Never to give over, nor in the least to slacken my fight with my corruptions, however unsuccessful I may be.

Resolved, After afflictions, to inquire, what I am the better for them, what good I have got by them, and what I might have got by them.

Jonathan Edwards

JANUARY 13

Father and Mother, Working Together

Two are better than one,
because they have a good return for their work.

ECCLESIASTES 4:9

The more we reexamine our male and female roles in Western society and the more we question the old stereotypes, the more we have to face the necessity for a new order. Some couples engage in writing marriage contracts, in which they spell out precisely who shall pay for what and who shall be responsible for the less exciting parts of running a household. It's all there in black and white. The contracts are rewritten from time to time as needs and feelings change.

Such an approach is probably an improvement over the old silent assumptions—but I think we Christians can do even better. We can, if we really want to, create a miniature of God's kingdom of love right here and now in our homes. Instead of worrying about the protection of egos, instead of searching for the perfectly just and equitable division of labor, instead of safeguarding against infringement of rights—we can surrender our rights and our lives to each other. This results in a *flow* of service unhindered by union rules; both husband and wife jump in and do whatever needs to be done at the moment. If a child's nose needs to be wiped or a flower patch needs to be weeded, either spouse responds without reference to a contracted list of duties.

There are times—not as many as I would like—when I sense Grace and myself flowing as a work team in an effective and strangely rewarding way. Walking in from an evening church service with three cranky children who need to get to bed, we both sort of spring into action. There's almost no conversation between us; we know the fifty-nine things that need to be done, and in what order, and we go at it. About twenty minutes later, when all three are down and the lights have been turned off, we meet each other in the hall, sigh, and usually say something inane like, "Hello—how are you?" Our work is done—notice, *our* work—and now we're ready to enjoy some adult time together.

I don't mean to imply that all things can be handled by instinct. Some parts of household life are complicated enough—menu planning, for example—that an administrator is needed. Somebody has to accept it as a responsibility and follow through more or less by himself or herself. But there are probably not as many of these as we think. The sensitive husband and wife can in most areas develop a synergistic approach that lightens the load and deepens the love of both.

As Ambrose Bierce, an American journalist of three generations ago, said, "Marriage is a community consisting of a master, a mistress, and two slaves, making in all, two.

Dean Merrill, *The Husband Book*

JANUARY 14
Change

Finally, be strong in the Lord and in his mighty power.

EPHESIANS 6:10

A ten-year-old boy went to the theater one Saturday afternoon to watch a movie about space aliens. The aliens were slaughtered by earthlings, and this upset the boy terribly. He decided to see the movie again the same day. In fact, he returned ten more times during the following week. Eventually the ticket-taker stopped the boy and said, "Son, I've seen you at this movie about ten times. Don't you think that's enough?"

The young fellow replied sincerely, "Sir, every time I see this movie the aliens are slaughtered at the end and I don't like it. I figure that if I just keep coming, one of these times the ending will be different. That will make me happy!"

I have heard many men say, "I have tried it all. Nothing will change!" Yet when I hear their stories, I discover they keep trying to change others (and a little of themselves) using the same old dysfunctional styles and systems.

The first step toward change that works is to admit *this movie will not change, but I can change.* Then get serious, saying, "Whatever is wrong with me is not her fault, the kids' fault, or the boss's fault. Sure, they have problems too, but I cannot control them or fix them."

The next step toward change is to go to a different movie. You can try a whole new way. So, once you have set your resolve and formulated your plan, do it! Don't expect magic; expect change. Change takes time and needs to be rooted. Yet every bit of change is significant. These two steps can provide significant change.

Some men reach a third level of change. This occurs when a man says, "I can actually write the script and direct the movie! That is, I can create a healthier life for myself which will impact others for good too!" Then, control, in the service of commitment, becomes a healthy tool for good. We experience true self-control in the service of God and others.

I pray for all men seeking personal peace, including you.

Dick Brian Klaver, Men at Peace

JANUARY 15   MARTIN LUTHER KING JR.'S BIRTHDAY
Joy

When your words came, I ate them;
  they were my joy and my heart's delight,
for I bear your name,
  O LORD God Almighty.

JEREMIAH 15:16

A middle-aged black man on skid row in Los Angeles recently paraded down the street with a sign that read, I NEED 'BREAD' TO GET ME TO THE MILLION MAN MARCH IN D.C. He held out a hat for donations to finance his trip to the 1995 event. Drugs and alcohol had failed, maybe he could fill the void in his heart by going to the march. He, like thousands of others, felt empty but didn't realize that you cannot find meaning in an ocean of lost souls.

This man's father had been in Washington in 1963, gathered with whites and blacks at the Lincoln Memorial with demands to pass civil rights legislation. And those demands were met. But what effect did this victory have for him? His only son was steeped in hate and was imprisoned for "wasting" a rival gang member. Three generations in search of imperishable food and all remaining empty. His father may have been searching for the right thing but did he go to the right place to find it?

Few will forget the surge of the crowd when Martin Luther King Jr., made his "I have a dream" speech, accompanied by white folk singers such as Joan Baez and Bob Dylan. One writer described the event as "in keeping with King's color-blind vision of the sons of former slaves and the sons of former slave owners sitting together to feed at the table of brotherhood." Even today I know few people who can't sit through a recording of that same speech without being captured by the beauty of the vision of a unified country. King's legacy will remain with us, but how many neighborhoods have become brotherhoods? Is this nation closer to judging people by the content of their character? The work has been done in the House of Representatives and the Senate of this great nation, but we have forgotten the greater work that must be done at the altar of repentance. Even with legislative victories, the insatiable hunger for meaning persists.

Rhetoric does not satisfy the soul. New laws will not feed people who are starving for purpose. Only Jesus does. Two thousand years ago He proclaimed that man shall not live by bread alone, but by every word that proceeds out of the mouth of God (Matt: 4:4).

Are you hungry? broken? dispossessed? searching for meaning? purpose? . . . Do you thirst for truth? God wants to speak to you straight from His heart. After hope and reason have failed, faith conquers.

Wellington Boone, *Breaking Through*

JANUARY 16

Discipline

No discipline seems pleasant at the time, but painful. Later on, however, it produces a harvest of righteousness and peace for those who have been trained by it.

HEBREWS 12:11

It is no mistake that in the Old Testament God chose to put the mark of His covenant with Israel on the male penis. He didn't put it on the arm, or on the elbow, or on the thigh. God demanded that every Jewish man be circumcised on his sexual organ to remind him of the fact that he belonged to God.

Too many evangelical pulpits are filled by men who have slept with women other than their wives. How many are there? I don't know, but one would be too many. Is it any wonder we are not having a greater impact upon our culture for Christ?

Yes, there is forgiveness and grace to the one who has committed adultery. God offers pure forgiveness and grace to cover all our sins. We cannot afford ever to lose that principle. . . .

If you are reading this and adultery is in your past or in your present, know there is forgiveness available as you simply call upon the Lord with a repentant heart. But forgiveness is not the only issue in this dialogue about the epidemic of adultery . . . especially when it concerns a spiritual leader. Forgiveness is available to all. But forgiveness does not automatically restore the privilege of leadership. Let me offer a critical principle: *In the New Testament, forgiveness is free, but leadership is earned.* It is earned by the power of a man's life. Sin, although forgiven, always sets off practical consequences. A mature, spiritual leader who sins and repents is forgiven, but he is not exempt from the series of aftershocks that will come his way from his disobedience.

I carefully chose the work "mature" in the previous sentence. A young man in his teens or early twenties is in the stages of developing character; that's why we normally don't put him in the upper levels of leadership. Several years ago, I had dinner with a group of men who all lead various ministries. The average age was somewhere around forty. As we ate, the conversation turned to our conversions and some of the foolish and wrong things we did as young believers in college. There was drunkenness, cheating in school, drugs, sexual immorality, bar brawls, and a few other activities (I was shocked to hear this since I have a completely spotless past. Ha!)

Let me hasten to add that the Lord disciplined every one of us as a father would discipline a young, immature son. God was disciplining us because He wanted to give every one of us spiritual responsibilities. But first we had to take some character examinations. If you don't pass on the first try, you'll take it again, and again, and again, until you do pass and God can entrust leadership into your hands. If you continue to fail these early tests of integrity, He never will entrust leadership to you.

Steve Farrar, *Point Man*

January 17
Priorities

Teach us to number our days aright,
that we may gain a heart of wisdom.

PSALM 90:12

Recently, my wife asked that I be home by 5:00 P.M. She and our boys needed to leave home by 5:30 to get to the church for a children's program rehearsal. She knew she had to ask me because I had been coming home later and later each evening. Sure enough, I was met with a church emergency at 4:30 and I came dragging home at 5:45. As I drove home, God's Spirit convicted me that I should have postponed solving the emergency until the next day. (Most "emergencies" can wait until the next day.)

As I walked into our kitchen, my sweet wife burst into tears. "You promised you would be home by 5:00. John almost killed himself by falling out the back door. Andrew and James are being rowdy. Grace Anne needs your attention. And I'm burning dinner!"

"But, sweetheart," I replied, "I was taking care of an emergency at church that came up and would not go away without my help. I had to help a person."

Still hurt because I was becoming too absentee, she said (tongue in cheek), "Well, maybe I need to set up an appointment to see you. That's the only way I'm going to be able to talk to you."

Ouch! (She was right.)

Men, our work *can* crowd out more important matters in our life. Like family. Like God. Maybe God Himself needs to say, "Well, maybe I need to set up an appointment to see you. That's probably the only way I'm going to be able to talk to you."

Maybe you can relate to how I blew it. We can let the tyranny of the urgent crowd out the best. When that happens, repeatedly buckling to the demands of work becomes a hindrance.

We must not allow the crunch of career demands to crowd out what is truly best in life. If we make that tradeoff, we will surely lose the race.

Steven Lawson, *Men Who Win*

January 18
A Natural Witness

Preach the Word; be prepared in season and out of season; correct, rebuke and encourage—with great patience and careful instruction.

2 TIMOTHY 4:2

I had breakfast with a young man recently who felt a desire to join a Christian organization, yet had some doubts about leaving his secular job. The more we talked the more obvious it became to both of us that he already had a tremendous mission field. He told me story after story of people who had come to know the Lord through his witness. He also had a great opportunity to advance quickly in the company and influence its direction. I haven't seen him since the day we had breakfast, but when he left that morning he was convinced he could touch many more lives through his secular job than he could with the Christian organization.

I didn't consider working in a Christian organization—even on a mission team—to be any more "spiritual" than working in a machine shop, driving a truck, being a nurse, or running an advertising agency. It really doesn't matter where we are. God has a mission field for us, and personally I feel one of the biggest mission fields today is among the hurting, searching, stress-filled people in business.

Our world can't understand the Christian's willingness to tell others about Christ. Religion is a private matter, we are told. But God commands Christians to share the Good News. Furthermore, I believe hell and eternal punishment are real, just as heaven is also a reality. God is just and fair, and everything He does is right, regardless of what man thinks or how foolish it sounds.

A Christian who manages a small business told me the other day that some of his employees were complaining about a co-worker who kept bugging them about the Bible. He wanted to know whether he should encourage the Christian to keep on in the manner he was, or ask him to stop. I advised him to ask the Christian to back off. I don't believe in bugging people to receive Christ. I think evangelism must be a natural part of our lives, like eating and breathing, and we need to use God's opportunities, rather than manufactured ones.

Chuck Snyder, *I Prayed for Patience*

January 19
Victory

*. . . for everyone born of God overcomes the world. This is the victory that has
overcome the world, even our faith.*

I John 5:4

Circumstances may appear to wreck our lives and God's plans, but *God is
not helpless among the ruins.* Our broken lives are not lost or useless. God's
love is still working. He comes in and takes the calamity and uses it victori-
ously, working out his wonderful plan of love. "All things work together for
good to them that love God." He is always master of the situation. There is
infinite resourcefulness in the almighty love. Many people have become great
in spite of, as well as because of, disaster. This is the victory of God's love, but
it does not come to all. It comes to those who keep their faith clear and
their lives clean toward God. It comes to those who keep in touch with the
divine love, are linked to the divine will, and look for chances of helping on
the purposes they are sure God still has for them.

Eric Liddell, The Disciplines of the Christian Life

January 20
His Sovereignty

*. . . for dominion belongs to the Lord
and he rules over the nations.*

PSALM 22:28

Not long ago the son of one of our church leaders was run over by a
motor boat. He lived, but his knees were badly damaged, and there were
superficial nicks on his chest and neck from the propeller. When his father
testified at a deacon meeting, he said that his main comfort and lesson was
the sovereignty of God. "God has his purposes for the life of my son," he
said, "and for the whole family. This will turn out for the good of all of us
as we trust in him. God could have taken my son with another half-inch
difference. But instead he said to the blade:'Thus far and no farther.'"

God does not always stop the blade. On December 16, 1974, he did not
save my mother's life. She was riding with my father on a touring bus head-
ing toward Bethlehem in Israel. A van with lumber tied on the roof

swerved out of its lane and hit the bus head on. The lumber came through the windows and killed my mother instantly. The death certificate said "lacerated medulla oblongata." When we saw her body ten days later, after the funeral home did the best it could, my sister fainted. We left my father to weep alone over the coffin for a long time.

Then I went in and shut it for the last time. We used pictures at the visitation.

What was my comfort in those days? There were many. She suffered little. I had her for twenty-eight years as the best mother imaginable. She had known my wife and one of my four children. She was now in heaven with Jesus. Her life was rich with good deeds and its good effects are lasting long after she is gone. And underneath all these comforts, supporting all my unanswered questions, and calming my heart, there is the confidence that God is in control and God is good. I take no comfort from the prospect that God cannot control the flight of a four-by-four. For me there is no consolation in haphazardness. Nor in giving Satan the upper hand. As I knelt by my bed and wept, having received the dreaded phone call from by brother-in-law, I never doubted that God was sovereign over this accident and that God was good. I do not need to explain everything. That he reigns and that he loves is enough for now.

So let us stand in awe and wonder of God—eternally happy in the fellowship of the Trinity; infinitely exuberant in the wisdom of his work; free and sovereign in his self-sufficiency. "Our God is in heaven; he does all that he pleases." Let us humble ourselves under his mighty hand, and rejoice that his counsel will stand, and that one day all the families of the nations shall worship before him; for dominion belongs to the Lord, and he rules over the nations!

John Piper, *The Pleasures of God*

January 21
A Day's Work

Then man goes out to his work,
to his labor until the evening.

PSALM 104:23

Prayers and working are two different things. Prayer should not be hindered by work, but neither should work be hindered by prayer. Just as it was God's will that man should work six days and rest and make holy day in His presence on the seventh, so it is also God's will that every day should be marked for the Christian by both work and prayer. Prayer is entitled to its time. But the bulk of the day belongs to work. And only where each receives its own specific due will it become clear that both belong inseparably together. Without the burden and labor of the day, prayer is not prayer, and without prayer work is not work. This only the Christian knows. Thus it is precisely in the clear distinction between them that their oneness becomes manifest.

Work plunges men into the world of things. The Christian steps out of the world of brotherly encounter into the world of impersonal things, the "it"; and this new encounter frees him for objectivity; for the "it"-world is only an instrument in the hand of God for the purification of Christians from all self-centeredness and self-seeking. The work of the world can be done only where a person forgets himself, where he loses himself in a cause, in reality, the task, in "it." In work the Christian learns to allow himself to be limited by the task, and thus for him the work becomes a remedy against the indolence and sloth of the flesh. The passions of the flesh die in the world of things. But this can happen only where the Christian breaks through the "it" to the "Thou," which is God, who bids him work and makes that work and means of liberation from himself.

The work does not cease to be work; on the contrary, the hardness and rigor of labor is really sought only by the one who knows what it does for him. The continuing struggle with the "it" remains. But at the same time the break-through is made; the unity of prayer and work, the unity of the day is discovered; for to find, back of the "it" of the day's work, the "Thou," which is God, is what Paul calls "praying without ceasing" (I Thess. 5:17). Thus the prayer of the Christian reaches beyond its set time and extends into the heart of his work. It includes the whole day, and in doing so, it does not hinder the work; it promotes it, affirms it, and lends it meaning and joy. Thus every word, every work, every labor of the Christian becomes a prayer; not in the unreal sense of a constant turning away from the task that must be done, but in a real breaking through the hard "it" to the gracious Thou.

Dietrich Bonhoeffer, Life Together

JANUARY 22

Written Prayer

But when you pray, go into your room, close the door and pray to your Father, who is unseen. Then your Father, who sees what is done in secret, will reward you.

MATTHEW 6:6

Six years ago I began, at the Lord's direction, to write down my daily prayers. I've done it almost every day since then. I simply write a letter to my Father in heaven, sometimes addressing Him as "Dear Lord Jesus," other times as "Dear Heavenly Father." There are times when I don't address Him at all; I just start writing to Him. The words and the form are not important. What is important is that I come into His presence to talk to Him, praise Him, worship Him, confess to Him, ask of Him, and to intercede before Him for someone else. Over the last six years I have spent an average of thirty to forty minutes in communion with Him each day. There have been many times when we have spent well over an hour together . . .

Writing your prayers does many things for you. In my life, the most obvious thing it has done is bring me the healing power of the Lord. All the old issues I struggled with for so many years have been cleansed away. Today when I speak on how prayer can change your life, there are always people who come up to me later and tell me the phenomenal changes that have occurred in their lives, too, as they have written their prayers.

Writing your prayers is also an important discipline; by dating your prayers you can see very quickly if you have missed any days. Second, it helps you focus your mind on the Lord and prevents your thoughts from wandering. Writing also helps keep you alert, in accordance with Colossians 4:2: "Devote yourselves to prayer, keeping alert in it with an attitude of thanksgiving" (NASB).

It also helps protect you from the flaming missiles of the evil one, who is very happy when Christians are not praying. Inevitably he tries to attack us as we endeavor to submit ourselves to the Lord and draw closer to Him.

Perhaps the most significant benefit of daily written prayer is a totally changed life! For verification that it has changed *my* life, you could ask my wife. She lives with me. She sees that the suppressed anger that once raged within me is gone. She no longer sees a critical spirit in me. Now she not only enjoys being with me, she misses me deeply on those few occasions when we're apart. Jesus said, "I have come to heal the brokenhearted, to set the captive free" (paraphrase of Luke 4:18). He has done that for me through written prayer simply because I was obedient to His offer to "Come unto me, all ye that labour and are heavy laden, and I will give you rest" (Matt. 11:28). God also kept the promise made in Isaiah 26:3: "Thou wilt keep him in perfect peace, whose mind is stayed on thee." Writing my prayers enables me to keep my mind focused, or "stayed on" Him . . .

I have developed a little system that helps me maintain the daily discipline of writing my prayers. It may also help you maintain good habits and can be used just as effectively to help you break bad ones. Each day in a small pocket diary I write down the number of how many days in a row I have spent time with the Lord in written prayer. There have been days when I wasn't able to get to my prayer time until late at night because of the complexity of our schedule that day. Now I will not allow myself to get in bed until I have had at least some time with the Lord. I'll admit I'm apt to be sleepy, and my prayer time may be a little shorter than usual or less intense that I would like, but I still take a moment to bring my spirit into communion with God. It's not that God needs to hear from me. It's that I need that time with Him, and I can't afford to miss even one day. Tomorrow might be just as hectic, and then I would have missed two! As I see that little number growing each day on my weekly diary, I don't want to have to go back to zero and start all over. It really works to give me that edge that I need in self-discipline. And the results speak for themselves!

Fred Littauer, *Wake Up, Men!*

JANUARY 23
A Defining Moment

Whoever finds his life will lose it, and whoever loses his life for my sake will find it.

MATTHEW 10:39

I met a sharp young businessman on a plane. He prayed to receive Christ, but a few weeks later said, "I just can't give up control." Another man, a stockbroker, wouldn't attend our large Bible study, but wanted to meet privately. He had to be in charge—to do it his own way. Today he is divorced.

Every man must answer the question, "Who's in charge?" It is the issue of who has control. The kingdom of God is not about "praying a prayer" and then everything will turn out all right. Rather, the kingdom is a turning from self to God, a total release. It is to say, "I will go anywhere You want me to go, be anything You want me to be, do anything You want me to do." Obedience to God is the trademark of a Biblical Christian. It is how we demonstrate our love for God.

If you have not made the decision to receive Christ as your Savior, every other decision you make will be different from what it would have been if you had. If you have salvation and know it, but wrestle against putting Christ in charge of your life, every decision you make will be at risk. Personally, I had been a follower of Christ for twelve and a half years before I settled once and for all who would be in charge of my life. It's a tough surrender to make. The irony, of course, is that surrender ends not in defeat but in victory.

Have you settled the issue of who's in charge? Have you really turned from self to God? Released totally? Said you will go anywhere, be anything, do anything? Made a commitment to obey God?

Or do you have your life all planned out?

Here is the issue: whether you know Christ already or not, will you say to Jesus, "Take control of my life; make me the kind of man You want me to be"? This issue is a defining moment.

Patrick Morley, *The Seven Seasons of a Man's Life*

JANUARY 24
Inner Praise

Through Jesus, therefore, let us continually offer to God a sacrifice of praise—the fruit of lips that confess his name.

HEBREWS 13:15

When we are busied, or meditating on spiritual things, even in our time of set devotion, whilst our voice is rising in prayer, we ought to cease for one brief moment, as often as we can, to worship GOD *in the depth of our being*, to taste Him though it be in passing, to touch Him as it were by stealth. Since you cannot but know that GOD is with you in all you undertake, that He is at the very depth and center of your soul, why should you not thus pause an instant from time to time in your outward business, and even in the act of prayer, to worship Him within your soul, to praise Him, to entreat His aid, to offer Him the service of your heart, and give Him thanks for all His loving kindnesses and tender mercies?

What offering is there more acceptable to GOD than thus throughout the day to quit the things of outward sense, and to withdraw to worship Him within the secret places of the soul? Besides by so doing we destroy the love of self, which can subsist only among the things of sense, and of which these times of quiet retirement with GOD rids us well-nigh unconsciously.

In very truth we can render to GOD no greater or more signal proofs of our trust and faithfulness, than by thus turning from things created to find our joy, though for a single moment, in the Creator.

Brother Lawrence, *The Practice of the Presence of God*

JANUARY 25
New Life

For God so loved the world that he gave his one and only Son, that whoever believes in him shall not perish but have eternal life.

JOHN 3:16

At the age of thirty-three, in 1974, I got the opportunity to go to the University of Michigan and be on the great football staff. I was the only high school coach Bo Schembechler ever hired. That was important to me.

I knew that once I walked into that big stadium of 100,000 and rubbed elbows with the winningest football coach in the country, everybody would recognize, once and for all, that Bill McCartney had arrived. But it wasn't long after I got there that I discovered everybody there knew more football than I did. I again realized that if I was going to get their attention, affection, or esteem, I would have to achieve great things.

Then I met Chuck Heater. I was thirty-three years old and there was a guy on our team who was nineteen. He was a sophomore, fullback-running back and I noticed a quality to his life, a dimension to him, that was very attractive to me. So, I approached him. I said, "Chuck Heater, I see in you a dimension that I know I don't have. You're such a great competitor. You're so fiery and yet there's a peace and serenity to you that's so beautiful. What is it about you?" Chuck stood back for a second and sized me up. He wasn't used to being approached by a coach on the Michigan staff quite like that. He said, "I'll tell you what, Coach. In two weeks eighteen Michigan athletes from all sports are having a conference in Brighton, Michigan. I'd like for you to come. Then, I'll try to answer your question."

What I heard at that conference changed my life, and it has never been the same. For the first time I was confronted with whether or not I had actually surrendered control of my life to Jesus Christ. I understood that if I would submit to Christ, Almighty God would take dominion in my heart and take over the direction of my life. Then, my life would start to gain some real satisfaction and fulfillment. That really appealed to me because in my work I had just entered into an arena where it was extremely competitive and I wasn't feeling good about myself.

I remember going home that day being excited because I had made a decision to give my life to Jesus Christ. It was something I had never done before. My wife, Lyndee, was in the living room with a lady from the neighborhood. I came bursting in the front door and told her what happened. I then excused myself and left the room. The neighbor reached over and tapped Lyndee in the ribs and said, "I've seen it before. Don't worry about it. It blows right over." But it didn't blow over.

One of the reasons it didn't blow over was because I immediately started getting together with other men—for encouragement, fellowship, prayer and Bible study.

Bill McCartney, *What Makes a Man?*

January 26

A Guarded Heart

*Above all else, guard your heart,
for it is the wellspring of life.*

Proverbs 4:23

The TV advertising rates for a Super Bowl separate the corporate men from the boys. The tab for the most recent gridiron extravaganza came to something over $800,000 a *minute*. For that kind of currency, the Madison Avenue gurus are expected to provide some pretty high-powered slogans, tunes, and jingles.

So when the Reebok athletic shoe company flashed its slogan before the millions of Super Bowl viewers, it hit on a proverb that cuts to the heart of our times: "Life is short. Play hard."

In other words, have fun. Go fast. Pile up the toys. Increase your pleasure. Do it *now*.

Financial pressures to appear more prosperous than our neighbors can claim a huge bite of our time and energy. Beyond our God-given responsibilities to provide food, clothing, and shelter for our families, it's easy to chase after [material goods] to somehow "prove ourselves" to our friends and peers. To many men, it becomes vitally important what kind of ink pen they carry, what kind of watch they wear, what kind of boat they tow behind what kind of car, and so on and so on. Things, things, things. But remember, life is short, so play hard.

We're working so long to buy our toys (or ignoring our families in our "hunt" for them), however, that what's really important in our homes slips out the back door while we're not looking. If we want to be men of [God], we can't close our eyes a moment to the danger of these pressures to "buy, buy, buy." Messages of "material fulfillment" literally saturate our society and will leave us . . .empty . . .the moment we drop our guard. . . .

History shows that at the beginning of every major revival, there has been a fresh realization of mankind's self-centered ways. When people finally understand how deeply they're concerned about pleasing themselves and how little they care about pleasing God, they begin to fall on their knees in repentance and seek each other's forgiveness. Almost immediately they go to their brothers and sisters, people in their churches, people in their neighborhoods and towns, and seek reconciliation. It's such a stunning, super-natural turn of events that it pierces to the heart of any community. And then the dam breaks, releasing a great torrent of God's grace and power.

It's time for a group of bold men to say, "I've had enough of this love affair with myself. I'm going to repent. . . . Even if no one else does it, I'm going to do it anyway. It has to start somewhere, so let it start with me. I'll admit it. I am self-centered. I want to confess that to God and to you. Will you forgive me, Lord? Will you forgive me, my wife, my children?"

Will you be one of those men?

Gary Smalley and John Trent, *The Hidden Value of a Man*

JANUARY 27

A Team Player

*How good and pleasant it is
when brothers live together in unity!*

PSALM 133:1

When I was in college, I competed in a sport called "crew" in an eight-man shell with coxswain. The hull of the boat was very sharp. The boat could tip over with the slightest movement to the side. When we first learned to row together it was extremely awkward, with the oars slapping from side to side and the boat rocking. After months of practice, the men were able to move and row with perfect balance, the keel of the boat would even out, and the boat would move with great speed through the water.

Even though each of the individual men was rowing with extremely violent force, the timing and cooperation was so perfect that there would be no side movement in the boat. When the rowing reached racing speed, the hull would begin to rise slightly up out of the water. There would be moments of poetic beauty that were experienced through the strength, speed, balance, timing, and rhythm.

Part of the beauty was an intuitive sense of teamwork and unity among the men. The slightest wrong move by any of the eight oarsmen could have ruined the race. We had spent months in grueling preparation for the few minutes of the race. We were all interdependent on one another. Not only was it a joy to win the race and compete well, but the privilege to experience that perfection of teamwork was an aesthetic and spiritual reward in itself.

The same could be said for any team sport or team activity. Serving in the kingdom of God should have the sweet spiritual reward of being a member of a team. There is a joy of fraternity and kinship in working together.

In a team spirit one is looking not so much for his own separate fulfillment, but for the good of the whole group together. Those who have played basketball remember times when a certain friend would desire to shoot the ball every time he got his hands on it. His desire was to build up his own score. While he may have achieved a higher score for himself, the team suffered overall . . .

In the body of believers, there are also different types of players. In a basketball team one might have forwards, guards, centers, coaches, managers, water boys, and members of the business part of the club. Even the owner and the fans themselves may be considered as part of the identity of the team. In the body of believers, we have deacons, elders, worship leaders, administrators, janitors, Sunday school workers, nursery attendants, sound equipment helpers, hospitality coordinators, and so on . . .

The three aspects of teamwork are the following: First, we must adopt the inner spirit of being a team player. We breathe the same air of the team spirit. We are motivated with an attitude of teamwork.

Secondly, we direct our goal for the good of the overall team. We do not see a separate achievement; our eyes are on the greater good of the victory of all of us together. Our goal is for the group, not individual success.

Thirdly, we are committed to learning how to interact with one another. We need to develop the ability to pass the ball back and forth. We must spend time training in interrelationship, communication and team play. It is not enough to have a team spirit; one must develop the techniques of team play.

The three aspects of teamwork are team spirit, team goal and team play. A covenant-oriented man is a team player.

Keith Intrater, *Covenant Relationships*

January 28

Practice

Although he was a son, he learned obedience from what he suffered . . .

HEBREWS 5:8

What makes a man a good athlete? Practice. What makes a man a good artist, a good sculptor, a good musician? Practice. What makes a man a good linguist, a good stenographer? Practice. What makes a good man? Practice. Nothing else. There is nothing capricious about religion. We do not get the soul in different ways, under different laws, from those in which we get the body and the mind. If a man does not exercise his arm, he develops no biceps muscle; and if a man does not exercise his soul, he acquires no muscle in his soul, no strength of character, no vigor of moral fibre, no beauty of spiritual growth. Love is not a thing of enthusiastic emotion. It is a rich, strong, manly, vigorous expression of the whole round Christian character—the Christlike nature in its fullest development. And the constituents of this great character are only to be built up by ceaseless practice.

What was Christ doing in the carpenter's shop? Practicing. Though perfect, we read that He *learned* obedience, and grew in wisdom and in favor with God. Do not quarrel, therefore, with your lot in life. Do not complain of its never-ceasing cares, its petty environment, the vexations you have to stand, the small and sordid souls you have to live and work with. Above all, do not resent temptation; do not be perplexed because it seems to thicken round you more and more, and ceases neither for effort nor for agony nor prayer. That is your practice. That is the practice to which God appoints you; and it is having its work in making you patient, humble, generous, unselfish, kind, and courteous. Do not begrudge the hand that is molding the still too shapeless image within you. It is growing more beautiful, though you do not see it, and every touch of temptation may add to its perfection.

Therefore keep in the midst of life. Do not isolate yourself. Be among men and among things, among troubles, difficulties, and obstacles.

Henry Drummond

JANUARY 29
Man-to-Man Relationship

In bringing many sons to glory it was fitting that God, for whom and through whom everything exists, should make the author of their salvation perfect through suffering.

HEBREWS 2:10

Contrary to popular belief, men aren't born. *Children* are born—men are *formed*. And the Bible says men help "form" each other: "As iron sharpens iron, so a man sharpens his friend" (Proverbs 27:17).

Carved, designed, and shaped—males are processed into true manhood. At the core of that process is one crucial component: man-to-man relationship. Prioritizing the cultivation of such relationships according to God's created order is in line with His blueprint for full manhood.

Ah, but we've hit a snag right there; snagged on the word "manhood." For many of us, the very term "manhood" may cause us to squirm, because it carries emotional baggage for some, and possibly conveys unachievable responsibility to others. Say the word "manhood" and some men may immediately recall the times in his childhood when he was picked last for the baseball team. Or it may bring back the fresh emotions of last month when he was laid off at work—"How can I face my peers as a failure?!" Say "manhood" and some women may instantly feel complex emotional recollections of all the times their "manly" husbands forced their desires and preferences on them to the annihilation of their own sensitivities or feelings . . .

True manhood is resourced in Jesus Christ. Don't let the simplicity of that statement blow by you. Since it *sounds* "religious" it might only conjure a mental dullness toward its earth-moving potential. But religious rhetoric doesn't change lives, God's *reality*—living truth does, and Jesus Himself is Truth Incarnate. . . . He is the only salvation for a battered or ambiguous male identity, and He's the provider of substance to bring definition to your manhood and mine.

It's God's intent to reproduce Jesus in us: "For it was fitting for Him, for whom are all things and by whom are all things, in bringing many sons to glory, to make the captain of the salvation perfect through sufferings" (Heb. 2:10).

That's God's design—getting the glorious image of Jesus Christ to be reproduced in any person who will ask Him to do so. It works for *both* genders! In Christ, women can be *truly* liberated and celebrated, and in Him men can finally escape the world of "self-help" programs and *machismo* power tactics. However, being conformed into the image of Jesus can't be done Lone Ranger style. One of the chief scalpels that God has chosen for shaping us into His image is the dynamic of personal friendships—man-to-man relationships. This is an essential, practical biblical principle, and one of a man's key starting places.

Jack Hayford, *A Man's Starting Place*

JANUARY 30
A New Nature

Therefore, if anyone is in Christ, he is a new creation; the old has gone, the new has come!

II CORINTHIANS 5:17

Nature defines character. Who we are determines what we do.

This "be to do" truth is reflected in the nature of all physical life. Species determine characteristics. Biological life is classified into distinct phyla based on this immutable fact.

Travel with me for a moment into the world of imagination to see this wonderful truth illustrated. A few years ago I went to the kennel in my yard to visit with my three dogs: Gus, Snow, and Scratch. Scratch was in the pits. Depression is too mild a word to describe his state; he was talking of suicide.

Here was the situation: Gus, the oldest dog in the kennel, had used his position to deceive poor ol' Scratch. He had told Scratch that he was a cat—and Scratch had believed it. Trying to be a good cat, Scratch had begun studying cat behavior and trying to act like a cat. But he wasn't very good at it. He tried to meow, but failed. He attempted to climb trees, but failed at that as well. He hated cat food and couldn't purr.

A failure! That was Scratch's final assessment of himself. He didn't deserve to live. He was taking up space that some good cat could occupy, eating food that some worthy cat should eat, Suicide was the honorable thing to do. But before he took that final out, he asked me for help.

"I can help you," I told Scratch.

"Really?" he prayed. "Please, anything. Put me on the couch. Cast out demons. Anything!"

"You got yourself into this mess," I said, "by believing a lie. You can get yourself out by believing the truth. You aren't a cat. You are a dog. Go be yourself."

Dogs like to bark. And strangely enough, they are equipped to bark. Dogs like to dig, and they have that capability. Scratch was a bird dog. This particular species has both the desire and ability to hunt quail. In the same way, cats meow. They like to meow. They're good at it. And birds fly. Fish swim.

You get the point. When God creates a species, he gives it the desire and ability to do what he intended it to do.

Now, here's another important consideration. Christians are a "new creature"—a "new species" (2 Cor 5:17). We have the very life of Christ in us. There has never been another species like the one created when God's Spirit becomes one with a human being's spirit, And this form of life has the capability and desire to live the same way Jesus lived on earth.

Our trouble comes when, like Scratch, we choose a course of action contrary to our nature. When dogs try to act like cats, they are contradicting their nature. When birds try to act like fish, they are miserable. And when Christians try to act like anything other than the new creation they are, they become paralyzed, because they have violated their nature. True freedom comes from choosing actions that are consistent with your nature.

Dudley Hall, *Grace Works*

January 31
The Promise of Our Word

Remember the day you stood before the Lord your God at Horeb, when he said to me, "Assemble the people before me to hear my words so that they may learn to revere me as long as they live in the land and may teach them to their children."

36 · PROMISES TO KEEP

A promise is a commitment for the future. Not much point in making promises about yesterday! A promise is very much like a goal. Both lie in the future. Both are statements about what I expect to happen. But a promise goes further than a goal. A promise says, "Within my ability and if circumstances don't stop me, I will do what I have said I will do." In recent years I have modified the business principle of management-by-objectives so it is more like management-by-promise-keeping.

There is something so much more ethically profound about making a promise as compared to committing to an objective. In business we are accustomed to being asked to do things and asking others to do things. If it's our boss who is doing the asking, we may agree even though we are not sure it's a very good idea. We may take on the task half-heartedly and perhaps find excuses why it shouldn't be done. On the other side of the coin, we make excuses for people who don't do what they said they would. Shifting our thinking to see a commitment to the future as a promise given and received can change our entire attitude about life. Let me recommend it to you as a business practice. There is no higher commendation that can be given to a business person than to say that he or she keeps promises. That applies in big and little things. In our culture it implies arriving on time, completing an assignment when it is due, producing quality work.

There is an ultimate promise we need to talk about. Of all the commitments we make, it is the only one that we make for life. It is the promise we give when as a couple we come before a pastor and exchange our marriage vows. It is the only promise we make that includes "until death do us part." I realize that in a day when many marriages seem like trial arrangements, such an idea sounds old-fashioned, out of step with the times. But it is the times that are out of step. God's design was that marriage should signify the commitment that Christ has made to his church (Eph. 5:22–23). The promise is "I will give you 100 percent. My dedication will not be conditioned on what you give in return. This is no 50–50 arrangement. I promise all of myself to you."

There is another promise we make that doesn't have the lifetime duration and impact that marriage does, but it is closely related. When you have children, you make a promise to them. You promise to house and feed them, to educate and train them. You promise to be a model for them, to love them and to give them time. In a day of two-income families this is not easy. Society is coming to realize that the primary danger to the family is the absent father, regardless of the reasons for his absence. Children need a father, a male role model.

What might that entail? For one thing, time. Schedule family devotional times. Get a Bible story book and read to your children every morning at breakfast (even if you or they have to get up early!). When that one is worn out, buy another one. Teach them Bible verses that speak of hope, joy, and caring.

Edward Dayton, *Succeeding in Business*

February

A Father's Love

So he got up and went to his father. But while he was still a long way off, his father saw him and was filled with compassion for him; he ran to his son, threw his arms around him and kissed him.

LUKE 15:20

I came home from work one day to find my wife, Amy, and my son, Bob, sitting in the living room. Amy was crying her eyes out, and Bobby looked as simple as a horse. He looked bleary-eyed, pale, and sick—which he was. It was the last day of school, so he and some buddies had decided to really celebrate. They got hold of some beer, which Bobby had never tried before, and made it their goal to get rip-roaring drunk. Bobby had gone along with the guys and was now paying the price. He had thrown up everything but his toenails, and I think he was working on those. He was positively green.

I had only a few seconds to decide how to respond, and there were a lot of things that could have crossed my mind. I could have been outraged, since I was, after all, a well-known minister. I was a Bible teacher and counselor, and I was on the radio every day talking about the Lord. I was a highly visible figure at a large church, which was known for being against alcohol consumption. If people found out what Bobby had done, it could reflect badly on me. Those are some of the things I could have thought. But the truth is, I thought about none of these. All I could see was my son whom I loved more than anything on earth. I immediately walked over and put my arms around him.

"Bobby," I said, "I love you. I hate what you did, but I love you."

We sat for a few minutes, and then Bobby said, "Daddy, let's pray." And we did.

Long afterward I learned what a significant experience this was in my son's life. A few years later, in a conversation, where we recalled the occasion, Bobby said, "You know something, Dad? All my life you told me you loved me. But that day I *knew* you loved me."

Bob George, *Growing in Grace*

FEBRUARY 2

Affection

His left arm is under my head,
  and his right arm embraces me.

SONG OF SONGS 2:6

To most women affection symbolizes security, protection, comfort, and approval, vitally important commodities in their eyes. When a husband shows his wife affection, he sends the following messages:

- I'll take care of you and protect you. You are important to me, and I don't want anything to happen to you.
- I'm concerned about the problems you face, and I am with you.
- I think you've done a good job, and I'm so proud of you.

A hug can say any and all of the above. Men need to understand how strongly women need these affirmations. *For the typical wife, there can hardly be enough of them.*

I've mentioned hugging often because I believe it is a skill most men need to develop to show their wives affection. It is also a simple but effective way to build their accounts in a wife's Love Bank.

Most women love to hug. They hug each other, they hug children, animals, relatives—even stuffed animals. I'm not saying they will throw themselves into the arms of just anyone: They can get quite inhibited about hugging if they think it could be misinterpreted in a sexual way. But the rest of the time, across most countries and cultures, women hug and like to be hugged.

Obviously a man can display affection in other ways that can be equally important to a woman. A greeting card or a note expressing love and care can simply but effectively communicate the same emotions. Don't forget that all-time favorite—a bouquet of flowers. Women, almost universally, love to receive flowers. Occasionally I meet a man who likes to receive them, but most do not. For most women, however, flowers send a powerful message of love and concern.

An invitation to dinner also signals affection. It is a way of saying to one's wife, "You don't need to do what you ordinarily do for me. I'll treat you instead. You are special to me, and I want to show you how much I love and care for you."

Jokes abound on how, almost immediately after the wedding, a wife has to find her own way in and out of cars, houses, restaurants, and so on. But a sensitive husband will open the door for her at every opportunity—another way to tell her, "I love you and care about you."

Holding hands is a time-honored and effective sign of affection. Walks after dinner, back rubs, phone calls, and conversations with thoughtful and loving expressions all add units to the Love Bank. As more than one song has said, "There are a thousand ways to say I love you."

From a woman's point of view, affection is the essential cement of her relationship with a man. Without it, a woman probably feels alienated from her mate. With it she becomes tightly bonded to him while he adds units to his Love Bank account.

Willard Harley, *His Needs, Her Needs*

FEBRUARY 3

Water into Wine

Thus, the first of his miraculous signs, Jesus performed in Cana of Galilee. He thus revealed his glory, and his disciples put their faith in him.

JOHN 2:11

After thirty years of research the medical college at The Johns Hopkins University released an interesting finding. They discovered that a lack of proper emotional life causes headaches, ulcers, heart disease, and even cancer. It was further disclosed that patients with cancer were generally introspective and lonely, and had not enjoyed good relationships with their parents and siblings during early childhood. Those who had never learned to share love and compassion were those who tended to disease and to poor health.

It was to remedy this lack that Christ performed His first miracle. In Cana He attended a marriage—the relationship with the greatest potential for satisfying depth or for devastating disaster. During the wedding feast a need arose, and Christ turned the water into wine.

By this miracle Christ symbolically showed us He has the power to transform our lives from tasteless water into tasty, profitable wine. By this miracle Christ assured us He could transform our lives of emptiness into lives full of love and compassion, satisfying the needs of those around us.

Christ loves you regardless of your education, your wealth, your place in society, your age . . .or your nationality. Turn your life over to Christ. Let Him flood you with his love. The love of Christ can restore your personality to wholeness, lift your feelings of acceptance, and bring healing to your body, soul, and spirit. . . .

To find true happiness establish a purpose with permanence, identity, and power. Through faith in Christ you can be freed from the bondage of guilt and the murk of meaninglessness, and released into the peace of mind needed for genuine happiness. When the final component of love and compassion is instilled into your life and attitudes you will find yourself enriched with one of God's greatest blessings, true and lasting happiness.

Paul Yonggi Cho, *Solving Life's Problems*

FEBRUARY 4

Trying

. . . for though a righteous man falls seven times, he rises again,
but the wicked are brought down by calamity.
PROVERBS 24:16

The greatest failure in life is to never try. The only difference between a winner and a loser is that the winner gets up one more time than the loser. As Proverbs 24:16 says, "For though a righteous man falls seven times, he rises again, but the wicked are brought down by calamity." The loser may also be the timid soul who knows neither victory nor defeat because he never enters the race. Remember, a mistake is never a failure, unless you fail to learn by it.

In the parable of the talents in Matthew 25:14–30, the slave was given only one talent, which he took and buried. His idea of duty, progress and stewardship was to slam on the brakes and throw the transmission into reverse! God considered him a wicked slave. He should have taken the talent entrusted to him and invested it in the Kingdom of God. The fearful person asks, "What do I stand to lose if I do?" A person of faith is someone who asks, "What do I stand to lose if I don't?"

Two types of people will never amount to anything: those who cannot do what they are told, and those who won't do anything unless they are told. In the parable, the slave with one talent had just as much responsibility as the one with five talents. Both were required to be submissive to the master. One took the risk of doing, while the other sought the security of hiding. I understand why people like to have the security of clinging to a tree trunk, but the fruit is always out on the end of the limb.

It's important to remember, however, that not everyone has the same level of giftedness. . . .

We should seek to live up to our potential and not look for excuses, but not everybody's potential is the same. The Lord hasn't equally distributed gifts, talents or intelligence. But He has equally distributed Himself.

Neil Anderson, *Living Free in Christ*

FEBRUARY 5

The Sanctity of Sex

Flee from sexual immorality. All other sins a man commits are outside his body, but he who sins sexually sins against his own body. Do you not know that your body is a temple of the Holy Spirit, who is in you, whom you have received from God? You are not your own; you were bought at a price. Therefore honor God with your body.

I CORINTHIANS 6:18–20

If one says nowadays that sex is sacred, one runs the risk of being ridiculed. But that is only because the job of demystification has been done so well. If someone managed to kidnap a princess, dressed her in rags and knocked her about the head so her speech was slurred, and then told his fellow thugs that this woman was a princess, they would likely not believe him.

Our society is in a similar situation with regard to sexual love. We find it difficult to see how anything that can be found in low places can also be found in the highest. Given the common and easily available state to which sex has fallen, it is not to be wondered at that the medical and psychological estimate would prevail: sex is not sacred at all. It is a natural thing, one more biological process among many. So let us eat and drink and sleep and have sex and be healthy.

Christianity won't go along with that. Neither did the pagan world for that matter. The Greeks believed love was a god and sex a goddess. The Romans felt that only virgins should tend the vestal fire. In our better moments we don't go along with the casual view of sex, either. We can see, though not so clearly as before, that sex is something set apart and not for the public realm, that what goes on behind closed doors is not meant to go on the movie screen.

I think we may go further and say that even our natural impulses reinforce this view. The sense of the sacred is conveyed, among other ways, by reticence and the fact that some things are not said—or said only with a sense of their specialness. The fact that we tend to blush and stammer or assume an awkward air of matter-of-factness when talking about sex does not mean we are holdovers from puritanism, but simply that we realize the subject matter we are tackling is not a purely biological phenomenon. No one, as far as I know, ever blushed when telling children how grapefruit should be eaten.

Unless you understand that Christianity considers sexual love to be a sacred thing, you can never fully understand why it insists that sex be set about with exclusions and restrictions. All sacred things are. It is not that it thinks sex is a bad thing, but a high thing. Like other high things, it deserves to be bounded by objective rules and not wafted about by gusts of changing emotion. The Christian position on this is quite clear. Sexual love is too important to be left up to spontaneity. The correctness of our sexual conduct must not turn on the intensity of the moment's feelings but rather on objective criteria: Whether we have made a vow and to whom. How else can it be? We are not allowed to plead our case on the basis of, "It's all right if you're in love." Much less on the defense, "It can't be wrong when it feels so right." Poached trout, as John White points out in *Eros Defiled*, tastes quite as delicious as the purchased kind, but it is still poached trout.

William Kirk Kilpatrick, *Psychological Seduction*

February 6

Morning Praise

Yet [Abraham] did not waver through unbelief regarding the promise of God, but was strengthened in his faith and gave glory to God, being fully persuaded that God had the power to do what he had promised.

ROMANS 4:20–21

I begin each day with a prayer of thanks to God—as soon as my eyes open and my feet hit the floor. I encourage you to do the same, even on Monday mornings.

Beginning your day with a prayer of thanksgiving to God isn't as easy as it sounds. Listen to yourself when you wake up tomorrow morning. For years I groaned about each new day. My prayers, when I prayed, were mostly complaints. "Lord, here comes another day. I don't feel up to the tasks before me. There are so many temptations. I don't want to lose my temper. Don't let me fail You. Don't let me grieve You. Don't let me dishonor You if an opportunity to witness comes up. . . ." On and on I went, groaning and moaning, wailing and pleading with the Lord.

I remember frequently praying, "Don't leave me, Lord," as if Hebrews 13:5–6 could be turned around to say, "I am going to leave you and forsake you. Don't count on me. Watch for what others are going to do to you!" God must have considered my prayers utter foolishness.

One day Fred Renich, who helped direct our missionary internship program, challenged us in this area. He claimed that "most of you probably start out the day groaning. The content, tone, and direction of your prayers are negative." And he was right. I hadn't realized how negative I was.

Renich made it clear he wasn't advocating positive thinking as a cure-all. "This is different. Pray on the basis of the promises and reality of God." He urged us to start each day saying things like, "Thank You, Lord Jesus. Here's a new day. Yes, I am weak, but You are strong, and all Your resources are my resources. I don't always know how to witness to others, but You will give me the right words. When temptation comes, Lord, I've got Your power. Thank You that You live in me. Thank You that Your resurrection life is real and that today you're going to prove it once again."

Why start the day with a prayer of unbelief? Why not start with a note of praise? If I understand Romans 4:20 correctly, Abraham grew strong in his faith as he gave glory to God. God had promised the impossible—that his wife, almost ninety years old, would have a son. The temptation to doubt God was incredible. But Abraham became "fully persuaded that God had the power to do what he had promised."

Are you convinced that the same power of God is in you? Then affirm it at the beginning of each day.

Luis Palau, Say Yes!

FEBRUARY 7

Wisdom

I have more insight than the elders,
for I obey your precepts.

PSALM 119:100

Wisdom is the skill for living life. The Hebrew word is the same as the word for a skill to make a chair out of a piece of wood or a tent out of animal skins. Wisdom is obtained from observing the regularities of life or learning from others who have already learned those skills by living longer. Since true wisdom also comes from God, it is looking at life's regularity from God's point of view as revealed in the Bible (Psalm 119:100). If we lack wisdom, we should ask God for it (James 1:5). But the wisdom God gives us will make sense and not contradict what He has given before. To learn wisdom is to learn the regular patterns of the way God does things . . .

A person will not choose the irregular and the regular at the same time. If a guy continually looks for irregular interventions of God into his life via signs, gifts, experiences, or messages, he will not tend to seek wisdom. If he seeks the regular patterns of life as God prescribes them (wisdom), he won't constantly expect God to be interrupting those regular patterns (although He may).

Guys seeking mystical signs remain boys. Guys seeking God's regular patterns (wisdom) become men. Some boys buy lottery tickets for the same reason other boys are mystics. They want to ignore the realities of life while expecting an intervention. I'm told that most people believe that there is a very good chance they will win the lottery and very little chance they will get in an automobile accident. Why do they believe that? Because they are boys. Boys live in chaos, chance, mysticism, and a fantasy world that does not exist. And it keeps them from the real world, which does exist. Men face the real world and learn its patterns. That's wisdom.

David De Witt, *The Mature Man*

FEBRUARY 8
A Time Alone

And without faith it is impossible to please God, because anyone who comes to him must believe that he exists and that he rewards those who earnestly seek him.

HEBREWS 11:6

We communicate with God through prayer and Bible study. The best way is to decide upon a definite time for your prayer time, preferably in the early morning, and keep it sacred. Build your life's habits around that period. Do not allow it to be crowded out by other things. Those who neglect the fixed time for prayer and say they can pray at all times will end in praying at no time. But if you keep the fixed period, it should influence the whole day.

In the beginning of the prayer period, be silent. Allow your mind to relax and to roam across your life. If it stops at anything wrong, determine in God's strength that you will right it. Make sure you do right it. If nothing is shown to be wrong, you are ready for bold praying. See I John 3:21.

Then bathe your thought in God's Word. It will cleanse your eyes and give you insight. Thus you will get right attitudes and will pray right prayers. God will be bringing your thoughts into line with his thoughts, your purposes with his purposes.

Write down what comes to you. Pore over God's Word. Your pen is a sign of your faith that something will come, and it will. Don't read hurriedly—each word is precious. Wait for the meaning to settle in. When a person hurries through a forest, few birds and animals appear. They go into hiding. But if the person sits down and waits, they come out. It will be so with reading the Bible and praying. "Prayer is a time exposure of the soul to God." Let your inmost self be exposed to God's Word. Be willing to obey, and *obey.*

The outcome of the prayer time should be action. You should have some definite, concrete work to do. Often the actions are small, but they demand some sacrifice of time, or they test your patience and love. Do them. Keeping a record may prove helpful.

I would suggest the discipline of rising half an hour earlier than usual and giving the time to prayer, meditation, and Bible study. Be careful, however, not to fall into the habit of thinking God can guide you only at this one special time or at any one special time. Be careful, too, about your attitude to others who differ from you regarding the time they find most helpful. Be prepared to change the time of your prayer if the circumstances of your life lead you to feel it necessary or advisable.

Eric Liddell, The Disciplines of the Christian Life

FEBRUARY 9

Forgiveness

This is how my heavenly Father will treat each of you unless you forgive your brother from your heart.

MATTHEW 18:35

On February 9, 1960, Adolph Coors III was kidnapped and held for ransom. Seven months later, his body was found on a remote hillside—he had been shot to death. Adolph Coors IV, then fifteen years old, had lost his best friend.

The Coors case attracted nationwide attention. A suspect, Joseph Corbett, was apprehended, convicted and sentenced to life imprisonment in the Colorado penitentiary.

For years, through service in the Marine Corps and on into adulthood, Ad Coors harbored hatred for the man who had murdered his father. "I would have done anything in my power to have taken him had I met him," Ad recalls.

Then, in 1975, Ad became a Christian. Soon afterwards, he became part of a fellowship group which included a friend, Dale Morris. "Have you ever forgiven that man?" Dale asked Ad one day. Ad thought a moment and replied, "Sure, Dale. In my heart I have."

Dale pressed the question. "I'm not talking about that, I'm asking whether you've ever gone to him and told him you've forgiven him—and asked for his forgiveness that you've hated him for so long . . ."

It was during this same exchange that Ad learned that Dale was regularly visiting the maximum security unit of Canon City Prison—where the man convicted of killing Ad's father was confined. "Come with me when I go down next Wednesday," Dale exhorted his friend.

"That invitation hit me right in the pit of my stomach," Ad remembers, "There have been few tougher decisions in my life." Three weeks later, Ad made his decision. Dale made arrangements for him to visit Joseph Corbett.

The men arrived at the prison only to learn that the convict had refused to see them. "The funny thing," Ad now recounts, "is that I wasn't relieved—I was disappointed." So he left Corbett a Bible and inscribed it as follows: "I'm down here to see you today. I'm very disappointed that I can't. As a Christian, I have been commanded by our Lord and Savior Jesus Christ to ask for your forgiveness. I forgive you for the sins you have committed against our family, and I ask you to forgive me for the hatred I have had in my heart for you."

To those attending our rally, Ad explained that "Hatred is like the barrel of a shotgun that's plugged. Pretty soon it's going to go off in your face. It hurts the hater more than the hated. It hurt me. It ate me alive, and it ate my family alive."

Remarkably, Ad also told the audience that "Tonight I have a love for that man that only Jesus Christ could have put in my heart."

"Sticking a man in prison and expecting him to reform doesn't work," Ad continued. "It can be done only by forgiveness and a tremendous amount of love, and a knowledge of what Jesus Christ has done for us. That is being done in a dramatic way by Prison Fellowship. That is why—and because of my experience—I feel so drawn to this ministry."

His own knowledge of the grace of Christ has prompted Ad to divest himself of all his interest in the Coors' brewery. Instead, he works as an independent investment adviser and has spent much of his time as a volunteer with Prison Fellowship and other Christian endeavors.

Stories like these, unexplainable apart from an active supernatural God, make me wonder how anyone can question whether Jesus Christ lives.

Charles Colson, *Who Speaks for God?*

A Home in Heaven

Do not let your hearts be troubled. Trust in God; trust also in me. In my Father's house are many rooms; if it were not so, I would have told you. I am going there to prepare a place for you. And if I go and prepare a place for you, I will come back and take you to be with me that you also may be where I am.

JOHN 14:1–3

My best and dearest friend since boyhood, Roy Hicks, Jr., suddenly left this world for heaven. While flying home alone from Los Angeles to Eugene, Oregon, late one night, Roy's small plane developed engine trouble and crashed in the southern Oregon mountains. Instead of flying home to be with his little family in Eugene, Roy flew all the way home to be with Jesus in our Father's house.

I love this man, and always will. We laughed together, played together, prayed together, and cried together. His abrupt homegoing has been more difficult and intensely painful for me than I can adequately put into words. I really haven't "gotten over it," the way some people who know me think I should have. I haven't worked through it all. I want to believe I'm doing better, but the wound is still fresh and deep. I still lay in bed at night and worry about waking Joyce because I can't stop weeping. Sometimes the pain has been so great I've wondered if I'm even going to make it. I've found myself saying, "I don't think life is going to be fun anymore. What will I do now when I'm in trouble? Who will I call now when I'm in a jam? Who's going to lose all those new golf balls with me out on the back nine?"

"Do not let your hearts be troubled . . . I go to prepare a place for you."

I've had to come back again and again to our Lord's own cure for a troubled heart. One of the things that has kept me in this most troublesome, horrendous of times, is that I know I'm going to see Roy again. The Lord has promised me that. One day, in the place prepared for us, I will be with my old buddy again. I don't know if we'll get to play golf together or not, but I'll know him and I'll be with him. We'll live together and laugh together and rejoice in the Lord's presence and in all the bounty of our Father's good house.

Ron Mehl, God Works the Night Shift

FEBRUARY 11
Our Sonship

For you did not receive a spirit that makes you a slave again to fear, but you received the Spirit of sonship, and by him we cry, "Abba, Father." The Spirit himself testifies with our spirit, that we are God's children. Now if we are children then we are heirs—heirs of God and co-heirs with Christ, if indeed we share in his sufferings in order that we may also share in his glory.

ROMANS 8:15–17

The Father wants us to take on the attitude of sonship, of heirs. We are heirs to His character and nature. He transforms us, as we totally surrender to His will and to the Lordship of Jesus Christ, into the image of Christ. His ways become our ways; His thoughts become our thoughts. He gives us the confidence to overcome the wounds, hurts, and wrong choices from the past. He gives us the ability to make the right decisions for the future, to stand for righteousness, and to do God's will. He establishes deep roots of His character in us so we can radiate the life and character of God to others.

When we are sealed as the adopted children of God, when we have that stamp of approval by the work of the cross and the Spirit of adoption upon our lives, we should radiate the life of God! People should see a radical difference in our lives. People should know! A person's born-again experience is verified by the radiance of the Holy Spirit upon his life, pointing to the work of the cross. We prove that the seal of adoption is on our lives when we are zealous, transparent, and bold enough to openly let God live in us!

Doug Stringer, *The Fatherless Generation*

FEBRUARY 12   LINCOLN'S BIRTHDAY
National Restoration

If my people, who are called by my name, will humble themselves and pray and seek my face and turn from their wicked ways, then will I hear from heaven and will forgive their sin and will heal their land.

II CHRONICLES 7:14

We have been the recipients of the choicest bounties of Heaven. We have been preserved these many years in peace and prosperity. We have grown in numbers, wealth and power as no other nation has ever grown.

But we have forgotten God. We have forgotten the gracious Hand which preserved us in peace, and multiplied and enriched and strengthened us; and we have vainly imagined, in the deceitfulness of our hearts, that all these blessings were produced by some superior wisdom and virtue of our own.

Intoxicated with unbroken success, we have become too self-sufficient to feel the necessity of redeeming and preserving grace, too proud to pray to the God that made us!

It behooves us then to humble ourselves before the offended Power, to confess our national sins and to pray for clemency and forgiveness.

Abraham Lincoln

FEBRUARY 13

Iron Sharpening Iron

As iron sharpens iron,
  so one man sharpens another.

PROVERBS 27:17

One night after the 1992 Promise Keepers conference in Boulder, Colorado, our little band of accountability amigos stayed up late and asked each other a few tough questions, such as: *What are the three things you don't want anyone to know about you? If you could identify three questions you'd prefer not to be asked on a regular basis, what would they be?*

It took hours to go around the room asking each other, but by the end of that time we had written down twelve questions, three for each of us. More importantly, we made the commitment to each other that when we got back to Des Moines, we would ask each other these questions during our weekly accountability lunches.

After our return, one of the guys took our questions and printed them out on green cards, the size of a business card. All our questions are listed under each of our names. *And these questions are fair game for any of us, at any time.* On Tuesdays, during our accountability sessions, one of us will often whip our card from our wallet, lay it on the table, and start that sometimes uncomfortable dialogue. I've had a few unsettling lunches on Tuesdays where the Italian food didn't want to slide down very easily. But as unsettling as those questions have been on my digestive system, they've been producing growth in my spirit.

What exactly do the questions say? Quite frankly, it's none of your business. It's the business of our little group—our mutual business, by common consent. Because what each of us wrote down is specific to the areas where God is challenging us in our personal lives today.

Do you have a friend or group of friends in your life willing to ask you the tough questions? Men who will love you enough to not only celebrate your successes but also stand by you in your failures? Men who will stick closely by you during the bad times as well as good times, but will not fall into the trap of telling you only what you want to hear? Men who are willing to look you in the eye and ask you questions like these:

How's your thought life?

How are you handling the balance between work and home?

Have you been in the Word over the last few days?

What has God been teaching you recently?

How are you doing in handling God's provision of time, talent, and money?

Are you being responsible in protecting your eyes, hands, feet, and mind with women other than your wife?

Are you shooting straight in answering the above questions—or trying to blow smoke?

To the point? Yes indeed. Metal on metal. Iron sharpening iron.

Gary Rosberg, *Guard Your Heart*

FEBRUARY 14   ST. VALENTINE'S DAY

Romantic Love

There are three things that are too amazing for me,
   four that I do not understand:
the way of an eagle in the sky,
   the way of a snake on a rock,
the way of a ship on the high seas,
   and the way of a man with a maiden.

PROVERBS 30:18–19

How was it with you when you first fell in love with the girl you married? Or (if you feel that you never were in love) look at her now through another man's eyes. Think about those thing that are attractive in her. Love her with a sensitive appreciation and watch her become beautiful as she reflects and radiates the love you have poured out to her. . .

As Christians we can be sure that romantic love is as old as Time itself, for it came into being in the Garden when the first man and women gazed on each other. We must recognize that it was our Creator who gifted us with the capacity for the intense and passionate emotions required to fall in love. Clearly, God intended for our emotional potential to be fully developed in marriage and to find its fulfillment in oneness with our beloved.

Ed Wheat, *Love-Life for Every Married Couple*

FEBRUARY 15
His Strength

I pray that out of his glorious riches he may strengthen you with power through his Spirit in your inner being . . .

EPHESIANS 3:16

Behold, Lord, an empty vessel that needs to be filled. My Lord, fill it. I am weak in the faith; strengthen thou me. I am cold in love; warm me and make me fervent that my love may go out to my neighbour. I do not have a strong and firm faith; at times I doubt and am unable to trust thee altogether. O Lord, help me. Strengthen my faith and trust in thee. In thee I have sealed the treasures of all I have. I am poor; thou art rich and didst come to be merciful to the poor. I am a sinner; thou art upright. With me there is an abundance of sin; in thee is the fullness of righteousness. Therefore, I will remain with thee of whom I can receive but to whom I may not give. Amen.

Martin Luther

FEBRUARY 16
A Good Soldier

Endure hardship with us like a good soldier of Jesus Christ.

II TIMOTHY 2:3

Soldiers are identified by their uniforms. Spies and undercover agents disguise themselves, hoping to slip in without being noticed. The Lord doesn't need undercover Christians, but those who wear his uniform and proudly identify themselves with him.

Do you act as a "secret believer"—one who unveils your Christianity only when it is nonthreatening, then in more hostile situations, covers up your true identity? This kind of clandestine discipleship makes it easy to deny the Lord in difficult times. When the apostle Peter tried to secretly follow the Lord at a distance, on three occasions he denied that he knew Jesus.

To come out of your foxhole, you must first decide to be identified with Jesus Christ as your Lord and Savior. No more secrecy, no more undercover discipleship. Straightforwardly proclaiming your allegiance to the Lord is practical evidence of saving faith. Christ identified with your sins, taking them upon himself. By faith, you identify with his righteousness. After you accept Christ as your Savior and Lord, then publicly profess your faith.

Christians are clothed with garments of righteousness and wear helmets of salvation. Put on the uniform, then. Identify yourself publicly as a disciple of Jesus Christ.

Carman, Raising the Standard

FEBRUARY 17

A Refuge

I will say of the LORD, "He is my refuge and my fortress,
my God, in whom I trust."

PSALM 91:2

Discouragement.

Where does it come from?

Sometimes it feels like a dry, barren wind off a lonely desert. And something inside us begins to wilt.

At other times it feels like chilling mist. Seeping through our pores, it numbs the spirit and fogs the path before us.

What is it about discouragement that strips our lives of joy and leaves us feeling vulnerable and exposed?

I don't know all the reasons. I don't even know most of the reasons. But I do know *one* of the reasons: We don't have a refuge. Shelters are hard to come by these days . . . you know, people who care enough to listen. Who are good at keeping secrets. And we all need harbors to pull into when we feel weather-worn and blasted by the storm.

I have an old Marine buddy who became a Christian several years after he was discharged from the Corps. When news of his conversion reached me, I was pleasantly surprised. He was one of those guys you'd never picture as being interested in spiritual things. He cursed loudly, drank heavily, fought hard, chased women, loved weapons, and hated chapel service. *He was a great marine.* But God? They weren't on speaking terms when I bumped around with him.

Then one day we ran into each other. As the conversation turned to his salvation, he frowned, put his hand on my shoulder, and admitted: "Chuck, the only thing I miss is that old fellowship all the guys in our outfit used to have down at the slop shoot (Greek for tavern on base). Man, we'd sit around, laugh, tell stories, drink a few beers, and really let our hair down. It was great! I just haven't found anything to take the place of that great time we used to enjoy. I ain't got nobody to admit my faults to . . . to have 'em put their arms around me and tell me I'm still okay."

My stomach churned. Not because I was shocked, but because I had to agree. The man needed a refuge . . . someone to hear him out . . . .

Where do *you* turn when the bottom drops out of *your* life? Or when you face an issue that is embarrassing . . . maybe even scandalous. Like:

- Your mate is talking separation or divorce.
- Your daughter has run away . . . for the fourth time . . . and you're afraid she's pregnant.
- You've lost your job. It's your own fault.
- Financially, you've blown it.
- Your parent is an alcoholic.
- Your wife is having an affair.
- You flunked your entrance exam or you messed up the interview.
- You're in jail because you broke the law.

What do you need when circumstances puncture your fragile dikes and threaten to engulf your life with pain and confusion?

You need a shelter. A listener. Someone who understands . . . .

Discouraged people don't need critics. They hurt enough already. They don't need more guilt or piled-on distress. They need encouragement. They need a refuge.

A place to hide and heal.

A willing, caring, available someone. A confidant and comrade-at-arms. Can't find one? Why not share David's shelter? The One he called My Strength, Mighty Rock, Fortress, Stronghold, and High Tower.

David's Refuge *never* failed. Not even once. And he never regretted the times he dropped his heavy load and ran for cover.

Neither will you.

Charles Swindoll, Growing Strong in the Seasons of Life

FEBRUARY 18

Understanding Your Father

Honor your father and your mother, so that you may live long in the land the LORD your God is giving you.

EXODUS 20:12

If your father is still alive and you are able to have contact, try to spend time with him—but . . . only for the purpose of gathering information, not to discuss your feelings or hurts with him. If it feels uncomfortable even to talk with him in this way, take some time to reflect on why this is so. Obviously if he abused you physically, sexually, or even emotionally, you have good reason to bypass this part of the process. Otherwise, ask him about his memory of those days as well as about his own childhood experiences with *his* father. His answers should give you some valuable insights.

If your father has died or cannot be contacted for some other reason, try to contact his siblings—your aunts and uncles. Ask for their memories of your father, and gather whatever information you can about his childhood and adolescence.

Several years ago I was able to travel to Ireland and visit relatives there. During that trip I learned more about the Irish custom that the youngest son cares for the widowed mother, which I had read of earlier in Leon Uris's book *Trinity*. Light bulbs went on in my head. My father had been the youngest son in his family, and his mother had been widowed while he was still living at home. It turned out that he had stayed at home and cared for her until he was thirty-five years old. Only after she passed away was he free to marry. That information helped me gain a new understanding of my father's life.

Once again, *understanding* is the key. The apostle Paul warned about people who are always learning, "but they never understand the truth" (2 Timothy 3:7). We need to gather facts, but we also need to work at understanding those facts. We need to apply them to ourselves and to our experience of our father.

In my case, learning that my father had spent so much of life caring for a strong, domineering woman helped me understand why it was so difficult for him to share himself emotionally with me. My sister always used to tell me how much Dad cared for me, but I couldn't connect with it; he never showed me his love in ways I could understand at the time. Her insistence that Dad genuinely loved me seemed to contradict my own experience—until I learned more about my father's past.

David Stoop, *Making Peace With Your Father*

FEBRUARY 19
Taking Fatherhood Seriously

The sleep of a laborer is sweet,
   whether he eats little or much,
but the abundance of a rich man
   permits him no sleep.

ECCLESIASTES 5:12

Jim worked seventy hours a week as a sales manager. He was committed to it—and proud of it. He believed it was the American thing to do. He believed he was being patriotic. He believed people respected him more for it. He thought people not as committed were slackers. His devotion had its effect. He was enormously successful at the professional level. He made gobs of money, and he earned many prestigious awards.

Yet, Jim never had much time for his three sons. He never could break free for parent-teacher conferences. He couldn't tell you the name or location of any of the professional caregivers for his boys, like doctors, dentists, barbers, and so on. Sunday mornings belonged to him—he usually played golf with buddies from work. He believed spiritual and moral instruction for his boys was paramount, but he delegated that responsibility to his wife.

If you asked Jim what drove him to work so hard, he would be hard-pressed to give you an answer. Let's face it. Workaholism is not rational. Here is a key idea: People don't always act *rationally,* but they do always act with *purpose.* In other words, there are reasons *why* we do *what* we do.

Men may work too hard because of fear, because of their values, because they selfishly enjoy work, or because they hope to escape conflict in the home. They may still be seeking to win the approval of their own fathers. Whatever the reason, it is not rational.

The Bible commends hard work. Our culture and society esteem hard work. Hard work, industry, initiative, excellence, and diligence represent the values that made America great. On the other hand, the family also made America great. But today the economy takes first place at the expense of the family. The family is hurting. When we get our work and family priorities out of balance, we tend to shortchange family.

Let's face it. You and I could work twenty-four hours a day. But for what! The Bible says, "Don't weary yourself trying to get rich. Why waste your time! For riches can disappear as though they had the wings of a bird!" (Prov, 23:4–5 TLB). And also:

The sleep of a laboring man is sweet,

Whether he eats little or much;

But the abundance of the rich will not permit him to sleep. (Eccl. 5:12 NKJV)

If you can't sleep, you may be trying to do too much.

... No amount of success at the job will compensate for failure at home. To succeed in work but fail at home is to fail completely.

Patrick Morley, *The Seven Seasons of a Man's Life*

Small Beginnings

He guides the humble in what is right
and teaches them his way.

PSALM 25:9

Once I was praying for the Lord to move mightily in my ministry. I had asked, fasted, and prayed. I had probably begged a little and foamed at the mouth too, but none of it hurried the plan of God in my life. After many days of absolute silence, He finally sent me a little answer. The Lord answered my prayer by saying, "You are concerned about building a ministry, but I am concerned about building a man." He concluded by mentioning this warning, which has echoed in my ears all of my life. He said, "Woe unto the man whose ministry becomes bigger than he is!" Since then I have concerned myself with praying for the minister and not for the ministry. I realized that if the house outgrows the foundation, gradually the foundation will crack, the walls will collapse, and great will be the fall of it!

No matter what you are trying to build, whether it is a business, a ministry, or a relationship, give it time to grow. Some of the best friendships start out gradually. Some of the strongest Christians once desperately needed prayer for their weaknesses. I am still amazed at who I am becoming as I put my life daily into His hands. He is changing me. He's not finished. There is so much more that needs to be done. Every day I see more immaturity in me. But what a sharp contrast I am now to what I was.

Humility is a necessity when you know that every accomplishment had to be the result of the wise Master Builder who knows when to do what. He knew when I needed friends. He knew when I needed to sit silently in the night, wrap my arms around my limitations, and whisper a soft request for help into the abyss of my pain. He is the One who rolls back the clouds on the storms and orders the rain to stop. Oh, how I trust Him more dearly and more nearly than I have ever trusted Him before. He is too wise to make a mistake!

T. D. Jakes, *Can You Stand to Be Blessed?*

February 21

The Craft of Fathering

Let us not become weary in doing good, for at the proper time we will reap a harvest if we do not give up.

GALATIANS 6:9

As I was growing up, I had the opportunity to do summer work for some licensed craftsmen, mostly electricians and bricklayers. I remember watching Jerry, my bricklaying boss, and the proficiency he'd developed over the years. From him I learned how to proportion the right amounts of mud, bricks, and wedges needed to complete a particular project. I watched Jerry take a brick in his hand. He seemed so agile and quick as he buttered the brick with mud and placed it into the right position. I noticed how he put everything he needed within reach, so he could get into a rhythm and have hundreds of bricks perfectly in place in what seemed like no time at all.

Or take Curt, the electrician I worked for. He would carefully roll his wire out on the floor before trying to pull it all through the conduit. Taking the time to unravel the kinks with his fingers assured him of a smooth pull through the pipe. Sometimes there were situations where he even had to pump soap into the pipe to make the pull easier. And then, after the wire was successfully through, he always double-checked the length before cutting it. "Measure twice, cut once," he would tell me.

There are many procedures these craftsmen have learned that make sense after you've seen them done. You say, "Of course, that's the best way to do it." But while they make sense, they aren't necessarily common sense. In other words, if you had been working alone, you probably wouldn't have done it that way. It would have become obvious to you only after you had gone through a long trial-and-error process yourself.

But what these journeymen represent are countless generations of experimentation, of searching for effectiveness and efficiency and *mastery*. They have wisdom and tricks of the trade handed down from journeyman to apprentice, journeyman to apprentice, journeyman to you. When you assist a journeyman, you learn his secrets of the trade.

As fathers, you and I need to become craftsmen. Maybe now we're apprentices, but we can *become* craftsmen.

In a moment of great love and affection, you conceived a human being, a child. What an incredible feat in and of itself! Here is flesh of your flesh, bone of your bone: a son or daughter. A miracle. Two eyes. A nose. (Your nose!) A living, breathing human being who will grow up and think thoughts, and cry tears, and shake hands, and tell jokes, and fall in love, and battle the odds. It's incredible: you've fathered a child!

But however incredible that may be, we have to admit that any halfway-interested male graduate of puberty can father a child. A man I know who came out of the ghetto says, "Anyone can make a kid, but it takes a man to be a father." *Fathers need to be craftsmen.*

A newborn child is a wonder in and of herself. But what makes for a great deal of the wonder is the amount of potential wrapped up in that wrinkly, purple skin. When the child takes her first breath of air, she lets out a wail, full and healthy. One day, that same child may sing a song where she hits a note so perfectly that all who hear her will suddenly realize that God is a God of incredible beauty and majesty.

That infant in the delivery room opens his eyes for the first time and blinks in discovery. Faint, blurry images, but he sees something; a light, a face, a table. Years later, that same child may open his eyes and suddenly see something he's never seen before. He may have insight into the way one chemical compound affects another and suddenly he knows: this is it, this is the cure for cancer.

In a newborn child, you have raw material that's beautiful in itself, but capable of so much more beauty. We need to shape that life and mold it. Anyone can hammer a nail into a board, but only a craftsman can build a cabinet, a house, or a home. Be a craftsman! Be skilled in your fathering! Produce in your family a thing of quality and usefulness and beauty.

Our society has shown us that trial and error doesn't usually work in the craft of fathering. By the time we learn how to do things the best way, our children may be grown—so now is the time to get started. In order to become skilled craftsmen, we must all begin as apprentices. We need to turn to other men and ask them, "Show me how to do this and do it well. What are your tricks of the trade? What are your secrets?"

Ken Canfield, *The Seven Secrets of Effective Fathers*

Humility

Humble yourselves before the Lord, and he will lift you up.

JAMES 4:10

[Editor's note: George Washington carried with him, in his field notebook, twenty-four pages of personal prayers he had handwritten. The first prayer, that follows here, was taken from that notebook. The second prayer is "Washington's prayer for the United States of America" and appears on a plaque at Pohick Church, Fairfax County, Virginia, where Washington was a vestryman from 1762 to 1784.]

Almighty God, and most merciful Father, who didst command the children of Israel to offer a daily sacrifice to Thee, that thereby they might glorify and praise Thee for Thy protection both night and day, receive O Lord, my morning sacrifice which I now offer up to Thee;

I yield Thee hearty and humble thanks, that Thou hast preserved me from the dangers of the night past and brought me to the light of this day, and the comfort thereof, a day which is consecrated to Thine own service and for Thine own honour. Let my heart therefore gracious God be so affected with the glory and majesty of it, that I may not do mine own works but wait on Thee, and discharge those weighty duties Thou required of me: and since Thou art a God of pure eyes, and will be sanctified in all who draw nearer to Thee, who dost not regard the sacrifice of fools, nor hear sinners who tread in Thy courts, pardon I beseech Thee, my sins, remove them from Thy presence, as far as the east is from the west, and accept me for the merits of Thy son Jesus Christ, that when I come into Thy temple and compass Thine altar, my prayer may come before Thee as incense, and as I desire Thou wouldst hear me calling upon Thee in my prayers, so give me peace to hear the calling on me in Thy word, that it may be wisdom, righteousness, reconciliation and peace to the saving of my soul in the day of the Lord Jesus.

Grant that I may hear it with reverence, receive it with meekness, mingle it with faith, and that it may accomplish in me gracious God, the good work for which Thou hast sent it.

Bless my family, kindred, friends and country, be our God and guide this day forever for His sake, who lay down in the grave and arose again for us, Jesus Christ our Lord. Amen.

Almighty God, We make our earnest prayer that Thou wilt keep the United States in Thy Holy protection; and Thou wilt incline the hearts of the Citizens to cultivate a spirit of subordination and obedience to government; and entertain a brotherly affection and love for one another and for their fellow Citizens of the United States at large, and particularly for their brethren who have served in the Field.

And finally that Thou wilt most graciously be pleased to dispose us all to do justice, to love mercy, and to demean ourselves with that Charity, humility, and pacific temper of mind which were the Characteristics of the Divine Author of our blessed Religion, and without a humble imitation of whose example in these things we can never hope to be a happy nation.

Grant our supplication, we beseech Thee, through Jesus Christ our Lord. Amen.

George Washington

FEBRUARY 23
Tears

He who goes out weeping
carrying seed to sow,
will return with songs of joy,
carrying sheaves with him.

PSALM 126:6

Why are we afraid to cry? Usually, because when you're crying, your defenses are never more fully down and you're wide open to getting hurt worse. Crying disarms you. Indeed, that's why the purest tears are spiritual weapons and most definitely not "the world's mighty weapons."

For the wounded, fearful man who has become so well defended that he can't access his own inner feelings, tears are a blessing that flush out his clogged spirit. Often trapped in loneliness, he wants to be disarmed, because he knows he can't either love or be loved when his energies are consumed in defending himself.

Holocaust survivor Elie Wiesel tells of a man who worried after seeing the death-camp horror, "Will I ever cry again?" Translation: Has living amid the inhumanity of Evil caused me to build such formidable defenses that I've become desensitized, and thereby dehumanized?"

Significantly, the man did not worry, "Will I ever laugh again?" Laughter is simply not the more reliable indicator of reality. If you can't cry, you've lost touch with your own heart and can't laugh genuinely. Satan laughs; he can deceive and manipulate, but can't cry heartfelt tears. I can't imagine Hitler's crying, yet I've seen photos of him laughing with Nazi henchmen.

When his friend Lazarus died, Jesus wept. Occasionally I read Christian commentators who wish the Scriptures said somewhere that Jesus laughed. I don't worry about that. I know he laughed heartily, because I know he cried deeply.

Gordon Dalbey, *Fight Like a Man*

FEBRUARY 24

Belief

Then the father realized that this was the exact time at which Jesus had said to him, "Your son will live." So he and all his household believed.

JOHN 4:53

How do you get to belief? You have a need; you risk; you invest your trust in the proper object; then the Father acts in ways that will simply leave you speechless. That's when you'll have that John 4 experience: "So he [the official] and all his household believed" (verse 53). That is the Father's surprise! Paul said it right, "Now to Him who is able to do immeasurably more than all we ask or imagine, according to his power that is at work within us" (Ephesians 3:20).

A mature Christian is not the one who says, "Lord, zap me with faith and belief so that I can do the mountain bit." The mature Christian is the one who has gone through the process of need, Christ-centered help, faith, and risk . . . and has seen God faithful.

The one sport I have ever excelled at is swimming. I have even taught many people to swim. If you are swimming in competition, I can show you how to cut time off your speed. Swimming is an experienced fact to me, but that maturity in swimming never came in shallow water. I'll never forget the day when I was very small and my father let go of me in water that was much deeper than I was tall. The realization that I was in deep water and swimming was an absolute thrill. That day I laughed and laughed. My father laughed with me.

In the area of faith, the heavenly Father laughs for the same reason. Have you heard Him chuckle lately?

Steve Brown, Jumping Hurdles

February 25
Individual Dignity

While Jesus was having dinner at Levi's house, many tax collectors and "sinners" were eating with him and his disciples, for there were many who followed him. When the teachers of the law who were Pharisees saw him eating with the "sinners" and tax collectors, they asked his disciples: "Why does he eat with tax collectors and 'sinners'?"

On hearing this, Jesus said to them, "It is not the healthy who need a doctor, but the sick. I have not come to call the righteous, but sinners."

Mark 2:15–17

People in Jesus' time who looked to him as their political savior were constantly befuddled by his choice of companions. He became known as a friend of tax collectors, a group clearly identified with the foreign exploiters. Though he denounced the religious system of his day, he treated a leader like Nicodemus with respect, and though he spoke against the dangers of money and of violence, he showed love and compassion toward a rich young ruler and a Roman centurion.

In short, Jesus honored the dignity of each person whether he agreed with him or her or not. Anyone . . . was welcome to join his kingdom. The person was more important than any category or label.

I feel convicted by this quality of Jesus every time I get involved in a cause I strongly believe in. How easy it is to join the politics of polarization, to find myself shouting across the picket lines at the "enemy" on the other side. How hard it is to remember that the kingdom of God calls me to love the woman who has just emerged from the abortion clinic (and, yes, even her doctor), the promiscuous person who is dying of AIDS, the wealthy landowner who is exploiting God's creation. If I cannot show love to such people, then I need to ask if I have understood Jesus' gospel.

A political movement by nature draws lines, makes distinctions, pronounces judgment; in contrast, Jesus' love cuts across lines, transcends distinctions, and dispenses grace. If my activism drives out such love, I betray his kingdom.

Philip Yancey, *Finding God in Unexpected Places*

FEBRUARY 26

A New Identity

"Where is your faith?" he asked his disciples.
In fear and amazement they asked one another, "Who is this? He commands even the winds and the water, and they obey him."

LUKE 8:25

When I was a boy, my hero was Superman. I often pretended to be like him. Imagining I was Clark Kent, I would get Mama's longest towel, shake it out real good, flip it back around and tie it under my neck. Then I would get up on top of something, usually the chest of drawers, make sure my cape was ready, hold up my arms, and loudly proclaim, "Da dum da dum da dum . . . here I am, faster than a speeding bullet, more powerful than a locomotive, able to leap tall buildings in a single bound." I was all primed for the moment, up, up and away! At least, I thought so! But soon it was down, down in dismay! I still have a scar today to prove it!

It is one thing to play like Superman, and another thing to be him. When it finally dawned on me I would never really be Superman, I realized I would have to settle for being just a mere man. But then I discovered God's plan, and found out I could be much more than just a mere man. God had a not-so-secret identity for me.

When Jesus calmed the stormy seas, His disciples exclaimed, "What manner of man is this! (Luke 8:25). Jesus had told them to go across the lake, but the nasty weather conditions caused fear to rise up in them and they forgot His words. Often in our own situations, even when we have heard the Word, stormy circumstances arise. When that happens we can unwittingly enter the danger zone. And the danger is we might allow our faith to be overcome by fear. We can forget what manner of men we really are. If we allow that to occur, then we are mere men.

Jesus knew who He was! He knew and operated in His authority and realized His supernatural abilities. A storm was not about to keep Him from accomplishing His goals. He was a SUPERNATURAL MAN and He knew it. What about us? Are we destined to be just mere men? Is there a new identity for us? Let us examine what God's Word says about us. Second Corinthians 5:17 says, "Therefore if any man be in Christ, he is a new creature: old things are passed away; behold, all things are become new."

New "creatures"—did you know that another way of saying new creature would be "a brand new species"? We are no longer mere men, but supernatural men, exactly like Jesus. We got that way by being born again of a supernatural God. Being born again by the Spirit of God puts us in a different dimension, a new level, a league by ourselves. We truly have a new identity.

Buddy Harrison, *Man, Husband, Father*

February 27
Going All the Way

Jesus replied, "No one who puts his hand to the plow and looks back is fit for service in the kingdom of God."

Luke 9:62

I believe the secret of the power of the Gospel is to be willing to go all the way with the Lord. I believe a man who is on the fence cannot enjoy the things of God. I believe when he tries to get betwixt and between, he gets into an awful mess.

We had an experience at Boulder Dam that illustrates this point. A group of powder men had been working all night drilling holes in the mountainside to blast away the rock. They wanted to make the big shot before the day crew came on. At last the holes were all dug, the dynamite was in, the wires connected with the power line. The man who was to set off the blast was short of wire and there wasn't time to send to camp for more. What wire he had wasn't long enough to let him get beyond the danger zone of falling rocks. He saw a little cave in the mountainside and thought he'd push the button and jump in there. So he pushed the button, the blast went off, he jumped in the cave—and there was a rattlesnake! He was betwixt and between. He couldn't go in on account of the snake and he couldn't go out on account of the falling rocks. What could he do? He saw a huge rock at the cave entrance. In less time than it takes to tell it, he picked up that rock, dropped it over the snake and jumped into the cave. The snake tattled and rattled but couldn't reach the man because it was pinned down by the rock.

I wonder sometimes whether some folks who say the are Christians really believe in the Lord or not. I don't know whether they have been born again. They're on the fence. They're betwixt and between. I want to say that you're like that man in the cave and you'll have to do something about it. If you get hold of the rock of Christ Jesus, that will save you. He can hold Satan down.

R. G. LeTourneau, *God Runs My Business*

FEBRUARY 28
Prayer and the Word

. . . and will give out attention to prayer and the ministry of the word.

ACTS 6:4

The idea continued to come to my mind, and finally—with real dread—I decided God was calling me to more extended times of prayer. I knew I must do my best to obey, whether or not I felt suited to the task and whether or not I had time, and regardless of how much I dreaded it! The next step, of course, was to decide just how much time God wanted me to spend in prayer each day. After some soul-searching I decided that for me, "longer prayer time" meant one hour a day on my knees, rather than praying while walking. Incredible! I felt I couldn't possibly do it, and yet I must. I resisted for several days, but at last I knew I must start the next morning, so I built that hour into my schedule and waited with trepidation.

I did it. And it was just a bad as I had feared. After five minutes I couldn't think of anything more to say. (I have read a survey that reveals the average Christian's daily prayer time is about three minutes—and that of a pastor about seven minutes.) I stuck with it, and the hour finally came to an end, but my relief was tempered by the knowledge that I must repeat the process the next day!

But I persisted, with the help of a prayer list and some favorite Psalms of praise. I was being welcomed into God's presence, His very throne room, and I began to feel at home. As the days went by, the terror of that time with God gradually changed to anticipation, and I now regret it when I miss my appointment.

Then, as should certainly be expected, my prayer list items began to be checked off. In fact, some quite amazing things began to happen—even things I had not prayed about. So, in addition to becoming better acquainted with my Lord and Savior, I had the added encouragement of seeing my prayers answered.

As my devotional life developed, I learned that prayer brings power, but character grows through reading and obeying the Word of God—the Scriptures. I learned this by the strange experience of coming from prayer tired, in a sense, and finding myself easily upset by minor household affairs, instead of being quiet and stable. Amazed at this condition, I took stock and realized that even extended prayer could not fulfill my need for regular spiritual food from the Bible, ministered by that same Holy Spirit of prayer. My extended prayer times had edged out my Bible reading, leaving me spiritually undernourished, so I began again to make time for regular reading of the Scriptures too.

I doubt that all of God's children should have the same kind of devotional life. I am only stating my own experiences for whatever value they may be to others. But my perception is that not enough praying is going on. God, for reasons of His own, wants His will and work known and empowered by the Word and by prayer, so these disciplines should occupy a place of great importance in our days.

Ken Taylor, *My Life: A Guided Tour*

FEBRUARY 29

A Cheerful Heart

A cheerful heart is good medicine,
but a crushed spirit dries up the bones.

PROVERBS 17:22

"I wish they'd have put the extra day
in the summer."

Bil Keane, *Count Your Blessings*

March

MARCH 1
Renewed Courage

So keep up your courage, men . . .

ACTS 27:25A

A decline in courage may be the most striking feature an outside observer notices in the West today. The Western world has lost its civic courage, both as a whole and separately, in each country, in each government, in each political party, and, of course, in the United Nations. Such a decline in courage is particularly noticeable among the ruling and intellectual elites, causing an impression of a loss of courage by the entire society. There remain many courageous individuals, but they have no determining influence on public life. Political and intellectual functionaries exhibit this depression, passivity, and perplexity in their actions and in their statements, and even more so in their self-serving rationales as to how realistic, reasonable, and intellectually and even morally justified it is to base state policies on weakness and cowardice. And the decline in courage, at times attaining what could be termed a lack of manhood, is ironically emphasized by occasional outbursts of boldness and inflexibility on the part of those same functionaries when dealing with weak governments and with countries that lack support, or with doomed currents which clearly cannot offer any resistance. But they get tongue-tied and paralyzed when they deal with powerful governments and threatening forces, with aggressors and international terrorists.

Must one point out that from ancient times a decline in courage has been considered the first symptom of the end?

Aleksandr Solzhenitsyn, *A World Apart*

MARCH 2
Dedicated Talent

May the favor of the Lord our God rest upon us;
establish the work of our hands for us—
yes, establish the work of our hands.

PSALM 90:17

You know you have *some* talent, and God knows you have it, for He gave it to you. The thing to do, then, is offer it back to Him, dedicate yourself and your talent to Jesus.

After dedication comes discipline—the hard grind to sharpen this tool that God has given you to work for Him. I learned very early that God had given me a very special talent. But I had to do the practicing. The Holy Spirit doesn't do this for you. What He does, though, is to give you a confidence, a poise when you really do your part. He helps you to feel inside, "I can do it. I *can*, for God, for his glory."

[To maximize your opportunities:]

Recognize that you do have a God-given talent. Remember, everybody does!

Dedicate the talent *and yourself* to the Lord.

Discipline yourself to train to be the best in your field, *for God.*

Believe you can do it.

Take every opportunity no matter how seemingly small. It might be the very door God is unlocking for some future big work for Him.

As we walk with the Lord in the light of His Word and try to be our very best for Him, it's exciting! We never know what God has in store for us. I just can't wait to see what He's going to do next!

Talent? Yes, it's important. But it's just one piece of the picture. We have to be on the alert to take and make opportunities to use this talent to glorify Jesus Christ.

Then—be ready for life with a capital *L.*

Dino Kartsonakis, *Dino*

MARCH 3
Being There for Our Children

Fathers, do not exasperate your children; instead, bring them up in the training and instruction of the Lord.

EPHESIANS 6:4

Last year, I spoke to seven hundred high school students about the importance of making amends with others. A sixteen-year-old boy moved close, looked around to see if anyone was listening, and said quietly, "My dad left us when I was a little kid. Who is going to teach me to be a man?" He began to cry. "I mess up every relationship I get into. I hurt the people I care the most about. I really hurt this girl. I need to make it right but I don't know how. Who's going to teach me how to relate to people?" The day that young man's dad walked away (for whatever reason), he sentenced his son to years, perhaps a lifetime, of trying to figure out how to relate to people.

According to the apostle Paul and the Bible, dads are responsible for the social condition of their children. Instead of exasperating children by being absentee or abusive fathers, we must equip children practically, positionally, and personally.

How can dads fulfill this incredibly difficult role? The answer lies in Paul's words, "in the instruction of the Lord." We need divine assistance in order to be people of faith—and good fathers.

Fortunately, men are recognizing this. During the past thirty years men have been great promise makers but lousy promise keepers. This is changing. All across the nation, thousands of men are jamming the country's largest stadiums to proclaim boldly their allegiance to the family and to call upon God for assistance. I heartily applaud the efforts of Promise Keepers and other similar men's groups—they are making a difference! Through God's grace there is continuing strength and help for dad—and much hope for the family.

David Moore, *Five Lies of the Century*

March 4
Men in Unity

My prayer is not for them alone. I pray also for those who will believe in me through their message, that all of them may be one, Father, just as you are in me and I am in you. May they also be in us so that the world may believe that you have sent me.

John 17:20–21

Rise Up, O Men of God

Rise up, O men of God,
Have done with lesser things,
Give heart and soul and mind and strength
To serve the King of Kings.
Rise up, O men of God.
His Kingdom tarries long;
Bring in the day of brotherhood
And end the night of wrong.
Rise up, O men of God
The Church for you doth wait,
Her strength unequal to her task;
Rise up, and make her great.
Lift high the cross of Christ,
Tread where His feet have trod;
As brothers of the Son of man,
Rise up, O men of God.

William P. Merrill

March 5
Encouragement

Therefore encourage each other with these words.

1 Thessalonians 4:18

I coached T-Ball for nine years, giving three years to each son (who conveniently have birthdays three years apart). We taught those five-to-eight-year-olds the fundamentals of baseball and also some of the fundamentals of life. But in my coaching career, the *most* important lesson was that of encouragement.

At the start of every season I always met with the parents, explaining that my purpose in coaching was to encourage these boys and girls and to provide a good experience with a sport. I did not yell at them and did not permit parents to yell at any child except in encouragement. I told the parents that I would personally go over to the rooters' section and sit with them, reminding them of this principle if they slipped. I trained my other coaches to always get down on their knees during practice so they could look the child in the eyes, and with a smile on their face affirm what he/she was able to do. We also made an effort to put a hand or arm around their shoulder, tousle their hair and give a quick hug. We believed in that type of affirming contact, for we not only gained the trust of the child but we earned the right to be heard when we needed to give suggestions and corrections.

Sometimes it was so hard to find something encouraging to say to these children that it bordered on the ridiculous. I remember one game in particular. The dad coaching first base was frustrated with one of our players, yet so determined to be affirming that he hollered, "Way to kick the dirt, son, that's the way to get the dirt out of the way!". . . Many parents have commented that as their child began playing football or soccer in high school, they would invariably make a comparison to their T-Ball experience and say, "Coach Rand would not have done this. And our coaches would not have yelled like that." Our prayer time together and simple Bible study with each of our sons made a difference.

After coaching for nine years, I was privileged to coach a championship team with my children in the final year. And I know that was no accident. I firmly believe that under the fruit of encouragement, our teams always peaked at the end of the season because the boys and girls believed in themselves. You can't convince me that it was my coaching prowess, because all of our kids weren't outstanding players. They knew that we believed in them, win or lose, so they could not fail.

Ron Rand, *For Fathers Who Aren't in Heaven*

MARCH 6

Contagious Confidence

So Pharaoh said to Joseph, "I hereby put you in charge of the whole land of Egypt." Then Pharaoh took his signet ring from his finger and put it on Joseph's finger. He dressed him in robes of fine linen and put a gold chain around his neck. He had him ride in a chariot as his second-in-command, and men shouted before him, "Make way!" Thus he put him in charge of the whole land of Egypt.

GENESIS 41:41–43

While growing up, I did not have very many adult men to model myself after, my parents having separated when I was only eight. Thus, the heroes of the Bible became my heroes in childhood, as well as my role models. I learned about Jesus Christ who gave Himself for other people feeling their hurt, and caring about their pain.

I used to think often about Daniel and the three Hebrew boys who believed in God and stayed with their principles—even when the king tried to put them to death.

The hero I related to most is Joseph in the Old Testament. Maybe I identified with him because he had to face the world without his family. I used to mull over his being alone and in prison in Egypt because his jealous brothers had sold him into slavery.

Somewhere during my childhood, and I am sure it was after I started to achieve in school, I sincerely believed that God was capable of taking any person from any circumstances and doing something with that life. Joseph started in slavery but eventually became prime minister of Egypt. Not a bad role model, was he?

It does not matter where we come from or what we look like. If we recognize our abilities, are willing to learn and to use what we know in helping others, we will always have a place in the world.

I start out each morning with prayer and reading from the Bible, mostly Proverbs. I pray and read Proverbs each evening. During the course of the day, I frequently ask the Lord to give me wisdom to use the knowledge that I have and to give me perspective and understanding, particularly when difficult situations arise.

God not only gives me those things, but along with them, a confidence that what I am doing is right. That confidence is contagious.

Ben Carson, *Think Big*

March 7
A Tender Warrior

Husbands, love your wives, just as Christ loved the church and gave himself up for her.

EPHESIANS 5:25

Men must develop a thorough, biblical, manly love. Now what is that? In a word—*headship*. It is leadership with an emphasis upon responsibility, duty, and sacrifice. Not rank or domination. No "I'm the boss" assertion. Most people who have to insist that they are leaders usually aren't. "Husbands, love your wives [*exactly*] as Christ also loved the church *and gave Himself up for her.*" Harsh dominance is not the way of Christ.

Note the linkage. Headship is linked to saviorship. The heart of saviorship is sacrifice. The key to leadership is serving—not "lording it over."

So color your headship in soft shades of the tender side—
providing
protecting
teaching
caring
guiding
loving
developing
freeing
sacrificing
leading;
rather than in the harsh tones of the warrior side:
ruling
presiding
directing
determining
bossing
deciding.

The essence of the tender tones is servanthood. The mature husband understands servant-leadership. Just like Jesus.

What does a healthy man look like? I can't help but recall a statement from a young guy who lives near us—a sixteen-year-old high school sophomore. His parents divorced when he was eight years old. His father left and has never returned. His stepdad, a tyrannical and poor excuse for a man, treats him poorly. Tells him to "shut up" all the time. Tells him he's worthless, stupid, and will never amount to anything.

But just ask the boy about his dream and his eyes will light up. This is what he'll tell you: "I'd like to find out where my real dad lives. And I'd like to move in next door without him knowing who I was. And—I'd like to just become his friend. Once I had become his friend, then maybe it would be okay for me to move on."

This same young man who has had all kinds of difficulty in his life was asked to write an essay on the subject "What is a man?" The following is his brief essay—written by a boy who has never really been around a man, never really seen one. But I think there is something so inherent, so in-grained, so intrinsic, so fundamental, that even a young boy who has never seen it modeled can put it into words. Here's what he wrote:

A real man is kind.
A real man is caring.
A real man walks away from silly macho fights.
A real man helps his wife.
A real man helps his kids when they are sick.
A real man doesn't run from his problems.
A real man sticks to his word and keeps his promises.
A real man is honest.
A real man is not in trouble with the law.

It's one lonely boy's vision of a man who *stays*. A man who is both an authority and under authority.

It's a vision of a Tender Warrior.

Stu Weber, *Tender Warrior*

Promotion

The LORD will make you the head, not the tail. If you pay attention to the commands of the LORD your God that I give you this day and carefully follow them, you will always be at the top, never at the bottom.

DEUTERONOMY 28:13

Believers should expect to rise toward the top of whatever field of endeavor their vocation is in. We should be the best workers on the job in any situation. When we have a covenant with God, we have not only the promise of eternal life later on, but also the assurance of victory in this life now. Rising to the top in our job field is a central promise of the covenant we have with God.

Deuteronomy 28:13 says that the Lord will make us *the head and not the tail.*

This is not some vague ethereal promise, but a contractual covenant in which He promises to help us be on top of the practical areas of business and life. The passage of Deuteronomy 28 is talking about such things as our work in the city, our work in the fields, our work in our household and our work in the military. A man of covenant will expect to excel in his job.

Promotion comes from the Lord (Psalms 75:6). If a man is walking in covenant, God will cause him to excel in his work. This excellence will bring him success. Proverbs 22:29 states:

See a man that excels in his work, he will stand before kings; he will not stand before unknown men.

Both Psalm 1 and Joshua 1 promise that if we will meditate continually on God's Word, He will cause us to prosper and have success in everything we do. A noncovenantal view of Scriptures will say that this success is only in a mystic realm. An understanding of covenant brings the blessings of God into a man's character and life, and thereby into his work and the world around him.

Believers should grasp the relationship between work and faith. A covenant attitude in the heart will produce an excellent quality in the workplace. Quality will cause promotion and blessing. We need to develop our faith that we will be promoted in the workplace. An example of this grace and favor is given us by the patriarch Joseph. Genesis 39:2–4 states:

The Lord was with Joseph, and he was a successful man . . . .and his master saw that the Lord made all he did to prosper in his hand. So Joseph found favor in his sight and served him. Then he made him overseer of his house and put all that he had in his hand.

The witness of the fact that Joseph was walking in covenant with God was that he was successful in what he did on his job. The quality of work at our job is the primary testimony that most people see about our faith in God.

Keith Intrater, *Covenant Relationships*

March 9
Reconciliation

Here there is no Greek or Jew, circumcised or uncircumcised, barbarian, Scythian, slave or free, but Christ is all, and is in all.

Colossians 3:11

In high school I used to go to an inner-city YMCA to play "city ball." That's slammin', jammin', no-blood, no-foul, and no-wimps-allowed basketball. It's a brutal sport, but great fun. I'm a white guy and a lot of the other teens were black. Every time I showed up at the "Y" my black friends would fill the air with fun-loving insults about the other players' abilities, the so-called "trash talk." When it came to trash talking with the white guy, racist talk was included. "White men can't jump," they said (and a whole lot more!). Long before they made a movie featuring that stereotype, I heard it on the "Y" basketball court.

Cultural stereotypes either leave you bitter or leave you better. Being told what you "can't do" because of your racial or ethnic group identification can move you to excel beyond your peers and your critics, or those stereotypes can become demoralizing, self-fulfilling prophecies. At the "Y," I tried to prove them wrong—that white men can jump. Yet I also wanted desperately to be accepted just for who I was—even if I couldn't out-jump all my inner-city friends. My strategy worked.

But while facing one cultural stereotype head-on and winning friends on the basketball court, I was facing another demoralizing stereotype in school. This one I succumbed to.

On the first day of my sophomore year in high school, I was ushered in to see the guidance counselor, who was also our school's football coach.

This unexpected appointment had me feeling curious and very anxious. Upon arriving at his office and taking a seat, I watched as he dramatized my fate. He pulled out a manila folder from his filing cabinet, opened it, shuffled the stack of papers, spread them on his desk, put his hand on them, and then made this chilling pronouncement: "Glenn, what's in this folder tells me you don't have what it takes to go to college. I suggest you learn a trade so that you will be able to make your way in this world."

I was quickly enrolled in a vocational/technical school, handed a piece of paper for my parents to sign, and encouraged to let them know that this move was best for me. Our meeting was over in all of ten minutes.

Whereas I had never set any academic records up to this point, I was devastated to hear a man I respected tell me I was not bright enough to pursue what was touted as a "real career." Ironically, he underestimated the power of the vocational/technical school, because most of those men I went to that school with are doing quite well today—many owning their own businesses.

Stereotypes are powerful weapons. They bind us to our past, making it difficult to achieve today. They make us question ourselves. We can succeed but we must dismiss these false labels to do so. And we must dismiss those stereotypes we have of men from other cultures. This is crucial to finding reconciliation, man to man, in America.

E. Glenn Wagner, from *We Stand Together*

MARCH 10

Godly Wives

But after he had considered this, an angel of the Lord appeared to him in a dream and said, "Joseph son of David, do not be afraid to take Mary home as your wife, because what is conceived in her is from the Holy Spirit.

MATTHEW 1:20

Now every one of you husbands, would you listen carefully? Over and over again, we men, like Joseph, need to hear this message from the Lord: "Fear not." When the women we love are wise, and start to get turned on to the Lord, something is conceived in them of the Holy Ghost. Perhaps they come back from a prayer meeting and they are just elated in the Lord – perhaps they begin a new Bible study where they become excited about the

Lord. If we are not careful, we will "think on these things" but then say, "I don't know if this is good for my wife. She's getting a little too spiritual." And we'll begin to squirm a bit when our wives tell us, "Something in me is being conceived – a passion for Jesus."

Wives, you know what this is? It's this weird male insecurity. You see, although we don't express it and maybe haven't even articulated it, the fact remains—sometimes to some of us, Jesus can be the Other Man in your life. That might be hard for you to understand. But sometimes we men can start to get a little insecure if you get too spiritual. We start to fear.

"You mean you're getting up early now and praying? When did *that* start?"

"What about my oatmeal?"

"You want to go to church *again*? We went last month!"

Somehow in women, who are oftentimes innately more spiritually sensitive than men, the Holy Spirit can begin to conceive something of Jesus. And we guys can start to freak out.

The Lord would say to you and me as husbands: "Fear not! Don't worry!" You see, the more your wife falls in love with that other Man, the Son of Man, Jesus Christ—her capacity will expand exponentially to love you along with loving Jesus.

There was a couple who had celebrated their golden anniversary with a big party. Presents were exchanged, and congratulations were expressed before they got in their car and drove home.

When they got home the woman made her way into the kitchen. As was her custom, she brewed some tea, and took out a loaf of bread, one of which she had baked daily for years. She cut off the heal, warmed it, and buttered it for her husband before cutting another slice for herself. Then she served him the warm bread.

Now, this guy who had been married for fifty years loved his wife greatly, but the stress of the day had taken its toll. And he blew up. He said, "Honey, I love you. You know that. But quite frankly this is it. For more years than I can even count, you have baked bread for me every day. But you always give me the heel. You always pass off that crusty piece of bread, that heel on me. I've had it! I won't take it anymore!"

And this is true—she looked at him, blinked back the tears and said, "But honey, that's my favorite piece."

She was giving him the best. And guys, if you want your wives to give you the best in any area, let them be expanded in the Lord. Don't fear!

Jon Courson, *Tree of Life Bible Commentary, Matthew*

MARCH 11

Hearing His Voice Again

If we confess our sins, he is faithful and just and will forgive us our sins and purify us from all unrighteousness.

I JOHN 1:9

When I first became a Christian, I thought if I did wrong, I would be killed in a plane crash, or a car would run into me, or I would have an accident of some sort. But that is not the way the Father disciplines His wayward children. Instead, He sends what I call the "Silence."

When I do wrong, God takes His peace away from me. He reaches down into my heart and takes away the joy that He put there when I became His child. He stops His voice in my life. I can no longer hear Him. Where His voice was there is only Silence, and that is a terrible, terrible feeling. It gives me a great restlessness. It tears me apart. I look at Jesus and I know that I have done an ugly thing to Him, that I have hurt Him.

It is similar to hurting one's wife. If a man loves his wife and does wrong to her, it hurts him. He feels miserable. That is how it is with sinning against the Father. I feel miserable. So I come back to the right path, not because I'm afraid of being zapped, but because of the love that God has taken away. The joy is gone. I want to feel that closeness again. My chest feels as if it will crush with the weight of that terrible Silence of God. I have that hurting pain inside because I know I have hurt my Father.

Have you ever had a time when God put that Silence in your life? When you almost think that He is not there at all, that He has gone someplace else? When you try to pray and you feel that nobody is listening?

I think to myself, *Nicky, you are a smart man,* and I try to work my way out of that Silence. I begin to call on every resource, to pull every string. I pull the theology string, the philosophy string, the psychology string. Then sometimes I try to do it by sheer force, to pray and shout and storm my way out of the Silence. I pray loud and hard, "Hallelujah, hallelujah," and all that. And nothing happens. I say, "Maybe I need to fast," and I fast, but it does no good. The Silence is still there.

And finally I am forced to look squarely at myself and see me as God sees me. I have to admit that I have been carnal and bad. With a heart that is bursting with sorrow, I confess my wrongdoing and I throw my arms around my Father's neck. I tell Him how I feel, and I rest in His arms, and the peace and joy come flooding back.

Nicky Cruz, The Magnificent Three

MARCH 12
God's Part in Salvation

For it is by grace you have been saved, through faith—and this not from yourselves, it is the gift from God—not by works, so that no one can boast.

EPHESIANS 2:8–9

Have you ever heard the story of the man who was wonderfully saved and arose in a class meeting to testify to his new found joy? His heart was filled with Christ and his lips spoke of Him and of Him only, as his Redeemer and Lord. The class leader was a legalist and said when the other had finished, "Our brother has told us what the Lord did for him, but he has forgotten to tell us what he did in order to be saved. God does His part when we do ours. Brother, did you not do your part before God saved you?" The man was on his feet in a moment and exclaimed, "I surely did do my part. I ran away from God as fast as my sins could carry me. That was my part. And God chased me till He caught me. That was His part."

Yes, you and I have all done our part, and a dreadfully sad part it was. We did all the sinning and He must do all the saving.

Harry Ironside, Full Assurance

MARCH 13
Respecting Creation

God made the wild animals according to their kinds, the livestock according to their kinds, and all the creatures that move along the ground according to their kinds. And God saw that it was good.

GENESIS 1:25

Christians, of all people, should not be the destroyers. We should treat nature with an overwhelming respect. We may cut down a tree to build a house, or to make a fire to keep the family warm. But we should not cut down the tree just to cut down the tree . . . To do so is not to treat the tree with integrity. We have the right to rid our houses of ants; but what we have not the right to do is to forget to honor the ant as God made it, in its rightful place in nature. When we meet an ant on the sidewalk, we step over him. He is a creature, like ourselves, not made in the image of God, but equal with man as far as creation is concerned. The ant and the man are both creatures.

One does not deface things simply to deface them. After all, the rock has a God-given right to be a rock as He made it. If you must move the rock in order to build the foundation of a house, then by all means move it. But on a walk in the woods do not strip the moss from it for no reason, and then leave the moss to lie by the side and die. Even the moss has a right to live. It is equal with man as a creature of God.

Hunting game is another example of the same principle. Killing animals for food is one thing, but on the other hand they do not exist simply as things to be slaughtered. This is true of fishing, too. Many men fish and leave their victims to rot and stink. But what about the fish? Has it no rights—not to be romanticized as though he were a man—but real rights? On the one hand, it is wrong to treat the fish as though it were a human baby; on the other hand, neither is it a chip of wood or a stone.

When we consider the tree, which is "below" the fish, we may chop it down, so long as we remember it is a tree, with its own value *as a tree*. It is not a zero. Some of our housing developments demonstrate the practical application of this. Bulldozers have gone in to flatten everything and clear the trees before the houses are begun. The end result is ugliness. It would have cost another thousand dollars to bulldoze *around* the trees, so they are simply bulldozed down without question. And then we wonder, looking at the result, how people can live there. It is less human in its barrenness, and even economically it is poorer as the topsoil washes away. So when man breaks God's truth, in reality he suffers . . .

I have this in common with the tree: we were made by God and not just cast up by chance.

Suddenly then we have real beauty. Life begins to breathe. For us the world begins to breathe as it never breathed before. We can love a man for his own sake, for we know who the man is—he is made in the image of God. And we can care for the animal, the tree, and even the machine portion of the universe, each thing in its own order—for we know it to be a fellow-creature with ourselves, both made by the same God.

Francis Schaeffer, *Pollution and the Death of Man*

MARCH 14
Living Water

Whoever believes in me, as the Scripture has said, streams of living water will flow from within him.

JOHN 7:38

Conversion to Christ means a return from an unnatural, foreign way of life to the truly natural way of life. The change called conversion, by dethroning the false unnatural life of sin and by giving us an infusion of the life of Christ, makes us supernaturally natural. The Christian is naturally joyous. He will laugh—even at himself. He is now not suppressing nature; he is expressing nature, in the way God intended nature to be expressed. Therefore he is not sitting on a lid. He is a unified person. He lets God pull out all the stops and play him all over—body, mind, and spirit. A friend spoke to a radiant Christian at breakfast: "Do you know, John, I thank God for you." And the reply: "Do you know, Frank, I thank God for myself." Natural and beautiful! I feel that way too—I'm grateful for myself.

A Hindu visited our Sat Tal Ashram and after he left he wrote back: "I expected to find Brother Stanley in deep tapasiya (austerities), but instead I found him a God-intoxicated child of nature." "A God-intoxicated child of nature"—that phrase has been running through my mind and heart like a refrain, a refrain of gratitude. I'm not striving to be good; I'm surrendered to goodness, incarnate goodness. I'm not trying to be happy; I just am happy, surrendered to happiness. I'm not striving to get to heaven; I'm in heaven now, at home. I'm not looking for reward; I have the reward now: Christ is my reward.

E. Stanley Jones, *A Song of Ascents*

MARCH 15
Ability

I can do everything through him who gives me strength.

As a teenager I often joked about my lack of mechanical aptitude. With a laugh and a lazy shrug I claimed that I could not be good at everything—and mechanics was one of the items on my "ineptness list." But in college and graduate school, I learned something amazing about myself. Being chronically short of money, I had to find ways to keep my car in running condition. By necessity I learned to do many mechanical chores I had once shunned: rotating tires, tuning the engine, cleaning the carburetor, changing the oil, installing brake linings. That forced me to conclude that my earlier claims of clumsiness were merely a cover for my lack of motivation to learn and to engage in a little hard work.

Similarly, when individuals claim that they have no options available to them in their circumstances, they are actually covering a lack of motivation for psychological and spiritual toil. Although these people are truly weary from the troubles heaped upon them, choices are available, though they may not necessarily be the preferred choices. The mindset of victimization and defeat is only an excuse to keep the person from saying "I will," in place of the complaint "if only."

Les Carter, *Putting the Past Behind*

MARCH 16
Setting an Example

I have set you an example that you should do as I have done for you.

JOHN 13:15

Life is like a relay race. God has handed us the baton of truth. He has entrusted us with the lives of our children and instructed us to pass the baton. Part of that exchange will involve verbal instruction. Part of that exchange will involve the process of discipline. Most of the exchange will be a matter of prayer and example. Our children will learn what they live. Giv-

88 · PROMISES TO KEEP

ing our children the gift of truth will require the ongoing discipline of working the truth out in our own lives.

Every once in a while we have an experience that lets us know how the "race" is going. One morning I was having my morning time of prayer and Bible study in my favorite chair in the living room. (. . . My favorite chair is an old overstuffed easy chair that my wife and I found at a secondhand store. We had it re-covered in black-and-white cowhide. It used to sit in our living room next to a 1952 Seeburg jukebox. We had an old Coke machine in one corner of the living room, and I kept my Harley-Davidson motorcycle in the other corner. This environment was highlighted by one wall of the living room that was all glass and looked out on a perfect view of the front range of the Rocky Mountains. This was the spot where I did my best praying, thinking, and writing.)

On this particular morning I had finished praying and was working on a chapter of a previous book. [My son] Baker came running into the living room as soon as he awoke. We were in a stretch where the first thing he wanted to do in the morning was climb into my lap and sit for a while. I took full advantage of this special period of grace!

Seeing my writing, Baker stopped and asked why I was working. I replied that I had not finished the work I needed to do the day before. He asked, "Are you not finished because I sat too long on your lap?" I saw an opportunity to use his question to affirm my love for him and his value to me, so I answered, "Nothing in the whole world is more important than you sitting on my lap." I saw a grin spread across his face as he said, "That's wrong, Dad." I was stunned, so I asked, "What do you mean?" Baker replied, "God is more important, Dad!" Pretty good theology for a five-year-old!

I had an idea of how I could use this reply to teach him another lesson, so I said, "Baker, do you know how Daddy likes to sit in this chair each morning and read his Bible and pray?" Baker shook his head in the affirmative. "Well, that's kind of like Dad sitting in God's lap," I said. Baker smiled broadly and exclaimed, "Cool, Dad!" That little encounter was a huge affirmation that the gift of truth was taking root in his life.

Bob Beltz, *The Solomon Syndrome*

MARCH 17 St. Patrick's Day
Christic with Us

Who shall separate us from the love of Christ? Shall trouble or hardship or
persecution or famine or nakedness or danger or sword?

ROMANS 8:35

> Christ, be with me, Christ before me, Christ behind me,
> Christ in me, Christ beneath me, Christ above me,
> Christ on my right, Christ on my left,
> Christ where I lie, Christ where I sit, Christ where I arise,
> Christ in the heart of every one who thinks of me,
> Christ in the mouth of every one who speaks of me,
> Christ in every eye that sees me,
> Christ in every ear that hears me
>> Salvation is of the Lord,
>> Salvation is of the Lord,
>> Salvation is of the Christ,
>> May your salvation, O Lord, be ever with us.

St. Patrick, a prayer

MARCH 18
God's Promise Kept

God is not a man, that he should lie,
*   nor a son of man, that he should change his mind.*
Does he speak and then not act?
*   Does he promise and not fulfill?*

NUMBERS 23:19

A long time ago I made a special promise to someone. For a number of
reasons, some my fault and some not, I ended up breaking that promise.
The feeling I felt afterward is impossible to describe. Remorse doesn't capture it. Nor does despair. The only way I come close is to say I felt less a person after I broke that promise. I learned from that painful experience that
when you make a real promise, a little bit of yourself goes along with it.

Promises are made with words. I might say, "I'll be there at three," or "I will never leave you." And that part of myself that goes with every promise is given to you through my words.

Our God is the great maker of promises. His Word, the Bible, is quite simply a collection of some of the promises He has made to us. In the beginning God told Adam and Eve, I will send someone who will crush the head of the serpent. A promise. Most of the other promises in the Bible— if you look closely at them—are only a variation on that same theme. They concern Jesus, who would come to be known after all as the "Promised One." Through all these promises, God was trying to give something of Himself to Adam and to Israel—and finally to us. The Bible tells us that when the Promised One finally came, the Lord poured all of Himself into Him.

In the fullness of time what God had desired to do through the ages happened: He gave all of Himself to us through Jesus Christ, the Word of God, spoken at an incalculable price. When the Promised One appeared, God knew the giving of Jesus' life was in view. It makes you realize in the end what a costly thing it can be to make a promise. Sometimes it can even cost you your life!

Michael Card, *Immanuel*

MARCH 19

Sleep

. . . he grants sleep to those he loves.

PSALM 127:2

The Bible chides the workaholic who cheats himself on sleep in order to make another buck: "*In vain you rise early and stay up late, toiling for food to eat—for he grants sleep to those he loves*" (Ps. 127:2).

In perfect balance, the Word of God makes fun of the person who sleeps too much: "*A little sleep, a little slumber, a little folding of the hands to rest— and poverty will come on you like a bandit and scarcity like an armed man*" (Prov. 24:33–34).

In harsher tones, God warns: "*Do not love sleep or you will grow poor; stay awake and you will have food to spare*"(Prov. 20:13).

Is it possible to sleep too much? Can we sleep less, feel just as good, accomplish more and hurt ourselves? For many people the answer to these questions is a resounding yes.

On vacation I can sleep nine hours every night. Why not? I have the time and enjoy the relaxation. The rest of the year I function well on seven hours sleep per night, sometimes less. The difference, obviously, is two hours per day. The exact amount of sleep needed varies, but the point is that most people can function well on less than their maximum sleep capability.

What could you do with two more hours per day, or even one, or a half hour? What if you spent it in prayer or worship or Bible study? What if you gave it to outreach ministry? What if you shared it with your family?

To reduce your sleep and increase your effectiveness try a few simple experiments:

Try setting your alarm for fifteen minutes earlier than you normally get up. Leave it at that spot for several days, even a week or two. If you function well, once you adjust, set it back another fifteen minutes. Keep this up until you find the right sleep level for maximum productivity.

Try going to bed earlier. Late hours spent before the TV often profit little. Early hours spent with the Lord profit much.

Try a twenty-minute nap during the day. Sleep experts (and short-nap lovers) know that this revitalizes energy. The key is to set an alarm so you don't sleep too long. All that is needed is enough time to doze off. Long naps slow down the system so much that they only produce a better feeling the next day.

Try making the Lord's Day—or your day off if you are a pastor—a real day of worship and rest. God made us to rest one day in seven. We violate ourselves when we ignore His built-in laws.

Sleep less. Rest more. Feel better. Enjoy the Lord and His life. This calls for careful balance, but the wise Christian will find it.

Charles Mylander, *Supernatural Energy for Your Race*

says, "I will lift up my eyes to the mountains." Jesus began His last prayer by "lifting up His eyes to heaven" (John 17:1). Our tradition has again put us upside down to the Bible.

Well, the other men opened their eyes, and soon they began to pray a second time. One said, "Look, the sun! Isn't it wonderful? Isn't that a miracle of God? Father, You're tremendous! You make things so perfect."

We started to walk around the park. We smelled the roses and talked about the wonderful power of God. One boy climbed a tree and began exclaiming, "All the wonderful things I see from this tree!" He began naming them off.

Soon we all were in the trees (it was a very unusual prayer meeting), shouting like a bunch of monkeys. "Look at that cow! Look at the corn growing by the power of God! Look at that man over there! Look at that couple in love! Praise the Lord for love!"

Then we came down, and soon someone said, "Look at this grass."

"What about the grass?" I said. "Haven't you seen grass before?"

"Yes," he answered, "but now I understand that this is the carpet God has made for all the world. Praise the Lord for His carpet!"

We ran around like this for four hours. It was the most useful prayer meeting we ever had.

Since that day we have prayed with our eyes open, and we've entered a whole new world of praise.

Juan Carlos Ortiz, *Disciple*

MARCH 23
Road Warrior

But seek first his kingdom and his righteousness, and all these things will be given to you as well.

MATTHEW 6:33

The "road warrior" has become a new business icon. Studies show that even when the frequent traveler comes to resent the stress placed on him by the competing demands of business and family, he very rarely discusses the difficulties he is facing with either his employer or his family. Instead, he stoically marches on, placing both family relationships and job in peril. He finds himself unable to prioritize needs, being constantly torn between

MARCH 20
Patterning

Only be careful, and watch yourselves closely so that you do not forget the things your eyes have seen or let them slip from your heart as long as you live. Teach them to your children and to their children after them.

DEUTERONOMY 4:9

The most compelling question that every Christian man must ask is this: What am I doing today that will be an influence for Jesus Christ in the next generation? The stakes involved have never been higher. Both the church and society are facing an unprecedented crisis of leadership. Yet all the evidence suggests that leaders cannot be produced apart from some form of mentoring.

So it boils down to this: We cannot hold onto the world, we can only hand it to others. It's as if you are a father with your arms wrapped around your young son's shoulders, helping him get the feel of the bat as older brother lobs a ball across the plate. Swing and miss. Swing and miss. Swing and connect. Swing and miss.

There is no glory in that moment—only hints of glory as a pattern is established. It may be years before little Casey can swing on his own and connect with the ball. It may be years more before he ever hits his first run. But the pattern is established.

Someday, he will stand at the plate where the balls are hard and fast. It's a game where they call real strikes, and some men strike out. One team will win, and the other will lose.

When your son hits that home run in the game that counts, you may not be around to see it. But there will be a piece of you in that swing. That's your reward for leaving the world in good hands.

Howard Hendricks and William Hendricks, *As Iron Sharpens Iron*

MARCH 21
Willingness

If you love me, you will obey what I command.

JOHN 14:15

Obedience is a willing or an unwilling carrying out of an order or a command. Most of our own experience from childhood up has been of the unwilling kind of obedience. This is one of the reasons "volunteer" has a better reputation than "obey." In our experience, volunteering always means being willing. Obedience always means to be unwilling. If, however, we had known something of willing obedience, then volunteering would be out completely. God does not ask for volunteers, nor does he challenge his own children. When Jesus called his disciples he did the choosing. He said, "Follow me." It was a simple imperative. There were also a great many volunteers who followed Jesus. The volunteers did not last. Perhaps you think that volunteering is a greater expression of love than obedience. What is your basis? Jesus said, "If you love me you will obey my commands," and "the man who has received my commands and obeys them—he it is who loves me" (John 14:15, 21, NEB). He made simple, absolute, and authoritative statements. These were not challenges seeking volunteers, nor were they goals, landmarks to stretch our reach, to make us try harder. They were imperatives of an absolute nature. Not to obey them was sin. Every imperative from God since has had an absoluteness in its nature and an unbendableness in its character that defies improvement of the commandment or satisfaction if one falls short of the requirement.

In order to get men into the Armed Forces, the Armed Forces put out recruiting posters. "Join the Action Army," "Join the Navy and see the world," "Let the world see you." These are challenges to appeal to the pride of men so that they will volunteer and join the Army. However, once the man volunteers, the whole system changes. He is no longer appealed to. He is commanded and he obeys. The Army could not command him into the Army, so they used the challenge in order to get him to volunteer. Once he is in, it is a different story. Enlisting in the Army is the beginning of a command-obedience relationship. There is also an upper limit to this obedience, not as clearly defined as the enlistment at the beginning. In fact, it is always defined after the fact. For instance, an Army captain calls for his own position to be bombed with Napalm in order to destroy the enemy who has his company outnumbered and is overrunning his position. He receives the Silver Star and is recommended for the Congressional Medal of Honor for "danger above and beyond the call of duty." In the Army there is a beginning to obedience and there is a place above and beyond obedi-

ence. Between the lower limit and the upper limit the relationship is command-obedience.

Is there a lower limit to obedience in our relationship with God? There may be a lower limit in our ability to obey, but not a lower limit in the requirement to obey. This ability begins when we know Jesus Christ.

Jim Wilson, *The Principles of War*

MARCH 22

Open Eyes

After Jesus said this, he looked toward heaven and prayed: "Father, the time has come. Glorify your Son, that your Son may glorify you."

JOHN 17:1

Once my group of disciples and I went on a retreat to a place two hours out of Buenos Aires, a very nice house in a park with pine trees, flowers, and birds. We began praying under an apple tree. It was September, which in my country is springtime.

The first person prayed, "Lord, we come to You today . . ." and he sounded just like he always did in the basement of our downtown church. The second one did the same.

When it came my turn to pray, I said, "Lord, we drove a long time to be here. If we wanted the same kind of prayer meeting like we always have in the church basement, we could have stayed in Buenos Aires."

I opened my eyes. The apple tree was full of flowers, and a little bird was sitting right there in the middle of it. I went on. "Lord, what fools we are to come so far to this park and then sit with our eyes shut. Lord, how beautiful this apple tree is. The flowers are just fantastic. Look at the bird You have made, Lord. Isn't it beautiful?"

The other men began to open their eyes to see what was happening their pastor! I kept going.

"Lord, look at those roses. Look at the pine trees. . . . Now I understand why we haven't had new words for praising. Now I understand why David praised so much—Lord, where in the Bible does it say we must close eyes to pray?"

I did a quick dash in my mind from Genesis to Revelation—I didn't any such rule. It's not there. In fact, the Bible shows the opposite; Psalm

his role as provider for the family and his role of participant as husband/ father. Out-of-control work habits can make a father absent more often than present even at his own family's dinner table.

At the same time, the wife and children may become "real troopers," refusing to voice their emotional needs because "Dad has to do this for the family." Such refusal may mean a temporary avoidance of conflict. But in reality, it is only postponing an inevitable showdown, a time when choices have to be made between the long-term well-being of the family and the demands of business. It is much better to have the problem stated and examined up front; the earlier the response, the less painful the result will be.

A dangerous lesson is also taught the children in the family. They learn to subjugate relational responsibilities to the demands of employment just as they have observed in their home. And so, the next generation is drawn up into the cycle. What was a habit for the father becomes a tradition for the family.

David Nowell, *A Man's Work Is Never Done*

MARCH 24
Championship Living

I press on toward the goal to win the prize for which God has called me heavenward in Christ Jesus.

PHILIPPIANS 3:14

I was taught to be a well-mannered youngster. I was coached to be a championship-level basketball player. I was inspired to be a good Christian. But when I finally gave God my life completely and let go, He developed me into something bigger and better than anything I was ever taught, coached or inspired to become. He will do the same for you.

As a kid I had no idea of what my life could become. I dreamed of being a winner, so I tried hard to win at the little playground sports we played. As I grew, I naturally leaned toward basketball. But when Jesus Christ became my best friend, my Lord, my Coach with a capital C, I found the larger purpose for my life and went on to pursue it as well as professional sports.

Basketball is my talent, but the gift God gave me is much larger than that. God uses my talent as a platform from which I can achieve my greater purpose. My goal is to influence others to fulfill their potential by pursuing their dreams in accordance with their gifts and talents. Young or old, male of female—you can achieve your purpose in life. A limitless God can make you a champion.

Generally, a champion is someone who reaches a victory. A teammate of mine who won several championships defined being a champion as being acknowledged above all peers and competition as the undisputed "number one." But I don't define *championship* based on competition or accolades. To me, champions are people who achieve their true purpose in life, who reach victory in many areas.

True champions measure themselves by a higher standard. Nobody's perfect. If we try to become champions by competing against imperfect people or measuring up to someone else's imperfect victories, we measure ourselves against imperfection. By accepting their weaknesses or failures, we keep ourselves from reaching our full potential. The only perfect man who ever walked this earth is Jesus Christ, God's Son. The champions I'm talking about compare themselves to Him and try to live up to the goals He sets. The best part is that He helps them do it. We don't need to compare ourselves with others or compete against them. To be true champions, we can measure ourselves against Him alone and compete against any force that would keep us from being like Him.

A. C. Green, Victory

MARCH 25
Hunger For Him

. . . your love is more delightful than wine.

SONG OF SONGS 1:2

Believers today are realizing that if our hunger for intimacy is ever to be satisfied, we must have Him whose affectionate love is far better than "churchianity" or the best wine of earthly experiences and possessions. Like the maiden who cried, "Your love is better than wine," believers are coming to the point where they realize that money and material things are never going to supply the needs of our spirits. Prominence in the church or the world will never do it. No sensual or romantic relationship with another human being will ever satisfy the deep cravings of our spirits. We're becoming tired of powerless religion that can't deliver us from sin or from ourselves; tired of leaders filled with anger, striving, and immorality, tired of churches paralyzed in apathy. We're weary of trying to draw water from a dry well in the name of Jesus.

An abandonment, a holy recklessness, is awakening in the spirits of God's people. The Spirit of God is calling us forth, taking the truths of time and eternity and using them to awaken us out of complacency. Before this world comes to an end, God will raise up a church full of people who are hungering for God-centered religion from among those who are satisfied with man-centered Christianity. The denominational label won't matter. If the Son of God is being ministered in power, and His personal beauty and loveliness are unveiled, people will flock to Him.

Why do we want Him? We've discovered that the love and affection of God are better than anything the world has to offer, and we're beginning to see a little bit of the splendor, majesty and matchless beauty of Christ Jesus.

Mike Bickle, *Passion for Jesus*

MARCH 26

Manly Comfort

Praise be to the God and Father of our Lord Jesus Christ, the Father of compassion and the God of all comfort, who comforts us in all our troubles, so that we can comfort those in any trouble with the comfort we ourselves have received from God.

II CORINTHIANS 1:3–4

God used the doubts I had about my manhood to show me what manhood really was. Don't kid yourself. A lot of people who hear my story can relate. There's nothing special about me or about the way I was taught to grow from boy to man. You know the shuffle—learning to hide your feelings, to prove who you are by being something you're not, the code with all its images and icons of macho. Of all the lives lived for better or worse on 187th Street and Crotona Avenue, mine was no different. Gangs, drugs, success itself warped my idea of what being a man was all about. And no one else seemed to know either—no one until [my friend] Jack, who climbed down into the trenches with me, who would have died for me, I think, to prove that love is real. That kind of man, if you let him, will lead you to another kind of man. . . .

It comes down to this: The most courageous thing a man can do is open his heart to God. And if the courage isn't there, God'll give that in His time, too. There's a prayer I wanted to pray—seeking to comfort instead of being comforted, understanding rather than to be understood, loving rather than to be loved. That's a tall order for most of us, but it's what being strong and wise is all about. Being a servant. I prayed for God's will to be done every day for ten years. That day I understood that His will was for me to love Jesus.

Dion DiMucci, *The Wanderer*

MARCH 27
Sacrificial Love

Greater love has no one than this, that he lay down his life for his friends.

JOHN 15:13

This story from World War II is reportedly true. I have no way to verify it, but it's a good one.

The fighting was heavy. A platoon of U.S. troops was driven back and one of their infantrymen was wounded in gunfire. As he lay on the battlefield, a friend and fellow soldier asked his sergeant in the foxhole, "Can I go get 'im?"

"There's no use. He's probably dead," the sergeant answered. "And even if he isn't dead, you'd never make it back alive. But if you want to . . ." Those last few words were all the friend needed to hear. Off he ran, dodging bullets. Crawling on elbows and knees, he reached the bleeding infantryman, hoisted him to his shoulders, and hobbled back, As he neared the foxhole, the heroic friend was hit in the chest with a bullet and the two friends collapsed in a heap. The sergeant tried to find the pulse of the infantryman and there was none. Dead. Then he told the soldier, "I told you it would be senseless. Your friend is dead, and now you've been shot." Fighting for air, the friend painfully explained, "No, I have no regrets. You see, when I first got to my friend he was alive. He recognized me and said, "Thanks, Jack. I knew you'd come." With those words the soldier friend died.

That is friendship. Friendship says, "I knew you'd come"—*I knew if I needed you, you'd be there for me. I knew I could count on you.*

That is what makes a good marriage—not heroics but faithfulness under fire.

Faithfulness under fire is what every man longs for. It is love that keeps its word even when it hurts. It is the integrity that is just as loyal on a business trip halfway around the world as it is sitting at the breakfast table with our spouse. It is the inner sense of equilibrium that knows how to fight off the molesting demands of an overloaded schedule in order to maintain a man's commitments. When so many different fingers are scrambling to get into the control center of our lives and push our buttons, faithfulness is able to ward off the intruders bravely. This is the kind of love that has sticking power. It is the kind that will still be there twenty years later after the hair turns gray and when the breasts sag, the belly is covered with stretch marks, and "cellulite" puts contours on the thighs. It will be there through the mood swings of menopause, the teenage children who forget the words "please" and "thank you," and the pains of the empty nest.

Faithfulness under fire is what separates a great marriage from a mediocre one. It is what every man and woman deep down longs for, but which very few seem to enjoy.

Fred Hartley, Men and Marriage

MARCH 28

Manly Virtue

. . . add to your faith virtue; and to virtue, knowledge. . . .

II PETER 1:5 (KJV)

When was the last time you heard men discussing virtue as a manly thing to pursue? Virtue links masculinity with moral excellence. *Vir* in Latin means "a man," not in a general sense of the entire human race, but specifically "a male." And the Latin *virtus* can mean "strength," "manliness," or "moral perfection."

In other words, though women are to be virtuous, don't think for a moment that virtue is only an adornment meant for women. Men have only two alternatives by which to walk: virtue or vice. Therefore, men need to willingly clothe themselves with a mantle of virtue because only virtue produces the true objectives of being responsible to both God and man.

And a man who wants to complete his manhood and image God the Father will seek virtue like a pearl hidden in a field.

Weldon Hardenbrook, *Missing in Action*

MARCH 29
Circumcision

In him you were also circumcised, in the putting off of the sinful nature, not with a circumcision done by the hands of men but with the circumcision done by Christ . . . .

COLOSSIANS 2:11

Circumcision is one of the most brilliantly conceived symbols of life in relationship to God. Semitic in origin, it has served that race for millennia as a symbol of a life intimate with God. Other religious rites combined with certain moral disciplines are also present, but over the centuries circumcision has acquired a singular prominence.

The symbolism of circumcision is both complex and obvious. There are layers on layers of meaning, but they are all accessible to the ordinary, reflective mind.

Circumcision is indisputably physical. Our relationship with God is not ethereal. It is not something that has to do with fine, mystical feelings. It is physical, earthy.

Circumcision is an operation on the most intimate member of the male body. It is not a decoration, like a tattoo. It is performed at the place which shows our essential identity, where we know and are known. Relationship with God is not embroidery; it constitutes our character.

Circumcision is a wound. The scar remembers the pain of being separated from one way of life and set apart for another. We are not born innocent and pristine and then gradually fall away into sin; our natural condition requires intervention and is marked by an encounter with the divine, the holy.

Circumcision is vicarious. Each person does not have to bear the symbol in order to be in relationship with God. Since the sign was only carried by males, it could not be regarded as necessary for females who were obviously God's people quite as much as males. In that way the sign could never be identified with the reality itself. It was both necessary and not necessary.

The circumcised person is whole but partial. The missing part is cut off by God's command, which command also supplies what is lacking. The visible sign of obedience to the command is also a sign of the invisible God who promises to redeem, to guide and to bless. God *cuts* his word into our lives, a covenant in which he commits himself to be our God. The circumcised person is a commanded person, an obedient person and a blessed person. Circumcision is a visible absence of flesh symbolizing the invisible presence of the Spirit, a sign of a life set free to be in right relation with God.

Eugene Peterson, Traveling Light

MARCH 30
A Man's Work

And we pray this in order that you may live a life worthy of the Lord and may please him in every way: bearing fruit in every good work, growing in the knowledge of God. . . .

COLOSSIANS 1:10

Today I clean the bathroom. Whenever I return to this task, I am reminded how stable my life is. To clean the bathroom demands a sense of peace, a place of peace, and a time of peace. I see the history of the world each day in the newspaper: a new battle, a new death caused by carelessness or evil. I am a careful listener, hearing a neighbor's explanation on the new tax hike, or my sister's recalling a day when she and I ate fresh peppers together at the edge of a distant farm that seemed to never have existed after all.

When I turn the bathtub faucet to the right, clean, cool water gushes out against my hands. In some parts of the world, water is almost as valuable as gold. In some homes in the world, water will determine if the children will live another month.

We who are civilized eat on porcelain plates and bathe in porcelain tubs. I watched a television program showing children bathing in gutter water and using their hands to brush away the dust in the road in search of single grains of rice to chew and swallow for their inflated stomachs.

I like to wash the bathroom floor. The soap foams up, and I take my socks and shoes off, and then I slide around as if I am skating, though I don't tell anyone about this habit. Remember the ancient man found in the frozen tundra? He had a grin of pain etched on his face. Man buried in the ice. Man skating on the ice field of a suburban bathroom.

The toilet is easy to clean because there is a constant source of fresh water to flush down the soap. The kings of the fourteenth century did not have flush toilets.

The bathroom tiles are the easiest to clean. A simple squirt with the spray bottle and a quick wipe with the sponge, and the tiles shine. Each time I drive to New York City, someone tries to wash my windshield with a spray of water and quick wipe with a squeegee.

Sometimes when I wash the sink, the cat jumps up and dabs her paw into the water. She sometimes falls in, scrambles out, jumps to the floor, and runs out the door, leaving a trail of water and paw prints on my fresh and clean floor.

Each time I wash the bathroom, I stop for a moment and stare out the skylight above my head. I cannot see much except the sky and the branch of an oak tree. Sometimes a bird flies overhead. In the winter the skylight is covered with snow, but I still look up and admire the underside of winter's blanket spread out upon the house. Lord have mercy.

The last thing I clean when I wash the bathroom is the mirror. I wipe the mirror's surface with a damp sponge, then, with broad strokes, I dry the mirror with a paper towel only to discover myself staring back at me.

Who is that in the mirror? My children call me Daddy. My wife calls me Chris. I consider myself to be a writer, a man full of joys and regrets, a man in the center of the bathroom, smelling the soap, feeling the sunlight against my head, a man in the center of a civilized world, daring to feel intelligent, satisfied, confident in my cleverness, and yet, I am a man full of weakness, realizing how grateful I ought to be for the peace and privilege to clean the bathroom.

It is easy for me to forget the source of all my happiness. It is easy to forget who gave me the ability to lift my hand and wash the bathroom walls.

I like to look at a map and trace where the great rivers of the world begin, for they all begin with a small stream of water at the top of a mountain that slowly rolls down to join other water and eventually becomes the

Mississippi River. How easy it is to forget that God is the source, that God is the water that holds us all together so that we can form the river of life on this earth.

It is easy to overlook His part in our daily work. Too often we believe it is the labor that is at the center of what we do. I believe the cause of that labor ought to drive our work, and I believe all good labor is accomplished in the name of God—even cleaning the bathroom.

Each of our routines can be an act of gratitude to our Lord Jesus Christ, who suffered and died for us so that we can know the true way through our workaday world.

God, trace my hands with your fingers so that I may be guided in my work today to do your will. Accept my efforts as a greeting and a sign of my gratitude.

Lord of all labor, I offer my work as prayer for those who are in pain, God of power and might, God of labor and mercy. Amen

Christopher de Vinck, Simple Wonders

MARCH 31
Listening

He who has ears, let him hear.

MATTHEW 11:15

Two stories illustrate the attitude necessary for a life of fullness and excellence.

A young man longed to see God. He had heard for many years of a wise old man who lived in the mountains nearby. After searching elsewhere for God in vain, the young man finally went to talk with the old man.

"Old man, tell me, how can I see God?"

The old man stopped, and looked at him deeply. He immersed himself in thought. The young man waited for what seemed like an eternity. Finally:

"Young man, I don't think that I can be of help to you, for you see I have a problem that is quite different. I can't *not* see Him."

The second fire, the touch of disciplined grace, washes away the imagined barriers between secular things and spiritual things and reintroduces the whole universe to us as God's. We begin to see the world and its people and events as Christ sees them. We allow him to be our 20/20 vision—and with a combination of discipline and grace we move closer to the central Yes of our lives.

The second story deals with our capacity to hear.

An Indian was in downtown New York, walking along with his friend, who lived in New York City. Suddenly he said, "I hear a cricket."

"Oh, you're crazy," his friend replied.

"No, I hear a cricket. I do! I'm sure of it."

"It's the noon hour. You know there are people bustling around, cars honking, taxis squealing, noises from the city. I'm sure you can't hear it."

"I'm sure I do." He listened attentively and then walked to the corner, across the street, and looked all around. Finally on the other corner he found a shrub in a large cement planter. He dug beneath the leaf and found a cricket.

His friend was duly astounded. But the Indian said, "No. My ears are no different from yours. It simply depends on what you are listening to. Here, let me show you."

He reached into his pocket and pulled out a handful of change—a few quarters, some dimes, nickels, and pennies. And he dropped it on the concrete.

Every head within a block turned.

"You see what I mean?" the Indian said as he began picking up his coins. "It all depends on what you are listening for."

As you seek to live a life of excellence, a life of godly intensity and verve, may you have eyes to see and ears to hear. But most important, may you have the wisdom to know what to look for and listen to.

Tim Hansel, *When I Relax I Feel Guilty*

April

APRIL 1
A Fool for Christ

For the message of the cross is foolishness to those who are perishing, but to us who are being saved it is the power of God.

I CORINTHIANS 1:18

The cross made [a profound] change in me at a home Bible study group in 1963. I remember that evening as though it were last night. I did not arrive having planned to turn to Christ. Over a three month period I had learned a lot *about* Christ and the cross—I could have passed an elementary exam on the atonement. But I did not understand that I was a sinner. I thought I was a good guy. Oh, I knew I had messed up here and there, but I did not realize how serious my condition was.

Then, suddenly, when I was least expecting it, [my wife] Carol went off the deep end. She announced to the leader, Gunner Payne, "I think it's time to do something about all these things we've been talking about." The next thing I knew, she was kneeling on the floor and, as far as I could see, praying to the ceiling, weeping and telling it how sorry she was for all her sins.

I just sat there and stared at her. "This is weird," I thought. "Why is she doing this? What has she done that's so awful? Has she done something I don't know about?" I could feel her pain and the depth of her prayers. Soon she was weeping and sobbing repeatedly, "I'm sorry for my sin."

There were six or seven people in the room, all with their eyes closed. I looked around at them, then it hit me: "*They've all prayed this prayer, too!*" As a musician, I had been on stage enough to know when it was about to be my turn. And it was my turn now. I started sweating bullets. I thought I was going to die. The perspiration ran down my face, and I thought, "I'm not going to do this. This is dumb. I'm a good guy. I've got to get out of here."

Then it struck me. Carol was not praying to the plaster; she was praying to a *Person*, to a God who could hear her. In comparison to him, she knew she was a sinner and in need of forgiveness.

In a flash the cross made personal sense to me. Suddenly I knew something that I had never known before: I had hurt God's feelings. He loved me, and in his love for me he sent Jesus. But I had turned away from that love; I had shunned it all of my life, I was a sinner, desperately in need of the cross.

To this day I cannot fully account for how I got out of that chair. All I know is that I ended up on the floor, sobbing, nose running, eyes watering, every square inch of my flesh perspiring profusely. I had this overwhelming sense that I was talking with Someone who had been with me all of my life, but whom I had filled to recognize. Like Carol, I began talking to the living God, telling him that I was sinner. I was trying to pray the "Sinner's Prayer," but all I could do was to blub the Sinner's Blub: "Oh God! Oh God! Oh God!"

I knew something revolutionary was going on inside me. I thought, "I hope this works, because I'm making a complete fool of myself." Then the Lord brought to mind a man I had seen in Los Angeles a number of years before. He was wearing a sign that said, "I'm a fool for Christ. Whose fool are you?" I thought at the time, "That's the most stupid thing I've ever seen." But as I knelt on the floor I realized the truth of the odd sign: the cross is foolishness "to those who are perishing" (1 Cor. 1:18). That night I knelt at the cross and believed in Jesus. I have been a fool for Christ ever since.

John Wimber, *Power Points*

APRIL 2

A Father's Affirmation

Fathers, do not embitter your children, or they will become discouraged.

COLOSSIANS 3:21

Somewhere between the ages of three to five, little boys are "discovered" by their fathers. To put it crudely, at that age, children begin to "function" better. Most men know better what to do with children when they function. Now that a little boy plays more productively, a father can step in and begin to teach him to "do" some things. About this time, a little boy also discovers his father. He recognizes a kinship with his father in sexual identity. He learns to discriminate male from female, and begins to form an identity as a male . . .

What does a little boy get from his father?

Our fathers teach us how to work. Daddy spends most of his time working. He spends a lot of time at work; he may even bring work home with him. When he is home, he has plenty of work to do—yard work, things to make, things to fix, Dads are busy.

Our fathers show us how to do things together. Watch the Dodgers play ball on television. Do yard work together. Fix things. Play catch.

Our fathers teach us to take risks. To venture out. To make things happen. To have courage.

All of these are great lessons. And if you were one of a fortunate few, perhaps your father was also tender and nurturing. He said, "I'm sorry, I was wrong," after hollering at you. He affirmed your base hit or piano recital without adding, ". . . but you could have done better." He asked how you felt about losing your new watch without screaming at you or "fixing" it by quickly buying you a new one. His affirmations helped your self-confidence to grow strong. You gained competence in social skills and problem-solving.

But if your father was emotionally remote, your self-confidence suffered. You may have become remote and/or aggressive. Even today, you might still work hard to earn self-esteem. The bottom line is this: if your father did not model emotional skills for you, the little boy in you could be stalled in his emotional development.

In most families, little boys do not get much verbal expression from their fathers. What they do get has more to do with functional things as they hear comments like;

- "Good shot!"
- "Try it this way."
- "That's no good."
- "That's right!"

Some boys get emotional expressions that are anything but constructive. Instead, they get powerful negative messages:

- "You throw the ball like a girl!"
- "Lose some weight. You're fat—get some muscle!"
- "Fight like a man!"
- "With grades like this, you'll amount to nothing!"

Sometimes they get silence on sensitive life subjects. This can be just as hurtful. For example, few fathers know how to speak comfortably with their sons about sexuality. The silence can be deafening! A father's awkwardness can be turned to an advantage if he can admit that he is still growing and learning as well. But that takes vulnerability.

Once a boy has distanced himself from his mother, if he does not find comparable emotional closeness and fulfillment from his father, loneliness can root itself in his growing personality. This loneliness sets up a "hunger" for approval from his father. His ego begins to measure how "good" or "bad" he is by his estimation of what his father thinks about him. He begins to measure himself by what he does right or wrong—according to Dad's standards.

Dick Brian Klaver, *Men at Peace*

April 3
A Sunny Disposition

. . . I know whom I have believed, and am convinced that he is able to guard what I have entrusted to him for that day.

II Timothy 1:12

Men love men of stability, of cheerfulness. It is our choice whether we will live on the sunny side of the street, scattering sunshine, or live in the cold, damp shadows, scattering doubts, chilling the faith of His dear saints, placing mountains in the weaker brother's pathway. We can be strong in God, able to do a full day's work, a long day's work, a hard day's work, and not complain, or we can be weak, not fit for anything. A strong man talks strongly, walks with a firm gait, breathes deeply, has a good appetite, enjoys his meals, eats what is placed before him. He is like a signboard, pointing out clearly what good things God can do for those who are strong in Him.

How are we to be kept from discouragement? The first thing is to be certain that we are right with God, that we are regenerated, born of the Spirit, begotten of God, brought from darkness to light, *know* whom we have believed, and are fully persuaded that He is able to keep that which we have committed unto Him against that day.

The second thing is to obey. Walk in all the light God gives, and then when you have done fully your part, wait with patience for Him to do His. Never become discouraged, always remember that the world was not made the first day. When the day's work is done, if we did all that was shown us, if we did our best, if we walked in all the light God gave, even though our work be awkwardly done, if it was our best, He will love us good because we did it to please and honor Him.

W. J. Harney, Praying Clear Through

APRIL 4

Sufficient Strength

Blessed are those whose strength is in you,
who have set their hearts on pilgrimage.

PSALM 84:5

A normal man who has adequately preserved the body God has given him is a perfect specimen for his work. He has a strong body which functions beautifully under normal strain. To see a man at his work, his muscles functioning in beautiful coordination, is to see the handiwork of God. He has great physical endurance, taking day-in and day-out toil which extends for a lifetime. He enjoys the flexing of muscles and the habit of work.

The man was blessed with the emotional make-up to endure the demands of his work—the stresses and strains of the marketplace, the roar of industry, the uncertainties of the crops in the field, and the financial challenges of the office. He can endure worry and has the capacity to overcome his obstacles, solve his problems, and thus succeed at his work.

He is competitive in temperament, a characteristic fitting him to gain his place in the working world. He is aggressive, decisive, and possesses all the qualities necessary in dealing with perplexing problems in a challenging world.

There are, of course, many men who succumb to the pressures of the working world. Statistics point out that the competitive business world is killing our men. Since the man's life expectancy is somewhat less than the female; his arduous lifestyle is said to be destroying him.

In reality men do not die so much because of their work as because of other things. He may not have taken proper care of his health, may have filled his body with bad food, drugs, alcohol, tobacco, etc. Or, he may be suffering from frustration engendered in the relationship with his wife and children. They may be making demands of him, demands which are unjust and unreasonable. Further frustrations occur because he has not assumed his rightful place as leader. If his home life is filled with turmoil and unpleasantness, he will feel strain in his work.

Or he may be working too hard and too long in providing the luxuries for his family. This has taxed his body beyond its God-given capacity. His work has been blamed for killing him, where in reality his "striving for luxuries" is doing so.

Any normal man, who has properly cared for his body and is in good health, has the capacity to provide the necessities of life for his family with reasonable ease. In addition he will have a reserve capacity, allowing for responsibility beyond his home as well as time for personal pursuits. God has blessed man with greater capacity than we sometimes suppose.

Aubrey C. Andelin, *Man of Steel and Velvet*

APRIL 5

A Charitable Heart

Again I tell you, it is easier for a camel to go through the eye of a needle than for a rich man to enter the kingdom of God.

MATTHEW 19:24

I remember walking away with a $150 check after I'd given my Christian testimony. What a joke. After my first or second season with the [Dallas] Cowboys the hypocrisy of what I was doing suddenly hit me. I was horrified and tried to remember some of the churches where I'd spoken so I could return the money. It wasn't *after* I had the money that I started thinking differently. I simply realized that money can't be the bottom line of what I do. Money is an excellent servant but a lousy master.

That has been true with me ever since. I never negotiate with the ultimate objective being the dollar bill. We have plenty of money. I've earned it, worked hard for it. I do things with money for people outside our family. The key thing is what the Bible says about it being easier for a camel to pass through the eye of a needle than a rich man to get into heaven.

That's where I draw the line. I would negotiate in my own way, on my own terms. I'd be paid well but not end up in a hassle where the dollar was ultimate. That became true with speaking engagements, too. I decided on a nice, solid fee for business deals but would accept nothing for charities such as the Fellowship of Christian Athletes, youth and church groups, the Salvation Army or senior citizen functions.

We never negotiate money with anyone. If a business group calls Roz and wants to know my fee she gives it to them. If a youth group calls and says it will pay me a fee, she tells them there is no charge and then whether I can do it or not. There's also a thing called the honorarium which normally is associated with charity events.

I've been offered honorariums to go on telethons. The leukemia telethon would have paid me $3,000. Can you see me going on TV with all those sick kids there, asking people to give money and then walking away with a $3,000 check? That doesn't make sense at all. It blows my mind to know people can accept money for something like that.

Roger Staubach, First Down, Lifetime to Go

APRIL 6
All Things Possible

Everything is possible for him who believes.

MARK 9:23

The most fantastic things happen to people who believe. No less of an authority than Jesus Christ himself says you do not have to be defeated. You can overcome illness, you can overcome weakness, you can overcome sin, you can overcome heartbreak, you can overcome failure. There is nothing or no situation you cannot overcome if you will believe.

Belief can change what appears to be an impossible situation. Belief unlocks the door to power beyond our own imagination. All things are possible—only believe. . . .

All things are possible if you believe in God. Believing in the New Testament means receiving Jesus Christ into your life as Savior and Lord. Everything good starts with a decision to believe Jesus Christ and invite him to come into your heart.

You want an unbeatable life? Believe in Jesus.

You want to be a child of God? Believe in Jesus.

You want to overcome defeat? Believe in Jesus.

You want to have a better life? Believe in Jesus.

You want to beat defeating selfishness? Believe in Jesus.

You want to eventually win? Believe and totally dedicate yourself to Jesus.

God has a plan for your life. Finding and following God's plan for your life is the soundest, surest way to self-confidence. There is no greater feeling than to be in right relationship with God. If you are not in right relationship, you can be—starting now.

Believe wholeheartedly in God—and for you life will become unbeatable. Make this the dominating thought of your mind—God and I together are undefeatable.

Dale Galloway, *Rebuild Your Life*

APRIL 7

Physical Trials

Blessed is the man who perseveres under trial, because when he has stood the test, he will receive the crown of life that God has promised to those who love him.

JAMES 1:12

There were trials ahead of me that I could not imagine, so many moments where my faith and strength would be tested, but none would be more crucial than the prayer we shared inside that ambulance. Because it was then and there that I found the inner core of peace that would see me through everything to come. It was at that moment, en route to the hospital, that I turned everything over to the Lord, that I put it all in His hands.

There's a power to a moment like that that can only really be understood by someone who's experienced it. In a way, it's a total surrender, a serenity that comes from letting go of pain or fear or sorrow and putting it all in the hands of something far stronger than anything we can feel or imagine, putting it in the hands of the Lord. But it's not a simple matter, achieving that serenity, making that surrender. It takes faith. It takes true belief, the kind of acceptance and assurance that's rooted deep in a person's soul, beyond words or even thoughts.

I had that faith. I had that feeling. I had no idea what lay ahead of me, but I knew this was going to be a test, a trial in my life for which I would need God's help and a strong faith. And I believed I had both those things. I had spent my entire life reading the Bible, studying the scriptures, learning about God and Jesus Christ. I understood that the Lord has plans for people and their lives that we sometimes have no way of comprehending. There had been plenty of times in my life when I'd had the opportunity to bail out, say, "Hey, God, why did you do this? Why did you do that?" But I never had bailed out before. And I wasn't about to now.

Dennis Byrd, Rise and Walk

APRIL 8

Scripture

All Scripture is God-breathed and is useful for teaching, rebuking, correcting and training in righteousness . . .

II TIMOTHY 3:16

The Bible is the Chief moral cause of all that is good, and the best corrector of all that is evil, in human society; the best book for regulating the temporal concerns of men, and the only book that can serve as an infallible guide to future felicity . . . It is extremely important to our nation, in a political as well as religious view, that all possible authority and influence should be given to the scriptures, for these furnish the best principles of civil liberty, and the most effectual support of republican government.

The principles of genuine liberty, and of wise laws and administrations, are to be drawn from the Bible and sustained by its authority. The man, therefore, who weakens or destroys the divine authority of that Book may be accessory to all the public disorders which society is doomed to suffer. . . .

There are two powers only, sufficient to control men and secure the rights of individuals and a peaceable administration; these are the combined force of religion and law, and the force or fear of the bayonet.

Noah Webster, from the Preface to Webster's translation of the Bible

APRIL 9

Belonging to God

When I consider your heavens,
* the work of your fingers,*
the moon and the stars,
* which you have set in place,*
what is man that you are mindful of him,
* the son of man that you care for him?*
You made him a little lower than the heavenly beings
* and crowned him with glory and honor.*

PSALM 8:3-5

Many of my clients tell me that they are not as smart or good-looking or witty as others and that they feel inferior. These people, incidentally, are not mentally ill. There was a time when you went to a psychiatric clinic only when you were suicidally depressed or hearing voices. But today our waiting rooms are filled with normal, functioning people who are simply unhappy.

I wish I could say to clients who feel inadequate and inferior, "Oh, come now, you are as smart as anyone," but in some cases it would be dishonest. Despite what the *Declaration of Independence* says, we are *not* all created equal. So instead I try to help them realize that they have been magnificently created by a great God, and for *that* reason they matter. We begin building self-confidence when we believe that we originated from a benevolent Creator.

Standing on the windswept shores of Lake Michigan one wintry night, ready to throw himself into the freezing waters, a thirty-two-year-old bankrupt dropout happened to gaze up at the starry heavens. Suddenly, he felt a rush of awe, and a thought flashed through his mind: *You have no right to eliminate yourself. You do not belong to you. You belong to the universe.* R. Buckminster Fuller turned his back to the lake and began a remarkable career. Best-known as the inventor of the geodesic dome, by the time of his death he held more than 170 patents and was world-famous as an engineer, mathematician, architect, and poet.

Buckminster Fuller's experience that night on Lake Michigan merely echoed the words of the ancient psalmist, who also contemplated the night sky and was awed by its grandeur:

> When I consider your heavens,
> the work of your fingers,
> the moon and the stars,
> which you have set in place,
> what is man that you are mindful of him,
> the son of man that you care for him?

The psalmist was inclined to feel insecure and inadequate in the face of such magnificence, but back came a resounding reply to his question:

> You made him a little lower than God
> and crowned him with glory and honor (Ps. 8:3–5).

Like it or not (for it does carry with it certain responsibilities as well as glories) we have been created by God, and our Creator has endowed us with remarkable capacities.

Alan McGinnis, *Confidence*

APRIL 10

Inner Prayer

After the earthquake came a fire, but the LORD was not in the fire. And after the fire came a gentle whisper.

I KINGS 19:12

Do not let your faults discourage you. Be patient with yourself as well as with your neighbor. Thinking too much will exhaust you and cause you to make a lot of mistakes. Learn to pray in all your daily situations. Speak, act, and walk as if you were in prayer. This is how you should live anyway.

Do everything without becoming too excited. As soon as you start to feel yourself getting too eager, quiet yourself before God. Listen to Him as He prompts you inwardly, then do only as He directs. If you do this, your words will be fewer but more effective. You will be calm, and good will be accomplished in greater measure.

I am not talking about continually trying to reason things out. Simply ask your Lord what He wants of you. This simple and short asking is better than your long-winded inner debates.

Turn toward God and it will be much easier to turn away from your strong natural feelings. Depend on the Lord within you. Your life will eventually become a prayer.

Francois Fenelon

APRIL 11

Being Found

For the Son of Man came to seek and to save what was lost.

LUKE 19:10

Think of a time when you were lost and scared. Maybe it was when you were a child on a camping trip. Maybe in the cold and dark of a blizzard. Maybe you think of being lost to bankruptcy or disease.

I think of a day when I borrowed a small boat with an outboard engine to take my wife and baby daughter for a ride on the Intracoastal Waterway and into the harbor of Boca Raton, Florida. Enjoying the beautiful day and the sparkling water, I decided to venture out of the harbor and into the ocean. But the ocean was far rougher than I had anticipated and the waves larger than they had looked from a distance. I realized that we were in a dangerous situation I could not handle and that I needed to head back into the harbor. Then came the horrible realization that I could not see land and I didn't know which way to go. The boat had neither radio nor compass. Just retelling the experience brings back the feelings of lostness—an indescribable mix of helplessness, panic, and desperation.

That day in Florida the potential for tragedy quickly disappeared when I saw other boats and followed them back to safe harbor. At the sight of land my emotions changed from panic to peace, from feeling scared to feeling safe. But I still remember what it was like to be lost, and it helps me value the safety of the shore.

In similar but much greater fashion, Christians value salvation because we know what it was like to be lost from God, lost in sin, lost forever. And once we have been saved from the lostness of sin, we forever value salvation. At least that's the way it should be. But it is easy to take salvation for granted, to become ungrateful. I've tried to figure out why.

Millions of Christians have benefited from growing up in Christian homes, going to church from infancy, and making personal commitments to Christ when they were very young. It is not unusual for these people to say, "I never murdered anyone, robbed a bank, or became sexually promiscuous. I became a Christian as a child and my life hasn't seemed a lot different than it was before." In instances like this there is a temptation, if not a tendency, to barely value salvation at all because there is minimal memory of ever being lost. . . .

To gain a proper perspective, we should ask ourselves, "What would I have been like if I had never become a Christian?" Imagine the loneliness, purposelessness, fear, and sin. Look around at people of similar age whose lives have been a disaster and who have no hope for the future. Taking time to imagine the way we would have been without salvation goes a long way toward understanding this wonderful gift of God and consciously being grateful for it.

Leith Anderson, *Winning the Values War in a Changing Culture*

APRIL 12

The Shortness of Life

. . . What is your life? You are a mist that appears for a little while and then vanishes.

JAMES 4:14

How deeply do you desire your mission?

Socrates was walking by the water one day when a young man asked him, "Socrates, may I be your disciple?" Socrates didn't say anything; he merely started to walk into the water. The young man followed, asking again, "Socrates, please let me be your disciple." But Socrates kept his mouth shut and walked farther into the water. The young man still followed, pleading "Socrates—" At that point Socrates turned around, grabbed the young man by the hair, pushed him under water, and held him there until he knew he could take no more. The man came up gasping for air. Socrates looked at him and said, "Young man, when you desire truth as much as you desire air, then you can be my disciple."

How desperately do you want something? After you have put your vision, purpose, roles, goals, and guiding principles into print, think about them all the time. Read them over and over. Rehearse them in your mind.

Pray for their accomplishment. Talk about them. Interact with people about them. Tell them what you want to do. Let others hold you accountable.

Remember that life is short. So, accomplish what you truly want to accomplish. Develop a deep sense of the preciousness and shortness of life. And live in the light of that!

Ron Jenson, *Make a Life, Not Just a Living*

APRIL 13

Guarded Eyes

I will set before my eyes
 no vile thing.
The deeds of faithless men I hate;
 they will not cling to me.

PSALM 101:3

Men, we live in the real world. Here, many women package themselves in ways that would make most advertisers green with envy. So we cannot always avoid "seeing" an attractive woman. It is the "gazing" that must be controlled.

One wise sage once said, "You cannot keep the birds from flying over your head. But you can keep them from building a nest in your hair." It was allowing a nest to be built in his hair that Job resisted. And so must we.

May I get specific? This means we must not linger at the magazine rack. Nor watch films or rent videos that sensually enflame lust. For some of us men who travel, our biggest struggle is with the television set in our hotel room and the lewd movies that are accessible to us. When no one is watching. "Five minutes free," the sign says. It should read, "Five minutes to bondage."

For others of us, the magazines we "read" are our downfall. Even once-reputable publications are now filled with sleazy advertisements and voluptuous swimsuit issues.

Cliff Barrows is Billy Graham's much-respected music leader. I like what Cliff does when he checks into a hotel room. He first drapes a towel over the television and then places his Bible on top of the towel. That way, he has to fight through the Holy Bible to get to the trash on the tube. May his tribe increase.

Let me tell you two things we do around our house.

First, whenever I watch television, I do so with a remote control always in my hand. By hitting one button, I can immediately change channels. Especially when I am watching a ballgame with my young boys, this is an absolute necessity. You cannot watch a major sports program these days without being bombarded with nudity, bedhopping, and adultery via the commercials. An escape valve called a channel changer is critically important.

Second, whenever my sports magazines are delivered to the house, my wife first "deprograms" them by tearing out all the pages that contain "smut." And that is no small assignment. One sports magazine that I received weekly since 1960 touts an annual swimsuit issue and is totally ripped apart.

Men, what about you? Have you made such a covenant with your eyes? Will you guard what you allow to visually come into your heart? Men who win do.

Steven Lawson, *Men Who Win*

APRIL 14

Rendering unto Caesar

"Is it right for us to pay taxes to Caesar or not?"

He saw through their duplicity and said to them, "Show me a denarius. Whose portrait and inscription are on it?"

"Caesar's," they replied.

He said to them, "Then give to Caesar what is Caesar's, and to God what is God's."

LUKE 20:22–25

Perhaps nothing represents a Christian business person's spiritual values more clearly than that person's attitude toward paying taxes. No one likes to pay taxes; even those people who recognize the necessity of collecting taxes for roads, schools, and defense rarely count taxpaying as a privilege. (After all, they claim their deductions to reduce their tax burden, just like everyone else.) But to actually cheat on income taxes or any other tax due is a sin, and sin separates us from God.

Unless you believe that your relationship with God is the most important asset you have in this world, sin will easily ensnare you. I personally believe that cheating on income taxes is the most common sin among Christians in business. Much, if not most, of it is so well concealed that even the best auditors cannot detect it—but God already knows about it.

Over the years I have probably heard just about every possible way to cheat on taxes. I have met professing Christians who never paid their apportioned amount and rarely, if ever, thought of their evasion as a sin. Many of these people were generous givers to God's causes. Many did wonderful jobs of speaking out for the Lord and working to spread the gospel. Yet all of them had one characteristic in common—a lack of peace and fulfillment in their spiritual lives. They might fake being dynamic Christians when they were out among others who fed their theatrical abilities, but when they were alone they realized that something was missing from their relationship with Jesus . . .

[I believe] that cheating on income taxes is one of the most common sins among Christian business people. I also [believe] that someone who cheats on income taxes (or in any other aspect of our business) is no longer useful to God's plan. Until they confess and repent from their sin . . . God will simply pass them by.

Larry Burkett, *Business by the Book*

APRIL 15
Calm Amidst the Storm

He reached down from on high and took hold of me;
he drew me out of deep waters.

PSALM 18:16

[Editor's Note: Shortly after midnight on this date in 1912 the "unsinkable" Titanic, on its maiden voyage from Southhampton to New York, sank after hitting an iceberg. More than 1,500 people were taken to a watery grave. Many men, turned away from overcrowded lifeboats, were left to drown. The first portion of today's reading is from an account of one of the last men to leave the sinking Titanic, Colonel Archibald Gracie, U.S. Army, ret. He never recovered from the exposure and shock of the night and died eight months after the disaster.

The second entry is from the Rev. Dr. Newell Hillis, and the third, from an anonymous source.]

Though I did not see, I could not avoid hearing what took place at this most tragic crisis in all my life. The men with the paddles, forward and aft, so steered the boat as to avoid contact with the unfortunate swimmers pointed out struggling in the water. I heard the constant explanation made as we passed men swimming in the wreckage, "Hold on to what you have, old boy; one more of you aboard would sink us all." In no instance, I am happy to say, did I hear any word of rebuke uttered by a swimmer because of refusal to grant assistance. There was no case of cruel violence. But there was one transcendent piece of heroism that will remain fixed in my memory as the most sublime and coolest exhibition of courage and cheerful resignation to fate and fearlessness of death. This was when a reluctant refusal of assistance met with the ringing response in the deep manly voice of a powerful man, who, in his extremity, replied: "All right, boys; good luck and God bless you." I have often wished that the identity of this hero might be established and an individual tribute to his memory preserved . . .

[Another man] "swam close to us saying, 'Hello boys, keep calm, boys,' asking to be helped up, and was told he could not get on as it might turn the boat over. He asked for a plank and was told to cling to what he had. It was very hard to see so brave a man swim away saying, 'God bless you.'"

Col. Archibald Gracie, *The Truth About the Titanic*

When Col. Gracie came up, after the sinking of the *Titanic*, he says that he made his way to a sunken raft. The submerged little raft was under water often, but every man, without regard to nationality, broke into instant prayer. There were many voices, but they all had one signification—their sole hope was in God. There were no millionaires, for millions fell away like leaves; there were no poor; men were neither wise nor ignorant; they were simply human souls on the sinking raft; the night was black and the waves yeasty with foam, and the grave where the *Titanic* lay was silent under them, and the stars were silent over them! But as they prayed, each man by that inner light saw an invisible Friend walking across the waves.

Henceforth, these need no books on Apologetics to prove there is a God. This man who has written his story tells us that God heard the prayers of some by giving them death, and heard the prayers of others equally by keeping them in life; but God alone is great!

Rev. Dr. Newell Hillis

Four years after the Titanic went down, a young Scotsman rose in a meeting in Hamilton, Canada, and said, "I am a survivor of the Titanic. When I was drifting alone on a spar on that awful night, the tide brought Mr. John Harper, of Glasgow, also on a piece of wreck, near me. 'Man,' he said, 'are you saved?' 'No,' I said, 'I am not.' He replied, 'Believe on the Lord Jesus Christ, and thou shalt be saved.'

"The waves bore him away; but, strange to say, brought him back a little later, and he said, 'Are you saved now?' 'No,' I said, 'I cannot honestly say that I am.' He said again, 'Believe on the Lord Jesus Christ, and thou shalt be saved'; and shortly after, he went down. There, alone in the night, and with two miles of water under me, I believed. I am John Harper's last convert."

Anonymous

APRIL 16

Occupying Until He Comes

So he called ten of his servants and gave them ten minas. "Put this money to work," he said, "until I come back."

LUKE 19:13

I have a friend who is a genius at the piano. He knows how to construct, repair, tune and play the piano with an intense concern for quality in every area. He has absorbed into his spirit the essence of the piano. . . .

I have another friend who has a deep concern for the oceans. He has a master's degree in oceanography, with an emphasis in policy making. He works with the Coast Guard and has a broad sense of the philosophical and creative importance of the seas. If [King] David could assign a man to be in charge of the stewardship for his fields, would not Jesus assign someone for stewardship over the oceans? In the kingdom of God, there will still be real life. God is using the experiences of our present life to train us for our future greater stewardship.

The parable of the ten talents explains that what we do in this lifetime is preparation for the extension of our authority in the kingdom of God. In Luke 19:17 Jesus addresses the one who had been productive in his labor by saying:

Well done, good servant; because you were faithful in very little, have authority over ten cities.

This passage can be seen as referring to ministry, faith and evangelism, but is also referring to our faithfulness in the practical tasks of our jobs.

Jesus looks at our jobs to determine what kind of spiritual people we are. Verse 15 states:

He then commanded these servants to whom He had given the money to be called to Him that He might know how much every man had gained by trading.

As we are called to go out into the world and take dominion, our jobs are part of that calling. We are to gain positions of authority and influence in the world. We are to be occupying forces in the real areas of life as we await the coming kingdom. Verse 13 states Jesus' directive to us:

Occupy until I come.

We are to do business and exercise godly dominion through our jobs.

Keith Intrater, *Covenant Relationships*

APRIL 17

The All-Sufficient One

"I am the Alpha and the Omega," says the Lord God, "who is, and who was, and who is to come, the Almighty."

REVELATION 1:8

You are holy, Lord, the only God,
    and your deeds are wonderful.
You are strong.
    You are great.
    You are the Most High,
    You are almighty.

You, holy Father, are
King of heaven and earth.
You are Three and One,
Lord God, all good.
You are Good, all Good, supreme Good,
Lord God, living and true.
You are love,
You are wisdom.
You are humility,
You are endurance.
You are rest,
You are peace.
You are joy and gladness.
You are justice and moderation.
You are all our riches,
And you suffice for us.
You are beauty.
You are gentleness.
You are our protector,
You are our guardian and defender.
You are courage.
You are our haven and our hope.
You are our faith,
Our great consolation.
You are our eternal life,
Great and wonderful Lord,
God almighty,
Merciful Saviour.

ST. FRANCIS OF ASSISI

APRIL 18

The Freedom of Self-Discipline

He who heeds discipline shows the way to life, but whoever ignores correction leads others astray.

PROVERBS 10:17

I stayed for a week in the home of the president of a theological college. In saying good-bye he said something that rather startled me: "You are the most disciplined person I have ever seen. You don't waste a moment and you don't waste a word, and yet you are relaxed." The reason why I was startled was this: I didn't feel disciplined. To be told I was disciplined was something different from what I was telling myself. I was telling myself: "You are free—and happy."

There is something in Jesus that is native to my blood, to my nerves, to my tissues, to my organs, to my relationships—to me as a total person. My blood is purer, my digestion is better, my brain is clearer, my nerves are calmer and steadier, my glands function perfectly, my being has a sense of well-being. He is "native" to me and I'm "native" to him. We are made for each other as the eye is made for light, the conscience is made for truth, as the aesthetic nature is made for beauty. So discipline is functioning in the way we are made to function. Therefore, discipline is delight. To have no discipline is destruction. There are no exceptions.

E. Stanley Jones, *A Song of Ascents*

APRIL 19

Freedom from Worry

Do not be anxious about anything, but in everything, by prayer and petition, with thanksgiving, present your request to God.

PHILIPPIANS 4:6

Worry is a nonproductive pastime. It has been said that worry is the advanced interest paid on troubles that seldom come. It has also been said that worry is like a rocking chair. You are always moving . . . but you never get anywhere.

Worry is something that can grip us and overpower us. It is interesting that the word *worry* actually comes from an old English word that means "to choke or strangle." Everyone knows how it feels to be choked and strangled with worries.

Maybe we should follow the example of a man I once heard about. He was a bit of a worrywart. One day a friend noticed that he was not gripped with worry, as usual, and inquired, "You're normally so worked up and worried about the future, but today you seem calm and reserved. What happened?"

"I just got tired of worrying—and hired someone to do it for me," he said.

"Really? And what do you pay this person?" the friend asked.

"I pay him $10,000 a month," said the worrywart.

"You pay him $10,000 a month to worry for you? You don't even earn that kind of money yourself. How are you going to pay him?" asked the friend.

"That's for *him* to worry about!"

Greg Laurie, *Life. Any Questions?*

APRIL 20

Deliverance from Idleness

Lazy hands make a man poor,
  but diligent hands bring wealth.

PROVERBS 10:4

God has given every man work enough that there is no room for idleness. Yet He has so ordered the world that there is space for devotion. He who has the least business of the world is called on to spend more time in the "dressing of his soul," and he who has the greatest amount of worldly business may so arrange it that it shall serve God. While those business affairs are blessed by certain periods of prayers and religious exercises, they are hallowed all day long by a holy intention. . . .

To a busy man, temptation is apt to come in connection with his business, where sin looks for an opportunity to creep in. To an idle person, however, temptation comes with open violence and urgent impudence. An idle person is so useless to any purpose of God or man that he is like one who is dead, unconcerned with the changes and needs of the world. He lives only to spend his time and eat the fruits of the earth. When his time comes, like the wolf or vermin, he dies and perishes, and in the meantime he does no good. He neither plows nor carries burdens; all he does is either useless or positively destructive.

Idleness is the greatest extravagance in the world: it throws away time, which is beyond value to the present, and when past, is recoverable by no power of art or nature.

Jeremy Taylor

APRIL 21

Obedience

And this is love: that we walk in obedience to his commands. . . .

II JOHN 6

OBEDIENCE

I said: "Let me walk in the fields."
He said: "No, walk in the town."
I said: "There are no flowers there."
He said: "No flowers, but a crown."

I said: "But the skies are black;
There is nothing but noise and din."
And He wept as He sent me back—
"There is more," He said; "there is sin."

I said: "But the air is thick,
And fogs are veiling the sun."
He answered: "Yet souls are sick,
And souls in the dark undone!"

I said: "I shall miss the light,
And friends will miss me, they say."
He answered: "Choose tonight
If I am to miss you or they."

I pleaded for time to be given.
He said: "Is it hard to decide?
It will not seem so hard in heaven
To have followed the steps of your Guide."

I cast one look at the fields,
Then set my face to the town;
He said, "My child, do you yield?
Will you leave the flowers for the crown?"

Then into His hand went mine;
And into my heart came He;
And I walk in a light divine,
The path I had feared to see.

GEORGE MACDONALD

APRIL 22
The Right Vocation

What does the worker gain from his toil? I have seen the burden God has laid on men.

ECCLESIASTES 3:9–10

The crux of the consideration for Christians who don't want to burn out may be to consider if they are in the job God has for them. If you think you'll be fired if you spend sufficient time with family and on rest and relaxation, then it is unlikely that it is the job God has for you. Before quitting the company, however, it may be fruitful to consider if there is another type of position in the same company that would suit you better. One young Christian accountant in a large company realized that his chosen career was giving him little opportunity to deal with people on a personal level. Because he needed such contact, he asked to be switched to the human relations or personnel department of the company as a trainer. Today, he has won many awards for his innovative work efficiency programs and methods of motivating factory workers.

When we put God, family and work in any other order, we have diminished our faithfulness to God and are saying, "I don't trust God to meet my needs." God would much rather we have less income and a more enjoyable lifestyle. If you quit the road to burnout, you may indeed face the possibility of being fired. However, you may be surprised to find that your rating in the company will go up instead of down, as you enter each day fresher and more ready to give your best to producing during the part of the day that should be allotted to work.

One former burnout victim and workaholic, a company chief executive officer, uses the following checklist to get his life in balance.

1. Realize that you don't have to be perfect to be "somebody." You are already "somebody" in Christ because He says you are.
2. Realize that you don't have to be completely neat in order to have other people and yourself approve of you.
3. Look at life from the eternity perspective. What will you take with you?
4. Learn to relax with activities that are relaxing to you.
5. Get in touch with your hidden anger, then forgive others for their part in it, and forgive yourself for having it.

Learning a new way of life comes hard for a workaholic, but it is necessary. A workaholic has to practice being relaxed, practice saying no to others' expectations of him, schedule time with God, schedule eight hours of sleep, and schedule time with family. The alternative is to become progressively less productive and of less benefit to loved ones and to himself as a result of burnout.

Frank Minirth, *How to Beat Burnout*

APRIL 23
Peaceable Man
Don't get into needless fights.
PROVERBS 3:30 (TLB)

To be masculine, a man should be peaceable. In Proverbs 3:30 it says, "Don't get into needless fights." (It doesn't say not to fight under any circumstances.) Probably the most famous fight of all times was not held in a boxing ring or on a battlefield, but in a temple. Jesus walked into this area, which was supposed to be sacred, and found it swarming with money changers, its places of worship surrounded by the great Jerusalem carnival attractions. He turned over the booths, knocking over the cash registers and scattering the contents of the tables over the cobblestones. This was not a needless fight, but a display of positive strength in confrontation with a specific evil.

When I see some pictures showing Jesus with feminine characteristics, I think that some of the painters must have used women as models. Jesus was the personification of masculinity. He was a carpenter's son, and the men in the building trades of that time couldn't go down to the Jerusalem Lumber Company and order twenty-five two-by-fours. They had to go out into the woods and chop a few trees and hew them by hand. They didn't have band saws. You could tell a carpenter, because he was a "big moose," he was the guy who swung the ax and pulled a mean saw. He didn't have to work out with weights in the gym, after work. He did it every day.

Visualize Jesus striding into the temple and saying, "All right, you guys—move!" They moved! He was the masculine guy with His strength under control. He didn't lose His head. When He was in the Garden of Gethsemane, Judas led a mob of angry men, brandishing swords and clubs, and surrounded Jesus with the brute force that imflamed tempers can bring. Jesus answered their shouts and accusations, and they were so astounded by His strength that they fell back! Even His friends beat it out the back door.

They could have stoned Him to death right then, but they didn't tangle with the carpenter's son. I think we have a mistaken viewpoint of what is masculine and what is godly. We somehow think that the two aren't compatible, but the Bible teaches otherwise. To really be performing God's role as a man is to be a masculine individual, with strength under control. This has nothing to do with size, although I have emphasized the physical strength of Jesus. Obviously, no one has complete control over his size. I'm talking about being the type of man who doesn't mind taking charge and doing what is right. This isn't the fellow who fades into the woodwork when the going gets rough. Proverbs 12:16 says, "A fool is quick-tempered; a wise man stays cool when insulted."

Bob Vernon, *The Married Man*

APRIL 24
Our Jobs in Context

Listen, my son, to your father's instruction
and do not forsake your mother's teaching.
They will be a garland to grace your head
and a chain to adorn your neck.

PROVERBS 1:8–9

Whenever possible, our children need to be brought into familiarity with our workplace. This begins long before they take a trip into the office. Conversations about Dad's work should be a regular part of the family discourse. From an early age, the idea that Dad and Mom are doing something important, contributing not only to the family but also to the community and society as a whole, needs to be a part of your child's worldview. As they grow older, they need to be integrated more and more into an understanding of the workplace . . . our children need to see our workplace. If company policies preclude regular visits during working hours, they need, at the very least, to be given a conversational knowledge of what it is our jobs demand of us and how our jobs contribute to society as a whole. At that point, our children can begin to respect us not only for who we are in the home, but also for our position in the world at large. They can get a glimpse of the interconnectedness of all we do and who we are. Take our daughters to work? Certainly. But let's take our sons along with them.

David Nowell, *A Man's Work Is Never Done*

APRIL 25
Finished Work

I have brought you glory on earth by completing the work you gave me to do.

JOHN 17:4

Quite a while ago, I consulted with a young man who had followed his father and grandfather into business. He had a nice income, a nice house, nice cars, and all the extras. However, as I got to know him, I soon learned things were not as they appeared. The young man was actually miserable. He had been seeking counseling for quite some time, and his marriage was in trouble. As we worked through the situation, it was clear that he had not been obedient to God in choosing a vocation. He had followed in his father's and grandfather's footsteps because that was the easiest path and he could make more money than if he started a new business, as he felt God wanted him to. Once he left the family business and started his own business, his life gradually came back into focus. He had less money, but he was content.

The world deemed this young man a success when he worked in the family business. Why? Because of the riches and material possessions he was able to accumulate as a result of his income. But was that the work God wanted him to do? Would this man be able to say to God what Jesus was able to say: "I have glorified You on the earth. I have finished the work which You have given Me to do" (John 17:4 [NKJV])?

We are all called to different vocations. We cannot all be doctors, developers, accountants, or lawyers. We also need cooks, letter carriers, police officers, grocers, plumbers, printers, and truck drivers. Therefore, regardless of a person's vocation, only God really knows if he or she is successful. We do not know the degree of someone else's obedience. We can measure his or her wealth and riches, but not his or her success; we are only successful if we are obedient.

Is an excellent teacher who makes thirty thousand dollars less successful than a professional athlete who sits on the bench and makes three hundred thousand dollars? In God's definition, their obedience and the degree to which they have maximized the abilities He has given them are the keys to their success. Their income has nothing to do with it. They both could be failures if they are not doing their best or if they disobeyed God in choosing their vocation. Since it is God who gives us the ability to make wealth (see Deut. 8:16–18) and God who designs each of us to perform different functions, then the income we earn cannot possibly be the measurement of success.

Russ Crosson, *A Life Well Spent*

APRIL 26
Working Unseen

But you are not to be like that. Instead, the greatest among you should be like the youngest, and the one who rules like the one who serves.

LUKE 22:26

Exalt Christ. Use a sharp knife with thyself. Say little, serve all, pass on. This is true greatness, to serve unnoticed and work unseen. Oh, the joy of having nothing and being nothing, seeing nothing but a Living Christ in Glory, and being careful for nothing but His interests down here.

J. N. Darby

APRIL 27
An Ongoing Work

Even to your old age and gray hairs
I am he, I am he who will sustain you.

ISAIAH 46:4

Retired people should never get the idea that God created them to work till their late fifties or early sixties and then quit. That was never the divine intention. If they are fortunate enough to be in a position to retire, wonderful. This means that they can channel their creativity and the wisdom they've accumulated over the years into new ventures, new personal goals, and new areas of ministry. Retirement should never mean that people stop being creative and productive or that they cease to invest their lives for God's glory and channel their energies to the benefit of the community. What it can mean is that they have more time to do it, and they can do it on a volunteer basis.

When the time comes that there is no need to maintain civilization and there are no more human needs to meet, it could possibly be argued that work will then be unnecessary. Until that day, however, work is in order, and workers are needed. Remember that Paradise wasn't a vacation—it was a vocation.

Stuart Briscoe, *Choices for a Lifetime*

APRIL 28
The Fear of the Lord

The fear of the LORD is the beginning of wisdom,
and knowledge of the Holy One is understanding.

PROVERBS 9:10

The wisdom of God can take even a poor man, train him in the ways of the Lord and give him a strategy to deliver a city. Throughout the ages the Lord has had His judges, generals and kings who delivered the nation of Israel. In more modern times God has had His Wesleys, His Martin Luthers, His Jonathan Edwardses, men who turned their countries toward heaven. The chaos of our cities is not greater than the chaos which covered the deep, formless, pre-creation void. God's wisdom brought creation to order, and His wisdom can bring the church back to order as well.

The Lord desires for you to possess His wisdom. How do you find it? "The fear of the Lord is the beginning of wisdom, and the knowledge of the Holy One is understanding" (Prov. 9:10). What is "the fear of the Lord"? It is the human soul, having experienced the crucifixion of self and pride, now trembling in stark vulnerability before almighty God. It is this living awareness: God sees everything. This penetrating discovery marks the holy beginning of finding true wisdom.

However, this perception of the living God is not a terrible reality, for it liberates the mind from the cocoon of carnality, enabling the soul to escape into the Spirit. For all the dynamic gifts through which Jesus revealed the Father's power, His delight was in the fear of the Lord (see Is. 11:1–3). Yes, it is the awe-inspiring wonder of man living in fellowship, not with his religion, but with his God. In such a state the obedient man is invincible.

Indeed, has this not been our problem: The enemy does not fear the church because the church does not fear the Lord? As the fear of the Lord returns to us, the terror of the Lord will be upon our enemies. The fear of the Lord is our wisdom.

Francis Frangipane, *The House of the Lord*

APRIL 29

The Diligent Man

Joshua son of Nun and Caleb son of Jephunneh, who were among those who had explored the land, tore their clothers and said to the entire Israelite assembly, "The land we passed through and explored is exceedingly good. If the LORD is pleased with us, he will lead us into that land, a land flowing with milk and honey, and will give it to us. Only do not rebel against the LORD. And do not be afraid of the people of the land, because we will swallow them up. Their protection is gone, but the LORD is with us. Do not be afraid of them."

NUMBERS 14:6–9

The diligent man never takes "no" for an answer. This doesn't mean he keeps bugging the same person over and over. But it does mean that a "no" answer from one person—or many—will not stop him. Sooner or later he will find the person who says "yes."

Don't take "no" as some sort of sign from God to stop. Don't take a slammed door or denial of opportunity as a sign from God. God's already told you to keep asking, keep seeking, and keep knocking.

Don't try to figure out why obvious doors remain shut, because the diligent man only knows to go to the next door. As you become successful, you will find many of those formerly shut doors are now opening to you.

Your true enemies are not the people who seemingly have the power to stop you. Your true enemies are found within you—discouragement, hurt feelings, laziness, self pity, withdrawal pessimism, and dejection.

Here is the perfect example of the true enemy being within your heart and soul. The Lord spoke to Moses in Numbers 13 and commanded him to send out spies into the land of Canaan. Moses chose two men from each of the twelve tribes of Israel. After forty days, the men returned and reported that the land "certainly does flow with milk and honey." The promises of God were both good and rewarding—if they could be taken.

But the men added, "We are not able to go up against the people, for they are too strong for us. . . . The land through which we have gone, in spying it out, is a land that devours its inhabitants, and all the people whom we saw in it are men of great size . . . we became like grasshoppers in our own sight, and so we were in their sight."

APRIL · 137

Two men, Joshua and Caleb, gave a different report: "We should by all means go up and take possession of it, for we shall surely overcome it."

An angry God responded by forbidding all Israelites from twenty years and upward from ever walking into the Promised Land. God was not about to send a band of negative, pessimistic, and discouraged people into a land that required great optimism and diligence.

We all know the outcome—the Israelites conquered the land of Canaan. This is a lesson for ~~you~~ *us* in ~~your~~ *our* walk into God's Promised Land and calling.

The true enemies are not the giants who are there to devour ~~you~~ *us*—and indeed they will if ~~you~~ *we* let them. The true enemy is within ~~yourself~~ *ourself*—the unwillingness to try, to fight, to conquer, to be diligent.

The diligent will rule—because they have the character to make it happen.

Martin Mawyer, Pathways to Success

APRIL 30
A Nurturing Father

A deacon must be the husband of but one wife and must manage his children and his household well.

I TIMOTHY 3:12

Husbands are given to take leadership in prayer—not to do all of it or to control it. In day-to-day life, that means the husband should take the responsibility to say table graces or delegate this privilege to a family member. He should pray aloud for his wife if she is ill, or say a blessing if she is to take a trip or speak before a group or minister somewhere. He should establish and maintain family prayer times. His reading of the Word and meditating upon the law of God provides the context and style of the family's life.

As the children experience the openness and humility of a father's carrying the family problems and concerns to the Father in prayer, as they hear him praise the Lord for His faithfulness in all things, as they sit beside him in church in shared devotion, they will receive his structure of godliness as a natural part of the fabric of their lives. If the head of the household is in tune with the joys and the sorrows of those in his charge, and meets them where they are, he will call forth from them an ability to respond to authority throughout their lives without fear and guile.

The husband is the first comforter of a child, not the laggard, nagged-at one who finally sees and does because his wife gave him no peace—"Jim, can't you see how your daughter is hurting and needs you?"

A Christian head of a household is one who knows his position is a God-given privilege, an opportunity to express and experience the creative nurturing grace of the Father, not a burden to be endured in the spaces between the times he calls his own. He is refreshed on the golf course, and by national championship ball games, no more than he is by finding quiet joy in shared thoughts and adventures with his wife and children.

John Sandford, *Restoring the Christian Family*

May

May 1

Know-So Christianity

Jesus replied, *"Blessed are you, Simon son of Jonah, for this was not revealed to you by man, but by my Father in heaven."*

MATTHEW 16:17

We believe in salvation *here* and *now*. We believe in feeling, knowing and partaking here on earth of the leaves of the tree of life, which are for the healing of nations. We believe in being healed and blessed, and filled with the glory of God and the peace and purity and power of salvation. While we struggle and suffer and fight and sacrifice, we want the comforting, sustaining, upholding arms of Jehovah bearing us up, and making us feel strong in the strength of the mighty God of Jacob.

There are *think-so* Christians, and there are *hope-so* Christians, and there are *know-so* Christians; thank God we belong to the know-so people—we know we are saved. And why not? Enoch had the testimony that he pleased God. Job new that his Redeemer lived. John knew that he had passed from death into life. Paul knew that when his earthly house was destroyed, that he had a building in the heavens. And we know in whom we have believed, and the Spirit answers to our faith, and testifies in our hearts that we are the children of God.

My brethren, if you have salvation, you are sure of it. Not because you have *heard* it preached from the street corner or from the platform of the church. Not because you have *read* with your eyes, or heard read by others, the wonderful story of the love of God to you. Not because you have *seen* with your eyes transformations of character brought about by the power of the Holy Ghost; changes as marvelous, as miraculous, as divine, as any that ever took place in apostolic or any other days.

These things may have led up to it. But these things, as wonderful as they may be, have not the power to make you *sure* of your part and lot in the manner of salvation. Flesh and blood has not revealed this to you, but God Himself, by His Spirit, has made this known.

Our work is salvation. We believe in salvation and we have salvation. We are not mere sentimentalists or theory people: we publish what we have heard and seen and handled and experienced in the world of life and the power of God. We aim at salvation. We want this and nothing short of this, and we want this right off. My brethren, my comrades, soul-saving is our vocation, the great purpose and business of our lives. . . .

Look at this. Clear your vision. Halt, stand still and fully comprehend your calling. *You* are to be a worker together with God for the salvation of your fellow men. What is the business of your life? Not merely to save your soul and make yourself ready for Paradise. If this were all, would it not be a menial and selfish lot for which to toil and suffer and pray and die? Would it not be completely unlike the Master's work? No, you are to be a *redeemer*, a *savior*, a copy of Jesus Christ Himself. So consecrate every awakened power to the great end of saving men.

Rescue the perishing. There they are all around you, everywhere, crowds upon crowds, multitudes. Be skillful. Improve yourself. Study your business.

Be self-sacrificing. Remember the Master. What you lose for His sake, you shall find again. Stick to it. Having put your hand to the salvation plough, don't look behind you.

William Booth, from *The Salvationist Magazine*, 1879

May 2
His Greatness in Us

You, dear children, are from God and have overcome them, because the one who is in you is greater than the one who is in the world.

1 John 4:4

I worked in an office where the men of the office would take lunch hours on Tuesdays and Thursdays to play basketball in a gymnasium across the street. Now, basketball is not my best game. When we chose up sides, it threatened to go this way: "Gentlemen, we had Gayle last time. It's your turn to take him. . . ."

So, you can see that I was mainly there for the exercise. However, there was one fellow named Dave who was six feet eighteen inches tall when he stepped onto the basketball court. I loved to get on his team. We would always win. All I had to do was get the ball to Dave and he would score. When we would get the ball back, I would dribble it around a while simply for appearance sake, lob the ball over to Dave and he would dunk it for another two points. Then I would say, "Aren't we good?"

That is much like the relationship we have with Jesus. He is the one who is at work in us to help us want to do his will and then to help even more as we try to do it. We are his workmanship. What we are is his full responsibility and he accepts it. Our job is to stay on the same team as he, cast our cares on him, and let him do the scoring against Satan for us: "The one who is in you is greater than the one who is in the world" (1 John 4:4)

So make yourself available to him. Permit his Holy Spirit to make you aware of the mind of Christ as it works its way out in your life. Give yourself away and keep growing!

Gayle Erwin, *The Jesus Style*

May 3
No Favoritism

Suppose a man comes into your meeting wearing a gold ring and fine clothes, and a poor man in shabby clothes also comes in. If you show special attention to the man wearing fine clothes and say, "Here's a good seat for you," but say to the poor man, "You stand there" or "Sit on the floor by my feet," have you not discriminated among yourselves and become judges with evil thoughts? Listen, my dear brothers: Has not God chosen those who are poor in the eyes of the world to be rich in faith and to inherit the kingdom he promised those who love him?

JAMES 2:2–5

Some years ago, we had a fairly wealthy man coming to our church and giving a fair amount of money. He wanted to know when I was going to make him a leader.

I said, "Excuse me?"

He said, "Well, you know, I give a lot of money and I'm a very noted person."

I replied, "That's nice, but that's not the criteria for being a leader. Your spiritual development has to determine that."

"Do you know how many churches would love to have me as a member?" he came back.

Now he's going down the wrong road with me, so I said, "Well, maybe you should start visiting some of them."

"You mean to tell me that you would stop me from being a leader based on some criteria you come up with or the Bible comes up with when I'm giving all this money?"

I said, "You are absolutely right, because when it comes to your standing before God, what your bank account looks like is irrelevant."

You are not to be intimidated by people because they have more than you have, because they have greater names, greater prestige, or greater power. Before God, all of stand as sinners in need of a Savior. We all stand on level ground at Calvary, and understanding this is absolutely critical.

That's why you can't be overly proud of your race. You are only black because God made you that way; you are only white because God made you that way. You can't get too proud about how God made you unless you think He endowed you with something that makes you better than the next man.

Black and white people and all colors in between will live both in heaven and in hell, because God is no respecter of persons. You cannot look at your race and find pride in that. Like Paul, you can only say, "I am what I am by the grace of God." That's what you are, and *that* you can be proud of because God has made you in His image.

Tony Evans, *Our God Is Awesome*

May 4
The Two Becoming One

Has not the Lord made them one? In flesh and spirit they are his. And why one? Because he was seeking godly offspring. So guard yourself in your spirit, and do not break faith with the wife of your youth.

Malachi 2:15

What happens to a couple when they fall in love, when they pitch head-long into this winepress of intimacy, is not simply that they are swept off their feet; more than that, it is the very ground they are standing on, the whole world and ground of their own separate selves, that is swept away. A person in love cannot help becoming, in some sense, a new person. After all, even to stand for five minutes beside a stranger in a supermarket line-up, without exchanging one word, is to be drawn irresistibly, uncomfort-ably, enigmatically into the dizzying vortex of another human life. It is to be subtly swayed, held, hypnotized, transfixed—moved and influenced in a myriad of ways, subliminal and seldom analyzed, but nonetheless potent. But marriage takes this same imponderable magnetism and raises it to an infinite power. The very next step in human closeness, beyond marriage, would be just to scrap the original man and woman and create one new human being out of the two.

But this is exactly what happens (both in symbol and in actuality) in the birth of a child! Eventually the parents die, leaving the child a living sign of the unthinkable extremity of union which took place between two distinct lives. The two became one: "Has not the Lord made them one? In flesh and spirit they are His. And why one? Because He was seeking godly offspring" (Malachi 2:15).

Mike Mason, *The Mystery of Marriage*

May 5
Value in Losing

"I tell you the truth, anyone who will not receive the kingdom of God like a little child will never enter it." And he took the children in his arms, put his hands on them and blessed them.

MARK 10:15–16

When my son Sean was twelve, he played on a Little League baseball team. A week before the season started, I got an idea about how to show him—and his teammates—acceptance. I bought twelve coupons good for ice cream sundaes at a local restaurant, and took them to his coach.

"Coach, these are for the kids," I said.

"Good," the coach said with a big smile. "This is great. I wish more dads took an interest like this. I'll take them for sundaes after our first win."

"No, Coach," I said quickly. "I want you to take them for sundaes after their first *loss*."

Sean's coach looked at me strangely. What I was saying wasn't computing with his concept of winning, losing, and rewards for good play. This is what I shared with him:

"Coach, I don't know about you, but as I raise my kids I don't want to acknowledge their success as much as their effort. And I don't want to acknowledge their effort as much as their being created in the image of God. I believe my son is created in the image of God and that he has infinite value, dignity, and worth, which all have nothing to do with playing baseball. If he never played baseball an inning in his life, I would love and accept him just as much."

Sean's coach looked at me for a long moment. Finally, all he could muster was, "Well, *that's novel.*"

The season started and Sean's team won their first few games. But they lost the third or fourth game, and the coach was true to his word. He gave each player an ice cream sundae coupon and they all went out to "celebrate" their loss.

Sean must have thanked me at least five times for the sundaes. In addition, over the next two weeks three of the kids on his team came up and thanked me for the special treat. I recall especially a boy named Jessie, who said, "Thanks a lot for the ice cream sundaes, Mr. McDowell. Wow! It doesn't matter to you if we win or not—you love us anyway."

Nothing could have made me happier than to hear that. What I wanted to communicate to Sean and his teammates is that their worth is not based upon their ability to play baseball. It's based upon the fact that they are each created in the image of God with infinite value and infinite dignity. Is that kind of lesson too difficult for a twelve-year-old to grasp? Obviously not, especially when you use ice cream to prove your point!

Josh McDowell and Dick Day, *How to Be a Hero to Your Kids*

May 6

The Way to a Christian Mind

Oh, how I love your law!
—I meditate on it all day long.
Your commands make me wiser than my enemies,
—for they are ever with me.
I have more insight than all my teachers,
—for I meditate on your statutes.

PSALMS 119:97–99

Lt. General William K. Harrison was the most decorated soldier in the 30th Infantry Division, rated by General Eisenhower as the number one infantry division in World War II. General Harrison was the first American to enter Belgium, which he did at the head of the Allied forces. He received every decoration for valor except the Congressional Medal of Honor—being honored with the Distinguished Silver Cross, the Silver Star, the Bronze Star for Valor, and the Purple Heart (he was one of the few generals to be wounded in action). When the Korean War began, he served as Chief of Staff in the United Nations Command—and because of his character and self-control was ultimately President Eisenhower's choice to head the long and tedious negotiations to end the war.

General Harrison was a soldier's soldier who led a busy, ultra-kinetic life, but he was also an amazing man of the Word. When he was a twenty-year-old West Point Cadet, he began reading the Old Testament through once a year and the New Testament four times. General Harrison did this until the end of his life. Even in the thick of war he maintained his commitment by catching up during the two- and three-day respites for replacement and refitting that followed battles, so that when the war ended he was right on schedule.

When, at the age of ninety, his failing eyesight no longer permitted the discipline, he had read the Old Testament seventy times and the New Testament 280 times! No wonder his godliness and wisdom were proverbial, and that the Lord used him for eighteen fruitful years to lead Officers Christian Fellowship.

General Harrison's story tells us two things. First, it is possible, even for the busiest of us, to systematically feed on God's Word. No one could be busier or lead a more demanding life than General Harrison.

Second, his life remains a demonstration of a mind programmed with God's Word. His closest associates say that every area of his life (domestic, spiritual, and professional) and each of the great problems he faced was informed by the Scriptures. People marveled at his knowledge of the Bible and the ability to bring its light to every area of life.

You must remember this: You can never have a Christian mind without reading the Scriptures regularly because *you cannot be profoundly influenced by that which you do not know.* If you are filled with God's Word, your life can then be informed and directed by God—your domestic relationships, your child-rearing, your career, your ethical decisions, your interior moral life. The way to a Christian mind is through God's Word!

R. Kent Hughes, *Disciplines of a Godly Man*

MAY 7
A Bold Faith

. . . the righteous are as bold as a lion.

PROVERBS 28:1

The existence of so many spiritually "soft" men reinforces the old stereotype that Christian men are wimps. When I wanted to find a friend in the faith, a Barnabas among some of the Christians on my brother's college campus, even he told me, "Ken, those guys are a bunch of wimps."

To some extent, I had to agree. But God didn't call us to be wimps as Christians. I realize it's a tough decision to hang tough as a man of God in this culture. Yet I don't think we have to look far to find men who are tough—both spiritually and in their life's work. . . .

You wouldn't dare call Reggie White a wimp. Or Tunch Ilkin. Or Anthony Muñoz. The world of sports is a showcase of powerhouse men who are stand-up guys for God. They know how to stay in shape physically and spiritually.

Look at these stats from the George Gallop Polling Agency. "Recent Gallop surveys report that by a margin of 46 percent to 38 percent, women are more likely than men to attend religious services in the past week. What's more, by a margin of 57 percent to 37 percent, women are more likely than men to say they give serious and consistent attention to "the development of their faith."

While we can be glad that women in our country are so dedicated to God, we cannot be satisfied with these numbers. Like a halftime report from the coaching staff that proves we've been sloughing off, this Gallop survey should wake us up to the fact that a comeback is in order.

As we hit the faith workout room, another voice of challenge belongs to Matt Millen. The NFL-great-turned-broadcaster gives us his best spiritual Howard Cosell monologue when he says, "I have a hard time with wimpy Christians. I can't stand it."

The words of Tom Petersburg, chaplain of the Cleveland Browns, have the shock value of truth we need. "The average Christian male wants enough of Jesus to make him successful, but not enough to interfere with his own selfish agenda."

Indeed, until we make our agenda line up with God's, we'll never have the strength, power, and dynamic faith to make a difference in this world.

Ken Ruettgers, Home Field Advantage

May 8

His Everlasting Love

The Lord appeared to us in the past, saying:
"I have loved you with an everlasting love;
I have drawn you with loving-kindness."

JEREMIAH 31:3

Reflect upon the everlasting love God has had for you. Before our Lord Jesus Christ as man suffered on the Cross for you his Divine Majesty by his sovereign goodness already foresaw your existence and loved and favored you. When did his love for you begin? It began even when he began to be God. When did he begin to be God? Never, for he has been forever, without beginning and without end. So also he has always loved you from all eternity and for this reason he has prepared for you all these graces and favors. Hence he speaks to you as well as to others when he says by the prophet, "I have loved you with an everlasting love, therefore have I drawn you, taking pity on you." Among other things, he has thought of enabling you to make your resolution to serve him.

O God, what resolutions are these which you have thought of and meditated upon and projected from all eternity! How dear and precious should they be to us! What should we not suffer rather than forget the least of them! Rather let the whole world perish! For all the world together is not worth one single soul and a soul is worth nothing without these resolutions.

Francis de Sales, *Introduction to the Devout Life*

May 9

Meditation on His Word

*I have hidden your word in my heart
that I might not sin against you.*

Psalm 119:11

To hide the Word in our heart is to do more than just read the Bible or to memorize it. To memorize or read the Word puts it in our head. However, everything must get from the head to the heart before it transforms us. The heart is who we are. When we allow the Word of God to get deep within our heart, we are allowing it to shape the very essence of who we are.

The Word of God is hidden deep within the heart through the practice of prayer. God speaks to us in many different ways and at many different times. However, if we will take the Word that God speaks to us into the prayer closet, and talk to Him intimately concerning that Word, we will rise as new beings. In the secret place of prayer, the spoken Word of God becomes our sustenance. It becomes the very thing that gives us life and liberty. Prayer takes the Word of God and brings life to us. That new life becomes the very thing that keeps us from going back to the old way of sin.

Equally powerful is that of praying the written Word of God. When we pray the written Word of God, we express things we do not ordinarily express. Praying the Word of God teaches us to say the things the Holy Spirit wants us to say. The value of it is that it brings us into the knowledge of God while increasing our desire for God. This knowledge and desire keeps us from sin.

David said, "But his delight is in the law of the Lord, and on his law he meditates." God has always intended for His children to hide the Word in their hearts. Meditation accomplishes this in a most effective way. Meditation is done through running a particular verse over and over in your mind.

Ron Auch, *The Heart of the King*

MAY 10
Nature

Let the heavens rejoice, let the earth be glad;
  let the sea resound, and all that is in it;
  let the fields be jubilant, and everything in them.
Then all the trees of the forest will sing for joy. . . .

PSALM 96:11–12

During one period of my early manhood I was sent by the government to serve for six months in a gigantic factory where thousands of employees were crowded together building aircraft. Not only were my immediate surroundings almost intolerable, but to compound the horror of the place it was located in a low-lying, swampy area where fog was common. Consequently, opportunities for finding fresh air, sunshine, or natural beauty to offset the steel and concrete walls of my world were very slim. I recall, clearly, however, my delight in discovering behind one of the huge hangars a few square yards of green grass that had escaped the bulldozers. It ran down to the murky river nearby; on the opposite bank a fringe of trees survived. Best of all, the grassy spot was a sun trap where one could go at noon and coffee breaks to escape the factory fumes and never-ending noise.

Those few yards of open ground, clothed in green grass, open to the sky, and overlooking the river, saved my sanity in that man-made inferno. More than that, they preserved my body from breaking down beneath the appalling pressures on me. My chum and I would slip out to our "sanctuary" at every opportunity. There we would soak up a little sunshine, breathe deeply of the open air, walk briskly on the soft sod, and fill our vision with the quiet views across the river.

Sunshine, fresh air, and moderate exercise can do more to relieve the strain of modern living than can anything else. Best of all, these are all for free, requiring no cost but the bare time required to take them. Of course there are those who will argue that time is very precious, that they haven't got any to spare, that if they did it would not be wasted on such trifles as sunshine, fresh air, or exercise.

My reply to these people is that if they prefer to break down under the tension of twentieth-century living, to have their cases carefully diagnosed by a well-paid physician, and finally to try to find their feet again by spending a spell in a hospital ward or at home in bed, that is entirely their business.

But to the rest I appeal in all simplicity to seek the sun, the open skies, some fresh air, and some physical exercise at every opportunity. At the very least, this is excellent health insurance. At best, it is a road which can very well lead to a life of new zest, eager vitality, reduced tension, and a relaxed frame of mind.

W. Phillip Keller, *Taming Tension*

MAY 11
Vigorous Exercise

For physical training is of some value, but godliness has value for all things, holding promise for both the present life and the life to come.

I TIMOTHY 4:8

Perhaps it's an echo of my Osage Indian heritage on my father's side, but my personal makeup is such that strength is important to me—both physical and spiritual. Strength has been one of God's best natural gifts to me. I know, too, that ever since God formed man from dust and breathed his personal spirit into him, body and spirit have been interdependent. Physical health profoundly affects spiritual health and vice versa. I was becoming desperately weak and sick in my body because of the stress in my life, and it was affecting me spiritually as well. . . .

My father (the earthly one) began to notice the deterioration in my health and purchased a membership for me in a local athletic club. Because he had spent money, my personal-obligation pattern clicked in—beneficially for once—and I began to exercise. I chose body building because that's what I enjoy. For you, it might be racquet ball or jogging or swimming. The point is that exercise is critical to the recovery of any Wounded Warrior.

I now spend eight hours each week pumping iron at a local gym. In the beginning, I felt guilty for spending so much time on something not directly related to ministry. I still wrestle with it from time to time, but it's one place where I don't have to talk "church" unless I choose to. In the gym I'm just another human being, not a ministry machine/superman. If I want to pray, I can do so even while grunting out that last repetition on the leg press machine.

Furthermore, my time in the gym is the only real contact I have with the world outside of the church that doesn't involve work on behalf of the church. It's both physically satisfying and tangibly rewarding, while most of the rest of my daily routine is mental and emotional and not immediately rewarding. Such contact keeps me out of the "ivory tower" and in touch with real people. And from time to time I do get an opportunity to share the gospel with some curious or hungry soul fascinated by the rare spectacle of a well-muscled and sweaty pastor. . . .

The procedure I recommend is that you see your personal physician for a complete physical exam in order to determine what kind of exercise you can safely undertake and at what levels of intensity. . . .

Then go to an athletic club or gym where good instruction is given. If options are available, shop around and ask questions until you find which club has the best instructors. Tell your instructor about the results of your physical exam, share whatever personal goals you have for exercising and let the professional design an enjoyable program appropriate and effective for you. Understand that, for the first month or more, you may feel ill both during and after your workouts. The exertion may cause headaches. Each of your early workouts will be a burden and you'll want to quit. There will be days when you feel you're just too tired to go. Ignore this, Your body is cleansing itself, and your cells are releasing those stored toxins into the bloodstream where your natural filters can eliminate them. Stick with it faithfully and you'll find yourself a confirmed "sweathog," addicted to the satisfying, full sensation of fatigued muscles. You'll look better and you'll feel better in every way. You'll notice your energy returning in a kind of "body joy" produced by the endorphins secreted by a healthy body when it exercises.

Don't con yourself into thinking you're too far gone or too tired to do this. Exercise is too important . . . for you to permit that kind of self-deception. . . . It's part of the balance of body and spirit that God intended for us to cultivate.

Loren Sandford, *Wounded Warriors*

MAY 12
Faith and Failure

The Lord delights in the way of a man
whose steps he has made firm;
though he stumble, he will not fall,
for the Lord upholds him with his hand.

PSALMS 37:23–24

I don't like to fail, but I can handle it. That hasn't always been true, but as a Christian of ten years, I know where my strength comes from. I know that even if I give up a home run and that makes me the goat, I'll survive. My wife and kids will still love me. God is still in His heaven. The world will not come to an end, regardless of my performance.

It's the same faith, though, that makes me determined to be a good steward of the mind and body I've been blessed with. If my faith merely made me accept defeat and failure, it would be a crutch—a weak, sad alibi. People who criticize Christians for being less competitive—and Christians who *are* less competitive—have missed the point of faith.

It's my faith that lifts me up when I've failed. It's my faith that reminds me of my true insignificance when the world has been laid at my feet because of my success throwing a ball. To call myself a Christian and then to not strive to be the best I can be and do the most I can with what has been given me would be the height of hypocrisy. Being a Christian is no excuse for mediocrity or passive acceptance of defeat. If anything, Christianity demands a higher standard, even more devotion to the task.

Orel Hershiser, Out of the Blue

MAY 13
Vocal Prayer

And when you pray, do not be like the hypocrites, for they love to pray standing in the synagogues and on the street corners to be seen by men. I tell you the truth, they have received their reward in full.

MATTHEW 6:5

One reason I believe prayer is so difficult for us is that private prayer is usually carried out silently. Silent praying, as with silent reading, is a modern phenomenon—the by-product of living close together in urban settings. In New Testament times, praying and reading was always done out loud. In fact, Jesus' admonition to his followers to go into a closet (off by ourselves) to pray was *not* an admonition to pray silently; it was a criticism of the hypocrites who prayed standing in public places. . . . We need a "closet" for prayers because our prayers make noise—or at least they ought to. Speaking your prayers out loud can be a refreshing and meaningful experience. You'll have to find a private place to do it, but I commend it as a helpful encouragement.

There are many books available to help you in your prayer life, so I won't attempt an exhaustive summary of help here. I will simply make a few suggestions for how you can improve your prayer life.

1. *Simplify your praying as much as possible.* Prayer takes many forms—contemplative, thanksgiving, requesting. It should also include waiting quietly so that you can be instructed by God.

2. *The attitude of prayer should always be the same:* a simple waiting upon God and an experiencing of his presence in humility.

3. *You should develop the prayer of "being" in addition to the prayer of "asking."* The prayer of "being" is the prayer that only asks to experience God's presence. Such a prayer is receptive rather than expressive. It does not command God. It asks for no benefit. It appreciates God for who he is, not for what he can give. This kind of prayer is a habit we neglect to our detriment. We are the losers for not being in communion with God.

Archibald Hart, *Healing for Hidden Addictions*

MAY 14
God As Our Source

He said to me: "It is done. I am the Alpha and the Omega, the Beginning and the End. To him who is thirsty I will give to drink without cost from the spring of the water of life."

REVELATION 21:6

We are lost males, all of us: cast adrift from the community of men, cut off from our masculine heritage—abandoned to machines, organizations, fantasies, drugs.

I realize the depth of our predicament when I describe [an] African male initiation rite to groups, for the most frequent question afterward is, "Does the mother *really* hold the boy behind her when the mask/spirit approaches her hut, and cry when the mask/spirit seizes him? Or isn't she just playacting, going along with the game, so to speak?"

I have come to regard such a question as kin to the unspoken attitude of Western Christians before the Eucharist: Does anything really happen to people who take the bread and wine? Or isn't the congregation just playacting, going along, as it were, with the game which the church insists on perpetuating?

God help us when we have so forgotten who we are, and so lost our experience of the event which brought us into being, that we wander in such spiritual amnesia.

Gently, I explain that yes, the drama of the initiation rite anticipates a certain response from the mother. But in doing so, the rite does not define that response, but authenticates it. In fact, no mother who has enjoyed the devotion of her son can readily give it up. The release and proper growth of the boy require a community-ordained ritual to which her natural, self-centered impulses must yield.

The ritual, through the spirit who initiates and presides over it, allows the individual mother both to express her genuine pain and to submit at last to the larger authority of the spirit—thus yielding to the boy's new emotional/spiritual "birth" even as years earlier she yielded the baby in labor, itself.

Clearly, without such a ritual, the mother is not likely to be confronted with this, her essential role—and her natural, self-centered desires for the boy then prevail over his life, even into adulthood. In a convoluted myopia, the boy in later physical maturity cannot look beyond the woman to find manhood, and therefore seeks it in women, through sexual relationships. If his manhood has never been confirmed by identifying with the larger community of men through his father, he constantly seeks it with woman after woman, remaining forever "invalid" in his manhood.

In the face of such realizations, I am overwhelmed. How in the world—indeed, how in *our* world—can we Western men begin to rediscover this basic male need and meet it? If in fact the father is the key to a boy's crossing the threshold into manhood, what can those do who had no father, or perhaps whose father did not appropriately call him out from his mother?

Certainly, a seed of hope may be found in the fact that the origin of manhood cannot lie in the father alone, but only in some greater masculine Source from which the father himself must draw. The father becomes the sole focus of manhood only in a society such as our own, which lacks bonds of male "tribal" fellowship—not in societies such as the Nigerian village, where the boy's father appears before the mother's hut as part of a larger group of men, who themselves stand in the background, behind the mask/spirit.

A man must beware the temptation to skirt the pain of being cut off from his father; to do so is to let that pain bind and control him from the deeper unconscious to which he banishes it. He must start where he genuinely is, however painful, if he is to get where he needs to go.

At the same time, he must beware the companion temptation to judge and condemn his father for what the latter did not give him. The man who confesses his pain by bringing it to Jesus at the cross will begin to see that his father was not called out by his own father, so didn't know how to call out his son. One's father is not the oppressor, but a fellow victim, a brother in mutual need of manly affirmation. When a man allows Jesus to carry his tears for his own loss into tears for his father's loss when the latter was also a boy, he has begun to become a man of God at last.

Weeping for generations of loss, however, cannot by itself make you a man of God. Perhaps more significantly, neither can it save your own son from being so wounded. The communal dimension of manhood, largely discounted by our "modern" society, must be rediscovered and reaffirmed, as must the larger Source of manhood which beckons both fathers and sons. When enough men have begun to face and cry out their longing for manly affirmation, the time comes to act. The man who would move through and beyond his individual pain into an authentic, viable manhood today must acknowledge and connect with the deeper masculine Source which calls a man out—even from his father—to fulfill his unique, individual calling.

The Christian man may trust that such a transcendent manhood is rooted in the Father God who created all men and beckons him through Jesus.

Gordon Dalbey, *Healing the Masculine Soul*

MAY 15
Refrain from Murmuring

Yea, they despised the pleasant land,
they believed not his word:
but murmured in their tents,
and hearkened not unto the voice of the Lord.
Therefore he lifted up his hand against them,
to overthrow them in the wilderness:
to overthrow their seed also among the nations,
and to scatter them in the lands.

PSALMS 106: 24–27 (KJV)

Some time ago while flying home from the East Coast, I was talking with a Christian doctor about his family. All of his children were grown, happily committed to Christ, and serving in their local churches. The doctor was obviously grateful and relieved that his children had gone on in the faith. As a father of three, I was intensely interested in knowing what he felt was the secret to the spiritual success of his children. He explained, "My wife and I covenanted that our children would never hear us complain or criticize the church, church leaders or another brother or sister in Christ." In essence, he had made a commitment not to murmur.

Murmuring is complaining with a critical spirit that harbors a negative attitude toward a situation or the people involved. It runs the continuum from complaining about the slow driver in front of me to murmuring against the Lord for things He has permitted to come into my life. Murmuring carries the potential for great damage. It is a direct violation of God's will.

My doctor friend had wisely realized that complaining about God's work, God's leaders, and God's people was a direct reflection on the value of God, His plan, and His people. What child wants to commit his life to a system and a people who are the constant object of their parents' complaints?

A wise parent teaches the principles of love and prayerful intercession in regard to imperfections around us. Murmuring about the family of God only gives excuses to the future potential of rebellion in a child's heart. . . .

Murmuring is always a godless pastime. It overlooks our potential in God. It refuses to believe that God can conquer any circumstances if He so desires. And it refuses to recognize that God may use negative circumstances to work His best in our lives and demonstrate His glory.

Joseph Stowell, *Tongue in Check*

May 16
Freedom from Bondage

It is for freedom that Christ has set us free. Stand firm, then, and do not let yourselves be burdened again by a yoke of slavery.

Galatians 5:1

Several years ago, I was asked to speak at a secular university on the subject of Christian morality in the context of marriage and sex. The classroom was predominantly filled with young ladies. There was one young man, however, who pulled his chair off into a corner and made a show of being unconcerned about anything I had to say. Occasionally, he would interrupt with a little arrogant statement. One young lady in the back of the room asked me what Christians thought about masturbation. Before I could say anything he piped up, "Well I masturbate every day."

I paused for a second, then I said, "Well, congratulations, but can you stop?"

I didn't hear another remark from him again until the end of the class when everybody left. He came up and said, "So why would I want to stop?"

I said, "That's not what I asked; I asked if you *could* stop. What you think is freedom, really isn't freedom at all—it's bondage."

Anybody who acts as his own God is in bondage to his sinful nature. We were sold into the slave market of sin. Jesus purchased us from the kingdom of darkness and saved us from ourselves. We are not our own; we were bought at a very high price, the precious blood of Christ. We are no longer slaves to sin but servants to Christ.

Neil Anderson, *Living Free in Christ*

MAY 17
Proper Priorities

Praise be to the God and Father of our Lord Jesus Christ, who has blessed us in the heavenly realms with every spiritual blessing in Christ.

EPHESIANS 1:3

Since I retired from baseball, I've had many people tell me, "That's fine for you, but I can't quit my job. I have to support my family." Some men have even told me that my story made them feel guilty for not giving up their jobs for their families.

Because of that, I want to make it clear that I'm *not* saying all men ought to give up their careers or stay home with their families all the time. I realize few are in a position to do what I did. And even those who could shouldn't necessarily do it.

What I am saying is this: All of us need to do a serious evaluation of our outward priorities. I say *outward* because I think that for years, in my heart, I believed in the importance of putting God first, Christine second, our children third, and my work fourth. But that wasn't how I was living.

For me, getting my outward priorities into proper alignment required my retirement from baseball. But I've since talked to other men who rearranged their priorities by rescheduling work travel to spend an extra day a week at home. Another man told me he had begun taking work home so he could spend more time with and around his family. So there are many ways to address work versus family priorities.

Of course, work isn't the only thing that can foul up our priorities. I find I still have to be careful with my leisure-time interests. I'm a big hockey and football fan; I love going to concerts, and I enjoy playing golf. Now that I have more time to pursue those interests, I have to remember not to let them take precedence over my time with God, my wife, and my family.

All in all, adjusting to life after baseball has been much easier than I expected. I've always been the kind of person who set goals and then worked toward them. So I simply changed my goals.

All my life, I dreamed of being a major-league pitcher. For eight wonderful seasons, I fulfilled that dream.

Now I have a bigger dream. I want to be a major-league husband and a major-league dad.

Tim Burke, *Major League Dad*

MAY 18
Character

Do not be deceived: God cannot be mocked. A man reaps what he sows.

GALATIANS 6:7

Habits make character. If one forms good habits, he will have good character. If he forms bad habits, he will have bad character, The word "character" comes from a word which means "to cut" or "to engrave." Each time an act is performed a deeper groove is made until one has done a certain thing so often in a particular way that it is difficult to change. H. W. Shaw said, "It is easy to assume a habit; but when you try to cast it off, it will take skin and all." The more that one has the same emotion or action the more it deepens the track and the easier it is to be repeated. This is true when a child is taught to eat, to button his clothes, to tie his shoes, to dress himself, etc. At first he has to think to do it. He does the same thing until it is done without his will or thoughts. He can now tie his shoes and never think what he is doing. He can walk with a thousand other things on his mind. He can dress himself without thinking. He has developed a habit. The action has been indelibly impressed on the nervous system. The parent who wants his child to grow up to be a good, strong person will be disappointed if he does not form the right habits in him. These habits must be formed by repetition until he does things entirely automatically with no thought or will behind his actions. Hence, his tasks are not performed by present effort but by past preparation. . . .

The more we live by doing right automatically and the more our good habits save us the making of excessive choices, the better we will be and the more we will do. Precarious is the life of a person whose daily actions have not become habitual and who must exercise his will every time he does something. He will become tired in his work, more laborious in his deliberations, and less efficient in all he does. Those who have to use their wills for every momentary matter of business without the help of habit are not as efficient as those who have learned to become disciplined enough to make their actions mechanical. Someone has said that habit is a labor-saving device that causes the disciplined person to get along with less fuel. The wise personnel officer checks concerning his applicant's habits; those of honesty, gambling, etc. Proper habits can write a check that is always redeemable.

Jack Hyles, *How to Rear Children*

MAY 19
Pleasing Your Wife

Husbands, in the same way be considerate as you live with your wives, and treat them with respect as the weaker partner and as heirs with you of the gracious gift of life, so that nothing will hinder your prayers.

I PETER 3:7

Affection is so important for women that they become confused when their husbands don't respond in kind. For example, a wife may call her husband at work, just to talk. She would love to receive such a call and is sure he feels the same. She often feels disappointed when he cuts it short because, "I've got all this stuff to finish by five o'clock." It doesn't mean the husband doesn't love her; he simply has different priorities because of a different set of basic needs.

When I go on a trip, I often find little notes Joyce has packed among my clothes. She is telling me she loves me, of course, but the notes send another message as well. Joyce would like to get the same little notes from me, and I have tried to leave such notes behind—on her pillow, for example—when I go out of town.

My needs for protection, approval, and care are not the same as hers, nor are they met in similar ways. I've had to discover these differences and act accordingly. For example, when we walk through a shopping center, it is important to her that we hold hands, something that would not occur to me naturally or automatically. She has encouraged me to take her hand, and I'm glad to do so, because I know she enjoys that and it says something she wants to hear.

When I try to explain this kind of hand holding to some husbands in my counseling office, they may question my manhood a bit. Isn't my wife "leading me by the nose" so to speak? I reply that in my opinion nothing could be further from the truth. If holding Joyce's hand in a shopping center makes her feel loved and cherished, I would be fool to refuse to do it. I appreciate her coaching on how to show affection. I promised to care for her when I married her, and I meant every word of it. If she explains how I can best give her the care she wants, I'm willing to learn, because I want her happiness.

Willard Harley, *His Needs, Her Needs*

MAY 20
Our Work

The LORD will fulfill his purpose for me;
your love, O LORD, endures forever—
do not abandon the works of your hands.

PSALM 138:8

Our work is meant to be an expression of who we are as God's handiwork. Because of who God is and how He sees us, as evidenced in the gift of His Son, Jesus Christ, we must be worth something. We have value, worth, dignity, and adequacy because God has declared that we have them. Instead of our work giving us a sense of value, worth, dignity, and adequacy as Christians, it is the other way around.

The *way* we do our job is an expression of the high value God has ascribed to us.

The *proficiency* of the level of our work is an expression of the high value God has ascribed to us.

We bring *dignity* to our work because of God's giving us a sense of dignity. As believers, we have the opportunity to do a job out of the sense of *adequacy* we have because of God's declaration that we are adequate. We should not be using our work to make us feel adequate. If we search the Scriptures, we discover that we are special and worthwhile only because of God.

Over the centuries, we have used many means in our attempts to feel worthwhile, but they are all temporary. None are permanent, except for God's declaration. This is the initial step in preventing or lessening our sense of loss when our work is no longer available to us. It is the same step in preventing or lessening our sense of loss when our ability, looks, or position in life is no longer a part of our life.

What would happen to you and the quality of your work if your attitude was this: My work is an expression of me and the presence of God in my life! It would be the beginning of feeling good about yourself in spite of what is going on at your job.

Norman Wright, *Recovering from the Losses of Life*

May 21
Confessing Our Secrets

This will take place on the day when God will judge men's secrets through Jesus Christ, as my gospel declares.

ROMANS 2:16

Every man questions whether he has what it takes to survive the challenge of looking honestly at life. Men with secrets are convinced they don't.

In conversations with themselves—which they sometimes don't consciously hear—men with secrets wonder, "How could a man like me handle the real challenges of life? How could I enter the messiness of relationships and hang in there with the power to do good, when I know what I'm really like? My only hope is to stay so far away from what I can't handle that I am never exposed to the inadequate man I am. The best I can do is find something I can do well, and put all my energies there."

Men who keep secrets are terrified at the prospect of exposure. But something else terrifies them more. The lesser fear—exposure of something they know but no one else knows—sometimes protects them from having to face the greater fear. Like a man so preoccupied with his sprained ankle that he doesn't notice the pain in his chest, men may focus attention on what they are hiding to keep them from facing something far worse.

When a man shares his secrets, his first reaction is often relief. But soon he becomes aware of a deeper fear. Men without secrets see more clearly the terrifying nature of existence, its profound uncontrollability, and its power to destroy every dream. When we get beyond our tightly held secrets, they seem petty in light of what we then begin to face. We slowly (sometimes over years) become aware of a yawning black hole that threatens to swallow us into its depths. The everyday pressures of life—unpaid bills, rebellious kids, relational conflicts—feel like only the tip of an iceberg. Something more is lurking beneath, a sinister force that is arranging for our lives to crumble around us and leave us in misery, alone, with no hope of escape.

Keeping secrets is cowardly. It helps us stay away from the far more significant challenge, which is to stare into the darkness of a life that make no sense and, in that darkness, to move with joy.

Larry Crabb, *The Silence of Adam*

MAY 22
Casting Off Illusions

My son, pay attention to my wisdom,
listen well to my words of insight. . . .

PROVERBS 5:1

When I was in high school I asked my dad if I could smoke. He said no. I asked him if I could quit school and join the Navy early. He said no. I asked him if I could hitchhike to New Orleans. He said no. I asked him if I could have a motorcycle. He said no. I couldn't understand why he was so unreasonable and mean-spirited. Jeepers, I just wanted to be like other guys and enjoy life!

Well, today I have a different opinion about my dad's guidance and counsel. All my old friends who smoked now wish that they hadn't. My high school diploma allowed me access to an advanced electronics school in the Navy. And while a chaplain for the Los Angeles sheriff, I saw the bloodied and broken remains of many motorcyclists and witnessed one boy die before my eyes. Dad wasn't really so stupid after all. I'm glad I obeyed (most of the time).

I had to abandon many juvenile plans as I grew up. And today I find that there are still illusions to be cast off. My biggest fallacy is that I can run my own life.

By the way, I asked God if I could be in control. He said no. But he said I could see New Orleans someday.

Jerry S. and friends in recovery, *Meditations for the 12 Steps: A Spiritual Journey.*

MAY 23
Stages of Life

He will endure as long as the sun,
as long as the moon, through all generations.

PSALM 72:5

Between the wanderings of the wilderness of "childish things" and the settled place of manhood, all men should aspire to become planted in the promised land.

For men, the promised land is the place of steadfastness. This is the place where the wanderings cease and the building begins. It was there that Israel began to build houses and throw away tents, and it is there that unstable things in us become solidified. It is the place where the irresponsible become committed. While in the desert, the Israelites owned nothing, conquered nothing, and acquired nothing! But in the promised land, the men of Israel rose up to confront enemies, subdue entire territories, and attain property by conquest.

The promised land is the place where we keep our promises to ourselves, to our wives, and to our children. It is the place where our words can be trusted. It is the place where we cease to wander in our marital commitment—whether we wandered in the secrecy of our own mind, or wandered literally, creeping stealthily home in the late hours of the night. The promised land allows us to keep our promises, while God keeps His!

We need to celebrate male adulthood by learning what it means and what it takes to be real men. We need to "continue our education" through all the rites and experiences of courtship, marriage, child rearing, and even grandparenting!

Every major stage of our lives brings *change,* and most of the time, we're unprepared for it! Many of us in our forties have families, yet we have never celebrated our manhood! If we celebrate manhood with all our strength and heart, and honor God as men who appreciate their masculinity, we will discover that the women in our lives will celebrate too! God made us to be men. It is time to take the challenge and live up to the manly destiny God has given us!

T. D. Jakes, Loose That Man and Let Him Go!

May 24
Prayer with Thanksgiving

I want men everywhere to lift up holy hands in prayer, without anger or disputing.

I Timothy 2:8

They say there are no atheists in foxholes. There aren't too many atheists in classrooms, either. Most students who haven't studied will toss a prayer to heaven before they take a test, regardless of Supreme Court decisions about prayer in public schools. And there probably aren't many atheists standing in unemployment lines.

No matter what your religious background may be, you probably came face-to-face with your own limitations when you realized that your job was fading into history. Where do you turn when all your efforts fail? I faced this foxhole issue when I knew my days at my former job were numbered.

As circumstances were coming to a head, I asked my editor to meet me in the conference room. What began as an outburst of anger with my job and a desire to leave it turned into an hour-long argument. The more I pressed my points, the more desperate I became. What had started as a venting of frustrations ended as a lost battle. Frightened of what I had initiated, I drove home, sat on my bed, and broke down. I didn't know what would happen next, but I knew that my days at the newspaper were numbered.

I can't recall any other time in my life when I cried so hard. Lungs and stomach expelled anguish and anger as I wailed, "God, does anybody want me?" My tears soaked my pillow, my breathing grew less labored, and my sobs gave way to sleep.

What else besides prayer is there at a time like that? No one else is listening. No one else *can* listen. Prayer—communication with God—fills in the void of our sorrow. In the most painful moments of our lives, we realize that our relationship with our Creator is the best thing we have.

At times such as these, however, it's easy to forget what else we have. We are the same people we were before we lost our jobs. We have the same talents, skills, and desires. We have the same place to live. We have the same friends and family who care for us more than we know. This is more than mere happiness. And it isn't denying our pain, either.

When you're pressed by the squeeze plays of life, give in to the impulse to pray. And count your blessings. That form of thanksgiving will ease the darkness of the loss you feel, or at least shed a little light to put it in perspective.

Many, many people have found that when they pray and count their blessings, they also find help to order their lives and begin to build a new career.

Tom Morton, The Survivor's Guide to Unemployment

MAY 25
Opening Our Hearts

What, then, shall we say in response to this? If God is for us, who can be against us? He who did not spare his own Son, but gave him up for us all—how will he not also, along with him, graciously give us all things?

ROMANS 8:31–32

I talked to a man who was on the edge of experiencing [the] gift of a heart truly open to God. He had lost his sixteen-year-old son. "I'm really angry at God for doing this!" he said. "How could He take this boy from me? He was a fine boy, believed in God, and had a great future. Now he's gone."

The man had three problems: the loss of his beloved son and the grief that was causing, the anger he was feeling that was blocking him from receiving the only source of comfort to endure his pain, and he was belaboring false assumptions that this life is the best of all lives and that his son was being denied a long life here. The man had not allowed himself to consider the blessing of heaven or the peace his son knew with our Lord. He was thinking only of himself and his loss. His plans for his lad would not be accomplished. He had planned to have him take over his business. Most of all, the man was aching over the denial of his enjoyment of his son. Very human reactions. But beneath all the grief was a hardened, self-determining will that had been threatened. Though the man claimed to be a Christian, he had never yielded the core of his heart to the Lord.

The bright side of the story is that the Lord did not leave the man to muddle in his grief forever. I did all that I could to help him to talk and cry out his grief and to gently clarify his thinking about death and eternal life.

One day I felt led to say, "My friend, the Lord is going to give you a burning desire to open your heart to Him. He knows your grief. He gave His own Son to deal with the problem of death and to open heaven to us. I promise you that before long you will realize you can't make it without Him. That will open you to receive what He has been longing to give you. You are angry with God because you think He canceled your plans."

Some days later the man suddenly felt differently inside. He was gripped by an undeniable desire to surrender his grief, confess how tenaciously he had held his own life and those he loved in his control. The Lord broke open the citadel of his heart and flooded it with His peace.

Lloyd John Ogilvie, *If God Cares, Why Do I Still Have Problems?*

MAY 26

Wisdom in the Time of Need

If any of you lacks wisdom, he should ask God, who gives generously to all without finding fault, and it will be given to him.

JAMES 1:5

Once when I was operating deep inside a brain, an artery broke loose in an area that I couldn't see. This resulted in vigorous bleeding. Because we couldn't see where the blood was coming from, it looked as though we might lose the patient. Without consciously deciding to do so, I just started praying for God's help. I have learned to act on intuition in such emergencies.

Just then I did something that, in the telling, seems almost irrational. I place the bipolar forceps into the pool of blood where the bleeding might be coming from. It started sucking away the blood. I pleaded, "God, You've got to stop this bleeding. Please, God, I cannot control it."

Strange as it may seem, at that instant the bleeding stopped without my ever being able to locate its cause. Afterward, the patient awakened and recovered fully.

At another time we had a man from Bermuda who had trigeminal neuralgia (an extremely painful condition of the face caused by irritation of the fifth cranial nerve). Before we had methods to treat this condition, many patients committed suicide because of the constant pain.

I had to put the needle into an exceptionally small hole at the base of his skull and pass it up to the level of the ganglion. This process requires a skill in which I had developed a great deal of proficiency during my days as a medical student. On that particular day, however, no matter what I did, I could not get the needle into the hole. I had worked at this for nearly two hours before it occurred to me that perhaps I should just give up.

Just before quitting, I finally prayed, *Lord, I cannot get the needle in. There is no way I can do it. I am going to take this needle and push it in one more time. I want You to guide it into the hole, because I cannot seem to do it.*

I took the needle, pushed it, and it went right through the hole as if it had a mind of its own. A feeling of deep gratitude came over me.

I feel that it is a little risky to relate an incident like this because I can almost hear skeptics say, "Oh, come on, Ben, that is ridiculous. Why would you even say a thing like that?"

Yet, for me it is *not* absurd; it is what I expect. In talking with other Christian surgeons, I have learned that some of them understand because they have experienced similar feelings of God guiding their hands.

When we develop a relationship with God and believe that He is working through us, we still have moments of helplessness—when God has an opportunity to do something for us. This happens when we give our best—which, at the particular moment, does not seem good enough. Ready to give up, we say aloud or silently, "I cannot do anymore, Lord. I need *You*."

At such moments we provide God with the opportunity to respond. Truly, "Man's extremity is God's opportunity."

Ben Carson, *Think Big*

MAY 27
A Lasting Marriage
. . . a husband must not divorce his wife.

I CORINTHIANS 7:11B

Many look at holiness as a bunch of rules. Believing that holiness is out of reach, the very idea gets dismissed. But the true believer has got to take personal holiness seriously. God demanded it, and it is the seed of the reality of God inside us. We are called to walk in holiness. Righteousness is the outward working of holiness, and in that context we walk in purity.

Christian men, we are no greater than we are pure. The most significant description a man can have said about him is that he is a man of God. He is righteous and honest.

In no way do we live in a gray-colored world. Our yeas are to be yeas and our nays should be nays. When Jesus becomes our standard, we do not commit sins of the body because it is no longer in our nature. There is no sex outside of marriage because we are determined not to break the covenant once we are married. Why does God hate divorce? Because He has established marriage as a physical manifestation of an invisible reality. Marriage models our relationship to Christ. Jesus married the church and will never divorce it. When we defy God and divorce we are mismodeling the church's relationship to Christ.

We learn to keep our word to our own hurt, even if we are not getting along in our relationships. When we become willing to be changed by constructive observations, we develop an awareness that opposites attract and likes often repel. Our differences may be used to make us one. In reality our purity is proof of our differences, not our agreements. We keep our covenants because we are men of integrity, not because we have to or are forced to by law, but because we want to. Jesus warns us to guard our hearts, our integrity, because out of them are the issues of life.

Wellington Boone, *Breaking Through*

MAY 28
Owning Our Wounds

He will wipe every tear from their eyes. There will be no more death or mourning or crying pain, for the old order of things has passed away.

REVELATION 21:4

A long time ago Doris and I lost our only biological child. We suffered together. But each of us also suffered alone. I raged; she accepted, But, when mourning time was over, I went on as if I had left my grief behind me.

Recently I visited the small spot of ground at the end of a graveyard where we buried his small body so many years ago. I was flooded again by my old sorrow. My grief surprised me, embarrassed me. I thought it had died and left me. Where did it come from, this old sorrow?

It came from me; it came from the wound that had been a part of me all these years. The wound was inflicted a long time ago; the terrible pain of that is long gone. But not the wound. Wounds can be reopened. All it takes is a new reminder. And it is honest and therefore healthy to own the wound, to let it identify us, to tell us who we are; for it is part of us forever.

Then there is the other kind of suffering, the unfair and deep pain we feel when someone betrays us, lets us down, brutalizes or demeans us. A parent molests us. A spouse is unfaithful. A friend is disloyal. Most of us will feel unfair pain sometime, if we just live long enough. This pain too leaves wounds that become part of who we are.

Some people hang on to their pain out of a sense of fairness. The person who hurt them does not deserve to be forgiven. So they will not heal themselves of the pain they did not have coming in the first place. Strange fairness, this, to condemn ourselves to perpetual pain that we do not deserve. But my concern here is not with people who either cannot or will not forgive.

I am concerned with people who do forgive and who expect that forgiving the person who hurt them will automatically remove the wounds.

People who forgive often have unrealistic expectations about the relief they will feel. They expect that once they have forgiven the person who hurt them, they will never feel the pain again. But forgiving does not take away our wounds; once wounded by another's unfairness and betrayal, we are forever wounded persons.

When we forgive we free ourselves from bondage to bitter memories. We release ourselves from the acute, wrenching nausea of betrayal. We begin a process of healing. But we do not take away the wound. Not ever. Our pain has been grafted onto our very beings. We will carry a residue inside of us as long as we live. Any chance reminder can open the wound again. And the pain will come back for a little while.

It takes courage to own our wounds, but we gain something important if we do. I believe that I have been more aware of other people's wounds since I discovered that the wound of my own pain is still part of me. I believe that anyone who is able to own the wounds that remain after forgiving someone who bruised them is better equipped to overcome similar

pains in the future. And better able, too, to help other hurting people overcome theirs.

Lewis Smedes, *A Pretty Good Person*

MAY 29
Being a Barnabas

*Joseph, a Levite from Cyprus, whom the apostles called Barnabas (which
means Son of Encouragement), sold a field he owned and brought the money
and put it at the apostles' feet.*

ACTS 4:36–37

Do you remember a man named Mordecai Hamm? I must admit that I
didn't when I first heard the name. Mordecai Hamm was the man who led
Billy Graham to Christ. How about the Biblical character, "Joseph, a Levite
from Cypress"? Again, I needed to be reminded that Joseph is better known
as Barnabas. Barnabas means "Son of Encouragement," and this Christian
name more accurately represents the nature of his gifts and character.

Very little is mentioned of Barnabas in Scripture. First, when the early
church needed money, he "sold a field he owned and brought the money
and put it at the apostles' feet." (Acts 4:37). Then when the great Pharisee
Saul of Tarsus came to Christ, the apostles avoided him like the plague,
"but Barnabas took him" (Acts 9:27).

He persevered with Saul, patiently being the link between him and his
destiny in Christ. He took Saul with him wherever he went, making the appropriate introductions and putting him forward until his place as one of
the leaders of the church was finally recognized. Eventually, Barnabas himself was far overshadowed by Saul of Tarsus.

The New Testament records one other man whom Barnabas influenced
during his lifetime—a washout of another's ministry, his cousin, John
Mark (Acts 15:35–40). What kind of impact can a man like Barnabas have?
What kind of impact can you or I have? You may not have very visible gifts,
but if God has given you His Word, His Spirit, and a heart for people, you
will have a lasting impact. God uses men of integrity and faith more than
men of position and title or the other attributes so valued today.

Some of you may feel like a Saul, a future leader waiting to emerge.
Then, like Saul, you need to find a Barnabas, or he needs to find you. Still

others are convinced that they are more modestly gifted. That was Barnabas—an average guy with average gifts. However, he had a major advantage. He knew that God wanted to use men like him to influence other men. Though we're certain he saw potential in Saul and John Mark, who would have guessed how far Barnabas' influence would eventually reach?

Saul of Tarsus is better known as the great evangelist and apostle Paul. He wrote half of the New Testament. As for John Mark, he became a traveling companion of Peter and under the inspiration of the Holy Spirit, penned the gospel according to Mark. You may not be a Paul or even a John Mark, but you can be a Barnabas, a brother!

Geoff Gorsuch with Dan Schaffer, *Brothers! Calling Men into Vital Relationships*

MAY 30 MEMORIAL DAY
Faithfulness

. . . if we are faithless,
he will remain faithful,
for he cannot disown himself.

II TIMOTHY 2:13

God's message to us is "You can walk away from me, ignore me or misrepresent me—but I'm not going to break my promise to you. I'll keep loving you and giving you chances right down to the finish line. I'm not going to break my promise to you because you broke your promise to me. If in the end you don't choose to return to me, them we'll both live with the consequences of your choice. But don't expect me to come down to your level. I cannot be unfaithful. It's not my nature. I don't have a bailout plan if you break faith with me. I will continue on regardless."

This is amazing! Do you see it? God is faithful and will not break faith with us. He is light, as John said, and there is no darkness in Him (I John 1:5).

When He says, "I'll be faithful," He isn't keeping some secret clause buried in fine print in the contract. *It's all on the table.* In plain view. And John warns us that if we say we're like Him but keep a little unfaithfulness tucked away in the dark, we're only lying to ourselves—and to God. And we're misrepresenting ourselves to the world. We're not being "light" to them.

Do you see why God places such a high value on faithfulness to Him? He wants to know if we'll really be His hands and feet to the people around us who live in darkness. And if we're not faithful, then we should beg God to teach us faithfulness. Beg Him to burn faithfulness into our character. People need to see the faithfulness of God in our faithfulness—to Him and to them.

Faithfulness means consistency. God can be counted on—He's not our friend one day and our enemy the next. He's loving, kind, gracious and compassionate. He demonstrated these attributes in Genesis, and He continues to demonstrate them today. God hasn't changed with the times.

How about you? Are you consistent? Can people rely on you? Can you be counted on when things are going well and when they're not? Or do you hide your Christian behavior depending on who you're with? Does your faith go up and down with the balance in your bank account? How do you react to God when your kids are sick? Does your love for God change according to your circumstances?

God wants us to be consistent in our love for Him regardless of our circumstances.

Keith Green, A Cry in the Wilderness

MAY 31
First Love

Everyone who competes in the games goes into strict training. They do it to get a crown that will not last; but we do it to get a crown that will last forever. Therefore I do not run like a man running aimlessly; I do not fight like a man beating the air. No, I beat my body and make it my slave so that after I have preached to others, I myself will not be disqualified for the prize.

I CORINTHIANS 9:25–27

One night [my wife] Anne and I were lying in bed challenging one another on this very piece of Scripture. What does it mean to discipline our bodies? How do we bring them into subjection to do the things they ought to do (spending time alone with God and His Word, loving and helping those who are naturally abhorrent to us) and not the things we want to do?

At one point Anne turned to me and exclaimed, "You know what? I love

Jesus more than I love you. Yes, that's the way He intended it to be. That we would first love Him with all of our heart, and soul, and mind, and strength."

Wham! I felt like I'd been socked in the belly with a baseball bat. It may have been a revelation to Anne, but for me it was devastating to hear those words spoken out of my wife's mouth! From my wife, who loved me and had stood by me through thick and thin. The pain must have shown all over my face. Yet once I recovered and could see what Anne really meant, it proved to be an awakening of where we as a family were headed. We were moving into a love relationship with the Lord of our lives. After the initial shock, I could see that her words represented my heart's attitude as well.

We were becoming one just as the Bible said we were meant to be, fitting our strengths and weaknesses together.

We had grown to the point where we loved the Lord with everything that was in us. And nothing—not even each other—could take the place of the Lord being first in our lives. And because we loved Him so much, we loved each other all the more.

Talking later about the parallels between athletics and the spiritual life, Anne commented in her casual manner with laughter interspersed, "It's really special how the Lord was really preparing you for a life with Him all along, especially through your running."

"Nothing in life ever happens by accident," I said. "I'm sure the discipline of all those early morning runs makes it easier now to get up early to spend time with the Lord every day. And all the verses in the Bible equating the Christian life with a race—'Run the good race . . . press on toward the prize . . . run with patience the race that is set before us . . . all the runners run the race, but only one wins the prize.'"

The race—the spiritual adventure—we are now involved in involves our whole family and every facet of our relationship together. Everywhere our spiritual horizons are being expanded. We are allowing God to map our own destinies in Christ Jesus. We are in the hold of God's Spirit, moving with Him wherever He takes us.

Jim Ryun, *In Quest of Gold*

June

A New Commandment

A new commandment I give you: love one another. As I have loved you, so you must love one another.

JOHN 13:34

. . . Jesus' disciples were in the upper room arguing about which of them would be the greatest in the kingdom. They were on an ego trip: they were being selfish, self-centered, self-indulgent, and insensitive to Jesus and the pain and sin He was about to bear. In their self-indulgence they wouldn't wash each others' feet. Finally, Jesus knelt down and washed their filthy feet and when He finished He said, "A new commandment I give you, that you love one another, even as I have loved you." And how had he loved them? Not by feeling emotional! But He washed their feet anyway, because love does not do what it *feels*, it does what is *needed*. Where there is a need, love acts, sacrificially. And that is the husband's part in marriage.

Husbands, you will never really know how to love until you've sacrificed yourself, crucified yourself, and died to yourself. Paul says true love "does not seek its own" (I Cor. 13:5). As long as a man is looking for what can be personally gained from marriage he will never know what it is to love his wife as Christ loved the church, and he can never experience the richness of self-giving and its amazing dividends.

Ask yourself a question: when was the last time you made a sacrifice for your wife? When was the last time you wanted to do different things and you said, "Honey, I'm ready to do what you want to do." Sometimes we need to lay aside our carefully made plans and do what she thinks we ought to do. The issue is sacrificial love. And husbands must die to themselves to have that kind of love. Our world tells us just the opposite: "Be the macho man, the big shot. Don't let anyone step on your territory, fight back, grab all you can get because you deserve it." But the Bible simply says, "Set yourself aside." Somewhere along the line if you are to love that woman in your house like Christ loved the church, you will have to see the death of your own selfish desires.

John MacArthur, Jr., *The Family*

JUNE 2
His Word As a Lamp

Your word is a lamp to my feet
and a light for my path.

PSALM 119:105

If religious books are not widely circulated among the masses in this country, I do not know what is going to become of us as a nation. If truth be not diffused, error will be;

If God and His Word are not known and received, the devil and his works will gain the ascendancy; If the evangelical volume does not reach every hamlet, the pages of a corrupt and licentious literature will;

If the power of the Gospel is not felt throughout the length and breadth of the land, anarchy, and misrule, degradation and misery, corruption and darkness will reign without mitigation or end.

If we work on marble, it will perish; if on brass, time will efface it; if we rear up temples, they will crumble into dust; but if we work upon immortal minds and imbue them with principles, with the just fear of God and the love of our fellow men, we engrave on those tablets something that will brighten to all eternity . . .

This is the Book. I have read the Bible through many times, and now make it a practice to read it through once every year. It is a book of all others for lawyers, as well as divines; and I pity the man who cannot find in it a rich supply of thought and of rules for conduct. It fits man for life—it prepares him for death.

Daniel Webster

JUNE 3

His Magnificent Works

How many are your works, O LORD!
 In wisdom you made them all;
 the earth is full of your creatures.

PSALM 104:24

I have a confession to make. *Ranger Rick* is one of my favorite magazines. When it arrives in our house with the address, "Piper Boys," I am one of the first Piper boys to take it to the couch. The reason is simple: in spite of its utterly unwarranted and unnecessary evolutionary bias, it inspires more praise in me than most other journals. It is a monthly record of man's discovery of incredible phenomena in nature that up till recently have only been enjoyed by God for thousands of years.

For example, I read about the European water spider that lives at the bottom of a lake, but breathes air. It comes to the top of the water, does a somersault on the surface and catches a bubble of air. Then it holds the bubble over the breathing holes in the middle of its body while it swims to the bottom of the lake and spins a silk web among the seaweed. It goes up and brings down bubble after bubble until a little balloon of air is formed under its silk web where it can live and eat and mate. When I read that, there was a moment of worship on our living room couch. Doesn't that make you want to shout, "O Lord, how manifold are your works! In wisdom you have made them all; the earth is full of your creatures" (Psalm 104:24)?

I sit there with my mouth open and I think God smiles and says, "Yes, John, and I have been enjoying that little piece of art since before the days of Abraham. And if you only knew how many millions of other wonders there are beyond your sight that I behold with gladness every day!"

God rejoices in the works of creation because they reveal his incomparable wisdom. This is the point of Psalm 104:24.

> O Lord, how manifold are your works!
> *In wisdom* you have made them all;
> the earth is full of your creatures.

"*In wisdom* you have made them all!" In other words the Lord delights in the expressions of his wisdom. This universe is a masterpiece of wisdom and order. Or if you just take a part of it, like the human body—what an amazing work of knowledge and wisdom! Who can fathom the human brain and the mystery of how mind and body work together? Whether you look near or far, whether you look for bigness or smallness, the wonders of nature stagger the mind with the wisdom woven through it all.

John Piper, *The Pleasure of God*

JUNE 4
God's Presence

For in him we live and move and have our being.

ACTS 17:28A

As a very small boy exploring the almost virgin woods of the old Carver place I had the impression someone had just been there ahead of me. Things were so orderly, so clean, so harmoniously beautiful. A few years later in this same woods I was to understand the meaning of this boyish impression. Because I was practically overwhelmed with the sense of some Great Presence. Not only had someone been there. Someone was there . . .

Years later when I read in the Scriptures, "In Him we live and move and have our being," I knew what the writer meant. Never since have I been without this consciousness of the Creator speaking to me . . . The out of doors has been to me more and more a great cathedral in which God could be continuously spoken to and heard from . . .

My attitude toward life was also my attitude toward science. Jesus said one must be born again, must become as a little child. He must let no laziness, no fear, no stubbornness keep him from his duty.

If he were born again he would see life from such a plane he would have the energy not to be impeded in his duty by these various sidetrackers and inhibitions. My work, my life, must be in the spirit of a little child seeking only to know the truth and follow it.

My purpose alone must be God's purpose—to increase the welfare and happiness of His people. Nature will not permit a vacuum. It will be filled with something.

Human need is really a great spiritual vacuum which God seeks to fill . . .

With one hand in the hand of a fellow man in need and the other in the hand of Christ, He could get across the vacuum and I became an agent. Then the passage, "I can do all things through Christ which strengtheneth me," came to have real meaning.

As I worked on projects which fulfilled a real human need forces were working through me which amazed me. I would often go to sleep with an apparently insoluble problem. When I woke the answer was there.

Why, then, should we who believe in Christ be so surprised at what God can do with a willing man in a laboratory? Some things must be baffling to the critic who has never been born again.

By nature I am a conserver. I have found nature to be a conserver. Nothing is wasted or permanently lost in nature. Things change their form, but they do not cease to exist.

After I leave this world I do not believe I am through. God would be a bigger fool than even a man if he did not conserve what seems to be the most important thing he has yet done in the universe.

George Washington Carver

June 5
Understanding God's Call

For those God foreknew he also predestined to be conformed to the likeness of his Son, that he might be the likeness of his Son, that he might be the first-born among many brothers. And those he predestined, he also called; those he called, he also justified; those he justified, he also glorified.

ROMANS 8:29–30

When I was a freshman in college, I learned firsthand that God's plans and my expectations aren't always the same thing. As a high school senior, I had yielded my life to Christian ministry and chosen to attend a private denominational university to prepare for my life's vocation. I had also received a football scholarship. My prayer was constantly, "Lord, help me to be a good football player, and I will use that athlete's platform to speak for you."

I honestly thought God and I had a deal. He would help me be a successful athlete, and I in turn would help him reach football-smitten youngsters with the gospel.

I was on the starting team most of my freshman year and showed great promise. Then, in the last game of the season, I was blocked from behind and suffered a fractured hip. After lying immobile in the hospital for several weeks, I was told by my doctor that I would never play football again.

I was devastated! "I can't keep my promise to God. What good will I be to him now? No one will want to hear my story. What kind of hero is a crippled freshman?" I visualized kids staying away from my speaking engagements in large numbers, mumbling, "Dudley who?"

I thought God wanted a football hero to put in a good word for the gospel. But he just wanted to love *me*. I shall never forget that day alone in hospital room number 101 when I admitted, "Oh, God, I can't do anything you wanted me to do!" And I heard God reply, "I love you just like you are. I don't want a hero. I just want you." My human expectations were replaced by a broader and deeper understanding of God's call and promise to me. He can be trusted.

Dudley Hall, *Grace Works*

JUNE 6
Not Fearing Others

Ignoring what they said, Jesus told the synagogue ruler, "Don't be afraid; just believe."

MARK 5:36

Fear paralyzes all our powers. We fail because we fear. If you feel afraid, stop, and quietly in God's presence ask yourself why. Be honest in giving the reason. Do not let your feeling of fear dictate your action. When convinced something should be done, go ahead and do it despite the feeling of fear. God's power is at your disposal. Paul said, "I can do all things [all things God wants me to do] through Christ which strengtheneth me" (Philippians 4:13). He had learned to appropriate the strength and power God had put at his disposal.

When a decision is made, do not be anxious or doubtful as to the result. Trust absolutely: remember God asks faithfulness; the rest can be left in his hands.

Each person has his own fears. Common ones are fear of what others will think or say; fear of making restitution; fear of apologizing, due to the loss of face it brings; fear of being different from others; timidity, or distrust of oneself; fear of the future.

Fear comes by looking at oneself or others instead of looking at Jesus. Jesus said, "Be not afraid I [of what the crowd thinks or does], only believe" (Mark 5:36).

Are you afraid in any situation? Stop a moment, surrender the feeling to God, *make a decision which fully satisfies your conscience,* and act quietly but firmly on it. This act is faith, the faith that overcomes the world of fear. God in this way will teach you to overcome all kinds of fear. *He can do this only with your trustful cooperation.*

Eric Liddell, *Disciplines of the Christian Life*

JUNE 7
Seeing Jesus

They came to Philip, who was from Bethsaida in Galilee, with a request. "Sir," they said, "we would like to see Jesus."

JOHN 12:21

It has been truly said that Jesus could go into any Army mess, into any factory dining-hall, into any business or professional common-room, into any hotel or boarding-house, into any students' hostel or college, and His presence would not make men uncomfortable. His second visit would be eagerly looked for. Why? Rarely did condemnation pass those gentle lips (unless men were religious hypocrites or cruel to little children); but in His presence men felt their inner, better selves suddenly revived within them. Jesus lifted up men's hearts. He saw all their dormant possibilities. What is more, He made men see them, and, what is more still, He made men desire, with a deep and passionate longing, that those possibilities should actualize, and His dreams for them come true; He made men believe that they *could* come true. His utter sincerity made men see their own sincerity, and instinctively turn from it with loathing and contempt. He made men want to be like Him and when He talked with them, men felt that likeness to Him had suddenly become possible, and that life would never be true or beautiful till they set this goal definitely before them.

So there is in the world today that same insistent—though sometimes inarticulate—cry: "Sir, we would see Jesus." He must shine again in all His winsome loveliness, not remote, but near; the ever available. . . .

Jesus has only to be truly seen to be loved, and when we love we shall be prepared to follow.

Leslie Weatherhead, *The Transforming Friendship*

JUNE 8
An Unplugged Life
Do not put out the Spirit's fire . . .

I THESSALONIANS 5:19

Out in Colorado they tell of a little town nestled down at the foot of some hills—a sleepy-hollow village. You remember the rainfall is very slight out there, and they depend much on irrigation. But some enterprising citizens ran a pipe up the hills to a lake of clear, sweet water. As a result the town enjoyed a bountiful supply of water the year round without being dependent upon the doubtful rainfall. And the population increased and the place had quite a western boom. One morning the housewives turned the water spigots, but no water came. There was some sputtering. There is apt to be noise when there is nothing else. The men climbed the hill. There was the lake full as ever. They examined around the pipes as well as possible, but could find no break. Try as they might, they could find no cause for the stoppage. And as days grew into weeks, people commenced moving away again, the grass grew in the streets, and the prosperous town was going back to its old sleepy condition when one day one of the town officials received a note. It was poorly written, with bad spelling and grammar, but he never cared less about writing or grammar than just then. It said in effect, " Ef you'll jes pull the plug out of the pipe about eight inches from the top you'll get all the water you want." Up they started for the top of the hill, and examining the pipe, found the plug which some vicious tramp had inserted. Not a very big plug—just big enough to fill the pipe. It is surprising how large a reservoir of water can be held back by how small a plug. Out came the plug; down came the water freely; by and by back came prosperity again.

Why is there such a lack of power in our lives? The reservoir up yonder is full to overflowing, with clear, sweet, life-giving water. And here all around us the earth is so dry, so thirsty, cracked open—huge cracks like dumb mouths asking mutely for what we should give. And the connecting pipes between the reservoir above and the parched plain below are there. Why then do not the refreshing waters come rushing down? The answer is very plain. You know why. *There is a plug in the pipe.* Something in us clogging up the channel and nothing can get through. How shall we have power, abundant, life-giving, sweetening our own lives, and changing those we touch? The answer is easy for me to give—it will be much harder for us all to do—*pull out the plug.* Get out the thing that you know is hindering.

S. D. Gordon, Quiet Talks on Power

JUNE 9
An Opened Door

Here I am! I stand at the door and knock. If anyone hears my voice and opens the door, I will come in and eat with him and he with me.

REVELATION 3:20

O God full of compassion, I commend myself to your keeping, to Thee in whom I live. Be Thou the Goal of my pilgrimage, and my Rest along the way. Let my soul take refuge from the crowding turmoil of worldly thoughts beneath the shadow of Thy wings; let my heart, this sea of restless waves, find peace in Thee O God.

Thou generous Giver of all good gifts, give to him who is weary refreshing food; bring our distracted thoughts and powers into harmony again; and set the prisoner free.

See, how I stand at thy door and knock; be it open to me, that I may enter with a free step, and be quickened by Thee. For Thou art the Wellspring of Life, the Light of eternal Brightness, wherein righteous men live who love Thee.

Be it unto me according to Thy word. Amen.

St. Augustine, a selected prayer

JUNE 10

A Living Sacrifice

Don't you know that you yourselves are God's temple and that God's Spirit lives in you?

I CORINTHIANS 3:16

When I was a member of a church during my college days, I had an interesting conversation one Sunday morning with an elder of the church, who was a good friend. We were standing on the church steps, about to enter the building. The elder was finishing a last cigarette before church.

I asked, "Why don't we go in? We're late, you know."

He replied, "I'd like to finish this smoke first. You go in, and I'll be there in a minute or so."

I asked, "Why don't you take your cigarette with you and go in now?"

He gave me a strange look and demanded, "Take this cigarette in there? Don't you know that our church is the temple of God?"

I offered, "That isn't the way I understand it. As I see it, you have that thing sticking in the temple of God right now!"

That was the last time he smoked a cigarette.

Now, I don't think he'll get to wear a gold medal on his chest in heaven because he quit smoking, but it is certainly commendable that he dealt with an important principle—a Christian's body is God's dwelling place and ought to be kept holy for his purposes.

Romans 12:1 indicates that every believer should present his body to God as a living sacrifice. Why? For God's use in manifesting himself on earth. Therefore, a believer should not do anything with his body that will detract from being a holy temple of God.

Yes, this means that there are some things I don't do. Not because God will love me more because I don't do them (he couldn't love me any more than he loves me in Christ), but because I love him enough to try to keep his residence on earth clean . . .

Your body wasn't given to you by a wonderful Creator for you to use as a garbage can. It belongs to him for his tremendous, holy purposes. And since he lives in your body, you will want to be extremely careful about what enters your body through the eye gate and ear gate, about what your mouth says, about what your hands grabs and where your feet go.

You are a temple of God on earth.

Earl Radmacher, *You and Your Thoughts*

June 11
Good Planning

Suppose one of you wants to build a tower. Will he not first sit down and esti-mate the cost to see if he has enough money to complete it? For if he lays the foundation and is not able to finish it, everyone who sees it will ridicule him, saying "This fellow began to build and was not able to finish."

Luke 14:28–30

Every business has to have a five- or ten-year plan. Then it needs to have specific goals and strategies for reaching its projected target. While I see the importance of doing that in my own business, I am poor at it when it comes to my personal life. This usually reflects a lack of interest or direc-tion for personal development.

Start by writing down where you would like to be in five or ten years. Make sure your goals are all things that are in your control—*not* "I want to be married in five years," but "I want to learn how to love others and be committed in a relationship."

These goals can cover several areas: your personal finances, your family, your career, your spiritual life, and your friendships or relationships.

Then write specific plans or strategies for accomplishing those goals. What will it take for you to accomplish this? What will you need to do? You may need the help of others, such as friends or mentors. If your goal is something you know little about, you may want to find people who are al-ready there and pick their brains a bit to find out what you need to do.

Choose an anniversary date for a review of these goals and your overall direction. I recommend a time that will be hard for you to forget, such as your birthday or New Year's Day. Then review your goals and your progress. Don't be surprised if you have to redo all of your strategies from time to time. My own five-year plan seems to change every six months. This is not a sign of failure but a sign that one is growing and changing. Some of your plans may be consistent throughout your whole life, but other things will change as your learn, develop, try new things, and explore new ideas.

Thomas Whiteman, Becoming Your Own Best Friend

June 12

Sending the Offense Away

But the goat chosen by lot as the scapegoat shall be presented alive before the Lord to be used for making atonement by sending it into the desert as a scapegoat.

LEVITICUS 16:10

What is forgiveness? Perhaps it is easier to explain what it is not. Forgiveness is not pretending something wrong didn't happen to us. Nor is it going to the other extreme and taking vengeance into our own hands. Forgiveness is not a matter of "forgive and forget." . . . memories are indelibly etched in the biochemical pathways of our brains. Often we are conscious of them, although sometimes they are "stored" in our subconscious minds where they can be called into the conscious whenever we choose to summon them. At other times they are in our unconscious and are almost impossible to retrieve. Nonetheless, they have a drastic effect on our emotions and lives.

Forgiveness is becoming aware of our anger toward someone, then choosing not to hold the offense against the person. It is deciding not to call up the memory of the offense, not to dwell on it, not to look for opportunities to take revenge.

In effect, this principle is illustrated in an event which took place annually in the life of Israel in the Old Testament. It was a tradition in those days to offer a ceremonial sacrifice by investing a "scapegoat" with all the wrongs done by the Israelites and then leading the animal into the wilderness. The scapegoat was taken to such a remote location that it would be impossible for it ever to rejoin the Israelite camp. This explains why the biblical word for forgiveness, used in both the Old and New Testaments, translates as "sending the offense away." In the New Testament this same principle is dramatically illustrated when Christ assumes the burden of human sin and makes the ultimate sacrifice of dying for our sin on the cross. He assures our forgiveness by taking our offenses away.

Today, when we choose to forgive an individual, whether for an insignificant slight or for a major offense, we are "sending away" that offense.

Frank Minirth *et al.*, *Worry-Free Living*

June 13
Skillful Hands

And David shepherded them with integrity of heart;
with skillful hands he led them.

Psalm 78:72

I once knew a man who had come to this country after World War II as a displaced person. He had been a skilled cabinetmaker in his home country but after the war had to settle for a job as sexton in a church. Not long after I became a pastor in that same church. I also became a father. Toys began to accumulate around the house. Knowing of his dexterity with tools and lumber, I asked Gus if he would throw together a toy box for me when he had a few minutes. I wanted a storage bin for the toys; I knew Gus could do it in an hour or so. Weeks later he presented our family with a carefully designed and skillfully crafted toy box. My casual request had not been treated casually. All I had wanted was a box; what I got was a piece of furniture. I was pleased, but also embarrassed. I was embarrassed because what I thought would be done in an off hour had taken many hours of work. I expressed my embarrassment. I laced my gratitude with apologies. His wife reproached me: "But you must understand that Gus is a cabinetmaker. He could never, as you say, 'throw' a box together. His pride would not permit it." That toy box has been in our family for over twenty years now and rebukes me whenever I am tempted to do hasty or shoddy work of any kind.

Eugene Peterson, *Run with the Horses*

JUNE 14
A Childlike Trust

Look at the birds of the air; they do not sow or reap or store away in barns, and yet your heavenly Father feeds them. Are you not much more valuable than they? Who of you by worrying can add a single hour to his life?

MATTHEW 6:26, 27

The mistake many people make when they start trying to be holy is they multiply religious practices and burden themselves with a host of activities, attending endless religious services, thinking that the more good things they do, the more spiritual they become. Spirituality doesn't work that way. The spiritual life is something that grows slowly, imperceptibly, way beneath the surface of our lives. Pressuring ourselves to do all kinds of nice things for people and performing a multitude of good works does not make us holy. It can, if we are not careful, make us extremely nervous and pressure us into commitments that can overload our already overburdened lives.

Real spirituality begins by finding God, feebly, perhaps, in the beginning, but then more confidently as we travel along the way. At first, we may be driven to Him out of desperation. But that's all right. God uses all kinds of circumstances to lead us to Himself. Or we may just feel a need to draw closer to God. Whatever the reason, God is calling us to a deeper intimacy with Himself. Jesus teaches us the attitudes we should have when we establish contact with His Father. We must have a childlike trust. This isn't a command, but His attempt to teach us how to establish a healthy relationship with His Father whom He knows so well. "Why are you all so worried?" He said to the crowd one day. "Look at the birds of the air. They don't sow and they don't reap and they don't gather into barns. Your heavenly Father takes care of them. You are worth more than all the flocks of birds and all you do is worry, as if you never had a heavenly Father. Stop worrying. Your heavenly Father knows what you need, even before you ask Him."

Joseph Girzone, Never Alone

JUNE 15
Boundaries

One who is slack in his work
is brother to one who destroys.

PROVERBS 18:9

If you are in a situation in which you're doing lots of extra work because you "need the job" and because you are afraid of being let go, you have a problem. If you are working more overtime than you want to, you are in bondage to your job. You are a slave, not an employee under contract. Clear and responsible contracts tell all parties involved what is expected of them, and they can be enforced. Jobs should have clear descriptions of duties and qualifications.

As hard as it sounds, you need to take responsibility for yourself and take steps to change your situation. Here are some suggested steps you may wish to take:

1. *Set boundaries on your work.* Decide how much overtime you are willing to do. Some overtime during seasonal crunches may be expected of you.

2. *Review your job description,* if one exists.

3. *Make a list of the tasks you need to complete in the next month.* Make a copy of the list and assign your own priority to each item. Indicate on this copy any tasks that are not part of your job description.

4. *Make an appointment to see your boss to discuss your job overload.* Together you should review the list of tasks you need to complete in the next month. Have your boss prioritize the tasks. If your boss wants all the tasks done, and you cannot complete these tasks in the time you are willing to give, your boss may need to hire temporary help to complete those tasks. You may also wish to review your job description with your boss at this time if you think you are doing things that fall outside your domain.

If your boss still has unreasonable expectations of you, you may wish to take a co-worker or two along with you to a second meeting (according to the biblical model in Matthew 18), or you may wish to discuss your problem with the appropriate person in your personnel department. If even then he remains unreasonable about what he thinks you can accomplish, you may need to begin looking for other job opportunities within your company or outside.

You may need to go to night school and get some further training to open up other opportunities. You may need to chase down hundreds of employment ads and send out stacks of resumes. . . . You may wish to start your own business. You may wish to start an emergency fund to survive between quitting your present job and starting a new one.

Whatever you do, remember that your job overload is your responsibility and your problem. If your job is driving you crazy, you need to do something about it. Own the problem. Stop being a victim of an abusive situation and start setting some limits.

Henry Cloud and John Townsend, Boundaries

JUNE 16
Remembering Good Fathers

The father of a righteous man has great joy;
he who has a wise son delights in him.

PROVERBS 23:24

Today is Father's Day. A day of cologne. A day of hugs, new neckties, long-distance telephone calls, and Hallmark cards.

Today is my first Father's day without a father. For thirty-one years I had one. I had one of the best. But now he's gone, He's buried under an oak tree in a west Texas cemetery. Even though he's gone, his presence is very near—especially today.

It seems strange that he isn't here. I guess that's because he was never gone. He was always close by. Always available. Always present. His words were nothing novel. His achievements, though admirable, were nothing extraordinary.

But his presence was.

Like a warm fireplace in a large house, he was a source of comfort. Like a sturdy porch swing or a big-branched elm in the backyard, he could always be found . . . and leaned upon.

During the turbulent years of my adolescence, Dad was one part of my life that was predictable. Girlfriends came and girlfriends went, but Dad was there. Football season turned into baseball season and turned into football season again and Dad was always there. Summer vacation, Homecoming dates, algebra, first car, driveway basketball—they all had one thing in common: his presence.

And because he was there life went smoothly. The car always ran, the bills got paid, and the lawn stayed mowed. Because he was there the laughter was fresh and the future was secure. Because he was there my growing up was what God intended growing up to be; a storybook scamper through the magic and mystery of the world.

Because he was there we kids never worried about things like income tax, savings accounts, monthly bills or mortgages. Those were the things on Daddy's desk.

We have lots of family pictures without him. Not because he wasn't there, but because he was always behind the camera.

He made the decisions, broke up the fights, chuckled at Archie Bunker, read the paper every evening, and fixed breakfast on Sundays, He didn't do anything unusual. He only did what dads are supposed to do—be there. He taught me how to shave and how to pray. He helped me memorize verses for Sunday school and taught me that wrong should be punished and that rightness has its own reward. He modeled the importance of getting up early and of staying out of debt. His life expressed the elusive balance between ambition and self-acceptance.

He comes to mind often. When I smell "Old Spice" after-shave, I think of him. When I see a bass boat I see his face. And occasionally, not too often, but occasionally when I hear a good joke, (the kind Red Skelton would tell), I hear him chuckle. He had a copyright chuckle that always came with a wide grin and arched eyebrows.

Daddy never said a word to me about sex nor told his life story. But I knew that if I ever wanted to know, he would tell me. All I had to do was ask. And I knew if I ever needed him he'd be there.

Like a warm fireplace.

Maybe that's why this Father's Day is a bit chilly. The fire has gone out. The winds of age swallowed the last splendid flame, leaving only golden embers. But there is a strange thing about those embers. Stir them a bit and a flame will dance. It will dance only briefly, but it will dance. And it will knock just enough chill out of the air to remind me that he is still . . . in a special way, very present.

Max Lucado, God Came Near

JUNE 17

Fathers on Their Knees

Come, let us bow down in worship,
  let us kneel before the LORD our Maker . . .

PSALM 95:6

I want to ask you, Dad: When was the last time your children saw you on your knees with an open Bible, seeking direction from God? That's an unmistakable lesson to a child. To be a spiritual man you must take time to talk to Him and to listen to him through His Word. The regularity of this meeting, not its length, is the important thing. When you're running late, I suggest you pause long enough to get on your knees and tell the Lord, "I am committing this day to you. Late as I am, I am not leaving this house without getting on my knees before You." God will reward that commitment.

The homes of fathers who are doing this are richly blessed. God is bringing them toward maturity because they are taking spiritual steps each day. If you can pause for only a prayer of commitment and a memorized Bible verse, that will launch you into the day and a later opportunity for a longer period of meditation and reading.

Your attitude of mind covers your home. When your attention is focused on Bible truths, you are exercising the mind of Christ, His thinking. When I think as Christ thinks, I am loving my wife and children more faithfully; I am more sensitive to the needs of those around me. Apart from the principles of the Bible, you cannot be the man, the husband, and the father you may be.

Charles Stanley, A Man's Touch

JUNE 18
Good Stewardship

A generous man will prosper;
  he who refreshes others will himself be refreshed.

PROVERBS 11:25

The most contented and successful businessmen of my acquaintance are those who say sincerely: "God owns my business." Each of them acknowledges a responsibility to be as good an employee as possible for God, while relishing the freedom found in being able to say to God, "I don't know why you've chosen to allow such a circumstance to exist or what your thinking is in causing such an unexpected event at this time, but whatever you think, after all, this is your business!"

What these men and women have learned is an attitude of trust—the belief that God knows what's best for us, His children. Putting our entire lives into His hands (yes, even our bankbooks and our mortgage payments!) will not result in some kind of catastrophe as a sadistic puppet master "tests" our faithfulness.

I must quickly point out that there is no time when one has "arrived" at complete trust. In my work, I counsel young couples on how to stretch $1000 to cover a month's worth of food, housing, transportation and insurance. Do they need more or less trust than the middle-aged professional whose monthly income need is $6000 and for whom a three-month illness would mean the loss of both present and future income?

Have you thanked God for your home? When you go to the grocery store, are you consciously grateful that you can pay for your family's needs? Have you asked God to bless your automobile with safety of operation? Have you offered to use it as He directs? Do you feel that tithing is giving God something of yours—or do you see it as returning to Him a fraction of what is already His?

Alone, or as a couple, take out a sheet of paper and begin making a list. What are the possessions God has given you—your home, your car, your income? What things are you most frightened of losing—your job, your savings, your standard of living? What financial plans are of greatest concern to you—your children's education, owning your own business, retiring comfortably?

This project may get completed in an evening or it may be that you will start the list and add to it as God brings things to your mind over a period of several days. When it feels complete, when you are satisfied that it is exhaustive, take it and your paycheck and lay them both on the altar of God's ownership.

You might want to pray a prayer something like this:

Heavenly Father, as I hold my paycheck and a list of concerns in my hand, may I be reminded that it is a gift from you, as are all my physical possessions. Help me to consciously dedicate them all to your service. Help me to show myself to be a good "employee" of yours, putting the things you have blessed me with to good use and management. At the same time, help me to trust you completely and to relax in your ownership and planning. Amen.

Brock Thoene, *Protecting Your Income and Your Family's Future*

JUNE 19

Immortality

I am not saying this because I am in need, for I have learned to be content whatever the circumstances.

PHILIPPIANS 4:11

Courage is a virtue that the young cannot spare; to lose it is to grow old before one's time. It is better to make a thousand mistakes and suffer a thousand reverses than to run away from the battle. Resignation is the courage of old age. It will grow in its own season, and it is a good day when it comes to us. Then there are no more disappointments; for we have learned that it is even better to desire the things that we have than to have the things that we desire. And is not the best of all our hopes—the hope of immortality—always before us? How can we be dull or heavy while we have that new experience to look forward to? It will be the most joyful of all travels and adventures. It will bring us our best acquaintances and friendships. But there is only one way to get ready for immortality, and that is to love this life and live it as bravely and cheerfully and faithfully as we can.

Henry Drummond

June 20

Complete Acceptance

. . . to the praise of his glorious grace, which he has freely given us in the One he loves.

EPHESIANS 1:6

My desire for the approval of others has often been so great that I sometimes joke about having been born an "approval addict." Growing up, I had the feeling that I didn't fit in; that I was "different" from others; that there was, therefore, something inherently wrong with me. I felt inadequate and tried to win the approval of others, desperately hoping that this would compensate for the negative feelings I had about myself.

But ironically, the conditional approval of others was never enough to satisfy me. Instead, being praised only reminded me of the disapproval I might encounter if I failed to maintain what I had achieved. I was thus compelled to work even harder at being successful. I occasionally find myself falling into this pattern of behavior even now, despite my improved knowledge, experience, and relationship with God. . . .

I don't believe that any of us will gain complete freedom from this tendency until we see the Lord. Our God-given instinct to survive compels us to avoid pain. Knowing that rejection and disapproval bring pain, we will continue our attempts to win the esteem of others whenever possible. The good news is that because we are fully pleasing to God . . . we need not be devastated when others respond to us in a negative way.

As we grow in our relationship with God, the Holy Spirit will continue teaching us how to apply this liberating truth to different aspects of our lives at an increasingly deeper level. In fact, one evidence of His work within us is the ability to see new areas of our lives in which we are allowing the opinions of others to determine our self-worth. With spiritual maturity, we will more often be able to identify these areas and choose to find our significance in God's unconditional love for us and complete acceptance of us. However, profound changes in our value system take honesty, objectivity, and prolonged, persistent application of God's Word.

Robert McGee, *The Search for Significance*

JUNE 21
Variety

The body is a unit, though it is made up of many parts; and though all its parts are many they form one body. So it is with Christ.

I CORINTHIANS 12:12

It seems safe to assume that God enjoys variety . . . He didn't stop with a thousand insect species; he conjured up three hundred thousand species of beetles and weevils alone. In his famous speech in the Book of Job, God pointed with pride to such oddities of creation as the mountain goat, the wild ass, the ostrich, and the lightning bolt. He lavished color, design, and texture on the world, giving us Pygmies and Watusis, blond Scandinavians and swarthy Italians, big-boned Russians and petite Japanese.

People, created in His image, have continued the process of individualization, grouping themselves according to distinct cultures. Consider the continent of Asia for a crazy salad. In China women wear long pants and men wear gowns. In tropical Asia people drink hot tea and munch on blistering peppers to keep cool. Japanese fry ice cream. Indonesian men dance in public with other men to demonstrate that they are not homosexual. Westerners smile at the common Asian custom of marriages arranged by parents; Asians gasp at our entrusting such a decision to vague romantic love. Balinese men squat to urinate and women stand. Many Asians begin a meal with a sweet and finish it with a soup. And when the British introduced the violin to India a century ago, men started playing it while sitting on the floor, holding it between the shoulder and the sole of the foot. Why not?

Whenever I travel overseas, I am struck anew by the world's incredible diversity, and the churches overseas are now beginning to show that cultural self-expression. For too long they were bound up in Western ways (as the early church had been bound in Jewish ways) so that hymns, dress, architecture, and church names were the same around the world. Now indigenous churches are bursting out with their own spontaneous expressions of worship to God. I must guard against picturing the Body of Christ as composed only of American or British cells; it is far grander and more luxuriant than that. . . .

Blacks in Murphy, North Carolina, shout their praises to God. Believers in Austria intone them, accompanied by magnificent organs and illuminated by stained glass. Some Africans dance their praise to God, following the beat of a skilled drummer. Sedate Japanese Christians express their gratitude by creating objects of beauty. Indians point their hands upward, palms together, in the *namaste* greeting of respect, that has its origin in the Hindu concept "I worship the God I see in you," but gains new meaning as Christians use it to recognize the image of God in others.

The Body of Christ, like our own bodies, is composed of individual, unlike cells that are knit together to form one Body. He is the whole thing, and the joy of the Body increases as individual cells realize they can be diverse without becoming isolated outposts.

Dr. Paul Brand and Philip Yancey, *Fearfully and Wonderfully Made*

JUNE 22

Preparation

Remember your Creator
* in the days of your youth . . .*

ECCLESIASTES 12:1

We are on a journey. We can only make it once. We cannot retrace our steps to make a single correction. How important that we be careful. God's Word is the only authoritative chart. It says, "Remember now thy Creator in the days of thy youth." "Seek ye first the Kingdom of God and His righteousness, and all these things shall be added unto you." All intervening history and the experience of all ages corroborates the truth and wisdom of these requirements. Some one says, "Why can we not have a good time, sow our wild oats, and then repent and be saved?" I answer: Why don't men do it? Experience has proved that the chances are very greatly against such a course. In all vocations in life, men must make careful preparation in order to succeed. The future physician, lawyer, or statesman must prepare now for his career. He must apply himself now to study and preparation. Then comes the possibility of the practice. So if God and heaven and eternal life be absolute verities and if it be true that heaven is as certainly prepared for those who prepare for it, as the opportunity to practice medicine or surgery, to say nothing of a successful practice thereof, depends on thorough preparation, how important that we prepare for heaven by the study and practice of the principles laid down in the only Text-Book ever given to point out the way to accomplish that preparation. What would you think of the lawyer who would say: "Yes, I intend to practice law, but I do not care anything about the law books. I do not intend to put into practice any of the principles taught in the law schools." Or what of the physician who would say: "I do not care anything about the knowledge of medicine as taught in the text-books. I do not care what others have said about diseases and their remedies. Yes, I am going to practice medicine, but I am going contrary to all teaching and all past experience."

Then what shall we think of the young man who says: "Yes, I want to be a man among men, but I will not be governed by the precepts of the Bible, nor the experiences of other men in the past."

James W. Anderson, *Thoughts That Breathe*

JUNE 23
A Man's Integrity

Therefore, holy brothers, who share in the heavenly calling, fix your thoughts on Jesus, the apostle and high priest whom we confess.

HEBREWS 3:1

Integrity is an inner quality that affects our outer deeds. It brings together all that a man is, from the inside out. In the compartmentalized, fragmented, and superficial culture, where men have learned to hide their feelings, carry incredible burdens, and stand alone in the face of a hostile world, integrity has taken a back seat. In nearly every business in this land, including the institutionalized church, power is often more highly prized than integrity. On the outside we are building our walls, boundaries, and kingdoms, but on the inside we are running as fast as we can just to keep up.

Our sons, however, deserve better than to be handed a legacy of deceit, fear, compromise, and isolation. They must be taught that weakness is not failure and that even failure is a gift in the journey of life. To need relationships, to cry out for help, to weep at pain and sorrow, to share honestly with others the condition of a wounded heart is not to be any less of a man. These are the marks of a man of integrity, a man who recognizes that failure and loneliness and need and fear are the building blocks of faith.

A man of integrity is man enough to admit that he doesn't have all the answers. A man of integrity makes a promise intending to keep his word, even if it costs him dearly. A man of integrity admits failure and asks forgiveness when even his best intentions cannot or are not fulfilled; he picks himself up in the light of grace and forges ahead, learning from his defeats. A man of integrity is committed to the law of loving his neighbor as himself, whoever that neighbor happens to be. Most of all, a man of integrity loves Jesus Christ with passion, trusts Jesus Christ with fervor, and follows Jesus Christ with focused dedication.

Call your son to integrity. Invite him into the turbulent waters of faith as he grows up. Allow him to see you struggle with compromise and failure and arrogance and fear. Grant him permission to care for you when you are in need, without burdening him beyond what he can bear. Give him the gift of a father who is authentic, a dad who is more concerned with truth that personal acclaim. Pass on to your son the torch of faith in Jesus Christ, the "high priest whom we confess" (Hebrews 3:1).

Steve Lee and Chap Clark, Boys to Men

June 24

An Object of a Man's Affections

The LORD God said, "It is not good for the man to be alone. I will make a helper suitable for him."

Genesis 2:18

As men we have an inbred desire to find an object for our affection. There is a sense in which this desire is so instinctive, it is an evidence of being created in God's image. Just as God desires intimacy with us, so we desire intimacy with each other. Even ancient Hebrew literature records, "And God saw it was not good for man to be alone" (Genesis 2:18). Because this desire for lifetime companionship is such a part of who we are, the level to which we successfully fulfill the desire is the extent to which we will be fulfilled.

A friend told me last week, "Fred, I feel like I should know all the answers. I've read the best marriage books, I've been to marriage enrichment seminars, I've taught the young married couples' Sunday school class—I've even counseled other couples having marriage problems. But meanwhile I lost it. I feel nothing for my wife. Last night she told me our marriage is dead. When she told me those words I felt nothing. Even though she never said them before, they sounded like old news. I don't know what happened, but for some reason all the answers I have heard over the years are doing me no good."

Sometimes we don't need answers—we need arms. We need passion and compassion that reaches out and draws our wives back to our side where they belong. Perhaps it's more than coincidence that the Bible indicates when God made a wife for Adam, He took her from the man's side. Ever since then, it has been man's joy and responsibility to draw his wife back to that original spot.

We call this inner desire in a man to find a single object of his affection *the desire to squeeze.* Don't misunderstand. This desire to squeeze is not simply physical or sexual. Our masculinity is not determined according to the size of our biceps. Instead, our masculinity is determined in part by how effectively we can embrace our wife and draw her close to our side. A squeeze that pleases only ourselves is no squeeze at all. It needs to transmit a level of pleasure to our wife.

To set the record straight, the squeezes I mean are not all physical.

- Catching each other's eye across a crowded room.
- A phone call in the middle of the day.
- A love note.
- Flowers, even when they are picked by the side of the road.
- A walk around the block.
- A back rub.
- Fulfilling a domestic duty—like washing her whitewalls.
- An "I-forgive-you,"
- A "can-we-pray-together?"
- An "it's okay—we-can-wait-till-tomorrow-night."
- A heart question.
- A "will-you-forgive-me!"
- An "I love you"—with no strings attached.

In order for a gesture to qualify as a legitimate squeeze, it must connect on both sides: It needs to mean love on the part of the husband, and it must be received as love on the part of the wife. Discovering which expressions connect is what I mean by becoming reattached.

This is the kind of love that healthy marriages are made of. It is healthy for the wives. They will thrive on it. But it is also healthy for us as men.

Fred Hartley, *Men and Marriage*

June 25
The Journey of Faith

The Lord had said to Abram, "Leave your country, your people, and your father's household and go to the land I will show you."

Genesis 12:1

It seems to me that the journey of faith is not such an easy-to-follow map. It is a one-step-at-a-time kind of experience. When God called Abraham to leave his hometown and follow him, Abraham was given no map, no set of directions. He didn't even know his destination. God just said, "Get up and go to a land that I will show you."

Abraham was expected to go where God led him, a step at a time, a day at a time. There were no guarantees that the journey would be easy. He had a lot of heartache along the way, his share of danger, and the painful introspection of living with postponed hopes.

Yet he is remembered as a man of faith.

God doesn't promise us a life full of mountaintop experiences. There will be valleys to go through, too. Dark valleys. Disorienting valleys. Valleys of depression and despair. What he promises is not a road map that will give us a detour around those valleys, but that he will walk through those valleys with us.

When we emerge from those experiences, we look back and realize that that is where the growth is. It isn't on the mountaintops, above the timberline; it's in the valleys.

Dave Dravecky, *When You Can't Come Back*

JUNE 26
A Wife's Embrace

. . . may her breasts satisfy you always,
may you ever be captivated by her love.

We have found in counseling that too few husbands know the virtue of nudity with their wives. Our spirits pour forth to one another much like electricity. We need the current of each other. Clothes tend to insulate. A husband needs the power of his wife's body against his, quite apart from sexual union.

All too few husbands and wives understand that verse, "Let her breasts satisfy thee at all times." During the day husbands need to hug their wives long enough to let that current which flows from her pierce the heart to refresh and strengthen. Woman was taken from the rib of man. Man protects woman by his strength and logic, but woman protects the heart area of man. Her breasts satisfy him when held against his chest. Her energy fills and warms all his thinking with wisdom and gentleness. In sexual embrace, husbands most often fail to touch, hold, and kiss the breasts long enough. Men need to feed, sensitively and quietly, a long time upon their wives' breasts. The command is to "*let* her breasts satisfy thee at *all* times." It is fulfilling and satisfying to both partners. A man who is fully satisfied in his wife's embrace, who truly feeds upon her love, is not easily tempted to another. Who would take a bologna sandwich to a banquet? Only his own wife is a fully satisfying banquet to his heart and soul and spirit and body. Let husbands pray that God will reveal to them the true gift and power of their wives' love for them. It is not that we are too sexual, but not sexual enough, because we do not discover how to meet and nourish, cherish, embrace, and feed upon one another's love as we ought.

John Sandford, *Restoring the Christian Family*

JUNE 27
Change Points

Why, you do not even know what will happen tomorrow. What is your life? You are a mist that appears for a little while and then vanishes.

JAMES 4:14

Because men are by nature more didactic than women, our search for meaning in the things that happen to us is often short-circuited. This also occurs because men are typically less process-oriented; we want to "fix" things that go wrong rather than explore the meanings behind them. In this way a man might never come to see that losing a job, a career, or a lifestyle could mean there is a better one for him in the next chapter of life.

Instead of rushing to "fix" changes that occur unexpectedly, take a time-out for a closer look and ask yourself these three questions, which always need to be asked at any change point:

- What does this change mean?
- What does this change mean to me?
- What does this change mean to those around me?

Answering these questions helps you search for the meaning in the event, itself, rather than the meaning of the event for those involved. For example:

- What does this change mean? *It may mean God is interrupting my life and plans.*
- What does this change mean to me? *It may mean that unused gifts, talents, and abilities in my life may be challenged for the first time.*
- What does this change mean to those around me? *Their lives may be forever different because of the changes I make.*

Abraham Lincoln is a vivid example of someone who found meaning in the events that happened to him. He lost some elections during his political career, hut those losses became stepping-stones to his ultimate victory when he became president of the United States. In an 1858 election, Lincoln ran as the underdog in a race against Stephen A. Douglas for a U.S. Senate seat—and Lincoln lost. But he found meaning in the campaign, itself, not just its outcome, and he used that insight to further his political aspirations.

Douglas, the incumbent, was well known, and Lincoln realized that merely by being on the same debate platform with Douglas he would share in the spotlight that perpetuated the renowned senator's fame. It was during this unsuccessful campaign and its seven debates that Lincoln began to make a name for himself as an inspiring public speaker. This led to his addressing a political rally in New York in February 1860. By May of that year, he was popular enough to be nominated as a candidate for the presidency.

Jim Smoke, *Facing Fifty*

JUNE 28
Provisionary

He who finds a wife finds what is good
and receives favor from the LORD.

PROVERBS 18:22

Men, if your family is lost in the woods, maybe it's time for you to climb a tree. Maybe it's time for you to get your head above the limbs and leaves, take a deep breath of fresh air, and scan the purple hills in the distance. The provisionary must know the difference between the forest and the trees. He needs to be able to scale the heights from time to time, and, with God's help, see the horizon.

It's not that men are genetically far-sighted while women are near-sighted. It has more to do with the God-given tendency of a man to look up and out and discern objects in the hazy distance and the tendency of a woman to read the fine print of relationships. A woman is simply a better reader. She has better focus on people and situations near at hand. She can read right away what's happening in the spirit, in a tone of voice, in a fleeting facial expression. That's why she so often tugs at the man. He gets so far "out there" in his provision role that he fails to see things under his very nose! Women place more emphasis on details, and on security.

I can remember when my wife didn't want to move into the new house we'd planned for months and months to purchase. When it came right down to signing the papers, she pulled up short. She didn't want to spend

the money it would take to make that little leap forward. She was more security conscious, considering our monthly budget, and I kept thinking of
long-term implications: *Where do we want our kids to grow up?*

Provisionaries need to use their God-given capacity for distance vision
to encourage and give hope and security to their families. When they cannot or will not, the people under their roofs suffer loss.

Stu Weber, *Tender Warrior*

June 29
Freedom from Legalism

*Now when a man works, his wages are not credited to him as a gift, but as an
obligation. However, to the man who does not work but trusts God who justifies the wicked, his faith is credited as righteousness.*

ROMANS 4:4–5

Although the workaholic may appear very confident on the surface,
deep within he hides tremendous feelings of insecurity and has a poor self-
image. To the public, he seems to be one of society's dedicated servants, but
his work and accomplishments, for the most part, are an unconscious
compensation for his insecurity, a means of fulfilling both his strong need
for society's approval and his driving urge to be perfect . . .

Because his parents were overly critical of him as a child, the workaholic
also develops an overly critical spirit. He is critical of himself because he is
not perfect. He is critical of others whenever they disagree with him or fail
to measure up to his impossible standards.

Not only does the workaholic feel insecure with himself, but also feels
insecure in his relationships with others, including God. . . . The workaholic whose parents gave love on a conditional basis views God the same
way. Because his parents were critical and unforgiving, the perfectionist
sees God as critical and unforgiving.

If the workaholic is a Christian, he is prone to put himself under a rigid
spiritual discipline. He gravitates toward a system of rules not only because
this makes him feel secure, but also because he believes that only as he conforms to a system of do's and don'ts will he be accepted by God. In essence,
the perfectionist somehow feels he must earn his salvation. Throughout his
Christian life, he is guilt-ridden by past and present sins; he is unable to

fully experience God's forgiveness. It is at this point that many obsessive-compulsives are drawn under the umbrella of legalism. Religious legalism makes the perfectionist feel that in some ways he is earning his salvation by making atonement for his daily sins through outward obedience to a given code of laws. He becomes proud of his ability to keep the rules and begins to measure his spirituality solely on the basis of his external obedience.

To make matters worse, the Christian workaholic will usually try to force everyone else to conform to his rigid pattern of spirituality. Soon other people who have similar personalities will be led down this road to bondage, hoping to feel accepted in the church and by God. By being good and performing well, they hope to ease the lingering accusations of a guilty conscience. And the cycle goes on and on . . .

The Christian perfectionist does not realize that his compulsions are leading him down the road to bondage. He is becoming a slave to the law and the flesh, from both of which he has already been delivered. It has been said that legalism is a fleshly attitude which conforms to a code for the purpose of exalting self. Because legalism finds its roots in the flesh, it can lead only to frustration and guilt. Legalism is directly opposed to the gospel of God's grace. For while legalism is based on the works of the flesh, grace is based on the work of the Holy Spirit. Legalism exalts self while grace exalts God. Legalism leads to slavery, but grace leads to freedom.

Frank Minirth *et al.*, *The Workaholic and His Family*

JUNE 30
Inner Strength

Instead, whoever wants to become great among you must be your servant . . .

MATTHEW 20:26B

Strong men—weak men. We males are born with the inner ingredients to be either or both. The choice is ours. Deep down, of course, we want to be strong. But what makes the strong men of today? Who are they?

Money gives a man the power to control others, but in itself money does not make a man strong.

Athletic skill wins the adulation of others, but so often today these "heroes" have feet of clay.

Political leaders learn the art of compromise, a trait that too often weakens them.

Do we receive some guidelines as we look at the greatest Man who ever lived, the Man who, the ages have confirmed, was God Himself?

Above all, He came to be the servant of all.

The strong man, Christ teaches us, will take unpopular positions on issues he believes in, then he acts boldly, knowing that mighty forces will come to his support. He readily admits his mistakes, is quick to praise an opponent, holds back any judgment. A strong man has a rock-like patience; he is not deterred by criticism, but examines it prayerfully to see if he can learn from it.

The strong man will be celibate when this is called for; as a son he honors his parents; he is a faithful husband, a father who would not only lay down his life for his wife and children, but also give them the time they need; the strong man is a caring brother; he seeks the Lord's guidance in his work; he leads others by serving them; when he goes to church, he seeks ways to minister to others. He has a tender heart for the weak.

The strong man knows his Creator, joyfully accepts the way he was made, delights in the special skills he has been given and learns to use them for the good of mankind.

Most important, we men who seek to be strong know it will never happen through our own power—only through His.

Leonard LeSourd, Strong Men, Weak Men

July

JULY 1
A Satisfying Job

Delight yourself in the LORD
and he will give you the desires of your heart.

PSALM 37:4

Many people would equate working for a living with "making money." The more money we have, the more flexibility we have to make choices about how we will live, where we will live, what we will buy. The turn-of-the-century phrase "to make your fortune" embodies the idea that one should have a fortune (a sum of money much greater than what most others have). Money supposedly gives us more freedom to make choices. Here again we let the world define freedom for us.

I hope *you* work because it is fun, not Disneyland kind of fun, but the kind we experience when we are with a group of friends and enjoying ourselves and someone says, "Hey, this is fun!" Or the kind of fun we are talking about when we do well at some sport and tell our coach, "That was fun!"

Life is not the proverbial bowl of cherries. It's tough. Success is not a feeling that comes from winning a one-sided game of golf with a novice or beating your ten-year-old at chess. There are mountains to climb, valleys to cross. There are times when all you worked for goes down the tubes. But if in balance you don't enjoy your job, quit it! If you are struggling to make ends meet as you read this page, that may seem like hollow counsel. I can only respond that if you are a Christian living in America, there are almost limitless opportunities open to you. As you set your face to lead a life that is pleasing to God I believe you will discover a "fun" job waiting for you.

Edward Dayton, Succeeding in Business

JULY 2
Helping Around the House

So the Twelve gathered all the disciples together and said, "It would not be right for us to neglect the ministry of the word of God in order to wait on tables. Brothers, choose seven men from among you who are known to be full of the Spirit and wisdom. We will turn this responsibility over to them. . . ."

ACTS 6:2–3

My dad is not a talkative person, but he can be emotional and sensitive. Housework was never beneath him and neither was taking care of babies, which my older brothers and I saw when our ten-years-later tagalong appeared. Here was dad, a police executive and ex-Marine, doing whatever had to be done to keep the house running while Mom recuperated.

Dad cooked meals, scrubbed floors, did laundry, washed dishes, changed the baby, and taught his ten-, twelve, and thirteen-year-olds to do the same. I get a kick out of hearing about husbands who have never changed a dirty diaper or washed a load of clothes. It may be nothing to brag about, but I'll bet my brothers have done as much of that as I have.

You'll do it too, if you plan to be fair and sensitive husbands. The day is long past where you can expect your wife to do typical "woman's work" alone. . . .

I have had to do this work at times, and I'll take managing, writing, editing, even manual laboring any day. The around-the-clock responsibility is too stressful and must, to many women, feel like jail. . . .

Develop sensitivity. Offer to help. Find out what she likes to do least, and do it for her once in a while.

Jerry Jenkins, Twelve Things I Want My Kids to Remember Forever

JULY 3
Passionate Christianity

. . . because you are lukewarm—neither hot nor cold—I am about to spit you out of my mouth.

REVELATION 3:15–16

Nothing in all creation is more significant to God than the soul of a human being. It is the seat of affections where love and true worship flow.

Who and what will possess people's affections are of grave concern to the Father. We were made in His own image and likeness, fashioned and uniquely designed for His holy purposes. God would not send His beloved Son to die for anything in all creation except priceless, eternal human souls.

God designed the human soul to be passionate, abandoned and committed. That is the way the soul functions best. It sinks into restlessness, boredom, passivity and frustration if it has nothing worthy of giving itself to or sacrificing itself for. In other words, if we have nothing to die for, then we really have nothing to live for. God intended our souls to be captured, consumed and enthralled with Jesus. Our highest development and greatest fulfillment lie in worshipping Him and serving Him with an abandonment that will sacrifice everything.

As an inheritance, God the Father has promised the Son a church filled with believers whose spirits are ablaze with affections and adoration for Jesus. The Father will never insult or sadden His beloved Son by presenting Him a church (the bride of Christ) that is bored, passive and compromising.

Passionless Christianity, so common today, is no threat to the devil. Focused on concepts and activities to the neglect of heartfelt affection and obedience to God, it brings no pleasure to God's heart. It doesn't even bring pleasure to the believer. But true Christianity sparks a flame in the human spirit. It ignites the heart with holy fervency for Jesus.

Mike Bickle, *Passion for Jesus*

JULY 4 INDEPENDENCE DAY

Patriotism

Blessed is the nation whose God is the LORD. . . .

PSALMS 33:12A

Patriotism is a positive attitude for believers. The Pledge of Allegiance reads:

I pledge allegiance to the flag of the United States of America and to the Republic for which it stands, one nation under God, indivisible, with liberty and justice for all.

Patriotism to our nation is a secondary allegiance under the general umbrella of covenant loyalty to God. We are submitted to God's authority, and are therefore submitted to every authority that He allows on earth (Romans 13:1–7).

In the allegiance to the country in which we dwell, we have a covenantal obligation to seek its welfare. In Jeremiah 29, the prophet writes to the Israelites who have been taken captive and are living in Babylon. They thought that perhaps they should rebel against the king of Babylon and try to return to Israel immediately. Jeremiah tells them that for the time being they should live in prosperity and seek the good of that foreign nation. Although Babylon was not their primary allegiance, they were to show loyalty, cooperation and a certain degree of patriotism. They realized that Babylon was not the kingdom of God; yet because they were a covenant people, they acted in integrity and showed loyalty to the country in which they dwelled.

Build houses and dwell in them. Plant gardens and eat their fruit . . . Seek the peace of the city where I have caused you to be carried away and pray to the Lord for it; for in its peace you will have peace (Jeremiah 29:5–7).

In the long run, the Israelites would be regathered out of that pagan nation. In the meantime, they had to cooperate with the authorities in their historical setting and physical location.

When we pledge allegiance to the flag of the United States, we are not doing it in a blind loyalty which says, "My country—right or wrong." We recognize the flag as a symbol of the nation in which we are living temporarily. As we show commitment and submission to every human organization, we also demonstrate our integrity by showing patriotism to our country.

Keith Intrater, *Covenant Relationships*

July 5

Nonnegotiables

There is a time for everything,
and a season for every activity under heaven . . .
ECCLESIASTES 3:1

When our son, Mark, was in high school, he was a successful athlete; our teenage daughter, Kristen, was an actress and musician. Both were in games and performances. It would have been easy to have missed those events had I not penciled the dates into the calendar weeks and weeks in advance. My secretary always kept the game schedules in the office calendar, for example, and knew full well not to expect me to commit to anything that would violate those times.

When someone would ask me to meet with him on the afternoon of a game, I was liable to take out my calendar and stroke my chin thoughtfully saying, "I'm sorry, I'm unable to do it that day; I already have a commitment. How about this as an alternative?" I rarely had a problem. The key was in planning and budgeting, weeks in advance.

What are your nonnegotiables? I discover that most of us who complain that we are disorganized simply do not know the answer. As a result, the important functions that will make the supreme difference in our effectiveness miss getting into the calendar until it is too late. The consequence? Disorganization and frustration; the non-essentials crowd into the datebook before the necessities do. And that is painful over the long run.

The other day a man caught up with me and asked if we could have an early morning breakfast on a certain day. "How early?" I asked.

"You're an early riser," he said. "Why not six?"

I looked at my calendar and said, "I'm sorry, I've already got a commitment for that hour; how about seven?" He agreed on seven rather quickly but looked quite surprised that my calendar might reflect plans for that early in the morning.

I did have a commitment for six that morning. In fact it started earlier than that. It was a commitment to God. He was first on the calendar that day where He belongs every day. And it is not the sort of commitment one compromises. Not if one wants to seize time and keep it under control. It is the start of an organized day, an organized life, and an organized private world.

Gordon MacDonald, *Ordering Your Private World*

JULY 6
Conversions, Great and Small

My brothers, as believers in our glorious Lord Jesus Christ, don't show favoritism.

JAMES 2:1

I'm always glad when famous people come to know Christ and tell others about Him. But sometimes it worries me, because sometimes the impression is left that if the famous sports player, singer, or actor knows Jesus, then people can rest assured that Jesus is okay.

Instead of Jesus validating an individual (as it should be), the individual validates Jesus. Now I'm sure the celebrity doesn't mean for that to happen. But as a society, we're so awed by celebrities that their conversion becomes greater news than the One who converted them. Listen to something important: Jesus doesn't need any help with His credibility, but we need a lot of help with ours. Celebrity conversions are great; they need Christ too. But let's never forget among all the hoopla who it is that does the saving.

Jesus Christ reaches out to people where they are: in the movies, on television, in sports, politics, business, the home. Wherever they are and no matter what they're doing, without Him they are all helpless, afraid, and lost. Yes, He seeks to win celebrities too, not because they're famous, but despite the fact they are. That makes me glad. If He didn't operate that way, He would never have noticed me.

Steve Brown, *Jumping Hurdles*

July 7
God's Handiwork

For you created my inmost being;
*   you knit me together in my mother's womb.*
I praise you because I am fearfully and wonderfully made;
*   your works are wonderful,*
*   I know that full well.*

PSALM 139:13–14

The first question we ask someone after learning his name is, "What do you do?" In getting to know God, then, we must ask that question. He may hide his face, but he has not hidden his work.

What does God do? He makes flowers and mountains and starry nights, the severity of the desert and the lushness of the forest meadow. In these he reveals himself as an artist of incomparable imagination. I have sometimes wondered: What if we had never seen a tree until, one day, someone presented one in the Museum of Modern Art? Would it not be a work of sculpture so splendid that all the other sculptors would put down their tools and come to stare? But that is only the beginning of the exhibition; next comes a whale, and after that a stone, and after that a star, and after that a seed, and after that . . .

But God's work is more than nature. He barely began there. People generally concede that you can know something about God through the universe he has made: "The heavens are telling the glory of God." But to know someone through his work you ought to concentrate on the work he loves best. God does not love stars as he loves me. The heavens, for all their splendor, will outlive their usefulness; they will be rolled up and taken away. So will the world we live in, for all its sensual glory and intricate ecology. They are like the scaffolding that Michelangelo designed for painting the Sistine Chapel—marvelous in its own right, but dismantled at the proper time so that the great work could be more clearly seen. When God had created everything else he went on to man and woman, creatures who sat up and talked to each other, who talked to him. He has been working to complete these creatures ever since. He even became one. His people are God's great work, to be displayed in an entirely new setting—a new heaven and a new earth.

To marvel at yourself is not far from marveling at God. This is the logic of the familiar Psalm 139: "You knit me together in my mother's womb. I praise you because I am fearfully and wonderfully made; your works are wonderful." (13–14). And then, three verses later, the psalmist lightly leaps to this: "How precious to me are your thoughts, O God! How vast is the sum of them!" From my own wonderful nature as a human being to the wonderful nature of God's thoughts—it is not a great leap, for the latter made the former. In this way, at least, a Christian is obliged to be a humanist. We are made in the image of God. As we observe ourselves, individually and socially, talking and singing, admiring babies and playing baseball, we strengthen our personal knowledge of God. This is not an abstract study. It is personal. It is personal because he made me and is working on me still. His hands are on me; I see the prints.

Tim Stafford, *Knowing the Face of God*

JULY 8
Stand!

. . . Stand firm and see the deliverance the LORD *will give you.*

II CHRONICLES 20:17

I am told that distance runners make long, steady strides and that their emphasis is on endurance, not speed. They take their laps and stretch their limitations, giving themselves over to committing their strength to a goal. Perspiration leaps out of their pores. The salty taste of exertion is in their mouths. Turning corners with agility, running shoes banging the pavement, heads high, backs straight—they are in pursuit of a goal. I am told that as they near the finish line, there is a final burst of energy that kicks in like the final cylinders in an engine. It is the last lap; there are no excuses; it's now or never. Now they go for broke! At least once, before they roll you in on a slab and put a name tag on your cold stiff toe, you owe it to your God and to yourself to experience in some area of your life that last-lap feeling of giving your all.

I want to warn you, though, that it hurts to push yourself. It is not easy to get up early every morning while others sleep and prepare for the challenge. Like Jesus in the garden of Gethsemane, it is difficult to find someone who will stand with you while you are in preparation. But there can be no celebration without preparation . . .

For many of us there is no option. We must go to the pinnacle of our own purpose, stand on the top of the mountain, and catch a glimpse of the other side. We are climbing up the mountain with tears in our eyes and dirt in our fingernails. In spite of bruises, cuts, and scrapes, there is a racing pulse and a pounding heart that exist in the chest of someone who has made up his mind, "I will go!"

The question is universal but the answer is totally individual. Can *you* stand to be blessed? If you answer yes, then I want to tell you this: The only way to be blessed is to stand! When you can't seem to put one foot in front of the other, stand. When days come that challenge your destiny, just stand. Realize that there has never been a day that lasted forever. You can't afford to crumple onto your knees like a weak, whimpering lily blown over by a windstorm. Bite your lip, taste your tears, but stand on what God showed you in the night until it happens in the light.

T. D. Jakes, *Can You Stand to Be Blessed?*

July 9

Faithfulness to Our Tasks

It was he who gave some to be apostles, some to be prophets, some to be evangelists, and some to be pastors and teachers, to prepare God's people for works of service, so that the body of Christ may be built up until we all reach unity in the faith and in the knowledge of the Son of God and become mature, attaining to the whole measure of the fullness of Christ.

EPHESIANS 4:11–13

The home is the model of the Church and all related levels of ministry. Our capacity to minister is developed in the home, where God's tools are sharpest and the heat is the greatest. If we cannot learn our lessons there, spurred on by love and the pain of failure, there is little hope for development of these capacities outside the home, where such incentives are lacking. If a man cannot submit to the demands of loving his wife and striving for her success, he will be of little help in praying and fasting for the success of anyone else in the Church! But through time, as he works diligently at his family tasks, he will develop increased capacity for ministry to other members of the body of Christ. Similarly, those who are unmarried who apply their gifts for the "work of service" (Eph. 4:11–13) before marriage will carry these capacities into marriage, to the blessing of their spouse and children and the work of God's Kingdom.

Work diligently at your tasks. Be faithful and patient in your trials. God intends to increase our capacities to minister to others until we become as Christ, whose capacity is limitless. Faithfulness to your tasks will enable God to supernaturally increase your time, your resources (finances, support, people to whom tasks can be delegated, etc.), your vision, and your power to hear the Father and minister His gifts according to His will! May this be your prayer and mine. Amen!

Karl Duff, *Restoration of Men*

July 10

Weeping

*Weeping may remain for a night
but rejoicing comes in the morning.*

PSALM 30:5

Do grown men weep? Sure. Should grown men weep? Of course. Anyone in touch with reality in this world knows there are lots of reasons to weep. We weep over triumphs and over tragedies. Most good people weep over admirable actions and deplorable ones.

Some people might say "Why should Max weep? He's the chairman and CEO. What problems could he possibly have?" Well, my joys and sadnesses may not be the same as everyone else's, but that does not make them any less real, believe me. Let me tell you about a good reason I had lately for weeping.

Our officers and director-level managers, sixty or seventy people, get together quarterly to review results, discuss plans, examine ideas and directions.

Shortly before one of those meetings, I had received a wonderful letter from the mother of one of our handicapped employees. It was a touching letter of gratitude for the efforts of many people at Herman Miller to make life meaningful and rich for a person who is seriously disadvantaged. Because we have a strong, albeit a quiet, effort going on in the company to empower the disadvantaged and to recognize the authenticity of everyone in the group, it seemed to be a good idea to read this letter to the officers and directors.

I almost got through this letter but could not finish. There I stood in front of this group of people—some of them pretty hard-driving—tongue-tied and embarrassed, unable to continue. At that point, one of our senior vice-presidents, Joe Schwartz—urbane, elegant, mature—strode up the center aisle, put his arm around my shoulder, kissed me on the cheek, and adjourned the meeting....

What *do* we weep over? What *should* we weep over? ... Here are some things we probably ought to weep about:

- superficiality
- a lack of dignity
- injustice, the flaw that prevents equity
- good news!
- tenderness
- a word of thanks
- separation
- arrogance
- betrayal of ideas, of principles, of quality
- jargon, because it confuses rather than clarifies
- looking at customers as interruptions
- leaders who watch bottom lines without watching behavior
- the inability of folks to tell the difference between heroes and celebrities
- confusing pleasure with meaning
- leaders who never say "Thank you"
- having to work in a job where you are not free to do your best
- good people trying to follow leaders who depend on politics and hierarchy rather than on trust and competence
- people who are gifts to the spirit

... What would you add? Why should you weep?

Max DePree, *Leadership Is an Art*

July 11

A Firm Foundation

Therefore everyone who hears these words of mine and puts them into prac-tice is like a wise man who built his house on the rock. The rain came down, the streams rose, and the winds blew and beat against that house; yet it did not fall, because it had its foundation on the rock.

MATTHEW 7:24–25

It is my firm conviction that mid-life crisis results from what the Bible refers to as "building your house upon sand." It is possible to be a follower of Jesus Christ and accept His forgiveness from sin, yet still be deeply influenced by the values and attitudes of one's surrounding culture. Thus, a young Christian husband and father may become a workaholic, a hoarder of money, a status-seeker, a worshiper of truth, and a lover of pleasure. These tendencies may not reflect his conscious choices and desires; they merely represent the stamp of society's godless values on his life and times.

Despite his unchristian attitudes, the man may appear to "have it all together" in his first fifteen years as an adult, especially if he is successful in early business pursuits. But he is in considerable danger. Whenever we build our lives on values and principles that contradict the time-honored wisdom of God's Word, we are laying a foundation on the sand. Sooner or later, the storms will howl and the structure we have laboriously constructed will collapse with a mighty crash.

Stated succinctly, a mid-life crisis is more likely to be severe for those whose values reflect the temporal perspectives of this world. A man does not mourn the loss of his youth, for example, if he honestly believes that his life is merely a preparation for a better one to follow. And God does not become the enemy of a man who has walked and talked with Him in daily communion and love. And the relationship between a man and wife is less strained in the mid-life years if they have protected and maintained their friendship since they were newlyweds. In short, the mid-life crisis represents a day of reckoning for a lifetime of wrong values, unworthy goals, and ungodly attitudes.

James Dobson, *Dr. Dobson Answers Your Questions*

JULY 12

Transcendence

It is God's will that you should be sanctified: that you should avoid sexual immorality; that each of you should learn to control his own body in a way that is holy and honorable, not in passionate lust like the heathen, who do not know God; and that in this matter no one should wrong his brother or take advantage of him. The Lord will punish men for all such sins, as we have already told you and warned you.

I THESSALONIANS 4:3–6

Rather than positioning sexuality and spirituality against each other as rivals, I see them as deeply related. The more I observe our society's obsession with sexuality, the more I sense in it a thirst for transcendence.

My neighbors, in their condominiums, high-rises, and even suburbs have little transcendence left in their lives. Few of them attend churches; they believe science has figured out most of the numinous mysteries of the universe, like disease and weather. Except for the New Agers among them, they tend to scoff at superstitious practices like astrology.

But sex—ah, there's a mystery to which normal principles of reductionism do not apply. Sex is not something you can "figure out." Knowing about sex, even taking a degree in gynecology, doesn't diminish its magical power. Probably the closest thing to a supernatural experience my male neighbors ever have is when they watch Michelle Pfeiffer in a clingy red dress, or when they pore over each microdot of the annual *Sports Illustrated* swimsuit issue. Is it any wonder these swimsuit models are often called "goddesses"?

In this view, sex is not a rival to spirituality, but rather a pointer to it. When a society so completely blocks the human thirst for transcendence, should we be surprised that such longings reroute themselves into an expression of mere physicality? Maybe the problem is not that people are getting naked, but that they aren't getting naked enough: we stop at the skin instead of going deeper, into the soul.

Philip Yancey, *Finding God in Unexpected Places*

JULY 13
Giving Up the Good for the Best

But whatever was to my profit I now consider loss for the sake of Christ.

PHILIPPIANS 3:7

If our years were allotted to us in the generous fashion which some of the patriarchs seem to have enjoyed, a man might find some opportunity for trying his hand at more avocations than one. As it is, however, the time is short. At seventy a man only begins to feel that he knows his work. There is no time for tinkering with many things or for trifling with one. The very brevity of life clamors for concentration and economy.

We have all read the affecting and informing and heart-searching correspondence of Dr. Marcus Dods. No man sounded the very depths of life's innermost experiences more terribly than did he. He felt called to be a minister. He buried every other inclination and possibility. Then came years of neglect and rejection. No congregation would call him. But, with a courage never excelled on a battlefield, he held on. He looked wistfully at the graves in which he had buried his earlier fancies. But he would allow no resurrection. And at last came recognition and reward. And out of that agonizing experience he wrote on the economy of life, and he deserves to be listened to with bated breath.

"Every man," the doctor says, "as he grows into life, finds he must employ such an economy on his own account. He is pressed to occupy positions or to engage in work which will prevent him from achieving the purpose for which nature has fitted him. He is offered promotion which seems attractive and has its advantages; but he declines it, because it would divert him from his chosen aim. Continually men spoil their life by want of concentration. They are greatly tempted to do so, for the public foolishly concludes that, because a man does one thing well, he can do everything well; and he who has written a good history is straightway asked to sit in Parliament, or the man whose scholarship and piety have been conspicuous is offered preferment which calls for the exercise of wholly different qualities . . .

Yes, it is good for the builder to bury the banker that he might have been. It is good for Paul to bury the Saul that he had been. But there is one man within us, whom we are most strongly tempted to bury, to whose funeral we must never, *never* go. He is the man of our ideal; the man of our prayers; the man we fain would be."

Frank Boreham, *The Luggage of Life*

JULY 14
Right Expectations

Every good and perfect gift is from above, coming down from the Father of the heavenly lights, who does not change like shifting shadows.

JAMES 1:17

The problem we face is that our culture fosters high expectations, even rights. We end up thinking that to be happy, we need to hold down a particular kind of job; therefore, we need to earn a particular level of income; therefore, we need to live in a particular kind of house in a particular kind of neighborhood; and therefore we need to drive a particular kind of car; and all by a particular age. Why? Simply because that's what we are programmed to expect when we adopt expectations from our culture.

When we set our expectations too high, we take risks that cause us to alternate between pursuing significance one day and survival the next. Yesterday we dreamed of building an empire with streets paved in gold; today we freeze with fear over how to meet payroll.

The siren song of our age is that "you can have it all"; moreover, you need it all to be truly happy. When we buy into this idea, our goals, plans, hopes, dreams, and expectations come from the culture, not from God. We are living by our own ideas. We must remember that not every good idea is a God idea.

Unmet expectations can lead to tremendous disappointment, anger, and even depression. Maybe it's a marriage that isn't working the way it's supposed to, a career that seems stalled too soon, or a teenager making horrible choices.

For two years I have been pondering a sentence that I believe answers a lot of questions about life. I reproduce it here, but ask you to not read past it quickly. You may find it valuable to do as I have done and write it somewhere for long-term reflection. Here it is: *All disappointment is the result of unmet expectations.*

Think about it. Whether it's a promotion that didn't go through, a wife that isn't sympathetic to your pressures, or a child hanging out with the wrong group—*all* disappointment is the result of unmet expectations. Knowing this can help us reevaluate many of our expectations and lower some of them.

The Bible says, "Every good gift and every perfect gift is from above, and comes down from the Father of Lights" (James 1:17 NKJV). Too often we don't show gratitude for the many blessings we do receive, and we become selfishly angered over the blessings we don't receive. Instead, we should receive everything with gratitude and humbly trust God when we don't get what we want.

How have your expectations led to disappointment?

Patrick Morley, *The Seven Seasons of a Man's Life*

JULY 15
Fasting

When you fast, do not look somber as the hypocrites do, for they disfigure their faces to show men they are fasting. I tell you the truth, they have received their reward in full. But when you fast, put oil on your head and wash your face, so that it will not be obvious to men that you are fasting, but only to your Father, who is unseen; and your Father, who sees what is done in secret, will reward you.

MATTHEW 6:16–18

After a certain period of time, many Christians realize that their witness is not effective and that their personal life lacks holiness. The joy which once filled them has waned, only to be replaced by a despondency caused through failure. This may well be due to the fact that true conversion has not taken place at all; it is possible for someone to want to become a Christian, and make all the mechanical moves toward this end, without being 'born-again,' through the operation of the Holy Spirit, in the individual life. On the other hand, a genuine believer can know times of deep despair and inward failure; Christian conversion does not hold out a promise of instant sinlessness or constant overflowing hopefulness.

However, God has provided a dynamic for every believer through His Gospel, and divine energy is still available today; we can share in the fullness of the Holy Spirit. Nevertheless, such an experience is valueless without discipline; there are many saints who face carnality. To maintain power over the desires of the flesh, and to be in constant victory over the egoistic self, we need much of the grace of God. To receive that grace in times of violent temptation, and to enjoy God's power when needed, there is no doubt that we shall find fasting necessary, sometimes. Fasting starves the flesh, allowing the mind to turn towards spiritual issues. If a man, when trying to pray, is constantly faced by pictures which make prayer a mockery, let that man fast—he will begin to taste the presence of God instead.

David Smith, Fasting: A Neglected Discipline

July 16

Openness

He who conceals his sins does not prosper,
but whoever confesses and renounces them finds mercy.

PROVERBS 28:13

God gave the husband and wife to each other to make them more than they could be singly. The completion of each cannot take place until they learn to share their innermost being and work for the good of the other. The personal areas that are kept private have no opportunity for growth. Why not try God's plan?

Marriage, love, and communication cannot be separated from God without shriveling them. There may be numerous areas of your life that you mark "off limits" to God as well as to your wife. Could they include fear of inadequacy, deeply rooted bitterness, feigned love, or a spirit of revenge? These are poisons in the soul that God and your mate can help dispel—if you seek help.

God seeks to develop your soul as well as your body. Many personable people are not using all their God-given gifts because their emotional life is constricted. They refuse to allow their emotions to be exposed and to be brought to maturity. Examine yourself for a moment; are you courageous enough to look inward to see what is really there? Then are you willing to talk to God and your wife about your hidden self? Little by little, you may be strengthened until you will care to say: "Honey, tell me exactly what you feel about me, about yourself, everything" and not say a word until she finishes! Only a real man can do that.

We men want to be masculine. A man has—or should have—emotions in the soul as well as muscles in the body. If you have not matured in this part of your being, pride or fear may be your enemy. Open your heart to the light of God and the sympathy of your mate, and you will see the enemy retreating. The fullness of emotional development and interrelationships can be yours.

Charles Stanley, *A Man's Touch*

July 17
Emotional Release

I am worn out from groaning;
all night long I flood my bed with weeping
and drench my couch with tears.

PSALM 6:6

Most men fear their feelings to some degree. Perhaps the great fear is that we might cry when someone is watching. As a result, we practice being dull to our feelings. After all, big boys don't cry—do they?

For most of us, there is a dammed-up torrent of feelings waiting to gush out. If you have been in denial of your feelings for so long that you can't agree with this statement, think again. The only men who really don't have feelings are psychopaths! They end up in prison because they have no feelings to help them discern the moral life. In other words, they hurt or kill without remorse. They don't fit into society.

You, of course, are not psychopathic. But you are dammed-up! And if you're like most men, you fear the dam. You're afraid that if a trickle of emotions is released, the whole dam might burst! If you know you are afraid of the dam, you are ahead of many brothers—at least you know the dam exists! If you, however, don't know what I'm talking about, then you may be protecting yourself with denial or repression. How deep is your hurt?

Fear is a natural, common emotion. Most of us are also frightened of fear. Facing our fears takes courage: the courage to see our defenses and the courage to explore and admit our fears. Knowing our fears frees us to enjoy an emotional life that is whole. Emotions give life zest and zeal. What are *your* fears? Speak about them.

Dick Brian Klaver, Men at Peace

July 18
Healing Grace

Therefore confess your sins to each other and pray for each other so that you may be healed.

JAMES 5:16

Some of us have misunderstood the doctrine of grace. We have supposed that since Christ died for us, God no longer recoils in loathing from our sinful actions. God forgives. He loves. We are his children. The death of his Son atones for us. Why then should God loathe our sinful actions? *We have forgotten that Calvary has made no difference to God's attitude to sin.* He cannot bear to look on it. That which cost him the death of his Holy One remains and ever will remain of utmost abhorrence to him.

We have subtly distanced ourselves from this aspect of his nature. We treat him with unconscious contempt. It would bother us to shock or grieve a friend. But God's grief and shock no longer affect us. We do not feel them. We say we reverence him and we believe what we say, but we do not even respect him. We would experience more relief from getting matters straightened out with an angry garbage collector than with an angry God. Our understanding of God's grace has become devalued to what Bonhoeffer derides as "cheap grace."

Here then is the rule: If it fills you with deep shame to confess to a close friend what is easily confessed to God, then your confession to God is in some sense unreal. The shame validates the transaction. Confession is not merely a verbal description of thoughts and actions. People who truly confess to God no longer care whether others learn their secret. The relief that floods them is such that it flushes away their shame as well as their guilt.

The practice of confessing our faults to another human being can in fact make the Godward transaction more real. Confession is meant (among other things) to heal. James's exhortation ends with the words ". . . and pray for each other, that you may be healed." Physical and emotional disease can arise from unresolved sin. Confession is meant to involve a real encounter with a real person. It is intended to produce healing. If the encounter with a fellow human can help the divine encounter become more real to us, then we had better take a serious look at the practice of confession.

John White and Ken Blue, *Healing the Wounded*

July 19

Victory in Our Personal War

I will ransom them from the power of the grave;
—I will redeem them from death.

Hosea 13:14

Many years ago I had the privilege of speaking across the length and breadth of the country of Vietnam. The year was 1971, and I was still an undergraduate in college when the invitation was extended to me to come and speak at the U.S. military bases and hospitals, as well as in other settings. It was an experience that changed my life. I recall numerous conversations with military personnel, and more often than not the conversation turned to the subject of death, and ultimately to God. Those conversations are deeply etched in my memory.

One of the memories of those years is a poem that was written by an American soldier and given to me. I have treasured it ever since and will summarize what he so painstakingly described with poetic beauty. He tells of a life-defining night when he was caught in the crossfire of a battle that raged around him and a war that he could not silence within him. One was a conflict of ideology for which the weapons of warfare now thundered forth their fury; the other, a struggle of the heart and mind as they dealt with matters of the soul. It was to that inner battlement he directed his attention.

The deafening noises of exploding shells and the sound of the signal to fight what could well have been his last battle did not daunt his yearning to settle that inner turmoil. Once again, within him he heard the voices of friends from the days of this youth who had convinced him of a mindless universe. But now, from his shellhole as he saw the starlit sky, he felt the skeptic had not called a spade a spade. In silence he peacefully surrendered to the Lord whose love he could resist no longer, and with the triumph of the soul, he said, "Now that I have I have met you I'm not afraid to die."

Ironically, several years later when I was in Syria, I heard a young officer testify to an identical struggle and to victory through Christ on a fateful night atop the Golan Heights. That battle, history records, exacted a terrible price in human life. Odd as it seems, such settings have settled wars of personal destiny for an astonishing number of soldiers. Victory over the grave puts every other battle in perspective.

Ravi Zacharias, *Can Man Live Without God?*

JULY 20
God in Our Dark Nights

He will not let your foot slip—
he who watches over you will not slumber . . .

PSALM 121:3

He was a strong man facing an enemy beyond his strength.

His young wife had become gravely ill, then suddenly passed away, leaving the big man alone with a wide-eyed, flaxen-haired girl, not quite five years old.

The service in the village chapel was simple, and heavy with grief. After the burial at the small country cemetery, the man's neighbors gathered around him. "Please bring your little girl and stay with us for several days," someone said. "You shouldn't go back home just yet."

Broken-hearted though he was, the man answered, "Thank you, friends, for the kind offer. But we need to go back home—where she was. My baby and I must face this."

So they returned, the big man and his little girl, to what now seemed an empty, lifeless house. The man brought his daughter's little bed into his room, so they could face that first dark night together.

As the minutes slipped by that night, the young girl was having a dreadful time trying to sleep . . . and so was her father. What could pierce a man's heart deeper than a child sobbing for a mother who would never come back?

Long into the night the little one continued to weep. The big man reached down into her bed and tried to comfort her as best he could. After a while, the little girl managed to stop crying, but only out of sorrow for her father. Thinking his daughter was asleep, the father looked up and said brokenly, "I trust You, Father, but . . . it's as dark as midnight!"

Hearing her dad's prayer, the little girl begin to cry again.

"I thought you were asleep, baby," he said.

"Papa, I did try. I was sorry for you. I did try. But—I couldn't go to sleep. Papa, did you ever know it could be so dark? Why, Papa? I can't even see you, it's so dark." Then, through her tears, the little girl whispered, "But you love me even if it's dark—don't you Papa? You love me even if I don't see you don't you, Papa?"

For an answer, the big man reached across with his massive hands, lifted his girl out of her bed, brought her over onto his chest, and held her, until at last she fell asleep.

When she was finally quiet, he began to pray. He took his little daughter's cry to him, and passed it up to God.

"Father . . . it's dark as midnight. I can't see You at all. But You love me, even when it's dark and I can't see, don't You?"

From the blackest of hours, the Lord touched him with new strength, enabling him to carry on. He knew that God went on loving him, even in the dark.

Ron Mehl, *God Works the Night Shift*

JULY 21

Running the Race, Unencumbered

Therefore, since we are surrounded by such a great cloud of witnesses, let us throw off everything that hinders and the sin that so easily entangles, and let us run with perseverance the race marked out for us.

HEBREWS 12:1

Come with me to the ancient Greek games. As the fastest runners in the Roman Empire gather at the starting line, the tension and pressure is mounting. They are about to run the race of their lives. The crowd rises to its feet in anticipation.

The runners begin to remove their outer warmup robes. Nothing must slow them down. They then remove their loose-fitting tunics. No garment must cause any wind drag.

Then, in a startling move, the runners remove the rest of their clothing. They strip down. Completely. To the buff.

They are totally nude.

This has become R-rated.

These Greek athletes have stripped down so nothing—absolutely nothing—will slow them down. They will do anything to gain an advantage over the competition. They are willing to risk the embarrassment of public exposure. To run without any encumbrance. All to win the crown.

This gives new meaning to the truism "Less is more."

Their bulging muscles and finely tuned bodies ripple in the open arena. With sculpted torsos that look like they have been chiseled out of marble, they resemble exquisite masterpieces. These are the finest athletes in the Roman Empire.

These naked runners are highly motivated to jump out to a fast start. If you fall behind this bare-bottomed pack, the view can be pretty rough.

Considered offensive by women and Jews, such nudity was the accepted practice of these world-famous athletic games. Nothing must be allowed to impede their speed. Not even clothing. Because winning was everything!...

These are men whose burning passion is winning. At any cost. So they remove all encumbrances that would hinder a swift performance. All to capture a crown, if not a cold.

Men, these are the bare facts. Very revealing.

Just as the first-century athletes stripped down to run with maximum speed, we must strip away every spiritual encumbrance that would impede our progress in God's race. Pursuing the ultimate prize requires laying aside anything that would slow us down.

I know what some of you are thinking, "If God wanted us to run naked, we would have been born that way." That's precisely the point.

Hebrews 12:1 (NASB) says, "Therefore, since we have so great a cloud of witnesses surrounding us, *let us also lay aside every encumbrance*" (emphasis added). This is a call for "spiritual streaking."

Too many of us run as if outfitted with layers of restrictive clothing and with heavy weights. We must strip down and run unencumbered. Take it all off!

Steven Lawson, *Men Who Win*

The Man of God Passing By

She said to her husband, "I know that this man who often comes our way is a holy man of God."

II KINGS 4:9

My first pastorate was a country church back in the twenties. I was a bachelor then, and I was a pedestrian. I didn't own a car. I didn't buy an automobile until I was sixty-six. I wanted to think it over. I did a lot of walking in those days. This is the day of the motorist, and any man who walks is viewed with suspicion. you see a man coming down the road now just meditating, and you figure he's either out of his head or out of gas, one of the two. He's such a rarity that dogs bark as though they'd seen a ghost, and policemen have been known to follow a pedestrian for blocks to make sure he isn't up to something.

One memory lingers from that pastorate. Along my route there was a grocery store, and the grocer said one day, "Preacher, I want you to know that many a time when things were not going well, I looked out my store window and saw you going by, and it helped. I felt better." He didn't elaborate on that, but I've never forgotten it. It's been my prayer that souls along my way, as I went through the years, might be able to say to some small degree what this Shunammite woman said, "I perceive that this is a holy man of God that passeth by us continually."

That ought to be the ambition of every Christian on his pilgrimage through this world. Luke tells us that when our Lord was on His way to Jericho, somebody told a blind man, "Jesus of Nazareth passeth by." He's still passing by, but not as then. He passes by in His people and particularly in His preachers. He has no hands, no feet but ours; and if this world reads the gospel, it'll be the gospel according to you and me—for most of them don't read Matthew, Mark, Luke, and John.

W. Phillip Keller, Taming Tension

JULY 23
Waiting Patiently

Be still before the lord and wait patiently for him;
do not fret when men succeed in their ways,
when they carry out their wicked schemes.

PSALM 37:7

If you have ever faced an hour when God seemed to have left you completely and your prayers seemed useless, you have been to Calvary. The man of God must face an hour of isolation.

In His time of forsakenness Jesus cried in anguish, "My God, my God, why hast thou forsaken me?" (Matthew 27:46) Although His entire life had been spent in doing His Father's will, at the end our Saviour seemed totally isolated and apparently abandoned.

Every true man of God knows what it is like to beseech God for deliverance and direction, only to be left with the cold feeling that God is no longer directing his life. He knows what it is like to make one mistake after another, to stagger on in faith that is very weak, to feel backslidden—tormented by the fact that although he loves God so much, he feels alone among crippling temptations.

In his isolation, Job cried out, "I cry unto thee, and thou dost not hear me . . ." (Job 30:20). David asked, "Is his mercy clean gone forever? Doth his promise fail for evermore? . . . Hath he in anger shut up his tender mercies?" (Psalm 77: 8, 9).

I dare you to look deep into the life of anyone God has ever used. You will find that he or she was often lonely and isolated. Yet in spite of this, his faith survived intact. Job testified: "But he knoweth the way that I take: when he hath tried me, I shall come forth as gold" (Job 23:10). David sang in his hour of trial, "But I have trusted in thy mercy; my heart shall rejoice in thy salvation" (Psalm 13:5). Peter came back from his denial to preach the powerful Pentecost sermon through which three thousand souls found Christ.

I have drunk from the cup of pain. I have faced nights of confusion and hours of isolation. No doubt there are more to come. But one thing is sure: I have learned to fear no evil. I am totally convinced that I shall come forth as gold and that the Lord's mercy endureth to all generations—especially to mine.

Do you have a problem? The hand of God has placed you in a divine crucible. You will come out of it like gold tried in the fire.

Meanwhile—stop trying to figure it all out.

Rest.

This is the Lord's commandment: "Rest in the Lord, and wait patiently for him . . . The steps of a good man are ordered by the Lord: and he delighteth in his way" (Psalm 37:7, 23 KJV).

David Wilkerson, *Man, Have I Got Problems*

JULY 24
Being Aware of Satan's Devices

Be self-controlled and alert. Your enemy the devil prowls around like a roaring lion looking for someone to devour.

I PETER 5:8

One of the hardest animals to hunt is the trophy white-tail deer. One misty day I had been sitting motionless for hours in the woods, hidden, watching a herd of these deer. A doe appeared. She couldn't have known I was there. Everything was still, and I was not upwind from her. Suddenly she stiffened. Her white tail drew up tight against her buttocks. She sensed danger.

The doe looked around. Her eyes froze. Her tail shot straight back. She knew an enemy was nearby. As I studied this beautiful creature, I asked God, "How does she know? Why is she so smart?"

"She's not so smart. She's alert," God replied. "That's what makes these deer so hard to hunt. From the day they are born almost everything around them—coyotes, bobcats and lions—tries to kill them, and they know it. They stay alert to stay alive."

In a sense, you and I are a lot like those deer. From the day we are born Satan schemes to claim our souls. From the time we are born again he works to destroy our testimonies and our lives. The tragic part is, unlike the white-tail deer, we too often don't know it. We are not alert.

Satan is very crafty. To overcome him we must learn to be spiritually alert. This doesn't mean harboring an undue awareness of the enemy. Rather, spiritual alertness grows out of a total consciousness of Christ—

loving God with all our heart. Nonetheless, winning any victory requires knowledge of how the enemy works. What is our enemy like? What is Satan doing?

James Robison, *Winning the Real War*

JULY 25
Loving by Faith

This is the confidence we have in approaching God: that if we ask anything according to his will, he hears us. And if we know that he hears us—whatever we ask—we know that we have what we asked of him.

I JOHN 5:14–15

Everything about the Christian life is based on faith. You love by faith just as you received Christ by faith, just as you are filled with the Holy Spirit by faith, and just as you walk by faith.

But if the fruit of the Spirit is love, you may logically ask, "Isn't it enough to be filled with the Spirit?" That's true from God's point of view, but it will not always be true in the actual experience.

Many Christians have loved with God's love without consciously or specifically claiming it by faith. Yet, without being aware of the fact, they were, indeed, loving by faith. Hebrews 11:6 reminds us that "without faith it is impossible to please God." Clearly, then, there is no demonstration of God's love where there is no faith.

How then do we love by faith in a practical way? It works like this: We know God has commanded us to love. We also know He promised in 1 John 5:14–15 that if we ask according to His command (His will), then we receive His love by faith according to His promise, knowing His promises are always true. Let me illustrate how this happens.

In one case, I was having trouble loving a fellow staff member. I wanted to love him, and I knew I was commanded to do so. But because of certain inconsistencies and personality differences, I found it difficult. Then the Lord reminded me of 1 Peter 5:7: "Let him have all your worries and cares, for He is always thinking about you and watching everything that concerns you" (TLB). So I decided to give the problem to him and love the man by faith—to act lovingly toward him regardless of my feelings, depending on God's love and strength within.

An hour later, I received a letter from that very man, who had no possible way of knowing what I had just decided. In fact, his letter had been written the day before. The Lord had foreseen the change in me. This friend and I met that afternoon and had the most wonderful time of prayer and fellowship we had ever experienced together. . . .

I encourage you to make a list of everyone whom you do not like and begin today to love them by faith. Include those people who have hurt you in the past. Pray for them. Ask for eyes to see them as Christ sees them. Act lovingly toward them no matter how you feel. We don't love people because they deserve to be loved—we love them because Christ commands it and empowers us to do so. Your relationships will change as God's love in you overflows to others. Further, you will be a channel of God's own life and power into this needy world, and loving by faith, you will please your loving Master. The greatest force in the world is love!

Bill Bright, *Seven Promises of a Promise Keeper—Promise 7: A Man and His World*

JULY 26
The Highest Flight

The day is yours, and yours also the night;
  you established the sun and the moon.

PSALM 74:16

[Editor's Note: On this date in 1971, the Apollo 15 mission to the moon was launched with astronauts Al Worden, Dave Scott, and Jim Irwin aboard.]

The excitement was overwhelming, but now I could let myself believe it. Dave and I were on the surface of the moon. We looked out across a beautiful little valley with high mountains on three sides of us and the deep gorge of Hadley Rille a mile to the west. The great Apennines were gold and brown in the early morning sunshine. It was like some beautiful little valley in the mountains of Colorado, high above the timberline.

There was the excitement of exploring a place where man had never been before, but the most exciting thing, what really moved me and touched my soul, was that I could feel God's presence there. In the three days of exploration, there were a couple of times when I actually looked up to see the earth—and it was a difficult maneuver in that bulky suit; you had to grab onto something to hold yourself steady and then lean back as far as you could. That beautiful, warm living object looked so fragile, so delicate, that if you touched it with a finger it would crumble and fall apart. Seeing this has to change a man, has to make a man appreciate the creation of God and the love of God....

I feel now that the power of God was working in me the whole time I was on the flight. I felt His presence on the moon in the most immediate and overwhelming way. There I was, a test pilot, a nuts-and-bolts type who had gotten rather skeptical about God, and suddenly I was asking God to solve my problems on the moon. I was relying on God rather than on Houston. Then there was my powerful desire to have a service on the moon, to witness. All this time God was taking over my life, and I didn't even realize it.

The Lord has found me a stubborn, hardheaded man. Mary [my wife] could see that something was happening inside me, but I didn't realize it. She has told me that she asked the Lord not to give me a minute's rest until I had completely surrendered my life to Him. And really, I didn't have any peace ... Now with the great flight to the moon over, and before I had realized that the highest flight of my life was still ahead of me, I began to reconsider everything about my life. I thought back to when I had accepted Christ at the little Baptist church. I tried to retrace my life from the beginning. For the first time, I was looking at myself introspectively to find out who I was and what was happening to me.

Jim Irwin, To Rule the Night

JULY 27

Saying No

Above all, my brothers, do not swear—not by heaven or by earth or by anything else. Let your "Yes" be yes, and your "No," no, or you will be condemned.

JAMES 5:12

Men need to relearn the manly art of saying no. Who knows how many marriages have gone down the drain because men, obsessed with some false concept of happiness, have not had the responsible courage to say that one little word? No!—to the big corporation that promises the "nice" increase in salary if a man will tear his wife away from her needed friends, yank his children from familiar schools, chop off the ties with the church, and uproot all community relationships. No!—to the committee that wants the last free night of a man's week for some "good cause" if it means being with his family is no longer possible. No!—to the young man who wants to live with his daughter rather than work out a proper courtship that leads to marriage. No!—to the flattering eyes of the adulteress.

Emphatically, with both feet planted firmly on the ground, men must commit themselves to saying no to things, good or bad, that would take them away from their patriarchal responsibility to make Christ and His kingdom the critical priority.

Weldon Hardenbrook, Missing from Action

JULY 28
Seeing Through Our Children's Eyes

Therefore, whoever humbles himself like this child is the greatest in the kingdom of heaven. And whoever welcomes a little child like this in my name welcomes me. But if anyone causes one of these little ones who believe in me to sin, it would be better for him to have a large millstone hung around his neck and to be drowned in the depths of the sea.

MATTHEW 18:4–6

Each Sunday, after church, we had a family habit of going out to lunch. Each week, it started out as a fun family time. But it seemed that we always ended up with tension in the air. I began to wonder why. As I thought about those lunches, I imagined a scene that had occurred many times. Bobby was an enthusiastic, growing young boy, and he really liked going out to restaurants. He especially liked ordering anything that included the word "deluxe." And that really irked me. It always seemed that Bobby couldn't just order a plain cheeseburger; he had to have a "deluxe cheeseburger." Of course, that was the most expensive one on the menu. And every week I would bawl him out about it, creating a "blue fog" over the entire luncheon gathering.

This was one of those times that, while there was no audible voice, it seemed that God and I carried on a conversation in my mind. He was asking me, "Bob, how much would you *like* Bobby to spend on lunch? What would make you happy?"

"I don't know, Lord. Maybe $2.25."

"Bob, how much is a 'deluxe cheeseburger'?"

"Well, about $2.75."

"How many times a year do you go out to lunch together?"

I thought, "I suppose about 50, if we went out every week."

"Why don't you figure out how much money that is."

I did. I got a piece of paper and multiplied out the difference between the lunch plates over a year. It came to about $25. I just stared at the paper. I felt ashamed and stupid. I didn't need an audible voice to know what the punch line of this conversation was.

"Bob, you are hurting the feelings of your son, whom you love more than anything in the world, and you are hurting your relationship with him over a measly $25 a year."

Without hesitation, I got up and drove home. I called Amy, Debbie, and Bobby together in the living room. "I've been spending some time with the Lord," I said, "and He showed me some things that I want to talk to you about. Especially with you, Bob.

"Do you know how I give you a hard time when we go out to lunch? How I say that 'you don't know what the right side of the menu is for'?" He nodded. "Bobby, when I yell at you because you order things that cost too much, does that hurt your feelings?" He didn't say anything, but big tears welled up in his eyes, and his lip began quivering.

"I had forgotten for a long time, but God reminded me this morning of something. When I was your age, my dad did the same thing to me. I didn't know what the right side of the menu was for either! And it always hurt my feelings, too, and made those family dinners not quite as much fun as they should have been.

"Bobby, I want you to know I'm sorry. I love you very much and I'm telling you now: If you want a deluxe cheeseburger, you can have a deluxe cheeseburger. And I am never going to bring it up again." We all hugged each other, and that was the end of the issue for good.

I'm sure that, to most other people, this is a trivial illustration. How important could a decision over a cheeseburger be? But the issue really isn't the cheeseburger or the menu. The issue is a love relationship. What law could have ever touched this situation? None, except the law of love.

Bob George, Classic Christianity

JULY 29
Abba

But God demonstrates his own love for us in this! While we were still sinners, Christ died for us.

ROMANS 5:8

Our physical fathers planted a seed that resulted in a child. However the response of some fathers to the fact that a seed was planted is, "Oh-no!" Some children are unwanted. Have you ever felt unwanted? Ever felt that you were stamped "not good enough" as a person by your father or mother? Ever felt "put-up-with"? God did something more than simply plant a spiritual seed. He wants you. He loves *you*—and He *likes* you!

As a kid I could throw a baseball a mile. Unfortunately, I couldn't throw it *straight*. And I couldn't field the ball very well, either. Some of the most painful, humiliating experiences I remember from childhood are the times when I either was *not* chosen for a team, or I was the *last* one chosen. But "He [the Father] chose us in him before the foundation of the world" (Eph. 1:4). Before the One who created *everything* there is created *anything*, He chose you and me.

You and I were God's first priority. Colossians 3:12 refers to us as "God's chosen ones, holy and beloved. . . ." Peter, in the second chapter of his first epistle, calls us a "chosen race." We all know the pain of not being wanted by someone; not being chosen by those to whom we are closest hurts even more. But you and I *are* wanted. We belong! We've been chosen, hand-picked, first team, by our new Father.

Romans 5:6, 8 says, "While we were yet helpless . . . Christ died for the ungodly . . . While we were yet sinners Christ died for us." He didn't wait until we cleaned up our act. He didn't ask for references. Romans 8:15, 16: "For you did not receive the spirit of slavery to fall back into fear, but you have received the spirit of sonship. When we cry, 'Abba! Father!' it is the Spirit himself bearing witness with our spirit that we are children of God."

"Abba" means daddy, and father (*pater* in Greek) means papa, the same word as in the Lord's Prayer. It's "Daddy, Papa" not "Scary Judge."

He chose you. He went through a lot to get you. And now you are His child. He is your dad. And He likes you a lot!

Jeff Vanvonderen, *Tired of Trying to Measure Up*

JULY 30

His Being Made a Curse for Us

Christ redeemed us from the curse of the law by becoming a curse for us, for it is written: "Cursed is everyone who is hung on a tree."

GALATIANS 3:13

Before [my experience with God], the Bible had meant nothing to me; it could have been written in Egyptian for all I knew! Now I started devouring the Word of God and had an incredible desire to read it. It was my hope, my faith, and my lifeline. The Bible opened up to me like some treasure that had been hidden in the earth for many years.

Whenever I read some new revelation, I thought: *Has this been here all this time?*

In Galatians 3:13, I read: "Christ hath redeemed us from the curse of the law, being made a curse for us."

The words, filled with truth and life, jumped out at me.

I had been under a curse, but I had done it to myself. I deserved "the curse of the law" because I had been in gross sin and had totally turned my back on God. Starting with my parents' divorce, I blamed God for all that was wrong with my life and had turned a deaf ear to His voice.

I read in John 10:10 where Jesus said the thief—Satan—comes to steal, kill, and destroy. I knew that had happened to me. Satan had tried to destroy me with drugs, with pain, and with sin; he had tried to steal my sanity; and he had tried to kill me with thoughts of self-hatred and suicide.

In contrast, Jesus said in John 10:10, "I am come that they might have life, and that they might have it more abundantly."

Life! Life! That was what I had been searching for!

Not just the promise of eternal life—although God promises that, too—but life in the here and now. An abundant life!

I learned that the word "gospel" means "good news," and I well understood that message, for the Word of God was such good news to me!

I've heard some people describe God as "the God of second chances." To me He became the God of a thousand chances!

All my problems didn't disappear overnight. Some of my weird mental quirks and the destructive patterns I had formed in life were not yet broken.

But I also had, for the first time, peace. The inner turmoil that had tortured me for so long was finally silenced.

Keith "Little Ricky Ricardo" Thibodeaux, Life After Lucy

JULY 31
Waiting

The LORD is good to those whose hope is in him,
to the one who seeks him . . .

LAMENTATIONS 3:25

One of the primary irritations confronting us in our fast-paced society is waiting. We wait for elevators and traffic lights, find ourselves placed on hold and waiting when using the telephone, stand in line and wait at the checkout counter of grocery stores, sit and wait in reception rooms of doctors' and dentists' offices, and otherwise occupy a great deal of time just waiting. Few of us enjoy it. Many of us become extremely impatient and irritated when forced to wait.

Yet one of the most important biblical principles found throughout the Bible involves waiting. . . . Waiting is an important ingredient in our personal spiritual growth and development. It is designed by God to build into our lives a number of important traits. He uses waiting to produce such important fruits of the Spirit as long-suffering, meekness, and self-control. . . .

The word used by Isaiah for "wait" is an illustrative Hebrew term describing a rope stretched taut. It is closely related to the term used for the scarlet thread, the cord hung from Rahab's home in Jericho in Joshua 2. The significance of that is that the waiting process is a stretching one, one that is often extremely difficult but one that ultimately has a good end.

Isaiah promises renewal of strength to those who wait upon and hope in the Lord. Here he utilizes another vivid Old Testament term that is related, in its root meaning, to the concept of "passing through." It was used of a change of clothes and of a knife cutting or passing through meat or other material. . . .

The significance of that term in today's burnout victim is important. Like an old and battered car, the burnout victim's strength is depleted. He has been many miles and feels he cannot long continue on. The Lord's promise is that waiting on Him will bring renewal of strength. His old, faltering strength will be traded in for God's limitless energy. Physically, emotionally, and spiritually, he will become like new by waiting upon the Lord.

Waiting thus becomes an expression of trust in the God who is described by Jeremiah as being "good to those whose hope is in [who wait on] him "(Lamentations 3:25) and who, according to David, strengthens the heart of those who wait on him (Psalm 27:14).

The picture of these Israelite individuals who were faint, powerless, weary, and experiencing complete disaster, now soaring as eagles, running long distances without growing weary, and walking without fainting, completes the description of a spiritual principle that, when applied today, provides a workable cure for the spiritual dimension of burnout.

Don't despair. There is hope! There is a solution available to the child of God. By turning attention away from self and one's seemingly hopeless, helpless condition and onto the everlasting God, the burnout victim can find strength renewed. By waiting on the Lord, he or she can find a constant supply of wisdom and strength from the God who faints not, who is never weary, and who Himself will never experience burnout!

Frank Minirth, *How to Beat Burnout*

August

AUGUST 1

Purifying Our Thought Life

Do not lust in your heart after her beauty . . .

PROVERBS 6:25

Most scientific advancements have involved man's imagination. Men "see" things before they do them. Inventors repeatedly tell of "seeing" a machine in their imagination long before they know how to build it. Inventors awaken in the middle of the night and write out solutions to problems they have "seen" in a dream. Men see solutions in the form of pictures and then work for years to materialize their visions. Men picture buildings in their minds and then set about making them a reality. There is something intriguing and mystifying about our ability to imagine things known and unknown. To God, that ability is sacred. He does not want it misused. And that is exactly why evil forces have an *intense* desire to see that ability misused. Our minds are the battleground; our imaginations are the trophy to be won.

If we use our imaginative power to visualize anything that represents lust or impurity, we are in *direct conflict* with God's will. Men enjoy using the power of imagination to create a multitude of images that God has forbidden. For example, when a man sees a woman who is attractive to him, he can disrobe her in his mind, bit by bit, until she is completely undressed. He then can use his imagination to feel what it would be like to touch her body. He can continue this mental activity until he has experienced every possible sexual act. He has taken God's special, holy gift and consumed it upon the altar of lust.

How do I know men do these things? First, I should confess that I engaged in such desecration of God's gift for much of my life. I continued doing this even after I became a Christian.

I have counseled with men by the hundreds on this subject, and invariably they confessed to having done the same thing most of their lives. . . .

Jesus taught us that there are sins so attractive and habit-forming that even if a man came back from the dead and warned us, we would not give them up!

No sin fits this category more clearly than that of immoral thinking.

Jesus explained, in a new way, a message God presented thoughout the Old Testament. He said: *Whosoever looketh on woman to lust after her hath committed adultery with her already in his heart.* (Matthew 5:28).

These are not the words of a wild-eyed radical. They need to be seriously considered by every Christian, yet I believe they have been glossed over. Men and women have thought that it would be impossible to eliminate lust in their hearts, therefore Jesus must have been saying that *everyone* has lust, so no one should fine fault with anyone else. I accepted this theory for most of my life, for it seemed an excellent way to handle my own moral dilemma. But now I know that Jesus is calling us to eradicate adultery from our hearts. This is what He says, and this is exactly what He means. The entire Bible is calling us to purify of heart and mind.

Merlin Carothers, What's On Your Mind?

AUGUST 2

The Common Man

The LORD turned to him and said, "Go in the strength you have and save Israel out of Midian's hand. Am I not sending you?"

"But Lord," Gideon asked, "how can I save Israel? My clan is the weakest in Manasseh, and I am the least in my family."

The LORD answered, "I will be with you, and you will strike down all the Midianites together."

JUDGES 6:14-16

In the Bible story of Gideon we are impressed by the fact that *the three hundred men who stood with him about the enemy camp with trumpet and pitcher in hand were common men—not professional soldiers in any sense.*

Some were tillers of the soil, others shepherds, and still others workmen in some trade. The world is filled with common men who go their quiet ways, turn the wheels of industry, produce crops, build our homes, and perform a multitude of everyday tasks. Geniuses are few and far between, only a few can be famous, and the rest of us must live our lives as just common people. We common folk are in the majority, which means that most of the work necessary to keep things going must be done by us.

Jesus honored the common man when He called the Twelve and assigned them an uncommon task. It is common people who found and maintain Christian homes, constitute the greater number of members of our churches, teach the thousands of Sunday School classes every Sunday, and, without fanfare, recognition, and sometimes without praise, carry on the indispensable work of the Kingdom of Heaven. This, no doubt, fairly expresses the experience of most of you. The work which engages your interest and claims your time as churchmen is purely a work of love. You devote yourself to it, and maintain your church, for the sole reason that you feel the Man of Galilee has called you to share His tender, unselfish ministry.

The joy of being His yoke-fellow, and the deep, abiding satisfaction in rendering a service to your fellow men is your reward. It is a high privilege we have.

J. C. Penney, *Lives of a Layman*

AUGUST 3
Going Higher

[Jesus] replied, "Because you have so little faith, I tell you the truth, if you have faith as small as a mustard seed, you can say to this mountain, 'Move from here to there' and it will move. Nothing will be impossible for you."

MATTHEW 17:20

In the early 1830s, my ancestors were brought on a boat across the Atlantic Ocean from Africa to America as slaves for men who felt they had the right to own other men.

In August of 1936, I boarded a boat to go back across the Atlantic Ocean to do battle with Adolf Hitler, a man who thought all other men should be slaves to him and his Aryan armies . . . a big part of Hitler's superiority idea was that his Nazis should rule not just because they were better and smarter, but because they were stronger and healthier. Though Hitler himself was short, dark, and anything but athletic-looking, he constantly talked of his "tall, blond, blue-eyed, Aryan supermen." Every newspaper was filled with his braggings of how the German Olympic team would prove him correct by "vanquishing the inferior Americans."

But when Hitler said "inferior Americans," he meant more than that. Our track and field squad—and the running and jumping events seemed to get more publicity than all the other sports put together—in 1936 happened to be made up mostly of Negro stars . . . We were everything Hitler hated. . . . But in particular Hitler hated my skin. For I happened to have been the one who had set world records in the 100- and 200-yard dashes less than a year before, and had been dubbed "the world's fastest human" because of it. Even more, I happened to have broken the world broad-jump record by more than half a foot. . . .

The day of the broad jump arrived. One by one, the other finalists fell by the wayside...But now it was my turn.

I took my time, measured my steps once, then again. I was tense, but that good kind of tense that you feel when you have to be tense to do your best. Deep, deep inside, under all the layers, there was a clear, placid pool of peace. . . . I didn't look at the end of the pit. I decided I wasn't going to come down. I was going to fly. I was going to stay up in the air forever.

I began my run . . . I went faster, precariously fast, using all my speed to its advantage. And then!

I hit the take-off board. Leaped up, up, up—

. . . My body was weightless . . . I surged with all I had but at the same time merely let it float . . . higher . . . higher . . . into the clouds . . .

I was coming back down! Back to earth.

I fought against it.

I kicked my legs.

I churned my arms.

I reached to the sky as I leaped for the farthest part of the ground.

The farthest—

I was on earth once again. I felt the dirt and the sand of the pit in my shoes and on my legs. Instinctively, I fell forward, my elbows digging in, the tremendous velocity of my jump forcing sand into my mouth.

It tasted good . . .

They measured.

I had done it. . . .

I had set a new Olympic record. I had jumped farther than any man on earth. . . .

Each new dawn, almost always without giving it a thought, you and I make the one choice on which every other choice is built. We choose to live. And all human lives, on the bottom line, are filled with the same tragedy and triumph, sorrow and joy, loss and love.

But as all of us strive to hold on to the gift, the challenge of life, each of us knows that someday our life on this earth will end. And it is no paradox that if you sincerely want to live, you simultaneously are prepared to die, if you must.

The key is belief.

This is what gives us our greatest, infinite joy. This is what makes the unbearable bearable.

The belief in that which is higher.

So, climb with me upon that summitless mountain. Go on higher, on, on higher.

Its cliffs are not paved with earthly matters—going higher, higher, and higher.

Climb not for the peak you see, but the one concealed to thee.

For true heaven lies infinitely, above the summit of the mountain.

Higher.

Higher.

Higher.

Amen.

Jesse Owens, *Jesse*

AUGUST 4

The Mystery of the Gospel

Pray also for me, that whenever I open my mouth, words may be given me so that I will fearlessly make known the mystery of the gospel, for which I am an ambassador in chains. Pray that I may declare it fearlessly, as I should.

EPHESIANS 6:19–20

To fight against the mystery of faith is foolish. The mystery of faith contains within it a reply all its own to the skeptical world it encounters. Bible-believing Christians cannot prove the existence of God by using the Bible, but neither can atheists answer all of their own questions. Which question is easier to answer, the mystery of the Trinity or the origin of the universe without God?

Once the atheist Robert Ingersoll met the great Congregational pastor Henry Ward Beecher. Ingersoll was renowned for his militant unbelief and his cutting debates with the pious, where he nearly always managed to "prove" there was no God. They once met in Beecher's study in Plymouth Church in Boston. A part of the decor of the study was a beautifully made celestial globe—an attractive piece of art, meticulously constructed. Ingersoll scrutinized it and said, "Henry, that's magnificent! Who made it?" The pastor answered with sparkling wit, "Why, Robert, nobody made it; it just happened."

Ingersoll and Beecher represent two poles, faith and anti-faith. Some, like Ingersoll, have a know-it-all attitude toward Christian mystery. But they cannot answer all questions satisfactorily. There are great questions about creation, destiny and meaning they can't answer. Neither can they answer many questions about personality, psyche or guilt. For such the universe itself is there, but without meaning.

Perhaps the major difference between Christians and skeptics is this: Christians accept the mysterious God and the universe is solved. Atheists deny God and must, therefore, live in a mysterious universe.

But the greatest barrier to skeptics' salvation is the failure of Christians to confront doubt with bold faith. We have kept the Christ in the crypt. The world is suspicious of all mention of God out of the proper Gothic context. Thus Jesus, like a medieval Bible, seems chained to the church.

St. Peter on his way into the city passed a cripple in a cranny of the city wall. In compassion and, more importantly, in the sunlight and fresh air of the outside world, he said to the man, "In the name of Jesus!" Today the cripple would say, "Please, not here . . . everyone is staring. Let's do it some other way—I'll meet you on Easter in church."

What happened that day was a thing of beauty. The lame man walked, even leaped. It all happened because the name of Jesus was spoken in courage to a hopeless soul.

Calvin Miller, *A Hunger for Meaning*

AUGUST 5
Little Rivers

Then he said to them, "Watch out! Be on your guard against all kinds of greed; a man's life does not consist in the abundance of his possessions."

LUKE 12:15

Little rivers have small responsibilities. They are not expected to bear huge navies on their breast or supply a hundred thousand horsepower to the factories of a large town. Neither do you come to them hoping to draw out Leviathan with a hook. It is good enough if they run a harmless, amiable course and keep the groves and fields green and fresh along their banks and offer a happy alternate of nimble rapids and quiet pools.

When you set out to explore one of these minor streams in your canoe, you have no intention of news-making discoveries or thrilling and world-famous adventures. You float placidly down the long still waters and make your way patiently through the tangle of fallen trees and carry your boat around the larger ones with no loftier ambition than to reach a good campground before dark and to pass the intervening hours pleasantly "without offense to God or man." It is an agreeable and advantageous frame of mind for one who has done his fair share of work in the world and is not inclined to grumble at his wages.

It is not required of every man . . . to be, or to do, something great; most of us must content ourselves with taking small parts in the chorus, as far as possible without discord. Shall we have no little lyrics because Homer and Dante have written epics? Even those who have greatness thrust upon them will do well to lay the burden down now and then and congratulate themselves that they are not altogether answerable for the conduct of the universe. "I reckon," said a cowboy to me one day, as we were riding through the Badlands of Dakota, "there's someone bigger than me running this outfit. He can tend to it well enough while I smoke my pipe after the round-up."

There is such a thing as taking ourselves and the world too seriously, or at any rate too anxiously. Half of the secular unrest and dismal sadness of modern society comes from the vain idea that every man is bound to be a critic of life and to let no day pass without finding some fault with the general order of things or projecting some plan for its improvement. And the other half comes from the greedy notion that a man's life does not consist, after all, in the abundance of the things that he possesses and that it is somehow or other more respectable and pious to be always at work making a larger living than it is to lie on your back in the green pastures and beside the still waters and thank God that you are alive.

And so I wish that your winter fire may burn clear and bright while you read these pages and that the summer days may be fair and the fish may rise willingly to your hook whenever you follow one of these little rivers.

Henry Drummond, *Who Owns the Mountains?*

AUGUST 6

Freedom from Racial Stereotype

There is neither Jew nor Greek, slave nor free, male nor female, for you are all one in Christ Jesus.

GALATIANS 3:28

Living under that negative stereotype that a "real" man went to a college (instead of a vocational school) placed upon me a heavy burden. When I finally graduated from high school, I tried a nearby junior college and didn't make it halfway through the first semester. I seemed bent on becoming what others told me I already was—a failure, someone who could never achieve or amount to much. I learned firsthand the sting and pain of having someone force their opinion on me and see it become a self-fulfilling prophecy.

Following my interrupted stint at college, I worked in a nearby factory. In my thirty-five-man work crew, I was the only white man. The first several weeks were extremely difficult. Through much tension and after much fighting, I was seeking to make a way for myself and to be accepted. Finally, Randy, a black man about thirty, took me under his wing. We became best of friends—I stayed at his house, ate with him, played with his children, and worked with him side by side. In both dangerous situations and fun times, we grew together.

When Randy introduced me to his larger circle of friends, I came to appreciate the great pain and difficulty these black men faced because of stereotypes foisted on them. We sat for hours talking about issues between whites and blacks and the injustices within our society. I struggled with their anger, their rhetoric, their strong positions. Because I was white, I was perceived as the one oppressing them and holding them down. It was as if I exercised all the power, while they had none.

That seemed like a stereotype too—that I was blamed for trying to hold them down. I was blamed for the injustice they experienced. I felt, at times, like I was put upon to solve their problems, to fix the political system that dealt so harshly with many minorities, to correct the economic disparities, and to help remove the barriers for advancement and employment. I was challenged time and time again with the statement "Whites simply don't care."

It didn't seem to matter that my mom had grown up in the inner city and was persecuted as a "minority" (my grandfather was an immigrant from Italy). It didn't matter that she had lived in poverty and had been forced to move eighteen times in the first ten years of her life—all because Grandpa had no job and no money to pay the rent. Was it a sin for me to be born white (as if I had some choice in the matter)?

Recently, in response to this question during a discussion at work on racial issues, a fellow staff member who is also an African American told me, "An M & M [candy] doesn't choose what color it's going to be." Simple words but true. His statement encouraged me and relieved much of my guilt and shame—feelings I had simply because I was white.

Many other whites are in need of that same release . . .

E. Glenn Wagner, from *We Stand Together*

August 7
Creative Thinking

Dear friends, this is now my second letter to you. I have written both of them as reminders to stimulate you to wholesome thinking.

II Peter 3:1

God has given us a marvelous ability to think original and creative thoughts, yet few of us spend enough time thinking. I believe that too many of us hurry through life with our minds preoccupied and overloaded with the cares of personal lives. We need to cultivate times to do creative thinking.

But creative thinking in solitude is difficult because it requires several important things:

Discipline. One must be willing to get alone and think on one subject without getting diverted because of self-defenses, negative thoughts, fantasies, and unconfessed guilt.

Courage. One must believe that there are solutions, answers, ideas, and concepts that are thinkable.

Hard work. Thinking creative thoughts doesn't just happen. It requires energy and a willingness to expend that energy on thought. Since it is easier in the short run to live with problems or poor designs, we tend to put off the expenditure of the energy it takes to think of good workable solutions.

Original thinking. One must believe that one can create whole new ideas where those ideas formerly did not exist. After an idea is developed people often say that the idea is simple and obvious. Fact is, it is obvious after it has been created. So the false impression is formed that new ideas are easy. Therefore most people think that hard, creative thought is unnecessary. However the one who did the original thinking knows just how hard it was and how hard it will be again.

Pen and paper. Without committing creative thought to paper one can easily lose the thought or the chain of thought. When it's on paper one can look at all of the alternatives and write out the expected results from each idea. It clarifies and objectifies the thought so that it isn't just fantasy or wasted daydreaming.

An action plan. I suppose I have spent thousands of hours in concentrated thought in my lifetime. I write out ideas, do calculations, design systems, write proposals, and create solutions to problems. Many of these thoughts never get shared because they aren't worthwhile. Some I try out on select people and go back to do more thinking. A few become solid and worth developing. When I develop an idea that I believe is sound, I not only think through what is to be done but also develop a complete plan for how it can be accomplished. This last step of developing an action plan helps one see the flaws and brings much reality to light regarding the idea.

The common activities that we use to fill our solitude are reading, praying, listening, or observing. These are all fine, positive, life-giving activities, but I would encourage you also to add more time to the creative act of thinking. Think about your own life and what you really would like to do, to make, to try, to change, and to develop. Think about your relationship with your family and the needs, opportunities, threats, and strengths that you have that require attention and creative solutions. Think about your church, your neighborhood, your support groups, and your world. And of course think about your work and the hundreds of opportunities for improvement in the quality and quantity of services or products you are producing.

It's generally in solitude that we drink from the deepest well of God's love, forgiveness, mercy, and grace. It is in the solitude of our minds that we can assemble our enormous capabilities to focus on a single person, an organization, or on a task. It is in solitude that we do most of our reading, thinking, and creating. It is in solitude that we learn from God to live a life of creativity, peace, and self discipline, which in turn ironically leads us to the full, rich life that Christ offers to us.

The choice is ours. We can use our solitude for self-indulgence, to berate others in the privacy of our minds, for character destruction. Or we can use our solitude as an opportunity to learn of God and be open to his voice. Solitude is, quite simply, an opportunity to choose to live more deeply and more fully.

Jim Carlson, *Choosing to Be Fully Alive*

AUGUST 8
Understanding the Brevity of Life

Moreover, when God gives any man wealth and possessions, and enables him to enjoy them, to accept his lot and be happy in his work—this is a gift of God. He seldom reflects on the days of his life, because God keeps him occupied with gladness of heart.

ECCLESIASTES 5:19–20

I go for long walks in the woods a lot, and I ask myself if I'm handling [all this success] the way it ought to be handled. I don't know why it happened to me. God has a purpose for it. We are able to contribute an awful lot of money to his work, and maybe that's why. But I firmly believe it will be over one of these days—five years from now, ten years from now. The books will stop selling for whatever reason. All this is temporary. . . .

One of my best friends in college died when he was twenty-five, just a few years after we had finished Mississippi State University. I was in law school, and he called me one day and wanted to get together. So we had lunch, and he told me that he had terminal cancer.

I couldn't believe it. I asked him, "What do you do when you realize that you are about to die?"

He said, "It's real simple. You get things right with God, and you spend as much time with those you love as you can. Then you settle up with everybody else."

That left an impression on me.

John Grisham, from an interview with Christianity Today

AUGUST 9

Commitment

Therefore, I urge you, brothers, in view of God's mercy, to offer your bodies as living sacrifices, holy and pleasing to God—this is your spiritual act of worship.

ROMANS 12:1

When the Spanish explorer Hernando Cortez landed at Vera Cruz, Mexico, in 1519, he was intent on conquest. To ensure the devotion of his men, Cortez set fire to his fleet of eleven ships. With no means of retreat Cortez's army had only one direction to move: into the Mexican interior. Cortez understood the price of commitment and he paid for it.

The apostle Paul also understood the price of dedication. After assuring us of our victory in Christ, he calls on us to burn our ships, bridges, or anything else that ties us to our destructive former life. Furthermore, he challenges us to commit ourselves completely to God: "Therefore, I urge you brothers in view of God's mercy to offer your bodies as living sacrifices, holy and pleasing to God. This is your reasonable act of worship." (Romans 12:1, my translation.)

Is Paul asking a lot? Yes! But he's not asking too much. He begins his exhortation with the word "therefore" because he wants to point us back to everything he's written in the previous eleven chapters. In those chapters he explained that God offers us forgiveness, acceptance, freedom from the dragon, a wonderful future, and the power needed for a victorious life. In light of all that, God wants our total devotion.

Earlier I mentioned that Paul found victory over his dragon through his relationship with Christ. To experience his victory, he had to be willing to devote himself completely to God.

It's important to realize that God will forgive and accept us whether or not we give our entire selves to Him. He extends His mercy without strings to all who believe (Ephesians 2:8,9).

But our refusal to devote ourselves to God short-circuits His power in our lives. As long as we cling to our addictive behavior, we alienate ourselves from the One who has the power to help us.

Bill Perkins, *Fatal Attractions*

AUGUST 10

Imitating a Good Father

Therefore I urge you to imitate me.

I CORINTHIANS 4:16

If you are one of the seventeen percent of this country's men who, as the Gallup poll suggests, characterizes his relationship with his father as negative, I would guess you are consciously trying hard not to pattern your life like your dad's. On some days you are pleased with your progress; other days you despair that you're caught in your father's web of inflicting pain on your kids. For some fathers, calling their dad's influence on them merely negative is putting it mildly; it's more accurate to say that their fathers ran them over, and the tread marks on their heart are proof. No pristine, solitary tracks of a tire in new snow, but the dark skid marks of more than one hit-and-run.

The images you carry of your father may have simply made you numb. You may have no feeling and little clarity about how your father imprinted you. You acknowledge the man as your father; but once you outgrew childhood, you made your own life. Your dad's fathering style, you believe, affects you neither one way or the other.

These very feelings belonged to a successful executive whom I visited. His father left him when he was eight. Yes, he has seen his dad a few times over the years, but he got the distinct impression that the relationship means little to his father. The imprint shows in the hurt he still feels from being abandoned. Yet this dad created a new pattern of fathering to overcome the pattern of abandonment his father left him with, a pattern more noticeable the more he speaks of his own children. He has aggressively poured himself into his son and daughter, taking delight in their activities and achievements.

Men floundering in deep fathering waters, with few or no models, are not alone. This decade is witnessing what may be the first generation of Americans in which a substantial number of dads have grown up without fathers in their homes. Two years after a divorce, one study shows, more than eighty percent of the noncustodial parents—generally the fathers—have little or no steady pattern of visitation with the children.

Men learn best how to be the father by watching and imitating a good one. The most important model, of course, is their own dad. Without a good dad to guide them—no matter how strong their desire to do a better job at fathering—boys usually grow up into fatherhood with much confusion.

So whether good, bad, or indifferent, your father has left his imprint on you. His presence or absence contributed to how you see yourself and how you perform a father's role. Recognizing and dealing with your father's imprint on you, particularly if it has been negative, is a prerequisite to acquiring the five key habits of smart dads.

Then, by accentuating the positive in your father's relationship with you and processing the negative, you unleash a power and freedom in you for shaping your own fresh fathering style.

Paul Lewis, *Five Key Habits of Smart Dads*

August 11

Afflictions

It was good for me to be afflicted
so that I might learn your decrees.

PSALM 119:71

Each person's relationship with God is a mystery, a mystery so deep we could never begin to fathom it. All we know for sure is that God is fashioning a masterpiece of unimaginable beauty way beneath what the human eye can see or the human mind can comprehend. Only in time as the plan begins to take shape will hints of what is taking place beneath the surface begin to emerge. I am sure each of us can see a pattern in the way He has been working in our lives, more so if we are older and have a better chance to view things from a distance. We can see the good coming out of the difficult and sometimes devastating experiences of our youth. I know I can. I went through a period of over ten years of the most intense depression in my older teen years until after my ordination. During that time I found it so difficult to feel there was a God. Not that I did not believe. My faith grew stronger than ever, but the darkness was almost impossible to bear, particularly since I had had such a warm relationship with God up until that point. Now I had to cling to God on sheer faith and in darkness and pain, even on the day of my ordination. Yet, those years were the most fruitful and productive years of my life spiritually, as God helped me grow in a deeper understanding of Himself and others, as well as myself. I do not think I would be capable of doing the work I do now if I had not gone through those experiences earlier in my life. What I learned then prepared me well for the future, although I doubt I would have the strength to endure that pain at this point in my life.

I do not think everyone would have to follow that route to God, but for me it was a necessity and it was effective. Others have radically different experiences depending on how God is molding them and where he is leading them. The important lesson is that each of us is unique and special and we must allow God the freedom to work in our souls in whatever way He pleases, knowing that He is an accomplished Master and will produce in us a masterpiece.

Joseph Girzone, Never Alone

Fellow Warriors

I went past the field of the sluggard,
  past the vineyard of the man who lacks judgment;
thorns had come up everywhere,
  the ground was covered with weeds,
  and the stone wall was in ruins.
I applied my heart to what I observed
  and learned a lesson from what I saw:
A little sleep, a little slumber,
  a little folding of the hands to rest—
and poverty will come on you like a bandit
  and scarcity like an armed man.

PROVERBS 24:30–34

Paul challenges all of us as men to finish the race and to be on our guard. Why does he do that? Because he knows that even if we've built a positive legacy to this point, there are wolves waiting at the door, ready to tear it from our grip and steal it away. He knows that we can lose our testimony, our counsel, and our influence as a role model *in a single unguarded moment.* What a frightening thought! One careless spilled bottle of black ink can seep through the pages of your entire life story. One drop of toxic selfishness can taint and poison the wellspring of your life. One moment of leaving the castle door unguarded can invite a cruel invasion.

That is Paul's sobering message to us. It's also Solomon's message.

Remember this little entry from his journal, recorded in the book of Proverbs?

I walked by the field of a certain lazy fellow and saw that it was overgrown with thorns, and covered with weeds; and its walls were broken down. Then, as I looked, I learned this lesson:

> A little extra sleep,
> a little more slumber,
> a little folding of the hands to rest

means that poverty will break in upon you suddenly like a robber, and violently like a bandit. (Proverbs 24:30–34, MTB)

Don't let anyone steal your legacy. Don't let anyone rob a lifetime of influence on your wife, your children, your friends, and your neighbors. Don't let moral poverty sneak up on you like a slinking wolf and rip away your witness for Jesus Christ. Guard your heart, man! Guard it with every ounce of energy you possess. Guard it in the limitless, fathomless, bottomless power of God's indwelling Spirit.

But don't stand guard alone.

You need some fellow warriors at your side. you need some buddies to watch your path. You need a few good men to pray for you, encourage you, teach you, walk with you, and remind you of what you already know. And by the way, there are some guys out there who need the same thing from you! A listening ear. A wise word. An arm around the shoulder. A brotherly nudge in the right direction.

That's the way it works. God equips each of us, and we equip each other. God strengthens each of us, and we strengthen each other. God warns each of us, and we warn each other. God encourages each of us, and we encourage each other.

Gary Rosberg, *Guard Your Heart*

AUGUST 13
A Kindred Soul

. . . the pleasantness of one's friend springs from his earnest counsel.

PROVERBS 27:9B

Friendship arises out of mere Companionship when two or more of the companions discover that they have in common some insight or interest or even taste which the others do not share and which, till that moment, each believed to be his own unique treasure (or burden). The typical expression of opening Friendship would be something like. "What? You too? I thought I was the only one." We can imagine that among those early hunters and warriors single individuals—one in a century? one in a thousand years?—saw what others did not; saw that the deer was beautiful as well as edible, that hunting was fun as well as necessary, dreamed that his gods might be not only powerful but holy. But as long as each of these percipient persons dies without finding a kindred soul, nothing (I suspect) will come of it; art or sport or spiritual religion will not be born. It is when two such persons discover one another, when, whether with immense difficulties and semi-articulate fumblings or with what would seem to us amazing and elliptical speed, they share their vision—it is then that Friendship is born. And instantly they stand together in immense solitude.

C. S. Lewis, The Four Loves

AUGUST 14

The Day and the Hour

You also must be ready, because the Son of Man will come at an hour when you do not expect him.

LUKE 12:40

Each morning remember that you may not live until evening; and in the evening, do not presume to promise yourself another day. Be ready at all times, and so live that death may never find you unprepared. Many die suddenly and unexpectedly; for at an hour that we do not know the Son of Man will come. When your last hour strikes, you will begin to think very differently of your past life, and grieve deeply that you have been so careless and remiss.

Happy and wise is he who endeavors to be during his life as he wishes to be found at his death. For these things will afford us sure hope of a happy death; perfect contempt of the world; fervent desire to grow in holiness; love of discipline; the patience of penance; ready obedience; self-denial; the bearing of every trial for the love of Christ. While you enjoy health, you can do much good; but when sickness comes, little can be done. Few are made better by sickness, and those who make frequent pilgrimages seldom acquire holiness by so doing.

Do not rely on friends and neighbors, and do not delay the salvation of your soul to some future date, for men will forget you sooner than you think. It is better to make timely provision and to acquire merit in this life, than to depend on the help of others. And if you have no care for your own soul, who will have care for you in time to come? The present time is most precious; now is the accepted time, now is the day of salvation. It is sad that you do not employ your time better, when you may win eternal life hereafter. The time will come when you will long for one day or one hour in which to amend; and who knows whether it will be granted?

Thomas à Kempis, *The Imitation of Christ*

AUGUST 15

Winning Souls

The fruit of the righteous is a tree of life,
and he who wins souls is wise.

PROVERBS 11:30

Nothing is more important than the salvation of one person, and we can have no greater significance than to be a witness.

While working as an engineer, I had my own encounter with this truth in what I now call the parable of the sunflower seed. I was acting as the lead engineer on an underwater fire control system. We had just built our first floor model, and I was assigned to get it up to specifications. I worked all day and most evenings, with a production engineer assigned to work with me on each shift.

The man who worked with me in the evenings was really no help at all. As I struggled late into the evening, he would sit and eat sunflower seeds. It was a most irritating habit, and it drove me nuts. As the hours increased, along with my fatigue, my tolerance to any distractions decreased. What's more, this man would call in sick more often than he seemed to be there. One night in sheer frustration, I asked him if he ever went to church. I was desperate for anything that would make him a better helper for me. Hardly the best motivation for good witnessing.

He said he didn't, but he and his wife had been thinking about it. I invited them to our church and was surprised when he and his wife came the following Sunday. Joanne and I escorted them to their proper Sunday School class and joined them later for the worship service.

The following Tuesday morning, I got a call from my pastor informing me that he had visited my co-worker and led him to Christ. I was overwhelmed with gratitude (and relief). My pastor also told me that my co-worker was an alcoholic! Suddenly, it all made sense. That was why he was absent so much. When my frustration factor had reached its limit, I finally did what I should have done from the beginning—be the witness that God had called me to be. That man's eternal life had far more value than the underwater fire control system I was working on, yet I had almost let that be more important.

I have had the privilege to be a pastor, seminary professor and now the founder of my own ministry, and I have determined that evangelism will always be on my front burner no matter what my place in life might be. There is no higher calling than evangelism. "He who wins souls is wise" (Prov. 11:30).

To this day, there is nothing more satisfying to me than leading someone to Christ or helping them find freedom in Him.

Neil Anderson, *Living Free in Christ*

AUGUST 16

Remembering God

Remember Jesus Christ, raised from the dead, descended from David.

II TIMOTHY 2:8A

When I was a teenager, I developed a case of severe acne on my chest. For more than a year, I kept medicated gauze on an open wound shaped like a rectangle, perhaps four by six inches in size. No one outside my family (except the doctor who was treating me) knew the secret that I kept hidden beneath my shirt. Before and after gym class, I changed quickly, facing the wall while I buttoned my shirt. I never showered at school.

I did whatever was required to keep my secret. And that task was far more meaningful to me than engaging in social opportunities. In every crowd, I was aware that I was hiding something that—if discovered—would set me apart as unusual, disfigured, hard to enjoy. I never relaxed enough to engage in community with the ease and naturalness I longed to experience.

Something similar happens to every man who keeps secrets, who lives to avoid exposure of that which he fears would mark him as an outsider. What he dreads comes upon him. He finds himself alone, isolated from the community he was designed to enter.

And it happens not only in community with people. It happens in relationship with God.

Grace makes it possible to stand unashamed in the presence of God. It restores the dream of belonging where one most wishes to belong. But men who keep secrets never realize that opportunity. Whatever their external posture might be, their inner man is always looking down, away from the possibility of contact with anyone's eyes, especially God's.

The effect is serious. Not only do secret-keepers feel that some part of them remains disengaged during routine conversations, but when the topic turns to spiritual things these men feel more like eavesdroppers than participants, like the kid pressing his face against the window of a closed candy store. They find little comfort in thoughts about God. Neither prayer nor Bible study connects with the hunger within them.

Forgetting God becomes a way of life, as natural and as necessary as breathing. Remembering God, thinking about him, speaking with others about him, feels stiff and forced. Sexual thoughts, or discussion about the last football game, connect far more powerfully with something deep inside. And keeping God out of our minds makes it easier to enjoy our secret sins.

Men with secrets do not remember God the way he wants to be remembered. They therefore fail to keep the memory alive or to pass it on to others.

Larry Crabb, *The Silence of Adam*

AUGUST 17

Holy Ground

"Do not come any closer," God said. "Take off your sandals, for the place where you are standing is holy ground."

EXODUS 3:5

Christian service means invading a battleground, not a playground; and you and I are the weapons God uses to attack and defeat the enemy. When God used Moses' rod, He needed Moses' hand to lift it. When God used David's sling, He needed David's hand to swing it. When God builds a ministry, He needs somebody's surrendered body to get the job done. *You are important to the Lord, so keep your life pure*: A holy minister [servant] is an awful weapon in the hand of God.

There is no substitute for Christian character. No matter how much talent and training we may have, if we don't have character, we don't have anything. . . .

Life is built on character, but character is built on decisions. The decisions you make, small and great, do to your life what the sculptor's chisel does to the block of marble. *You are shaping your life by your thoughts, attitudes, and actions and becoming either more or less like Jesus Christ.* The more you are like Christ, the more God can trust you with His blessing.

The person who cultivates integrity realizes that there can be no division between "secular and sacred" in the Christian life; everything must be done to the glory of God (1 Corinthians 10:31). God reminded two of his greatest leaders, Moses (Exodus 3:5) and Joshua (Joshua 5:15), that the servant of the Lord is *always* standing on holy ground and had better behave accordingly. If anybody else is watching, God is; and He will be our judge.

Warren Wiersbe, *On Being a Servant of God*

AUGUST 18

Green Pastures

He makes me lie down in green pastures,
he leads me beside quiet waters. . . .

PSALM 23:2

In the realm of his physical life David declared of God, "He makes me lie down in green pastures" (Ps, 23:2, NEB). When sheep lie down in green pastures it indicates that they have everything they need, that they are satisfied. We are the sheep of our heavenly Shepherd-Father. He lets us lie down in green pastures of restoration. Here David uses the language of faith to paint a picture of peace, an expression of God's goodness. Daily, you and I should make that same declaration.

Many people are prone to make negative declarations. They speak continually of how bad their business is, of how the economic situation is growing worse and worse. Those negative declarations, however, will not help them. By their negative declarations they bring a destructive power into their lives.

Instead of making negative declarations we must be determined to give affirmative confirmations—confessions of creation, victory, and abundance.

Envision yourself resting in the green pastures of your business or job, and watch how satisfied you will become. Feed this language of faith into your soul, visualizing God's daily provisions. Then, like David, sing out that you are satisfied every day in the green pastures of your life.

Paul Yonggi Cho, *Solving Life's Problems*

AUGUST 19
God at the Hub

He is before all things, and in him all things hold together.

COLOSSIANS 1:17

On my Honda Gold Wing motorcycle, power comes to the rear wheel through the hub. The hub at the center of the wheel receives the power and transmits it through the spokes to the rim. The wheel then moves. Think of our lives as that wheel. The hub is the center of our lives, what motivates and drives us. The spokes are the specific areas, such as our personality, character, and activities. The rim is the outer part of our lives that shows action. If our spokes aren't firmly connected to God at the hub of our lives, we won't move.

We may have action. The hub moves; the spokes may even flop around. But the rim doesn't move. Despite the activity, little is accomplished. However, when all the pieces of our lives are connected to God, we can have peace and harmony. Our lives may never slow down; we may not be able to escape the pace of life. But we can unify everything under Christ.

We're not torn in two directions, or even twenty, all at the same time. We go in one direction with God. We evaluate all activities out of a desire to please him. . . .

Anxiety over paying the mortgage doesn't possess our thoughts. We trust in God's promise to meet our needs when we put him first. We're not in constant fear over health issues. Either we die, which brings us directly to the love of our life, or we live and serve God here on earth. If our health improves, we're pleased; but if it doesn't, we know that God's power is made perfect in our weakness. Concern over government officials and school boards doesn't bring depression: what person can oppose what God truly wants done?

Instead of worrying or feeling rushed, we focus on pleasing him. By relying on God as the center of our lives, all the pieces of our existence connect. We have completeness. We have peace. We trust in God's love and power and yield personal responsibility for how things develop.

Tim Riter, *Deep Down*

AUGUST 20

Finding True Joy

The ransomed of the LORD will return.
  They will enter Zion with singing;
  everlasting joy will crown their heads.
Gladness and joy will overtake them,
  and sorrow and sighing will flee away.

ISAIAH 51:11

Among my patients and my friends, I've met few men who consider themselves to be having a joyful life. Many have lost the smile of a younger life. They are like Mitch, the sad central character in the movie *City Slickers*. Mitch (played by Billy Crystal) has a wonderful wife, two healthy children, a well-paying job, and two close friends, Ed and Phil. He is also discouraged, depressed, and hopeless. The three men have traveled around the world trying to find something to give them meaning and purpose in life. In fact, the movie begins with the trio in Pamplona, Spain, for the running of the bulls. They had thought that being chased by bulls might do the trick.

Later, Mitch throws one more birthday party, but Phil is depressed. Afterward, Mitch's wife, Barbara, says, "I just know you're not happy here, you're not happy at work."

Mitch pauses. "I just feel lost," he says. Barbara tells him not to go with the family to visit her folks in Florida. She encourages him to join Ed and Phil on a two-week cattle drive. "Go ahead and find your smile," she tells him.

"What if I can't?" he asks.

"We'll jump off that bridge when we come to it."

I've talked to hundreds of men who have lost their smiles. Some can't even remember the last time they had theirs. Oh, if they see a funny movie or hear a funny joke the corners of their mouth may turn up rather than down, and they probably laugh. But it doesn't last long. Like Mitch in *City Slickers* they have lost their joy, their intensity, their reason for living.

For some men the older we are the better we understand what true joy is. Joy comes from serving people. As we enjoy family and friends, we enjoy life, for the essence of living is people. If success is viewed in terms of growth and becoming conformed to Christ, then every man can be a success.

Success and joy are closely related. Success starts with who we are and what we are becoming. Successful men are those who express and experience the deep joy that comes from knowing we are becoming the kind of men God created us to become. The first step to becoming this kind of man is for us to choose to come home to God and to make an intimate, growing, love relationship with Christ a priority.

Gary Oliver, Real Men Have Feelings Too

AUGUST 21

The Body of Christ

. . . there should be no division in the body, but that its parts should have equal concern for each other. If one part suffers, every part suffers with it; if one part is honored, every part rejoices with it.

I CORINTHIANS 12:25–26

Because I am a surgeon and not a prophet, I tremble to make the analogy between cancer in the physical body and mutiny in the spiritual body of Christ. But I must. In His warnings to the church, Jesus Christ showed no concern about the shocks and bruises His Body would meet from external forces. "The gates of hell shall not prevail against my church," He said flatly (Matt. 16:18). He moved easily, unthreatened, among sinners and criminals. But He cried out against the kind of disloyalty that comes from within.

I must concentrate on how I, as an individual cell, should respond to the crying needs of the Body of Christ in other parts of the world. Beyond that, I cannot and should not make sweeping judgments about what the response of other Christians should be.

But I must say, from the perspective of a missionary who spent eighteen years in one of the poorest countries on earth, the contrasts in resources are astonishingly large. At Vellore we treated leprosy patients on three dollars per patient per year; yet we turned many away for lack of funds. Then we came to America where some churches were heatedly discussing their million-dollar gymnasiums and the cost of landscaping and fertilizer and a new steeple . . . and sponsoring seminars on tax shelters for members to conserve their accumulated wealth. As I saw those churches' budgets for foreign missions and for inner city work, I could not force a telling image from my mind—the memory of the Madras woman slowly starving to death while her lipoma grew plump and round.

The problem is not just an American problem or even a Western problem. I could easily point to examples of hoarding in every society I've seen: in the cruel Iks of Africa, in Soviet Russia, in the disparity within the Christian community in India. The warning applies to all of us. My only message is the caution of a doctor: remember, the body will have health only if each cell regards the needs of the whole body.

Paul Brand and Philip Yancey, Fearfully and Wonderfully Made

AUGUST 22

Environmental Stewardship

His master replied, "Well done, good and faithful servant! You have been faithful with a few things; I will put you in charge of many things. Come and share your master's happiness!"

MATTHEW 25:23

Creation is a trust from God. When Christ returns, He will ask what we have done with it. He will want to know if we watered it, nurtured it, and encouraged its fruitfulness, or if we abused it, forsook it, and ignored its needs.

God expects us to take what He has given us and do more than just return it to Him the way we received it. He expects us to care for His creation, to bless it, and to make it more fruitful. He expects us to be faithful servants who attend to His creation.

One day, God will call us before His judgment seat, and we can be certain that He will ask us to give an account of what we have done to the world which He has entrusted into our hands (Matthew 25:14–30).

A preacher once made a call on one of his neighbors, a farmer who, sad to say, had never had much time for the church.

The preacher found his neighbor out in his fields checking on the wheat growing there. Trying to get the farmer talking on religious things, the preacher said, "That's a fine field of wheat you and the Lord are growing together!"

There was no response from the farmer who acted as though the preacher wasn't even there. So the preacher let his well-chosen words fly a second time. "That's a fine field of wheat you and the Lord are growing together!"

Still there was no response. The old farmer acted as though he hadn't heard a thing.

But when the preacher made the same pronouncement a third time, the old farmer answered, "You should have seen this field last year when the Lord had it all to Himself."

Both the farmer and the preacher have truth to give us. The preacher was right to remind the farmer that all he ever could hope to accomplish would be because of a partnership with God. The farmer might till the soil and plant the seed, but God makes the rain fall, the sun shine, and the wheat grow. On the other hand, the farmer was right to acknowledge that without the proper development, the land would not produce much and indeed would be little more than a field overgrown with weeds. Faithful stewardship requires that we take what God places in our hands, especially His creation, and care for it as a faithful service to Him.

Tony Campolo, *How to Rescue the Earth*

AUGUST 23

Aging with Grace

When I was a child, I talked like a child, I thought like a child, I reasoned like a child. When I became a man, I put childish ways behind me.

I CORINTHIANS 13: 11

The pressure of time running out brings the facts of life into a brutal clash with the fantasies a man has had since youth or young manhood.

"Someday" he was to become king of this or that; "someday" he was to be a millionaire, a sports hero, an actor or poet or singer or writer; "someday" he was going to be a great lover. "Someday" he was going to be—as my oldest daughter often says—"rich and famous." But suddenly *now* is upon him. He's reached mid-life—and he begins to realize that the future is here, that all he is ever going to achieve must happen now. It's got to be by forty or at least forty-five.

His young-adult dreams and fantasies are confronted with the reality that he has a job, but he is never going to become boss or the president. He has a house in the suburbs, but he is never really going to be a millionaire. He can watch a lot of football on Sunday afternoon, but he is never really going to be a professional quarterback. He may have actually reached the top in his work and arrived at his goals, but he still isn't as happy as he thought he'd be. He comes for the first time to face the facts of his life and compare them to the fantasies that have motivated him over the past twenty years. . . .

It is this very comparison of dreams versus the demonstrated accomplishments of life that causes men in the mid-life crisis to experience depression. Only as a man can successfully face the facts of who he is and what he can do will he be able to graciously move to the next era in life.

Jim Conway, *Men in Mid-Life Crisis*

AUGUST 24

God Room

Jesus looked at them and said, "With man this is impossible, but not with God; all things are possible with God."

MARK 10:27

While traveling with Bob [Pierce, founder of World Vision], I learned many of life's lessons. But the lesson Bob taught me that stands out above all else is what Bob called "God room."

"What do you mean?" I asked him once when he started talking about "God room." He gave me a glance that was close to disgust, almost as if to say, "Don't you know?" He took a deep breath and sighed before he said, "'God room' is when you see a need and it's bigger than your human abilities to meet it. But you accept the challenge. You trust God to bring in the finances and the materials to meet that need.

"You get together with your staff, your prayer partners, and supporters, and you pray. But after all is said and done, you can only raise a portion of the resources required.

"Then you begin to watch God work. Before you know it, the need is met. At the same time, you understand you didn't do it. God did it. You allowed Him room to work."

Bob was on one of his many rolls. His eyes sparkled and the words tumbled out: "Many times I went to places like Vietnam, where I'd see people who needed help. I would commit a hundred thousand dollars for the project. Then I'd go home, knowing that Samaritan's Purse didn't have the money. I certainly didn't have the money. But I believed that through praying and trusting God, He would provide.

"You know, Franklin, you always have to have 'God room'!"

I stopped him and asked, "Does this always work? I'm not sure I've got that kind of faith."

Again he flashed a look that seemed to say, "Aren't you listening? . . . "

"You see, Franklin," Bob continued, "faith isn't required as long as you set your goal only as high as the most intelligent, most informed, and expert human efforts can reach."

Bob illustrated what he meant by telling me of a church in the United States that had set a goal to raise one hundred thousand dollars to refurbish the church. The church leaders appealed to the congregation and collected seventy-five thousand. They still needed twenty-five. So what did they do?

"They formed a committee, and members of that committee visited each church member and encouraged them to give more so they could meet their obligation. And they met it. Okay, that's what human strategy and planning can do. Nothing wrong with that, Buddy, but just don't call it faith."

"They reached their goal, didn't they? Wasn't that faith?" I asked.

"Naw, that's just good sense at work. Now, here's how faith works." He told me about another church, which outgrew its building and needed to enlarge. Members pledged two hundred thousand dollars for the expansion.

"About that time, a missionary couple from India came home on furlough and worshipped with the congregation. They told about the hellhole of Calcutta. The people could hardly believe what they heard. The couple never asked for anything, just shared the needs of the homeless, starving children they were trying to care for.

"You know what, Buddy? The board of the church got so involved with that vision, they voted to take the entire two hundred thousand dollars and give it to the missionaries for their work." (Later on I learned that this church became one of the fastest growing congregations in the United States and completed several building programs.)

"Their giving the money to the missionaries—that was faith." Then Bob got to his point: "That's where 'God room' comes in. Nothing is a miracle until it reaches the area where the utmost that human effort can do still isn't enough. God has to fill that space—that room—between what's possible and what He wants done that's impossible. That's what I mean by 'God room.'"

Franklin Graham, Rebel with A Cause

AUGUST 25

A Reason for the Hope

But in your hearts set apart Christ as Lord. Always be prepared to give an answer to everyone who asks you to give the reason for the hope that you have. But do this with gentleness and respect. . . .

I PETER 3:15

Unfortunately, when Christians switch from talking about football to talking about Christ, they often kick into a "religious twang" or a "stained-glass voice." It doesn't help. Sometimes they flip their argument switch when the subject touches religion, as though evangelism were an intellectual wrestling match. We argue as though Jesus needed defending. We do it, I think, because our ego is at stake, and we must engage and defeat the adversary at all costs. We wind up shooting ourselves in the foot.

Generally speaking, a highly argumentative nonbeliever isn't anywhere near the Cross. Entering into heated debates with him will drive him further away. Gently tell such a one to go, sell all he has, and give it to the poor. If he sticks around and persists in debate, tell him, "I know how you feel, but isn't it wonderful that God loves you and has a plan for your life?" Watch him melt.

There is a basic principle of communication interwoven in this discussion. The louder the noise, the weaker the argument. That's why a confident, gentle spirit can be so powerful. It exasperates the opposition. Your opponent wants you to join him in the shout and shove match. Don't! You both lose. . . . The supernatural wardrobe of a "meek and quiet spirit" can do what nothing else can.

Joseph Aldrich, *Gentle Persuasion*

AUGUST 26

The Lion and the Lamb

Then one of the elders said to me, "Do not weep! See, the Lion of the tribe of Judah, the Root of David, has triumphed. He is able to open the scroll and its seven seals."

Then I saw a Lamb, looking as if it had been slain, standing in the center of the throne, encircled by the four living creatures and the elders.

REVELATION 5:5–6A

Our richest model of manhood is Jesus Christ. More than any other man, Jesus demonstrated perfect balance in what I call "the duplex nature of a man," the perfect pattern of holistic masculinity.

One absolute prerequisite to the celebration of manhood is that there must be a *lion and a lamb* in every man. David was both poet and warrior, shepherd and general, priest and king. Jesus Christ was both God and man, lion and lamb. The art is to have both and to know when to be which.

There are some things that Christ did as a lion that He could not do as a lamb. There are also some things that He did as a lamb that He could not do as a lion. If Jesus had roared on the cross as the Lion of Judah, He would have been weak. His strength in that situation was rooted in His identity as the sacrificial Lamb of God Who was to take away the sins of the world by giving Himself up to death—the Innocent taking the blame for the guilty.

Yet, when Jesus comes again, if He whimpers as a meek Lamb, He won't fulfill His destiny as the supreme King of kings and Lord of lords, Whose name is above every name! The sacrificial Lamb of God will return as the triumphant Lion of Judah!

Similarly, there must be a tightrope within every man, a dichotomy of two completely different natures. One is so lamblike, vulnerable, fragile, and meek that we are willing to lie down so others can nail us to a cross. At the same time, there is another part of us that roars like a lion, that comes alive in a fight, that is mighty in battle. True men can't be ashamed of either side of their nature. We just have to hold them in tension. The true definition of meekness is strength under control. We can only celebrate masculinity after we recognize and walk in that duplex nature within us.

Man of God, you must walk a tightrope between being a lion and a lamb, and only the Holy Ghost can give you true balance in that walk.

T. D. Jakes, *Loose That Man and Let Him Go!*

AUGUST 27
Godly Dreaming

He fulfills the desires of those who hear him;
  he hears their cry and saves them.

PSALM 145:19

The secret of accomplishment lies in goals that are big enough. Let yourself go! Allow your imagination to run wild. Courageously dream great dreams. Think creatively into the distant future. What do you *really* want to do and become in the Lord? Do you believe He is able to achieve it?

Imagination is the cornerstone of achievement. Most of us do not experience great fruitfulness because we have not cultivated our ability to dream purposefully. We live merely coping with the endless specifics of life, rather than standing back to examine the pattern into which they fit. Setting goals channels our imaginations and dreams into definite and directed paths. Focusing the imagination in a pre-set direction ensures that actions will follow.

Christians are often reluctant to dream. They misunderstand the paradox that while God is sovereign, He has yet given men freedom to develop gifts and talents and to use them creatively—God often expects us to take a large share of the initiative in getting things done. There is no desire God has placed into a human heart for which He has not also provided the means to accomplish it.

Mike Phillips, *Getting More Done in Less Time and Having More Fun Doing It!*

August 28
Hope

Why are you downcast, O my soul?
Why so disturbed within me?
Put your hope in God,
for I will yet praise him,
my Savior . . .

PSALM 42:5

Recently I heard someone say another person was hopeless. Something inside of me cried out, That's not right. To my mind the most profane word in the English language is not a four-letter word, but the word "hopeless." To say a person is hopeless, or a situation is hopeless, is a direct denial of the power of God. In Psalm 42:5, we read this powerful statement: "Hope thou in God."

No man can live long without hope. Psychiatrists have discovered no matter how deeply a person is depressed, no matter how despondent, if somehow they can inject a ray of hope in a person's mind, he will begin to recover. There was a time in my life when some people said, "There's no hope for him." They were talking about me. But because Jesus Christ is alive, I still held onto hope. I refused to believe them. And now I am the useful pastor of a great, growing church.

Many a person in our society today feels hopeless for one reason or another. Never before in the history of the world have people been so beaten psychologically. It is our unwavering belief that in Jesus Christ we have hope that all failure, all sins are forgiven. Now that biblical word *hope* is not something you wish for or dream of, but it is the assurance of the fact that God keeps his word.

God promises us that if we confess our sins, he is faithful and just to forgive us our sins. Good news: No one has to be beaten down by his sins another day. If you are beaten by your sins, your failures, confess them all to God and he will forgive you for every wrongdoing. I have never yet met a person who is hopeless. If you are alive, there is hope—there is Jesus!

If I could give to a man only one thing, I would give him hope. The kind of hope the Psalmist wrote about when he said: "For in thee, O Lord, do I

276 · PROMISES TO KEEP

hope" (Psalm 38:15). Hope in God is the only firm basis for achieving worthwhile aspirations.

Dale Galloway, *Rebuild Your Life*

AUGUST 29

Healing from Betrayal

All a man's ways seem innocent to him,
  but motives are weighed by the LORD.

PROVERBS 16:2

Several years ago I was betrayed by a friend and business associate. This betrayal caused a great deal of pain and harm to me and others. My friend's actions produced one of the greatest wounds in my life and jeopardized a lifetime of work and diligence on my part. At the time I plunged into depression, fear, shame, and worry. I doubted my ability to continue my work and seriously considered selling everything I owned, taking my wife and children to a remote part of the country, and finding some other way to support my family.

As you can imagine, I am not fun to be around when I am in that state of mind. I live on the verge of making bad decisions that could affect the rest of my life. I am tense and cannot sleep. Sadly, the people I love feel the impact of turmoil within me. During times like these my only solution is to turn to God and to other men. Just as David needed Jonathan, I need men who are deeply committed to me and will stand by me—men who will help me work through my fear and worry and help me grow into a different spiritual, emotional, and physical state.

I was fortunate to have had two friends who stayed close beside me throughout that horrible time. These men had every reason to abandon me, for my depression was deep and my feelings of shame were strong; but they stuck with me through the trouble, affirming me, encouraging me and strengthening me. They helped to set realistic boundaries with the friend who had betrayed me, identify the limits of my responsibility, and enabled me to see how I had overlooked my friend's dark side. As these two friends walked with me, the bond between us grew stronger, and God's ministry of grace became more real to me.

Earl Henslin, *Man to Man*

Racial Reconciliation

For he himself is our peace, who has made the two one and has destroyed the barrier, the dividing wall of hostility. . . .

EPHESIANS 2:14

Reconciliation involves more than just getting whites and blacks to live and work side-by-side. It means accepting each other as human beings made in the image of God. It also involves an active concern for the welfare of each other.

The place to begin is with vulnerability. If folks from different races really want to communicate with each other, they've got to be honest and genuine. Blacks, for example, often need to take the initiative to ask questions, to discuss issues, to show concern. Perhaps the habit of deferring to whites has made us afraid to speak up. As a result, we too often hang back and appear silent or disinterested. I recall how the death of Martin Luther King prompted me to start making myself heard and known at [college]. Once I did, I found a whole new set of relationships with the white students. We got into some great discussions in which a lot of misinformation and misunderstandings got cleared up and new ideas got formed.

Whites, on the other hand, often seem to float right by black people as if they don't exist or don't matter. Perhaps they're afraid of getting involved or getting hurt. But reconciliation can't occur unless we risk ourselves with others.

Another way to break down barriers is to develop common meeting places. This has already happened through the public schools. But one place it hasn't happened very much is in the church. By and large we still have segregated churches. For that matter, we still have segregated communities. As a result, we're not around persons from other races and backgrounds enough to know what life is like for them. It's easy to ignore them—and to misunderstand them. At Mendenhall Bible Church we have a predominantly black congregation. But there are few whites, plus frequent white visitors. That has helped all of us to get to know each other in a way that respects racial differences yet overlooks them enough to treat each other as people with dignity.

I remember preaching once in one of the largest churches in California. My theme was loving your neighbor. Afterward, a white woman came up to meet me. She was blind. "I want to give my life to Christ as a result of what you said today," she explained. I learned that she had spent most of her life in Mississippi. Yet here she was in California, asking for spiritual help from a black man! I felt stunned. God had brought us both thousands of miles in order to "cross the tracks" and talk! She was reconciled to God that day. And I took a giant step forward in my own reconciliation toward Southern whites. . . .

Dolphus Weary, *I Ain't Coming Back*

AUGUST 31
Remaining Faithful

Wine is a mocker and beer a brawler;
  whoever is led astray by them is not wise.

PROVERBS 20:1

Ernest Hemingway's parents came from a strong Christian lineage in Oak Park, Illinois. His paternal grandfather served the YMCA as general secretary and developed a lasting friendship with evangelist Dwight L. Moody. Ernest's uncle worked overseas as a missionary physician in China. Hemingway's father, Dr. C. E. Hemingway, practiced medicine. Along with his wife, Grace, Dr. Hemingway demanded strict obedience to the Christian faith. To give the Hemingway children a lasting impression of the consequences of sin, they carted them off to visit the state prison. There the children could see and feel the harshness of iron bars and barbed wire.

As an adolescent, Ernest read every word of the King James Bible to win a Bible-reading contest. At fourteen, he played the lead role in a Sunday school play at the Third Congregational Church of Oak Park. But near the end of his life he said, "I live in a vacuum that is as lonely as a radio tube when the batteries are dead and there is no current to plug into." Somewhere between early adulthood and the Sunday in 1961 when he blew his brains out in the Sawtooth Mountains of Idaho, he rejected the Christianity of his parents. Instead, Hemingway embraced an all-out pursuit of adventure, hunting, fishing, eating, and drinking with friends—anything that would bring pleasure. He measured life with what he experienced, what he absorbed. Eventually the glass from which he drank consumed him. . . .

Ernest Hemingway was selfish. If he had exchanged his selfish pursuits for a heart large enough to embrace others, the vacuum tubes in his radio would never have gone cold.

Larry Kreider, Bottom-Line Faith

September

SEPTEMBER 1

A Purpose for All Things

. . . for it is God who works in you to will and to act according to his good purpose.

PHILIPPIANS 2:13

I can remember when I wanted to be accepted more than anything else. I wanted so much to be popular and have all the things that money could buy. I wanted to be liked by the "right" people, invited to all the "right" parties, belong to all the "right" clubs, and so on. Yet no matter how many parties I attended, no matter how many clubs I joined, and no matter how many other accomplishments I realized, there never seemed to be any real satisfaction. I knew there had to be more to life. I just didn't know what the "more" was.

This feeling continued for a long time—long after I was married, had three children, and owned my own business. Then one day doctors told my wife and me that our ten-year-old son, Craig, would be blind within two weeks. There was no logical explanation for this tragedy. He hadn't been sick. Something just went wrong inside his little body and his optical nerve began to die. The doctors told us there are only 105 cases of this particular disorder recorded in medical history—our son is one of them. We took him to other doctors, refusing to accept this unwelcome news. But everywhere we went, the answer was the same: There was no hope.

My perspective on life changed suddenly and drastically. I found myself . . . wondering why I even tried. Like Solomon, I wondered if it was all useless. It seemed as though no matter how hard I tried or how much

I struggled, the bottom always dropped out eventually. And I felt it had been that way all my life.

I recalled my earlier, more athletic, days when I occasionally got the breath knocked out of me. I wanted to get up off the ground. I wanted to move. But I couldn't—at least not until I caught my breath again. As I watched my little son slowly lose his eyesight, I felt that way again. I felt emotionally paralyzed, unable to "catch my breath." The money I had, the clubs I belonged to, the people I knew could not help. I felt helpless and without hope. During this time I searched for God and wondered where His goodness and mercy were—the same goodness and mercy that are supposed to "follow me all the days of my life." I needed help, and I felt God was off doing something for someone else.

If you read between the lines here, you will see that I thought I knew the aspects of God's character—those aspects *I* thought He should reveal to me. But God knew better. He waited patiently while I floundered in desperation and until I'd reached the point where I realized I could no longer handle the situation on my own. I finally stopped wondering where God was and stopped trying to control God and what I thought He should be doing for me. Instead, I began allowing God to control me, and I began making a concerted effort to live the way I thought He would want me to live. When I did that, I began to see other aspects of God's character that I had not seen before.

For example, God knows what we need to go through in order to prepare us for things we will encounter later in life (I learned this through hindsight). He also knows what we're capable of enduring. *He will never allow us to go through something beyond our endurance.* God has a plan for all of our lives and a *purpose* for everything that happens to us along the way to fulfilling that plan.

Lewis Timberlake, *It's Always Too Soon to Quit*

SEPTEMBER 2

Self-Acceptance

... *love your neighbor as yourself.*

LEVITICUS 19:18B

For much of my life, I saw myself as a complete failure. I tried to live up to other people's standards, and I could not do it. I desperately wanted to be better, smarter, funnier. Here and there, people tried to build me up, but it didn't work. I had no hook on which to hang their encouragement.

If only a friend could crawl inside my skin and be there with me—then I might be able to hear. It's great for all those people to show up and tell George Bailey [from the movie *It's A Wonderful Life*] how terrific a guy he is, but even that won't work unless there's someone *on the inside*. George needs *George* to affirm him, or at least to accept the affirmations of others. And I, in my attempt to earn the favor of others, came to a dead end. I got some positive feedback, but it didn't count. I wanted more. I needed more. I had a Teflon self-image—nothing stuck. It was like trying to store a computer document in a directory that does not exist. You have to create the directory first. It was like trying to deposit money in an account that hasn't been opened. There's nowhere to put it.

I needed to be my own friend. I needed to muster the courage to accept myself, with all my strengths and weaknesses, to give *myself* the affirmation I needed.

Becoming your own best friend does not mean shutting out the rest of the world, or the rest of your friends. It does mean establishing that core self, that germ of self-acceptance that can begin to grow within you. Once you get a friend "on the inside"—yourself—you can replay *It's A Wonderful Life* whenever you need to. You can call up all the affirmations you need from that computer directory marked "Self-Esteem."

It was only when I began to treat myself as my own best friend that I began to be comfortable in relationships with others. My friendships were deepened and energized by my self-acceptance. Certainly, there have been times when life has been especially *un*wonderful, but friends help friends get through such times. And if you are your own friend, it will be much, much easier.

Thomas Whiteman, *Becoming Your Own Best Friend*

Overcoming Procrastination

If a man is lazy, the rafters sag;
  if his hands are idle, the house leaks.

ECCLESIASTES 10:18

Men, it may be a hard pill to swallow, but laziness is a learned activity. Even for committed procrastinators, however, there is hope. Without exception, the men we've seen in counseling who struggle with a lack of motivation *are not in small groups.* But we've seen time and time again that when men finally join a healthy group, things begin to change. Why? Because of that same, powerful one-two punch of loving support and healthy accountability that brings things in the darkness into the light—and works equally well on both of them.

Waiting on an unmotivated, undisciplined man to follow through is one of the most frustrating things a wife can experience. And what often happens is that when such a man gets convicted and starts to take some small steps toward responsibility, the wife is so angry by then that she criticizes his baby steps, hindering any attempts he makes to walk!

The positive atmosphere of a small group provides the antidote to this extremely hurtful problem. The man gets the support and encouragement from the group to take those first steps toward change, and he receives applause when he takes them. The wife gets the support and accountability to hang in there with him, to talk about frustration, and even to learn to encourage his efforts, which can then lead to greater successes.

We live in a hostile world. Most of us don't have a week go by in which we're not blasted, bounced, or criticized by someone. But what a breath of fresh air it is to know there's a rest stop in your week, surrounded by the positive elements of a small group!

Gary Smalley and John Trent, *The Hidden Value of a Man*

SEPTEMBER 4
Being His Witness

But you will receive power when the Holy Spirit comes on you; and you will be my witnesses in Jerusalem and in all Judea and Samaria, and to the ends of the earth.

ACTS 1:8

The kingdom of God is real. At this very moment Jesus sits in the seat of cosmic authority. He is now the supreme ruler of the world. He stands over the governments of this world. He is King. . . . The Dalai Lama of Tibet must answer to Him. The Prince of Morocco must answer to Him. The President of the United States must answer to Him. But there is one big problem. His kingdom is *invisible*. Not everyone knows about it. All over the world people are living as if Jesus were not King.

Some people believe that there is no God. Others say that there are many gods. Some folks believe that man is supreme. Others believe that man is worthless. Many people believe there is a God, but they live as if there were no God. Still others ask, "What difference does it make?"

Where Christ is invisible, people perish. Where His reign is unknown or ignored, people are exploited. They are demeaned. They are enslaved. They are butchered. They are aborted. They are raped. They are casualties of war. They are robbed. They are slandered. They are oppressed. They are cheated in marriage. They are cheated in their wages. They are left to go hungry, naked, and unsheltered. They are consigned to loneliness. They are ridiculed. They are frightened—that and a whole lot more, is what difference it makes.

In all of life's situations we are to be His witnesses. Our job is to *make the invisible reign of Jesus visible*. The world is shrouded in darkness. Nothing is visible in the dark. No wonder then that we are called to be the light of the world. Every single one of us has a mission. We have all been sent to bear witness to Christ. That means simply that we are all missionaries.

R. C. Sproul, Lifeviews

September 5
Doing Good

Let your light shine before men, that they may see your good deeds and praise your Father in heaven.

MATTHEW 5:16

> Do all the good you can,
> By all the means you can,
> In all the ways you can,
> In all the places you can,
> At all the times you can,
> To all the people you can,
> As long as ever you can.

JOHN WESLEY, selected

September 6
Doing for Others

Do nothing out of selfish ambition or vain conceit, but in humility consider others better than yourselves.

PHILIPPIANS 2:3

As head football coach of the University of Colorado Buffaloes, I have an intense desire to beat our arch-rival, Nebraska, every time we play them. Unfortunately, when we were facing them in 1991, we had not won when we played in Lincoln for twenty-three years. So, on Thursday night before the Nebraska game on Friday, I had the team come together in one room and I explained to our guys that I had heard somewhere that we spend 86 percent of our time thinking about ourselves and 14 percent thinking about others. I then told them that if you could ever get a guy to stop thinking about himself and start thinking about others, there's a whole new energy source available to him. With that in mind, I said, "Men, I've ordered sixty footballs and we're going to put the final score of Saturday's game on these balls. On Monday, we're going to send each ball to a person you've designated in advance. Here's what I'm asking you to do. By midnight tonight, Thursday night, I'm requiring any guy who wants to get on that airplane to Nebraska to dedicate this game to somebody other than himself. I want you to call that person and tell him (or her) that he ought to watch you on every play. If he can't be at the game, then tell him to watch it on television. Tell him you are going to show how much you love him, that you're going to play with all your heart, and you're playing this game for him. It might be your mom or dad. I want you to call tonight. Then, I want you to demonstrate that love on Saturday."

Do you remember what happened in that game? The Colorado Buffaloes broke a twenty-three year losing streak in Lincoln and won the game 27–12.

Christian men all over our nation and around the world are suffering because they feel they are on a losing streak and they can't break the pattern. The Adversary has us where he wants us—feeling defeated. It need not be that way.

Bill McCartney, What Makes a Man?

September 7
God Using Ordinary Men

When they saw the courage of Peter and John and realized that they were unschooled, ordinary men, they were astonished and they took note that these men had been with Jesus.

Acts 4:13

In a worldly point of view the Disciples were a very insignificant company indeed—a band of poor illiterate Galilean provincials, utterly devoid of social consequence, not likely to be chosen by one having supreme regard to prudential considerations.

Why did Jesus choose such men? Was He guided by feelings of antagonism to those possessing social advantages, or of partiality for men of His own class? No; His choice was made in true wisdom.

If He chose Galileans mainly, it was not from provincial prejudice against those of the south; if, as some think, He chose two or even four of his own kindred, it was not from nepotism; if He chose rude, unlearned, humble men, it was not because He was animated by any petty jealousy of knowledge, culture, or good birth.

If any rabbi, rich man, or ruler had been willing to yield himself unreservedly to the service of the kingdom, no objection would have been taken to him on account of his acquirements, possessions, or titles.

The case of Saul of Tarsus, the pupil of Gamaliel, proves the truth of this statement. Even Gamaliel himself would not have been objected to, could he have stooped to become a disciple of the unlearned Nazarene. But, alas! neither he nor any of his order would condescend so far, and therefore the despised One did not get an opportunity of showing His willingness to accept as disciples and choose for apostles such as they were.

The truth is, that Jesus was obliged to be content with fishermen, and publicans, and quondam zealots, for apostles. They were the best that could be had.

Those who deemed themselves better were too proud to become disciples, and thereby they excluded themselves from what all the world now sees to be the high honor of being the chosen princes of the kingdom. The civil and religious aristocracy boasted of their unbelief.

The citizens of Jerusalem did feel for a moment interested in the zealous youth who had purged the temple with a whip of small cords; but their faith was superficial, and their attitude patronizing, and therefore Jesus did not commit Himself unto them, because He knew what was in them.

A few of good position were sincere sympathizers, but they were not so decided in their attachment as to be eligible for apostles. Nicodemus was barely able to speak a timid apologetic word in Christ's behalf, and Joseph of Arimathea was a disciple "secretly," for fear of the Jews. These were hardly the persons to send forth as missionaries of the cross—men so fettered by social ties and party connections, and so enslaved by the fear of man. The apostles of Christianity must be made of sterner stuff.

And so Jesus was obliged to fall back on the rustic, but simple, sincere, and energetic men of Galilee. And He was quite content with His choice, and devoutly thanked His Father for giving Him even such as they. Learning, rank, wealth, refinement, freely given up to His service, He would not have despised; but He preferred devoted men who had none of these advantages to undevoted men who had them all.

A. B. Bruce, *The Training of the Twelve*

Never Forsaking Us

No one will be able to stand up against you all the days of your life. As I was with Moses, so I will be with you; I will never leave you nor forsake you.

JOSHUA 1:5

Never has there been a greater model for friendship than Jesus Christ. Jesus was always there when He was needed. Strong, stable, caring, He touched everyone He met at his or her own private level of need—the woman at the well, Nicodemus, Zaccheus, the woman taken in adultery, the disciples with all their confused, misguided thinking. There was even a special word to the rich young ruler. To those who suffered physical affliction Jesus not only spoke but also healed. Jesus was a friend to all while He physically walked our earth. The miracle of all miracles is that the Incarnation continues in the lives of His people today. He is still that friend who sticks closer than a brother.

He is a permanent, unchanging friend in a world that steers itself on a wildly swerving collision course with the future. As we immerse ourselves in His boundless love, He gives us the thrill of being surprised by an unspeakable joy. He gives us the courage to reexamine our views. He somehow makes it easy for us to admit that we don't yet understand a thing. He upsets our tidy, carefully designed prisons and sets before us mansions of grace and beauty.

All the time He is saying, "I will never leave you or forsake you." Right now He wants to help you and me turn our troubles into triumphs, our failures into faith, and our mental and spiritual paralysis into limitless possibilities for good. He also wants us to be His hands, His feet, His heart to men and women, boys and girls who don't have a friend . . . to be there to care when we're needed most. It's one of the most simple, yet most profound, principles of all when it comes to learning the fine art of friendship.

Ted Engstrom, *The Fine Art of Friendship*

SEPTEMBER 9
Not Missing the Sunset

I want to know Christ and the power of his resurrection and the fellowship of sharing in his sufferings, becoming like him in his death. . . .

PHILIPPIANS 3:10

Most men are strangers to God today. Some are acquainted with Him, but only a few are intimates—those who have made it their business to know Him. Forgetting the bad behind them, they press through the good around them to reach the best before them; and for that they are predestined to be conformed to the image of His Son.

My pastor used a good illustration the other night. He said there was a young art student whose teacher put him to painting a sunset. He sat on the brow of a hill, looking across, trying to capture on canvas the glory that filled the west. But he spent too much time working on one detail. The old teacher came along and said, "Look, the sun is almost down, and you are spending your time putting a roof on a barn."

The application is clear for all of us. The sun is going down. "Fast to its close ebbs out life's little day." What a tragedy to shingle a barn and miss the sunset—to let the bad or even the good keep us from the best. There is nothing wrong with painting the barn, but everything is wrong if it makes you miss painting the sunset.

God save you from stopping at any lesser goal than to know Him, and the power of His resurrection, and the fellowship of His sufferings, being made conformable unto His death.

W. Phillip Keller, Taming Tension

SEPTEMBER 10
Being Pliable

Yet, O LORD, you are our Father.
   We are the clay, you are the potter;
   we are all the work of your hand.

ISAIAH 64:8

My young boys love Play-Doh, that squishy man-made clay that comes in beautiful colors. For hours they will mold it, pound it flat, and cut out figures with cookie cutters and other kitchen tools. I've rolled awkward lumps into round balls numerous times for them when their little hands could not manage the clay. We have gone through dozens of cans of the stuff, because my boys have a recurring challenge—they forget to put the Play-Doh back into its containers, or fail to put the lid on properly. Play-Doh dries out. It gets so stiff and hard that you cannot mold it into various shapes or roll it in your hands.

The older we get, the less flexible we naturally become. Arthritis sets in; we feel stiffer. At midlife we realize that we take longer to recuperate from the previous day's exercise. We need more time to loosen up to jog that three miles. Mentally, the older we get, the more we tend to enjoy routine. We have a harder time coping with different ideas and cultures and ways of looking at life.

The same tendency for decay occurs spiritually. There is the temptation to lose our flexibility. That's when breaking occurs. Jesus warns us about putting new wine in old wineskins. New wine creates a chemical reaction resulting in an expansion of gas. Old wineskins are brittle and inflexible. When new wine is poured into them they burst, wasting the wineskin as well as the wine. Jesus talks about the foolishness of applying a new patch to an old garment. The new patch will shrink and tear an even bigger hole into the clothes that needed mending (see Matt.9:16–17).

Consistently we see Jesus' disdain for those who were inflexible. The Pharisees and scribes refused brokenness in their legalistic, empty religiosity. On the other hand, the adulterous woman responded with humility to being broken. Jesus esteemed the man praying out of a broken attitude in the temple, but condemned the proud Pharisee flaunting his self-righteousness. Jesus turned down the man who wanted to follow Him, but who would not give his riches to the poor. Peter received more than one rebuke from the Lord when he refused to be sensitive to the Spirit and boldly took a rigid stand. Peter eventually learned brokenness, and only then was he able to be used mightily after Pentecost. Jesus associated with the tax collectors and other sinners because they responded to Him with flexibility. They were willing to change, to let Him be Lord of their lives.

Someone closed the sliding door of a van on our boy's fingers when he was young. Nancy rushed him to the doctor. Although the pinch was bad, the doctor reassured us that infants and toddlers seldom break their bones since they are so pliable. Old people break their bones frequently because they are brittle. Such is our spiritual tendency as we age. Jesus calls us to come as little children, pliable.

Alan Nelson, *Broken in the Right Place*

SEPTEMBER 11

Honoring Your Father

Honor your father and your mother, as the LORD your God has commanded you, so that you may live long and that it may go well with you in the land the LORD your God is giving you.

DEUTERONOMY 5:16

I know how it is for many adults—especially those in their twenties, thirties, and forties. They feel consumed by responsibilities at work, in their marriages, with children, at church. And it's easy in the midst of a busy and hectic schedule to leave parents in the dust. They reason, "They'll always be there, won't they? Once I get past that next deadline . . . once we finish this vacation . . . once the kids grow a little older . . . then I'll spend some time with my parents."

If your relationship with your parents is difficult—or if anything with your parents remains unresolved—it is even easier to shove the problem into a corner of your mind. "I'll have the chance to talk with them some-day. But I'm just not ready now."

I know of one man who was motivated to honor his dad even though he'd only seen him twice since he was ten years old—at his sister's graduation and at her wedding. "I'd seen him two times since then, but I didn't want to live with the regret that the last time I would see him would be standing over his casket at his funeral. I knew Christ and he didn't. My responsibility to love him began to grow within me. God has forgiven him. I might be the only one in my family to share with him God's love and forgiveness in Christ."

This man has sought to honor his father through numerous visits. And he calls and writes to him regularly. Today that man has no regrets.

Dennis Rainey, *The Tribute*

A Father to the Fatherless

A father to the fatherless, a defender of widows,
  is God in his holy dwelling.

PSALM 68:5

By his nature, Bill's father was a highly critical, unhappy man. Even earning a Ph.D. didn't gain Bill much attention from his father. When Bill married, his father never quite accepted his wife, often severely criticizing her. After his father died, Bill regretted that he had never been able to talk through his feelings with his dad and be reconciled. His brothers shocked him further when they told him that their dad had written Bill out of his will and never told him.

After months of feeling depressed, Bill sat down one day and wrote his father a long letter. A few days later, he slid behind the steering wheel early in the morning and made the long journey to the next state where his father was buried. Bill spent several hours alone, grieving at the grave of his father. Finally, he placed the letter he had drafted on top of the cold tomb and set it on fire. He watched it burn, hoping to put his pain in the past. Today he would tell you that, to his constant regret, some kinds of pain never go away.

For some men, other key relationships go unreconciled in the pedal-to-the-floor race to keep on top of our responsibilities. Some unresolved issues relate to tasks, but by far the majority deal with relationships. We tend to take care of our tasks at the expense of our relationships. In the process we wound and damage the feelings of our loved ones. Remorse goes unexpressed. Forgiveness is not sought. Relationships break down.

What are the unresolved issues in your life? Better yet, who are the unresolved issues in your life?

Patrick Morley, *The Seven Seasons of a Man's Life*

Praying for Spiritual Leaders

Brothers, pray for us.

I THESSALONIANS 5:25

Imagine what would happen if you and the other men from your church determined to pray for your pastor. The whole dynamic and atmosphere of your church would be different.

What would it look like to start such a prayer ministry? In the church I serve, men are asked once a year to sign up to be prayer partners with me. At least one man is assigned to pray for me each day of the month. When that list is drawn up, I pray for the man who is praying for me on that day as well. To further assist my prayer partners, I regularly send them a letter to keep them current on answers to their prayers and new things for which they can be praying.

The entire group that signed up is also divided into four teams. Each team is assigned one Sunday a month to come to the church and pray for me. Fifth Sundays are left unassigned, and any team member can come. Usually, the meetings are packed! The men arrive at 8:15 A.M., as our first service is at 9:00. They disperse throughout the entire church facility. Some stay in the worship center, praying for the worship team, and others participate in the service. Others move through the classrooms, praying for teachers by name. Still others walk in the parking lot, asking God to keep things organized and friendly, and that the sweet Spirit of Jesus will be sensed by folks as they pull into the lot. At 8:30, we all gather in my office, and they pray for me. I tell them what I think God wants me to do that day, plus how I am feeling both physically and spiritually. Then I kneel and men gather around, lay hands on me, and begin to pray.

The results have been dramatic. I have sensed a new power and authority in my preaching. The men who pray have a sense of personal ownership of Sunday mornings. They know their prayers are essential if anything of eternal significance is to take place. Further, the Lord has built a wonderful sense of teamwork through this prayer partnership. Sometimes as I'm preaching, I catch the eye of one of them, and he'll wink or give me the thumbs-up sign. When that occurs, I know they are praying and are *for* me, and then I really "go to preachin'!"

Dale Schlafer, *Seven Promises of a Promise Keeper—*

Promise 5: A Man and His Church

SEPTEMBER 14

Being Faithful to Our Children

Let us lie down in our shame,
  and let our disgrace cover us.
We have sinned against the LORD our God,
  both we and our fathers;
from our youth till this day
  we have not obeyed the LORD our God.

JEREMIAH 3:25

What makes gangs so powerful? One word: *acceptance*. When a kid joins a gang, he or she is part of the team. What makes kids so vulnerable to the power of a gang's acceptance? *Dad's missing acceptance.*

Find an adult working with urban youth and ask, "What is the number-one reason for the breakdown of the family and the buildup of gangs?" and you will hear one primary answer: the missing dad. . . .

Listen again to the young people who face gangs on a daily basis.

Diego: "People join gangs for protection, to stand out, to have friends."

Anthony: "Kids who don't get no attention at school join gangs to get attention. That's the worst thing about school, the gangs."

Where do these precious young boys find the acceptance they desperately need from Dad? A child lacking acceptance from his or her dad is wide open to destructive behaviors and/or people who will bring acceptance. Remember, kids take on the values of those who consider them valuable. With an empty spot for love and acceptance, the young person is driven to fill the void. The cost to the child seeking acceptance is secondary to the benefit of belonging. Find me a young girl lacking her father's acceptance, and I will show you a female on the threshold of sexual promiscuity and teenage pregnancy.

Dad, you hold the key. You and I matter. We fathers possess the most powerful position on the earth. With the investment of paternal acceptance, we can literally change the face of our globe's social landscape. If you're feeling guilty right now, it may be appropriate. Face the facts. Do you find rebellion in the kingdom? If you ask your child what he or she thinks about you and the response is filled with ugly colors, low numbers, and disheartening comments, listen up!

I am not striving to leave a pile of fathers stacked in a heap of guilt. We've got enough pain and despair in our world. . . . You and I matter, possibly more than we will ever realize.

Doug Webster, *Dear Dad: If I Could Tell You Anything*

SEPTEMBER 15
Excellence

In every matter of wisdom and understanding about which the king questioned them, he found them ten times better than all the magicians and enchanters in his whole kingdom.

DANIEL 1:20

The exercise of self-discipline should yield the fruit of excellence. Excellence should be part of every believer's vocabulary. We are not called to do a second-rate job at anything. The old adage that "anything worth doing is worth doing well" is certainly a biblical concept. Too often believers have used a phony form of spirituality to excuse second-rate effort and shoddy workmanship. We are the workmanship of God; therefore, everything that we do should reflect a workmanship of excellence. We are motivated to do everything in a first-class manner.

The prophet Daniel had this heart for excellence. His self-discipline produced the excellence. Everything he did was ten times better than anyone else around him.

The magicians and astrologers here are the professional advisers of the king. They might be the equivalent of modern scientists and government leaders. We should operate according to the Daniel standard. Our standard should be an excellence ten times better than the best of the standards the world has to offer.

Excellence is demonstrated in every aspect of life. We should have excellence in our school curriculums, musical performances, manner of dress, use of grammar and vocabulary, posture and demeanor, upkeep of lawns and houses, clarity of thinking, marital relations, courtesy in driving, business records, work for our employers, ability to handle stress, promptness, cheerfulness and so on. We should manifest first-rate quality in everything.

Keith Intrater, *Covenant Relationships*

SEPTEMBER 16

A Personal Experience

Search me, O God, and know my heart;
test me and know my anxious thoughts.

PSALM 139:23

I have met many who never see any further than their own sinfulness. Each time they hear forthright preaching, or read some article or book which stresses human failure, they come under extreme conviction. They never seem to be able to turn away from their own need, and their poor efforts, and gain a healthy understanding of the atoning work of Christ in His Cross. There are times when they are extremely busy and active in evangelistic endeavor, because deep down underneath they feel compelled to do something to gain God's favor. Such folks are restless, and hectic. They live on feelings. They must always be seeking advice in some new quarter. They are always looking for some new experience, not recognizing that a man may run the whole gamut of so-called spiritual experiences, and be far from God. "The object of Christ's work on earth," wrote Brownlow North, "was not only to make a way by which man could approach God, but by which, as a God of mercy, God could get access to man. It was man's sin that put the barrier between himself and God, *and to remove that barrier Christ died.* Christ shed His blood to satisfy the claims of God's justice against man: and so, putting away sin by the sacrifice of Himself, made a way by which God could return to man. God left Adam because he sinned, and thus (as to be without God is death) Adam died: God comes back to the child of Adam when he believes in Jesus, and thus (as to have God is life) the child of Adam lives." It is this sweet sanity of a knowledge of God's mercy, which a man must have in himself first, before He can dare to preach to others. He must become "a pattern" showing to men the reality of the mercy and long suffering of God.

J. C. Metcalfe, *There Must Be Heresies*

Private Worship

The LORD has heard my cry for mercy;
the LORD accepts my prayer.

PSALM 6:9

Private worship, or closet time, is the primary way you develop your relationship with the Lord. It is where you can fine tune you ear to hear His voice. It is where He will whisper secrets and share His heart with you.

Also keep in mind that there is a special way in which only *you* can touch God's heart. You are a unique individual created by Him and only you can worship Him like you do. There is a special place in God's heart that only you can fill through your worship time alone with Him.

The same applies to corporate worship, there is a way in which a church fills God's heart. Every church has a special purpose in God's plans. It does not matter if it's a small congregation or a church of five thousand members—there is some special project that each church is called to do, special people that each church is called to reach out to.

And just as we have corporate mandates, things the Lord calls us to do as a body—we also have individual mandates—things you were born to do that neither I nor anyone else for that matter can fulfill.

It is in the place of intimate worship that the Lord gives many of those mandates. Enter in and find out what special things He wants you and your church to do.

Ron Kenoly, *Lift Him Up*

SEPTEMBER 18

Loving Your Neighbor as Yourself

If you really keep the royal law found in Scripture, "Love your neighbor as yourself," you are doing right.

JAMES 2:8

The love I felt from my parents, the examples they set for me, and my Christian faith were instrumental in molding the kind of person I am today. It was by example that my philosophy on race relations was formed, and my mother was largely responsible. A black family was moving in close to our neighborhood, and people were upset about it. I recall my mother chastising the neighbors about their prejudice. I was in another room but I could hear everything going on in the house.

"How can you call yourselves Christians?" mother said. "How can you hold something over blacks because of the color of their skin, whether they want to move in next door or whatever they want to do? It goes against everything we believe as Christians."

Mother not only talked a good game but practiced it and tried to get others to practice it. That always stood out in my mind. In forming opinions about other people you must have understanding. You have to put yourself in their shoes. I was taught to judge a person on who he is and what he stands for instead of his color.

Like my mother, I am upset by religious hypocrisy more than anything. Jesus Christ would jump out of His skin at such a two-faced attitude. The second greatest of the Ten Commandments is to love your neighbor as yourself. Yet there have been Christians through the years who've prevented people from joining their church because of skin color. This is a disgrace. There is no worse hypocrisy in all of life than a Christian prejudiced toward another human being.

Everything we do on earth is temporary. We have our temporary joys and sorrows, for which there are temporary solutions. The permanent solution is that relationship with Christ. That is the bond which extends beyond this earth.

Roger Staubach, *First Down, Lifetime to Go*

SEPTEMBER 19
Lord of Prime Time

Do not conform any longer to the pattern of this world, but be able to test and approve what God's will is—His good, pleasing and perfect will.

ROMANS 12:2

I was at a dinner, seated next to the president of one of the three major networks. *A tremendous opportunity*, I thought. I told how millions of Christians were offended by the kind of programming the networks provided.

Knowing TV executives are keenly interested in profit and loss statements, I suggested it would be good business to air wholesome family entertainment. "After all," I said, "there are fifty million born-again Christians out there."

He looked at me quizzically. I assured him that was Gallup's latest figure.

"What you're suggesting, Mr. Colson, is that we run more programs like, say, *Chariots of Fire*?"

"Yes!" I exclaimed, "That's a great movie with a marvelous Christian message."

"Well," he said, "CBS ran it as a prime-time movie just a few months ago. Are you aware of the ratings?"

All at once I knew I was in trouble.

He then explained: That night NBC showed *On Golden Pond*; it was #1 with 25.2 percent of all TV sets in America tuned in. Close behind was *My Mother's Secret Life*, a show about a mother hiding her past as a prostitute. It was #2 with 25.1 percent.

And a distant third—a big money loser—was CBS with *Chariots of Fire*—11.8 percent. In fact, of the sixty-five shows rated that week, "Dallas" was #1, *Chariots of Fire*, #57.

"So," my companion concluded, "where are your fifty million born-again Christians, Mr. Colson?"

Good question. Where are we?

If even half of Gallup's fifty million born-again Christians had watched the show with the Christian message, *Chariots of Fire* would have topped the ratings. But the disturbing truth, as studies by the secular networks as well as the Christian Broadcasting Network show, is that the viewing habits of Christians are not different than those of non-Christians!

Since TV is a business, it gives its customers—the public—what they want. It is but a mirror image of us. How then can we complain, mount petition campaigns and boycotts when we are watching—along with the rest of the crowd—the very thing we're protesting?

So what does the Lordship of Christ mean in the TV age? First, we need to examine ourselves; values inevitably change as God works in one's life. If we aren't being offended by much of TV (not just the sex and violence, but the intelligence-insulting banality), we need to question whether we are really being "transformed by the renewing of [our] minds." Our discernment as Christians should cause us to turn off offensive programming. It should also make us question whether we are being good stewards of our time. After all, there are some good alternatives to TV. We can read the Bible, explore good Christian writing, spend time with our children, parents, friends.

If we can't turn it off, it may be because TV is addictive. One friend who discovered he was hooked did what any addict must do: abstain. He took the TV out of his house altogether: "If your eye (cathode) offends you, pluck it out." For ten years now my friend and his family have not only survived the TV's loss, but have actually flourished.

When we arrive in heaven and account for the stewardship of our time, will Christ say, "Well done" to, say, one and a half years of TV commercials?

Christ must be Lord of all, yes, even of prime time.

Charles Colson, Who Speaks for God?

SEPTEMBER 20

The Father As Giver

Which of you fathers, if your son asks for a fish, will give him a snake instead? Or if he asks for an egg, will give him a scorpion? If you then, though you are evil, know how to give good gifts to your children, how much more will your Father in heaven give the Holy Spirit to those who ask him!

LUKE 11:11–13

The earthly father must not only take the Father in heaven as his model and guide, but he must so reflect Him that the child may naturally rise from him whom he sees, to the unseen One whom he represents. A child loves his parents by natural instinct; as the child sees in the father all that is holy and worthy of honor, natural love becomes the homage of an affectionate and enthusiastic admiration. In a Christian father a child ought to have a better exposition than the best of sermons can give of the love and care of the heavenly Father and all the blessing and joy He wants to bestow.

But to attain to this the parent must consciously and distinctly aim at making himself and the name he bears the ladder by which the child can climb to the Father above. It is when the bright, living, happy piety of the parents, a mingling of holy reverence to God with childlike love, shines on the children from their early youth that the name of God as Father will become linked with all that is lovely and holy in the manner of a child. It is not so much a matter of reflection or thought but as the life-breath taken in all unconsciously that the fatherhood of earth will have been the gate of the Father's home above.

And it is possible so to live that all this shall be true? The one thing the Father loves to give, the sum and center of all His good gifts, is His own Holy Spirit—His Father-Spirit to be in us. And we have but to believe, and as we believe, to receive, and as we receive, to yield to and live in the Spirit; and He will make our fatherhood the image of God's, and from us too there will flow streams of living water to bless our children.

Andrew Murray, *How to Raise Your Children for Christ*

September 21

Forsaking All Others

The integrity of the upright guides them,
* but the unfaithful are destroyed by their duplicity.*

PROVERBS 11:3

A man who keeps his word and can be trusted is a man of integrity. In my work [as a police officer], when a man promises he will have four squads of men there within thirty minutes, if I can just hold on with the ten men I have, I know he is the type of man who will deliver. Lives are depending on him.

A man of integrity keeps and honors his promise to his wife to "forsake all others." He is committed to her.

Too many times the image of the real man is the "man of the world," the one who has more conquests than Don Juan. However, when marriage fidelity is taken lightly, no one wins. . . .

A guy who is loose in his morals and cheats on his wife will have every other aspect of his life influenced. I can spot the fellow in my organization who is messing around with his affections. All he can think about is the next gal he can make. It affects the way he works and the attitudes he has toward his job.

Someone who is really masculine is pure; he does not commit adultery. He is an honest man who doesn't steal the affections of the woman who is not his wife.

If a man is placed in a position of leadership by his church, company, or any other organization, and begins to center his attention of the woman who "understands him better than his wife," his personal leadership ability will begin to dissipate. Remember Delilah? In my opinion, the culprit in that familiar story was not the woman, but Samson, who ignored God's warning concerning the source of his strength and therefore relinquished his leadership as a man of responsibility and character. Delilah was the temptation, but Samson had the choice.

A man of integrity keeps his commitments to his wife, his children, his boss, and his friends.

Bob Vernon, *The Married Man*

SEPTEMBER 22

God's Name

You shall not misuse the name of the LORD your God, for the LORD will not hold anyone guiltless who misuses his name.

EXODUS 20:7

One Saturday afternoon, after returning from the warehouse, I was in my bedroom with my older brother, Dan. Regrettably, Dan thought it was his responsibility to do to me what every big brother does to his younger brother—degrade and humiliate me! I recall he took that responsibility very seriously; he made it clear that he considered me a real loser, a nerd, a wimp. Nothing I did ever impressed him or made him proud of me. Everything I did was minor-league kid's stuff . . . until that particular Saturday afternoon.

As usual, we were in my room, when I accidentally dropped a model I had been building on the floor. In frustration, I blurted out a new word I had learned from the dockhands. Boy, was Dan surprised—and impressed. He stared at me with eyes as big as saucers, and slowly a giant smile spread across his face. I could tell he thought that was just about the neatest thing I had ever said. I went from the minor leagues to the majors.

During the next forty-five minutes I used that word over and over again. And each time Dan smiled as if to say, "You're really something, Billy. You've got guts for a little guy!"

At dinnertime, Mom, Dad, and all five of us kids sat around the big kitchen table the way we always did, a perfect picture of a nice Norman Rockwell family. Near the end of the meal, my dad asked what Dan and I were going to do after dinner. Dan shrugged his shoulders as if he didn't care, but I decided to be a little more expressive. Leaning back in my chair, I jauntily cocked my head to the side. Then I casually said one of my newly acquired words—the way I'd heard the dockhands say it to express an "I don't care" attitude.

I looked at Dan to catch his smile, but for some reason he wasn't smiling. On the contrary, he looked horror-stricken. As my eyes darted around the table, I saw that my older sister was gasping for air, my mother was starting to cry, and my dad was slowly backing out of his chair, coming my way. I knew then that I'd been had.

My dad grabbed me by the shoulders and carried me about six inches off the floor all the way down to my bedroom. I turned around for one last look; my brother was beaming from ear to ear.

All the way down the stairs I begged for mercy. "Dad, I didn't know. Dan tricked me. He thought it was cool. I didn't know. I didn't know. I didn't..."

I honestly didn't know that the word was a problem. In my naiveté I thought anything so commonly used and so obviously impressive had to be all right. I was genuinely ignorant of the truth.

Perhaps some of you have slipped into the careless use of God's name. After all, it's commonly used in school, in the marketplace, in the neighborhood. Perhaps you have been unaware, though, that this is a grievous sin—a sin so serious that in the Old Testament it led to death. In this matter there is not room for ignorance.

If you have dishonored God's name in ignorance, I challenge you right now to implore His forgiveness and commit yourself to obedience. Decide right now that you're never going to profane His name again.

You are no longer ignorant.

Bill Hybels, *Laws of the Heart*

SEPTEMBER 23
Truth

I have chosen the way of truth;
I have set my heart on your laws.

PSALM 119:30

> Seek the truth
> Listen to the truth
> Teach the truth
> Love the truth
> Abide by the truth
> And defend the truth
> Unto death.

JOHN HUS, selected

SEPTEMBER 24
Potential for Greatness

And the angel of the LORD appeared unto Gideon, and said unto him, "The LORD is with thee, thou mighty man of valor." (KJV)

JUDGES 6:12

Gideon was a young man with no vision. He saw himself as weak, poor, and unable to do anything about his circumstances. One day the angel of the Lord came to him while he was hiding in a winepress, threshing out wheat to make some bread. He was afraid that the Midianites would find him and take away what little wheat he had for his family. This was not a man who was making plans for his future. Gideon was just trying to make a living.

The angel of the Lord said to Gideon in Judges 6:12: "The Lord is with you, you mighty man of valor!" These words were totally contrary to Gideon's mind-set, his feelings, and his lifestyle. He had never been mighty as a champion, a warrior, or a leader. He had never been a man of valor, honor, esteem or influence. He was a scared little guy, trying to get through life. But God said, "You are a mighty man of valor!" In the next few chapters of the book of Judges, we see the Lord take Gideon through a series of events that helped him renew his mind to God's Word, and purpose for his life.

Gideon argued with God that he was not a mighty man but a loser and a failure, but the Lord would not allow him to hang on to his mediocre lifestyle. Finally, Gideon began to accept what God said about him and reject what he had believed for so long. There were three areas that God led Gideon to change before he could fulfill his destiny:

1. His self-esteem,
2. His vision for life, and
3. His relationship with people.

Gideon had to renew how he thought about himself, how he thought about his future and who he was involved with. With these changes made, he went on to defeat his enemy, the Midianites, deliver his nation from bondage, and be one of the greatest judges of Israel.

Gideon had the potential for greatness in him all the time. It wasn't that God made him something he had not been before. Everything that he needed was on the inside of him. God simply led him to renew the things that were holding him back and go on to fulfill his destiny.

Casey Treat, *Renewing The Mind*

SEPTEMBER 25

A Companion

Though one may be overpowered,
two can defend themselves.
A cord of three strands is not quickly broken.

ECCLESIASTES 4:12

What do you do to render a man worthless? Unrecognizable? A thin shadow of his glorious potential?

Nothing.

Nothing at all.

Just leave him alone. Don't let him rub shoulders with another man. Isolate him. Don't let him come into regular contact with other growing, capable men. Let him stay isolated, and before long people may well be asking him, "What kind of a man are you?" Certainly not a healthy man.

It is not good that man be alone. Period. We weren't made for it. And left to it, we die. Perhaps that's why solitary confinement is considered "cruel and unusual" punishment by some. Isolation breaks a man down. Ask any POW and he'll tell you the roughest part is the aloneness.

So where, for crying out loud, did we ever get the idea that real men stand alone? That the real cowboy rides by himself? That the real hero has few friends? And that "strong, silent, and independent" are the hallmarks of true masculinity?

It may have begun with the Industrial Revolution ripping men out of their "natural habitat." It may have been fostered by the great war. But it was most certainly popularized by Hollywood.

Somewhere along the line there developed the myth of "The Man Alone." Somewhere over the years we learned to think that true men were to be "rugged individualists." John Wayne usually rode alone. So did Clint Eastwood. Ditto the Marlboro man. And mega-selling Western novelist Louis L'Amour constantly had his hard-bitten characters telling us that to the degree a man depends on anyone or anything else, he's that much weaker. I wonder if old Louis really believed that himself. This is the same author who created the wildly popular Sackett version of Westerns. And one thing you could always count on about that far-flung, hard-riding clan: When one of the Sackett Boys was hurt, in trouble, or in a tight spot, every other Sackett across the wide West would come a'ridin' with his Colt on his hip and his Winchester in the saddle boot. An insult or injury to one of the Sacketts was an insult or injury to all of 'em, and cowboy, you'd better check your passport, because America just ain't big enough to hide in.

Nevertheless, generations of men have bought into the dominant mythology that "masculinity carries it alone." And it's *killing* us. When men began to stumble toward isolation, when men began to lose touch with each other and the home, that's when men, marriages, families, and an entire culture began to die.

Stu Weber, *Locking Arms*

September 26

Fatherless No More

I will be a Father to you,
and you will be my sons and daughters,
says the Lord Almighty.

II Corinthians 6:18

A few years ago I went to a meeting that was being conducted by Edwin Cole in Dallas, Texas. Ben Kinchlow, one of the speakers, asked the fathers and sons who were present to come to the front and pray together. As I witnessed this, I began to weep. I had never really had a healthy father-son relationship with my own father. I never learned how to golf, ski, or swim; I never had anyone show me how to do hobbies. I wept because I had never really experienced what it meant to have a daddy, a papa, someone into whose lap I could crawl and not be rejected. I didn't have that father to say to me, "Son, I love you. Talk to me. Tell me what is bothering you."

All of a sudden, as I was weeping, the Holy Spirit spoke to me. "I'll be your Father. I have a desire to be a Father to the fatherless. I will teach you what a father is to be like. *I* will be your Father. Is there anything you would like to do? *I* will help you. I will give you wisdom. I will give you instruction. I will give you discipline. I will do hobbies with you. I'll teach you to swim if you want to learn. I'll teach you to snow ski and water ski and to do all these things."

In my mind I questioned, "How can this be? How can God do those things for me? Maybe He means that He will bring earthly men of God who will be like fathers to me, but that is still not the same."

The Spirit spoke back to me, "No. *I* will be your Father. I have heard your cry, 'Abba, Father.' You will be My son, and I will be your Father."

By the next year I had gone snow skiing for the first time. I'm sure I looked like an idiot, but I didn't care because Daddy was with me. I went deep sea fishing for the first time when I was in Australia and I caught the biggest fish in the group. I even went water skiing, not knowing how to swim, and had a wonderful time with my life jacket on. Daddy was with me. While in Australia, I also went golfing for the first time. I did a lot of "worm burning," hitting the ball across the ground rather than in the air. I also hit the same kangaroo twice, but Daddy was with me.

As I look back on that time, I realize that God was teaching me what it was like to be a son. He was teaching me what it was like to have a daddy who cared—no matter what struggles, faults, insecurities, and pressures I had. He said, "Forget all that and just get alone with Me."

Doug Stringer, *The Fatherless Generation*

SEPTEMBER 27

Regeneration

No one who is born of God will continue to sin, because God's seed remains in him; he cannot go on sinning, because he has been born of God.

I JOHN 3:9

Several years ago a new Christian asked me about some changes that had come into his life since he had been converted. For years he had dropped by the same bar every day after work, more for friendship than for beer. The Monday after his conversion he walked in as usual and his friends asked, "How's it going?" He ordered a beer and proceeded to tell them about how he had given his life to Christ. Suddenly his friends lapsed into a stony silence. He started feeling uncomfortable, out of place. Over the next day or two he noticed that the cigarette smoke bothered him, the beer did not taste as good as it used to, and the coarse language was suddenly foreign to him. By midweek he realized he no longer belonged there. He wanted to know how his desires could change so quickly and radically. "That's easy," I told him. "You've been regenerated, born again. You're a new man, with a new heart and desires. You'll never enjoy the old life again."

When we look at the idea of "regeneration," we leave the legal terminology of justification and come to that of childbirth. Whereas Paul normally talks about adoption into God's family, John speaks of being "born again," born of the very seed of God: "No one who is born of God will continue to sin, because God's seed remains in him; he cannot go on sinning, because he has been born of God" (1 John 3:9). When we are regenerated, our "I've-got-to-sin" nature is fundamentally changed. We are still tempted to sin, but in our hearts we want to please God.

John Wimber, *Power Points*

September 28

The Creational Male

So God created man in his own image,
in the image of God he created him;
male and female he created them.

Genesis 1:27

To be a creational male means to realize we as men have not been created for ourselves. The prophet Jeremiah declared that "Adam was not created for himself and therefore should be very fearful about trusting in himself" (Jeremiah 10:23, 17:5). Moses made it very clear that "man does not live by bread alone" (Deuteronomy 8:3). We are made in God's image and as such, we are made to have a relationship with our Creator. This strikes very deep at the heart of male independence, especially the rank independence from God we see in many men. But to be creational means that we as men owe something back to God. We are not created and given life in order to go our merry way without even saying so much as "thank you."

Inherent in the concept of being made in "God's image" is that we are His representatives on earth. In one sense, we show forth to the world and perhaps angels what God is like. In ancient cultures, images were personal portraits of the kings that allowed the citizens to know what their ruler looked like (see Daniel 3:2). If this is true, the King of creation has made us humans to rule as His vice-regents on earth and show forth what His rule should look like on earth. It is awesome to think that God is looking to me to reveal what He is like, but that seems to be the intended meaning of the term *image of God*.

Having a relationship with the living God also means that in this ruling function we as men must form a certain benevolent relationship with the earth and our fellowmen. Our joint rulership (men and women) of the earth suggests not the progressive environmental rape that we have seen by the "Christian" industrial nations. The rulership envisioned in Genesis 1:28 implies the rule of wisdom, care, and stewardship of God's territory. When the law was given, respect for property, boundaries, and natural resources was given with as much authority as were the Ten Commandments. . . . In modern terms, as trite as it might seem, this means that it is manly to recycle and have genuine concern for the welfare of the planet. I don't want my grandkids to live in the trash heap that our lovely earth could become if we merely do nothing.

This accountability is also extended to those living on the earth. The question from the early chapters of Genesis still echoes down through the hallways of history. Cain, in feigned innocence, asked the Lord, "Am I my brother's keeper?" (Genesis 4:9). The answer is obvious . . . for all times. Yes!!! I am my brother's keeper. I am held accountable for how I treat my fellow man.

Robert Hicks, *The Masculine Journey*

September 29
Perfect Peace

You will keep in perfect peace
  him whose mind is steadfast,
  because he trusts in you.

Isaiah 26:3

A few years ago, a man from the West Coast dropped by our office to visit. He said he was familiar with our ministry and had seen me a few times on television. He had ordered some tapes and listened to messages I had given, and he had a question.

"You seem to have found something of the secret of resting and being at peace. So, how do you do it? What is the secret of living without turmoil? Talking to you is like sitting by still waters."

I laughed and told him that might not be a compliment; after all, a mud puddle is still water. But then, in seeking to answer his question, I was called to verbalize succinctly something I had never really tried to verbalize before.

I heard myself saying to him something like this. "By temperament, I am not an aggressive or excitable person. But all my life, I was well acquainted with inner strife and anxiety. From an early age, I'd had a desire to know God and follow his ways. I spent many years seeking to discover all his principles and to live by them. I wanted to become an expert in understanding the ways of God.

"I reached a point, however, when the principles I was discovering turned out to be too many, and I realized I just did not have the mental capacity to decipher the multifaceted wisdom of Almighty God. It was during that time that I had a brief glimpse of God himself that completely overturned my perception of reality and taught me the secret of internal rest.

"I can't really say it was a vision, for I don't remember actually seeing anything, but somehow I was given an acute awareness of who God really is. I saw him with the eyes of my spirit, and I discovered was that *he is very big and very good.* Ever since that day, my perspective has changed. I've been able to keep my focus simple. And when I do that, I am able to be at peace."

"Very big and very good." What poor words to describe what I really saw! To say that God is big is the greatest understatement that could ever be made. To say that he is good does not begin to describe the character of our Father. But the point is: I began to be free of inner turmoil not when I focused on the complexity of God's principles, but when I perceived the awesomely simple truth of who he is. And that change of perspective dramatically changed the way I looked at everything else in my life.

Dudley Hall, Grace Works

SEPTEMBER 30
An Easy Yoke

Take my yoke upon you and learn from me, for I am gentle and humble in heart, and you will find rest for your souls. For my yoke is easy and my burden is light.

MATTHEW 11:29–30

His yoke is easy because his yoke is my yearning. It gives me the very thing I'm made for—creative activity. When I surrender to him, it is the same surrender a wire, unattached and noncreative, makes when it surrenders to a dynamo: it throbs with light and power. The same surrender which paint makes when it surrenders to an artist: mere color becomes a living picture which ink makes when it surrenders to a writer: mere color becomes words that burn and bless and enlighten. When you surrender to Christ, you surrender to the most creative and dynamic Person on this or any other planet. You begin to be alive with his life, enlightened with his light, loving with his love. You have surrendered to creativity. Therefore his yoke is easy, for you are made by the Creator for creation. His yoke fits you.

You are made to belong, and when you belong to him, you know instinctively that this is the right belonging. . . . When Jesus came to the disciples as they were distressed in rowing, bucking a heavy headwind and getting nowhere, they were frightened, thinking he was a ghost—something alien. But finally, after his assurance, "It is I," they gladly took him into the boat; and "immediately the boat was at the land whither they were going." They were going nowhere until they took him in, and then the boat was "immediately at the land whither they were going." You strive to get to the land of self-realization and can't, and then you take Jesus in as Lord, surrender to him, and immediately you are at the land whither you were going—the land of self-realization. You have been striving to get to the land of total meaning and can't get there. You take Jesus in, and immediately you are at the land whither you were going—you've found the land of total meaning, the Kingdom of God. You have arrived at the land of fulfillment when you are in him. You don't have to travel—you're here!

E. Stanley Jones, *A Song of Ascents*

October

OCTOBER 1

Keeping Hope Alive

Hope deferred makes the heart sick,
but a longing fulfilled is a tree of life.

PROVERBS 13:12

One day when I was about forty-eight, I was thinking about my wish to play the trumpet. Then I thought, *Well, what's keeping you from playing?* And I responded, *Nothing.* So I found a teacher, rented a trumpet (and eventually purchased one), and for a few years I took lessons. Then I stopped, for several reasons. I had learned enough to play some tunes (in key), and that was fulfilling. In fact, it was a real boost to me when the dogs quit leaving the room when I practiced. But in addition to being fulfilled, the realities of what I wanted to do hit me as well. At my age, my lip muscles were not going to respond as well as if I had started when I was a child. I didn't have the amount of time to put in each day to achieve the level I had once dreamed of when I was younger. Putting all of that together helped me make my decision to stop. I had realized a dream, although not to the extent of what it was at one time. This is a process that all of us have to face in many areas of our lives as we become older.

Growing older doesn't have to mean the death of our dreams. They can be revised, reshaped, and refashioned to meet the reality of who and what we are as well as our abilities. I have met people in their fifties, sixties, and seventies who still had dreams. These people are survivors.

Norman Wright, *Recovering from the Losses of Life*

OCTOBER 2
A Man's Movement

And let us consider how we may spur one another on toward love and good deeds.

HEBREWS 10:24

We must understand a simple principle: every man is moving. Movement defines a man's existence. But all movement is not good. Therefore, when a man is not moving as he should, he will moves in ways he should not. *When good movement stops, bad movement begins.* Good movement is movement through personal unhappiness toward God. Bad movement is movement aimed at nothing higher than relieving personal unhappiness.

Because men, like women, are fundamentally relational beings, all movement will be seen most clearly in the way a man relates. A man will either call forth life and beauty in the people he knows or he will destroy that same life and beauty. A man's effect on others may be imperceptible or dramatic, but it is there. No interaction of more than a few seconds, no conversation beyond the most casual, leaves the other person unchanged.

Manly men release others from their control and encourage them with their influence. They touch their wives, children, and friends in sensitive ways that free them to struggle with *their* loneliness and selfishness and pain. Manly men nudge their family and friends to the same crossroads where they, as men, have found that trust or unbelief must be chosen.

Unmanly men require their friends and family to meet their demands. Men who move with control, anger and terror deaden others into conformity or incite them to self-preserving rebellion.

Larry Crabb, The Silence of Adam

OCTOBER 3
Our Personal Strength

Each one should use whatever gift he has received to serve others, faithfully administering God's grace in its various forms.

I PETER 4:10

Know your strength, and then go with your strength. That's crucial in making good personal decisions. And remember that each of us has different strengths to bring to the different situations we face.

A concert violinist had a brother who was a bricklayer. One day a woman gushed to the bricklayer, "It must be wonderful to be in a family with such a famous violinist." Then, not wanting to insult the bricklayer, she said, "Of course we don't all have the same talents, and even in a family, some just seem to have more talent than others."

The bricklayer said, "Boy, you're telling me! That violinist brother of mine doesn't know a thing about laying bricks. And if he couldn't make some money playing that fiddle of his, he couldn't hire a guy with know-how like mine to build a house. If he had to build a house himself he'd be ruined."

If you want to build a house, you don't want a violinist. And if you're going to lead an orchestra, you don't want a bricklayer.

No two of us are exactly alike. None of us has every gift and ability. Our responsibility is to exercise the gifts we have—not the ones we wish we had.

And when it comes to making decisions about your own life and the direction it should take, focus on your strengths—not your weaknesses. Know yourself. Know what you do well, and then go with your strengths and shore up your weaknesses.

Haddon Robinson, *Decision-Making by the Book*

OCTOBER 4
Spiritual Markers

Choose twelve men from among the people, one from each tribe, and tell them to take up twelve stones from the middle of the Jordan from right where the priests stood and to carry them over with you and put them down at the place where you stay tonight.

So Joshua called together the twelve men he had appointed from the Israelites, one from each tribe, and said to them, "Go over before the ark of the LORD your God into the middle of the Jordan. Each of you is to take up a stone on his shoulder, according to the number of the tribes of the Israelites, to serve as a sign among you. In the future, when your children ask you, 'What do these stones mean?' tell them that the flow of the Jordan was cut off before the ark of the covenant of the LORD. When it crossed the Jordan, the waters of the Jordan were cut off. These stones are to be a memorial to the people of Israel forever."

JOSHUA 4:2–7

I have found it helpful to identify "spiritual markers" in my life. Each time I encounter God's call or directions, I mentally build a spiritual marker at that point. A spiritual marker identifies a time of transition, decision, or direction when I clearly know that God has guided me. Over time I can look back at these spiritual markers and see how God has faithfully directed my life according to His divine purpose. When I review my spiritual markers, I can see more clearly the directions in which God has been moving my life and ministry.

At times I may face several options where I could serve God. I need to know which of these good things is what God desires of me. When I face a decision about God's direction, I review my spiritual markers. I don't take the next step without the context of the full activity of God in my life. This helps me see God's perspective for my past and present. Then I look at the options that are before me. I look to see which one of the options seems to be most consistent with what God has been doing in my life. Often one of these directions will be most consistent with what God already has been doing. If none of the directions seems consistent, I continue to pray and wait on the Lord's guidance. When circumstances do not align with what God is saying in the Bible and in prayer, I assume that the timing may be wrong. I then wait for God to reveal His timing.

Henry Blackaby, *Experiencing God*

OCTOBER 5

Pure Love

Love never fails. But where there are prophecies, they will cease; where there are tongues, they will be stilled; where there is knowledge, it will pass away.

I CORINTHIANS 13:8A

Nothing breaks up the joyous nature of a home so much as having to hide things from one another. Husband and wife should be able to face *everything* together, keeping nothing back. It is a sad day when this crystal clear relationship is broken. It is a sad day when the child has to hide anything from the parents. It is a sad day when the parents have to deceive their children or frighten them in order to gain their obedience.

There must be loyalty. Loyalty often demands courage. Stand by one another in difficulty, hardship, and loss. Stand by one another when the world cheers, ridicules, or neglects. Trust grows out of honesty and loyalty. A trusting and confidential environment makes for happiness. Children, honor your parents with obedience. Parents, by transparent honesty, inspire your children to trust.

Love is the essential element in the Christian home. Efficiency, cleanliness, luxury cannot make up for the lack of love. . . . Love is interest in what the other members of the family do—joys and sorrows, struggles and achievements are shared by all. Love anticipates. It sees beforehand how it can help to lighten another's load; it is always willing to go out of its way or to make time to help. Love never harbors resentment, is not easily hurt, is always ready to forgive. Where love is, God is.

Remember the marriage vow—the twofold, lifelong promise given. "Wilt thou love, comfort, honor her [him], and keep her [him], in sickness and in health; and forsaking all others keep thee only unto her [him] so long as ye both shall live?" "*I will.*"

Ask yourself, "Am I keeping this promise in the letter and in the spirit?" When love is dethroned and the relationship is wrong at the center, how can the home be happy? Love is the secret of a happy home.

Eric Liddell, Disciplines of the Christian Life

OCTOBER 6

The Godly Heritage

Sons are a heritage from the Lord,
children are a reward from him.

PSALM 127:3

I had finally had it. The children were loud, cranky, impossible. I was tired and fed up. My wife was tired and fed up. I decided that I was going to run away from it all and have a day just for me. I wanted to spoil myself. I wanted to have a day in which I did just what I wanted to do. I was going to live it up and be as greedy as I pleased. I wasn't going to tend to anyone except myself.

I zoomed out of the house with fifty dollars. *There! I did it!* I said to myself as I drove to the highway and headed north.

Well, I drove to a mall and had a wild time in a bookstore and bought the collected poems of Walt Whitman. After that I drove and drove to a

McDonald's and ordered *two* hamburgers, my *own* large fries, and my *own* large soda. I ate everything *without* being interrupted, without giving my pickle to *anyone*, without wiping someone's mouth, nose, lap. Then I bought the *biggest* chocolate ice cream I could find.

I was free. I was out on the town, so I drove to a movie theater and watched a movie without buying popcorn, without someone sitting on my lap, without escorting someone to the bathroom. I was a free man. I was living it up. And I was miserable.

By the time I had returned home, everyone was asleep. As I slipped into bed, my wife whispered, "We missed you."

"Me, too," I answered. I never ran away from home again.

If you are in the middle of the pressures of raising a family, remember, it's no fun being alone.

"Children are a reward from the Lord," wrote the psalmist. So take the kids today to McDonald's, or to a bookstore, or to the movies. Take them anywhere except out of your heart.

Lonely in my heart, Lord. Lonely in my heart. I am not lonely in my heart because of the children on the swing, the children under the blankets, because of the children in the house, the house of the Lord, my Lord, You who have blessed me with the children, Lord, the children. I am not lonely. Amen I say to You with gratitude for the children. For this I pray. Amen.

Christopher De Vinck, Simple Wonders

OCTOBER 7
Being Unashamed

If we are out of our mind, it is for the sake of God; if we are in our right mind, it is for you.

II CORINTHIANS 5:13

A Christian should never be ashamed or inhibited. True humility is not weakness. A prudent man is one who recognizes his unworthiness to be called a child of God and to be a member of the family of God, but yet stands straight, with shoulders back and head held high. He has achieved that divine balance in his life between being a man whose gifts and abilities God can use and a man who gives all glory and honor to Jesus Christ. Paul himself did not hesitate to commend himself when falsely accused and belittled. But he made sure that his motives were understood—that he was doing so because of what God had done in *his* life.

In writing to the Corinthians and defending his apostleship against those who falsely questioned his motives, he said: "For if we are beside ourselves, it is for God; if we are of sound mind (prudent) it is for you" (2 Cor. 5:13). In other words, said Paul, you may think we are bragging and are proud. If so, it is because of what God has wrought in us. We are only glorifying the work of God in our lives. And from your viewpoint, Corinthians, we want you to see us as sober, prudent and sensible men, humbly acknowledging that we are what we are because of God's marvelous grace. (2 Cor. 11–12).

Gene Getz, *The Measure of a Man*

OCTOBER 8

Searching with All Your Heart

You will seek me and find me when you seek me with all your heart.

JEREMIAH 29:13

North of the village, and over a hill, lay a piece of woods, in which I was in the almost daily habit of walking, more or less, when it was pleasant weather. It was now October, and the time was past for my frequent walks there. Nevertheless, instead of going to the office, I turned and bent my course toward the woods, feeling that I must be alone, and away from all human eyes and ears, so that I could pour out my prayer to God.

But still my pride must show itself. As I went over the hill, it occurred to me that some one might see me and suppose that I was going away to pray. Yet probably there was not a person on earth that would have suspected such a thing, had he seen me going. But so great was my pride, and so much was I possessed with a fear of man, that I recollect that I skulked along under the fence, till I got so far out of sight that no one from the village could see me. I then penetrated into the woods, I should think, a quarter of a mile, went over on the other side of the hill, and found a place where some large trees had fallen across each other, leaving an open place between. There I saw I could make a kind of closet. I crept into this place and knelt down for prayer. As I turned to go up into the woods, I recollect to have said, "I will give my heart to God, or I never will come down from there." I recollect repeating this as I went up— "I will give my heart to God before I ever come down again."

But when I attempted to pray I found that my heart would not pray.... I said to myself, "I cannot pray. My heart is dead to God and will not pray." I then reproached myself for having promised to give my heart to God before I left the woods. When I came to try, I found I could not give my heart to God. My inward soul hung back, and there was no going out of my heart to God. I began to feel deeply that it was too late; that it must be that I was given up of God and was past hope.

The thought was pressing me of the rashness of my promise, that I would give my heart to God that day or die in the attempt. It seemed to me as if that was binding upon my soul; and yet I was going to break my vow. A great sinking and discouragement came over me, and I felt almost too weak to stand upon my knees.

Just at this moment I again thought I heard someone approach me, and I opened my eyes to see whether it were so. But right there the revelation of my pride of heart, as the great difficulty that stood in the way, was distinctly shown to me. An overwhelming sense of my wickedness in being ashamed to have a human being see me on my knees before God, took such powerful possession of me, that I cried at the top of my voice, and exclaimed that I would not leave that place if all the men on earth and all the devils in hell surrounded me. "What!" I said, "such a degraded sinner as I am, on my knees confessing my sins to the great and holy God; and ashamed to have any human being, and a sinner like myself, find me on my knees endeavoring to make my peace with my offended God!" The sin appeared awful, infinite. It broke me down before the Lord.

Just at that point this passage of Scripture seemed to drop into my mind with a flood of light: "Then shall ye go and pray unto me, and I will hearken unto you. Then shall ye seek me and find me, when ye shall search for me with all your heart." I instantly seized hold of this with my heart. I had intellectually believed the Bible before; but never had the truth been in my mind that faith was a voluntary trust instead of an intellectual state. I was as conscious as I was of my existence, of trusting at that moment in God's veracity. Somehow I knew that that was a passage of Scripture, though I do not think I had ever read it. I knew that it was God's word, and God's voice, as it were, that spoke to me. I cried to Him, "Lord I take thee at thy word.

Now thou knowest that I do search for thee with all my heart, and that I have come here to pray to thee; and thou hast promised to hear me."

That seemed to settle the question that I could then, that day, perform my vow. The Spirit seemed to lay stress upon that idea in the text, "When you search for me with all your heart." The question of when, that is of the present time, seemed to fall heavily into my heart. I told the Lord that I should take him at his word; that he could not lie; and therefore I was sure that he heard my prayer, and that he would be found of me.

He then gave me many other promises, both from the Old and the New Testament, especially some most precious promises respecting our Lord Jesus Christ. I never can, in words, make any human being understand how precious and true those promises appeared to me. I took them one after the other as infallible truth, the assertions of God who could not lie. They did not seem so much to fall into my intellect as into my heart, to be put within the grasp of the voluntary powers of my mind; and I seized hold of them, appropriated them, and fastened upon them with the grasp of a drowning man.

Charles Finney, *Charles G. Finney: An Autobiography*

OCTOBER 9
The Prayers of a Righteous Man

The prayer of the righteous man is powerful and effective.

JAMES 5:16B

The human body can take a tremendous amount of stress. I played twenty-two years of football, twelve as a pro and ten in school. I wasn't injured badly enough to miss a game until the last part of that twenty-second year when I had a couple of broken ribs and had to miss the last four games of that year. Only once did I push myself too hard in a game—I passed out from heat exhaustion. Most of the time I paced myself too much. But the amazing thing about the body is that the harder you push it, the stronger it becomes. The more you stretch the body, brain, or soul, the more it grows.

In high-pressure jobs, such as sports, nervousness can become counterproductive. The athlete can't afford to choke. It short-circuits his abilities. The victory is dependent upon a two-and-a-half-hour period which comes only once a week. But what does the athlete do with all the other time the rest of the week? First, he works himself to the point of exhaustion so that he sleeps well and is too tired to be nervous about the upcoming game. However, as great as physical exertion is, there is a point of diminishing returns when we overdo it. A person's body can become so weary it needs complete rest in order to recover and grow stronger. But, more often than not, we are usually too easy on ourselves.

When your body does need rest, concentrate on working your mind. Visualize yourself in vivid detail doing your job in winning form. Do this repeatedly. Anytime the job crosses your mind, make very sure it is in the form of powerful pictures. The second-mile work effort can move from the physical to the psychological, and more importantly, on to the spiritual. Make everything you do an object of prayer. . . .

In all his wisdom Solomon said, "With all of thy getting, get wisdom." But then came One wiser than Solomon who said, in essence, "with all of thy getting, get going." Action and second-mile effort must be added to words, thoughts, and visions so that dreams become hard reality.

Like a determined farmer, you need to give your crop a chance to come up, then water and cultivate it. It won't happen overnight, but it will follow as certainly as the night follows the day. Your harvest is inevitable!

Bill Glass, *Expect to Win*

OCTOBER 10

Sexual Purity

You have heard that it was said, "Do not commit adultery." But I tell you that anyone who looks at a woman lustfully has already committed adultery with her in his heart.

MATTHEW 5:27–28

Our sexuality and desires are a wonderful gift from God, and He knows they can best be enjoyed in the context of sexual purity—in both thought and action. It is vital to remember that sexual intimacy is *pure* in the truest sense only when exercised appropriately. While writing an encouraging letter to a friend is a good thing, it is not appropriate while driving down a busy highway during rush hour. Circumstances do matter, even for good things, and this is particularly so with our sexuality.

For the single man, this means a willingness to wait until marriage for sexual intercourse. God's call to virginity before marriage is unequivocal. For those who have made a mistake already, it means making a commitment today to a "second virginity" that will wait for your spouse. When our repentance is sincere, God can and will forgive and restore us from *any* sin. It is never too late to begin obeying God and enjoying the fruits of our faithfulness.

Purity also means obeying Jesus' command not to lust after that which is not ours. . . . This is tough! It means not putting ourselves in a position to use women sexually either by thought or action (e.g., pornography is an exploitive form of mental intercourse). For the single man, it means treating every woman he dates in a manner that respects and preserves her purity for her future husband. Purity also means seeking to follow Christ's call in spirit, not just by the letter of the law. It does *not* mean trying to find a thin line marking the boundary of what's acceptable and crawling right up to the edge (and maybe even peering over a few times).

For us married men, sexual purity means reflecting God's absolute faithfulness to us in our faithfulness to our wives. Adultery can take many forms. Watching racy movies on a business trip in an airport motel, with or without masturbation, is a form of emotional adultery that will eventually weaken the marriage. Every man faces this challenge when he travels alone overnight. Real intimacy is not just a function of sex—it permeates our lives only when emotional, spiritual, and sexual faithfulness characterize our relationship with our spouses.

Jerry Kirk, *Seven Promises of a Promise Keeper—Promise 3: A Man and His Integrity*

OCTOBER 11
Physical Contact and Eye Contact

He took a little child and had him stand among them. Taking him in his arms, he said to them, "Whoever welcomes one of these little children in my name welcomes me; and whoever welcomes me does not welcome me but the one who sent me."

MARK 9:36–37

Last summer my eight-year-old son played Peanut League Baseball, and I sat on the bleachers to watch him play. During the games I especially enjoyed watching one father who had discovered the secrets of eye and physical contact. Frequently his boy would run up to tell him something. It was obvious that there was a strong affectional bond between them. As they talked, their eye contact was direct with no hesitation. And their communication included much appropriate physical contact, especially when something funny was said. This father would frequently lay his hand on his son's arm, or put his arm around his son's shoulder and sometimes slap him on the knee. Occasionally, he would pat him on the back or pull the child toward him, especially when a humorous comment was made. You could tell that this father used physical contact whenever he possibly could, as long as he and the boy were comfortable and it was appropriate.

Occasionally, this same father's teenage daughter would come to watch her brother play. She would sit with her father, either at his side or directly in front of him. Here again, this caring and knowledgeable father related to his daughter in an appropriate manner. He used much eye and physical contact but because of her age, did not hold her on his lap or kiss her (as he would have done if she were younger). He would frequently lightly touch her hand, arm, shoulder, or back. Occasionally he would tap her on the knee or briefly put his arm around her shoulder and lightly jerk her toward him, especially when something funny happened.

Physical and eye contact are to be incorporated in all of our everyday dealings with our children. They should be natural, comfortable, and not showy or overdone. A child growing up in a home where parents use eye and physical contact will be comfortable with himself and other people. He will have an easy time communicating with others, and consequently be well-liked and have good self-esteem. Appropriate and frequent eye and physical contact are two of the most precious gifts we can give our child.

Ross Campbell, *How To Really Love Your Child*

OCTOBER 12   Columbus Day

Wonderful Deeds

They that go down to the sea in ships, that do business in great waters; these see the works of the LORD, and his wonders in the deep.

PSALM 107: 23–24 (KJV)

At a very early age I began to sail upon the ocean. For more than forty years, I have sailed everywhere that people go.

I prayed to the most merciful Lord about my heart's great desire, and He gave me the spirit and the intelligence for the task: seafaring, astronomy, geometry, arithmetic, skill in drafting spherical maps and placing correctly the cities, rivers, mountains and ports. I also studied cosmology, history, chronology and philosophy.

It was the Lord who put into my mind (I could feel His hand upon me) the fact that it would be possible to sail from here to the Indies. All who heard of my project rejected it with laughter, ridiculing me.

There is no question that the inspiration was from the Holy Spirit, because he comforted me with rays of marvelous illumination from the Holy Scriptures, a strong and clear testimony from the forty-four books of the Old Testament, from the four Gospels, and from the twenty-three Epistles of the blessed Apostles, encouraging me continually to press forward, and without ceasing for a moment they now encourage me to make haste.

Our Lord Jesus desired to perform a very obvious miracle in the voyage to the Indies, to comfort me and the whole people of God. I spent seven years in the royal court, discussing the matter with many persons of great reputation and wisdom in all the arts; and in the end they concluded that it was all foolishness, so they gave it up.

But since things generally came to pass that were predicted by our Savior Jesus Christ, we should also believe that this particular prophecy will come to pass. In support of this, I offer the gospel text, Matt. 24:25, in which Jesus said that all things would pass away, but not his marvelous Word. He affirmed that it was necessary that all things be fulfilled that were prophesied by himself and by the prophets . . .

I am a most unworthy sinner, but I have cried out to the Lord for grace and mercy, and they have covered me completely. I have found the sweetest consolations since I made it my whole purpose to enjoy His marvelous presence.

For the execution of the journey to the Indies I did not make use of intelligence, mathematics or maps. It is simply the fulfillment of what Isaiah had prophesied. . . .

No one should fear to undertake any task in the name of our Savior, if it is just and if the intention is purely for His holy service. The working out of all things has been assigned to each person by our Lord, but it all happens according to His sovereign will even though He gives advice.

He lacks nothing that it is in the power of men to give him. Oh what a gracious Lord, who desires that people should perform for him those things for which He holds Himself responsible! Day and night, moment by moment, everyone should express to Him their most devoted gratitude.

Christopher Columbus, Book of Prophecies

OCTOBER 13
The Spirit of His Son

Because you are sons, God sent the Spirit of his Son into our hearts, the Spirit who calls out, "Abba, Father."

GALATIANS 4:6

Our understanding of God as the Father is affected by our experiences with our earthly fathers. Few people really understand what a father is or is supposed to be. Even fewer realize what a godly father is. Some people did not even *have* a father. Many fathers have been abusive or even "absent"—spending more time with the television than with their children.

So many young people in America today grow up without a father figure. Can we blame them for not understanding the heavenly Father? People view God as a mean umpire—grouchy and authoritative—one eager to call them "out"! Others see Him as a rigid disciplinarian, ready with a baseball bat.

Thank God, He is not anything like that. In actuality He says, "If you will listen to me, I will seal you with My Spirit of adoption. You will be a joint heir through Christ. You will no longer be an orphan, but My child." God seals us by His Spirit.

God desires an intimate relationship with His children. Through this intimacy, God can shape our view of Him and our view of how we think He sees us. We will begin to realize our high value to God. We can experience the depth of His unconditional love for us.

With that kind of confidence, we can go boldly into His presence, addressing Him with the intimate "Abba, Father." We can enjoy the knowledge that He will hear us, speak to us, and meet our needs.

Doug Stringer, The Fatherless Generation

OCTOBER 14

Physical Touch

How delightful is your love, my sister, my bride!
How much more pleasing is your love than wine,
and the fragrance of your perfume than any spice!

SONG OF SONGS, 4:10

Physical touch is often withheld by men until they suddenly turn "touchie" because it's time, in their minds, to be sexually involved. However, many of these men receive a stiff-arm instead of a warm embrace from their wives. Why?

The average woman needs time to warm up to the sexual experience, in some cases taking as long as two days before she's ready to respond! Her desire grows as she is hugged or touched without sexual connotations attached; as she is praised, encouraged, and helped with things important to her. If a man has supplied these warm-up touches and actions, in most cases he will meet with a warm response from his wife.

As the leaders in our homes, we need to find out how our wives like to be touched, how often, when, and where.

Does your wife want to be touched by you to comfort her when she's hurting?

Does she appreciate an encouraging hug that says, "You can do it! I believe in you"?

Does holding her hand in public provide a great source of security and blessing to her, or would she rather you just sit near her on the couch after the kids have gone to bed and watch a favorite television show?

Men do have testosterone-driven sexual desires that need to be expressed regularly in the marriage. The Scriptures are clear that regular sexual involvement is crucial not only to enrich the marriage, but also to protect a couple from temptation and sexual sin. However, quoting Bible verses to our wives about how they aren't to "deny" us usually isn't helpful in increasing a woman's sexual response. Again, a woman needs to be treated with honor, respect, and warmth, and then she is almost always ready to respond.

Gary Smalley and John Trent, *The Hidden Value of a Man*

A Good Name

A good name is more desirable than great riches;
to be esteemed is better than silver or gold.

PROVERBS 22:1

No matter how hard a man works, no matter how much wealth and notoriety a man accumulates, no matter how many frequent flier miles he logs, it is always a fair question to ask, *What will I leave behind?*

What we leave behind is called *legacy.* It's more than bank accounts, IRAs and real estate. It is more than "Salesman of the Year" plaques. More than newspaper clippings. And certainly more than a wooden box planted six feet deep in the earth when it is all over. More than a fleeting memory, a legacy is an indelible impression. It is the mark we make in life that lives far longer than forty, fifty, or eighty years. It's the footprints we leave at a workplace or institution, and the fingerprints we leave in the lives we love. It's the way we do things and the reason we do them. Legacy is as close as we can get to immortality this side of eternity.

Deep in the soul of every man is the desire to leave behind a good name. A name that rings true. A name that makes people nod in affirmation. Few men lust for a name that makes people stand up and clap. For most of us a pat on the back from a family member is fine. If we hear a word of encouragement, it may be enough to get our heart out of rhythm. For a man to be able to look into the eyes of his wife and children and to be able to see them looking back with respect, admiration, trust, loyalty—that is enough to make most of us hallucinate. That is a living legacy. And that is what every man longs for.

A living legacy doesn't grow in a vacuum. Neither does it grow in a petri dish. A living legacy is the product of the consistent hard choices we have been talking about—integrity, sensitivity, humility, responsibility, fidelity, and charity. There are no shortcuts. No such thing as microwave maturity. A good name doesn't grow on trees and it is not for sale at any price. It is not just given to an elite few, nor is it withheld from others. It is held out to each of us—ours for the taking—as long as we are willing to pay the price.

Fred Hartley, *Men and Marriage*

OCTOBER 16

The Supreme Nurturer

God is our refuge and strength,
an ever-present help in trouble.

PSALM 46:1

Boys and men long to be nurtured. This includes touch. This includes intimacy. This includes feeling fulfilled.

We look to women for this filling. Yet—with respect and appreciation for many wonderful women—no woman can be our total fulfillment! This is a fantasy expectation. A partner can give us wonderful moments. A partner can care for us and give us great fulfillment. But she cannot be our *total* fulfillment.

God is our Supreme Nurturer. Unfortunately, we tend to re-create God in macho images while our passions long for tenderness—the feminine side of God. Perhaps that is what Catholic theology allows by revering the holy Mother Mary. Protestant men have no parallel means to revere the feminine characteristics and nature of the Divine. In our deepest reaches, it is our Creator that we long for. God is our first and ultimate lover.

Jogging late at night I can feel intimate with the Creator. I tell God about my hurts and hopes, my fear and fantasies. On occasion, I have burst into tears while running. God is there. I sense His presence. I respond.

Parents were meant to give us hints, glimpses, and tastes of God's nurturing. Committed to a woman, we can experience hints, glimpses, and tastes of God's love. God does not love us invisibly, silently, alone. He calls us to commune with other believers in order to experience aspects of His love. Of course, these relationships do not give us the entire wealth of God's deep love for us—some of this we experience while in communion with God Himself. Yet we can't deny that, through our fellowship with other human beings, God uses the people in our lives to illustrate and to express His love for us.

Sexuality has to do with the whole of our being. It impacts, and is impacted by, the body, mind, emotions, behaviors, styles, attitudes and beliefs. Sexuality includes our expression of feelings and thoughts via words and touch. Sexuality includes commitment to a lover through the intercourse of our bodies and souls. Sexuality teaches us about God.

God is sexual. God created sexuality. The Trinity is more than just "God in three persons": the Father, the Son or Word, and the Spirit or Breath. God is also the interaction of these "persons" of the Godhead. God is expressed in the Scriptures through male, female, and nonsexual pronouns and images. In the sense that our sexuality is part of the image of God, we can sense something about the passion and love of God.

Dick Brian Klaver, *Men at Peace*

OCTOBER 17

Husbandly Affection

The husband should fulfill his marital duty to his wife, and likewise the wife to her husband.

I CORINTHIANS 7:3

Men must get through their heads this vital idea: *Women find affection important in its own right.* They love the feeling that accompanies both the bestowal and the reception of affection, but *it has nothing to do with sex.* Most of the affection they give and receive is not intended to be sexual. You might better compare it to the emotion they exchange with their children or pets.

All of this confuses the typical male. He sees showing affection as part of sexual foreplay, and he is normally aroused in a flash. In other cases men simply want to skip the affection business; they are aroused already.

Let's look in on a hypothetical couple we'll call Brenda and Bruce. They have been having tension lately because Brenda hasn't responded with much enthusiasm to Bruce's request for sex. As our scene opens she senses Bruce has that look in his eye again, and she tries to head him off at the pass: "Bruce, let's just relax for a few minutes. Then maybe you can hold my hand, and we can hug. I'm not ready for sex just like that. I need a little affection first."

Bruce bristles with a bit of macho impatience and says, "You've known me for years. I'm not the affectionate type, and I'm not going to start now!"

Does this sound incredible or farfetched? I hear versions of it regularly in my office. Bruce fails to see the irony in wanting sex but refusing to give his wife affection. A man growls, "I'm not the affectionate type," while reaching for his wife's body to satisfy his desires for sex, is like a salesman who tries to close a deal by saying, "I'm not the friendly type—sign here, you turkey. I've got another appointment waiting."

Although they shouldn't have a hard time understanding this simple logic, men lose track of Harley's First Law of Marriage: *When it comes to sex and affection, you can't have one without the other!*

Willard Harley, His Needs, Her Needs

OCTOBER 18

Top Pop

The righteous man leads a blameless life;
  blessed are his children after him.

What will your children remember about you?

Some years ago a newspaper ran an interesting . . . contest in which children were to write essays on "My Pop's Tops." (Sorry, I don't know the name of the paper, nor the name of the small boy winner.) But here is his prize entry:

"We have so much fun with my dad that I wisht I had known him sooner. He is a farmer. He smells like a cow, and when I smell that cow in the house, I know Pop is home and I am glad.

"My pop's tops because every time I ast for a knickel he will start preeching that when he was a boy he had to earn his knickels, and at the same time he is putting his hand in his pocket and pulls out a knickel for me.

"My pop's tops because he was a brave soldier. He didn't see me till I was three years old, yet he is just as good to me as if he knew me all my life."

Well, that *is* a winner, isn't it?

Wouldn't any dad like his children saying, "My pop's tops"? But doing a retake on his essay, it's evident this little guy was judging his dad by the common everyday things. A smell, a nickel, the feeling inside.

Do we tend sometimes to overconcern ourselves with details like food, shelter, clothing, and the strong protector bit?

Sure, these are important. I want to be a good provider. So do you. But really! Does anything matter more than living so our children could say,

"We have so much fun with my dad, I wisht I had known him sooner."

Charlie Shedd, A Dad Is for Spending Time With

An Ark of Salvation

The Lord then said to Noah, "Go into the ark, you and your whole family, because I have found you righteous in this generation."

GENESIS 7:1

May I, without irreverence, venture to recast a Bible story? If the account of Noah and the flood went something like this, what would you think of it? Suppose that after the ark was completed God said unto Noah, "Now, get eight great spikes of iron and drive them into the side of the ark." And Noah procured the spikes and did as he was bidden. Then the word came unto him, "Come thou and all thy house and hang on to these spikes." And Noah and his wife, and the three sons and their wives, each held onto a spike. And the rains descended and the flood came, and as the ark was borne up on the waters their muscles were strained to the utmost as they clung to the spikes. Imagine God saying to them, "If you hang on till the deluge is over you will be saved!" Can you even think of such a thing as anyone of them going safely through?

But oh, how different the simple Bible story. "And the LORD said unto Noah, Come thou and all thy house into the ark." Ah, that is a very different thing than holding on! Inside the ark they were safe as long as the ark endured the storm. And every believer is in Christ and is as safe as God can make him. Look away then from all self-effort and trust Him alone. Rest in the ark and rejoice in God's great salvation.

And be sure to remember that it is Christ who holds you, not you who hold Him. He has said, "I will never leave thee, nor forsake thee." "For if, when we were enemies, we were reconciled to God by the death of his Son, much more, being reconciled, we shall be saved by his life" (Rom. 5:10). He who died for you now lives at God's right hand to keep you, and the Father sees you in Him. "He hath made us accepted in the beloved." Could anything be more sure?

Harry Ironside, Full Assurance

OCTOBER 20

Exploits

And such as do wickedly against the covenant shall he corrupt by flatteries:
but the people that do know their God shall be strong, and do exploits.

DANIEL 11:32 KJV

The scantiness or the fullness of your life all depends upon how large a God you have! The God of most Christians is not much larger than the dumb idol of wood or stone the heathen worships and then takes down from its pedestal and scolds if it does not answer his prayers or meet his expectations. The God of Paul was a very glorious and mighty Being, and it was the greatness of his God that gave greatness to his character and life. He was but a vessel to receive and reflect the glory of God. "The people that do know their God shall be strong and do exploits." The souls that have learned to clothe themselves with His Almightiness are the people of enlarged vision and victorious faith. Human heroes are honored for what they have become or achieved. God's heroes are honored for the measure in which they have dropped out of sight and simply magnify Him. It is not Elijah, but Elijah's God that we remember. It is not Paul, but Paul's Christ that we want.

A. B. Simpson

OCTOBER 21

Being Still

"Be still, and know that I am God. . . ."

PSALM 46:10A

Each person who wishes to be creatively Christian must learn the discipline of silence. He must learn to get his body still and he must learn to get his mind still. Apart from this the deeper messages of the still small voice will not be heard. In countless churches, services of worship begin with the words, "The Lord is in His holy temple; let all the earth keep silence before him," and then, instead of obeying these sacred words, the congregation immediately does something noisy. We say, "Be still and know," and then proceed to talk. It is not likely that we can cultivate the art of listening apart from silence. One danger is that we tend to become restless and make the silence brief. It is important to recognize that "a moment of silence" is almost worthless. Long experience indicates that an hour is required for the emergence of the best, which this method makes possible.

Elton Trueblood, *Alternative to Futility*

OCTOBER 22
Doing What We Say

As the body without the spirit is dead, so faith without deeds is dead.

JAMES 2:26

I'll never forget the day I looked out of our living room window and saw Mark, our youngest, walking home from school in the driving rain. Mark was in third grade, and he was allowed to ride his bike to his grade school, located right within our subdivision. I happened to be home from the church early that day, and I was sitting in an easy chair by the window. I looked outside at the pouring rain and saw my boy in the distance, trudging his way through the downpour. His clothing was absolutely drenched and his hair was plastered against his head. I opened the door for him, and he looked up at me with a little smile, his face red from the cold.

"Hi, Dad!" he said. "You're home early."

"Hi, Son," I replied. "You're soaked to the skin."

"Yeah, I know."

"Umm, Mark, you know, if you'd ride your bike you'd get home faster. You wouldn't get so wet."

He looked at me rather sheepishly as rivulets of rain streamed from his hair down across his face. "I know, Dad."

I was puzzled. "Well, Son, if you *know*, why in the world didn't you do it?"

Then he hung his head, just a bit, and it hit me. Boy, did I feel like crawling under a table and hiding out for a while. He had told me several times before that his bike had a flat tire. He had asked me, "Dad, could you please fix it for me?"

"Sure, son," I'd promised him. "Don't worry. I'll get after it right away." But I never did. I'd forgotten all about it.

As he stood there in the entryway, dripping and shivering, he could have said, "I couldn't ride my bike today because someone promised me he'd fix it and never did." He would have had every right to say that. But he didn't. What he did say remains printed indelibly on this dad's heart.

"Aw, Dad, I know how busy you are and everything, and—I just didn't want to bother you with it again."

I thought, *Son, your dad isn't too busy; he's just too selfish.*

For me, a bike tire was no big deal—just one more thing on a long "to do" list. But for Mark, it meant more than transportation. It meant more than a long walk home in the rain. It meant trusting his father to meet his every need.

I'm sure glad my heavenly Father doesn't forget. He knows about my flat tires. He knows about the things that matter most to me. He never fails to weigh and consider my hurts, my worries, and my pressures.

Ron Mehl, *God Works the Night Shift*

OCTOBER 23
Living Again

I am the resurrection and the life. He who believes in me will live, even though he dies. . . .

JOHN 11:25

The search for [my son] Ross and his friend continued; and grace abounded in my life and relationships. They found Ross' body in the spring, more than four months later, about ten miles downriver. Before his body was recovered, we had found on his desk at home in Denver a hand-written copy of his will, dated February 20, 1986, less than a year before the river swallowed his body. Through that long winter of fear and uncertainty, his words were also a grace to me.

"Well, if you're reading my will, then, obviously, I'm dead," Ross began. "I wonder how I died? Probably suddenly, because otherwise I would have taken the time to rewrite this. Even if I am dead, I think one thing should be remembered, and that is that I had a great time along the way. More importantly, it should be noted that I am in a better place now."

The will directed how he wanted his earthly goods distributed, and Ross concluded the document with this benediction: "In closing, I loved you all and thank you. You've made it a great life. Make sure you all go up instead of down and I'll be waiting for you at heaven's gate. Just look for the guy in the old khakis, Stetson, and faded shirt, wearing a pair of Ray-Bans and a Jack Nicholson smile. I also thank God for giving me the chance to write this before I departed. Thanks. Adios, Ross."

As horrifying and sad as it was, and is, to have lost him, Ross' disappearance and death also provided the greatest moments of rare insight and grandest gestures of immeasurable grace and joy that I ever hope to experience. Utter emptiness and brokenness left me feeling awful and wonderful at the same time. Close and silent embraces from friends, letters and phone calls of concern and empathy, and gifts of meals prepared and brought to our home were much-needed signs of love. . . .

There is a simple Quaker prayer about giving and receiving that I uttered the night after I lost Ross and that I pray often to this day. Because the Quakers use their hands as a type of religious artifact or symbol, the first part of the prayer is done with your palms up, visualizing yourself receiving all that you need from God. The second part is prayed with palms down, visualizing all your cares and concerns being left in the lap of a benevolent and loving God.

I used this physical prayer when I spoke at church two and a half weeks after we buried Ross.

"God," I began, "you have given my life into my hands. I give it back to you. My time, my property, my life itself. . . knowing it is only an instant compared to my life with you (and Ross) in eternity."

With palms down, I concluded, "Father, to you I release the cares and concerns of this world, knowing you loved me enough to give your only Son in my behalf. I'm a sinner in need of a Savior and, once again, I accept what you have done for me as sufficient. In Jesus' name. Amen."

I live in two worlds. One is the world of distraction and busyness. It's the world of deal-making and score-keeping, of stock market booms and busts. That world is like a cloud; it's going to perish. The other world I live in is where Ross is now—the world of the eternal. And it's the reality of that latter world that allows me to respond, with confidence: "Adios, Ross, for now."

Bob Buford, *Half-Time*

October 24

A Great Savior

In him we have redemption through his blood, the forgiveness of sins, in accordance with the riches of God's grace that he lavished on us with all wisdom and understanding.

Ephesians 1:7–8

John Newton, an Englishman who lived from 1725 to 1807, ran away to sea as a young boy and eventually went to Africa to participate in the slave trade. His reason for going, as he later wrote in his autobiography, was that he might "sin his fill." And sin he did! But the path of sin is downhill, and Newton's path descended so low that he was eventually reduced to the position of a slave in his master's African compound. This man dealt in slaves, and while he was off on slaving expeditions, Newton fell into the hands of a slave trader's African wife, who hated white men and vented her venom on Newton. Newton was forced to eat his food off the dusty floor like a dog, and at one point he was actually placed in chains. Sick and emaciated, he nearly died.

Newton eventually escaped from this form of his slavery. But he was still chained to sin and again went to sea, transporting slaves from the west coast of Africa to the New World. It was on his return from one of these slave voyages that Newton was wondrously converted.

The ship was overtaken by a fierce storm in the North Atlantic and was nearly sinking. The rigging was destroyed, water was pouring in. The seamen tried to seal the many leaks and brace the siding. Newton was sent down into the hold to pump water. He pumped for days, certain that the ship would sink and he would be taken under with it and be drowned. But as he pumped water in the hold of that ship, God brought to Newton's mind some verses he had learned from his mother as a child, and they led to his conversion. The ship survived the storm. The sailors were saved. And sometime later, after Newton had left the slave trade, this former "slave of slaves" studied for the Christian ministry and finally became a great preacher. He even preached before the queen.

What was Newton's motivation? It was a profound awareness of the grace and mercy of God toward him, a wretched sinner. Newton wrote,

Amazing grace—how sweet the sound—
That saved a wretch like me!
I once was lost, but now am found,
Was blind, but now I see.

Newton never forgot God's mercy to him. Once a friend of Newton's was complaining about someone who was resistant to the gospel and living a life of great sin. "Sometimes I almost despair of that man," the friend remarked.

"I never did despair of any man since God saved me," said Newton.

In his most advanced years, Newton's mind began to fail and he had to stop preaching. But when friends came to visit him he frequently remarked, "I am an old man. My mind is almost gone. But I can remember two things: I am a great sinner, and Jesus is a great Savior."

James Boice, *Mind Renewal*

OCTOBER 25

The Just for the Unjust

For Christ died for sins once for all, the righteous for the unrighteous, to bring you to God. He was put to death in the body but made alive by the Spirit.

I PETER 3:18

How then does the cross reconcile man to God? For long centuries God sought to humble man and get him to accept the blame of his sin in order that God might then forgive him and restore him to Himself. He brought many and grievous disciplines upon the race to that end, but all to no avail: man would not be broken—he persistently refused to take the blame and return to the Lord. At last it was as if God said, "If man will not be broken, I will be. If man will not take the blame, I will take the blame." That is what happened at the cross; it was God in Christ taking the blame, He the just for us the unjust. This was the divine strategy to bring man back to Himself. And it worked in a way no other way had! For whenever a man is given a real sight of the Cross, of God taking the blame that was his, he is broken, melted, finished, and cries out, "Oh my God, that is my place; Thou art not the wrongdoer, I am! Mine the blame, Thine the love!" And immediately there is reconciliation between them; man surrenders and God forgives. The brokenness of the Deity has provoked the brokenness of the creature!

Roy Hession, *Forgotten Factors*

OCTOBER 26

A Brother in Need

Jonathan said to David, "Whatever you want me to do, I'll do it for you."

I SAMUEL 20:4

All men need relationships with other men who have what it takes to keep their commitments to each other during difficult times—men who are not afraid to be truthful and real. Many men carry deep, deep hurts that need to be healed. Sometimes a man begins to remember the sexual or emotional abuse he received as a young boy and feels as if he is losing control of his anger and fear. Sometimes a man loses his job and is so overwhelmed with shame from his past that he cannot bring himself to get out of bed in the morning and look for work. Sometimes a man reaches a crisis in midlife when he feels as if time is running short, so he plunges into a destructive whirlwind of adolescent-type activity.

In all of these situations and more, men need to be ministered to by other men. They need the support of men who will offer comfort in their pain and encouragement as they struggle toward healing. Ministering to another man may mean holding and comforting him when he has flashbacks of sexual abuse. It may mean gently listening to a man who for decades has never revealed the fearsome details of his darkest combat days in Vietnam. It may mean affirming a man who is apprehensive about making a career change. It may mean sharing tears with the man who helplessly watched his buddy die following a mortar attack.

This is what I believe men's ministry is all about. Men are naturally afraid that other men will reject them if they share their deepest feelings and most intense struggles, so they keep their emotions to themselves for a long time. It takes a greatly hardened heart and/or tremendous amounts of alcohol, drugs, food, work or sex to keep these feelings locked inside. The ongoing ministry of a community of Christian men can do much to help men heal from the wounds in their hearts—old wounds as well as new. It can help them grow more fully into Christian manhood, can help put into action what Christ planted in their hearts when they became Christians.

Earl Henslin, *Man to Man*

OCTOBER 27

Nonaggressive Behavior

But he said to me, "My grace is sufficient for you, for my power is made perfect in weakness." Therefore I will boast all the more gladly about my weaknesses, so that Christ's power may rest on me.

II CORINTHIANS 12:9

Often we men recognize the need to rid ourselves of aggressive behavior. But giving up aggressive behavior isn't easy. We may realize that aggression creates personal stress and upset in others. We may know it alienates others and keeps others at a distance. But we are comfortable being able to control others. We have a sense of power. As aggressors, we can let off steam; and besides, others may get the (false) impression that the aggressor is a person of power.

How does a man come to want to forsake willingly his aggressive behavior? You will want to give up aggression when you discover that real power is not exercised through being aggressive and you are ready to reject several misbeliefs. You must feel secure about yourself, not needing to control others. That occurs when you discover your value and worth, which comes from God's perspective, not society's.

We also must learn to accept our imperfections and still feel good about our identity. We need to recognize we can never fully control our life or others' lives. The nonaggressive man is a true man—willing to become a risk-taker and discover new ways of relating to other people. His security comes through trusting the Person of Jesus Christ in his life, feeling secure in God's love shown through Christ.

Gary Oliver, *Real Men Have Feelings Too*

OCTOBER 28
A "Whole" Man

"My food," said Jesus, "is to do the will of him who sent me and to finish his work."

JOHN 4:34

A worthy goal for a man, which may run counter to his early learning, is to become a "balanced man." And that is where Christianity comes in by eliminating a man's inner conflicts and bringing about this balance as seen in Jesus Christ.

Jesus' personality had several facets, but he did not hide them from anyone. He could chase the corrupters out of his temple in righteous anger, displaying his manhood in what might be called "masculine" ways—and yet later he wept over Jerusalem, displaying what is considered a "feminine" side.

He met the challenge of the enemy and faced them in open debate; and yet he could hold children on his knees and in a moment of tenderness express how precious they were to him and to the kingdom of God.

He walked the bloody highways of Palestine, littered with the flotsam of man's inhumanity to man, pursued, harassed and carrying a price on his head; and yet he could sit and allow a woman to wash his feet and dry them with her hair and rebuke those who thought it inappropriate.

On more than one occasion, he lashed out with a sharp verbal lance, even calling the religious leaders a bunch of "vipers," thus taking the wind right out of them and leaving them dumbfounded; and yet he dealt mercifully with a frantic father who honestly confessed his inability to believe that Jesus could heal his son, touching the boy in tenderness, compassion and power—making him whole.

He had all the legions of heaven on his side and could have, in one master stroke of his manliness, wiped out his enemies. Yet he stood mute before the Roman court, refusing to give dignity to a mob.

Here is the Son of God, Jesus, the Man, who was not asexual, but who never used his sexuality to prove his manhood.

Here is the king of the universe, sweating blood during the deep revulsion he felt in Gethsemane concerning the death that faced him, and yet pressing on to take that death on the cross without wilting.

There is no greater picture of the "whole man"—a man who was "masculine" in terms of strength, muscle, sinew and courage and yet was not ashamed to show his "feminine" side in terms of tears, compassion, gentleness and peace. He said, "I must finish the task," which in essence means, "I must win for humanity the redemption God designed through me." He won that redemption in the end on the strength of his total manhood, which was beautiful, dynamic and sensitive.

Norman Wright, *Understanding the Man in Your Life*

October 29
Garbage In, Garbage Out

As he thinketh in his heart, so is he.

PROVERBS 23:7 (KJV)

GIGO. Sounds like a Greek verb, doesn't it? Or is it an Italian food you haven't tried yet? Well, before you reach for a Greek lexicon or rush to the nearest Italian restaurant, let me assure you it is neither of these. GIGO is a computer term, an acronym for *Garbage In, Garbage Out*. Computer programmers know that whatever they feed into a computer will inevitably show up in the printout. So, if "garbage" goes in, "garbage" will come out—GIGO.

The human mind is a fabulous computer. As a matter of fact, no one has been able to design a computer as intricate and efficient as the human mind. Consider this: your brain is capable of recording 800 memories per second for seventy-five years without ever getting tired. Although there are a number of computers on the market today with amazing capabilities packed into them, not one of them can match the service record of the human brain. God has certainly placed a phenomenal, one-of-a-kind piece of equipment in the human cranium.

Now, here's something on the plus side for the average computer: its engineers and programmers, understanding the meaning of GIGO, do their dead-level best to keep "garbage" out of the program so they do not get "garbage" in the printout. Human beings, on the other hand, don't exercise very much care about what they feed into God's computer, the brain. It's amazing how much "garbage" some persons will program into their brains as they sit for hours in front of the TV. It has been estimated that by the time a person in our society reaches the age of eighteen he has watched 25,000 hours of television, including 350,000 commercials. (You know how intellectually stimulating commercials are!)

Am I overly concerned about the adverse effect of television on the human mind? I don't think so. Some time ago I was reading *Media and Methods*, the stock and trade magazine for communications people, when I came across a provocative statement by Herbert Marshall McLuhan, who [was] a giant in the field of communications. McLuhan affirmed, "Only madmen would use television if they knew the consequences."

Certainly the Bible confirms the principle that what we feed into our minds will come out in the life. We can place McLuhan's alarming observation about TV squarely in line with what King Solomon observed about 3,000 years ago. "As he thinketh in his heart, so is he," Solomon wrote in Proverbs 23:7

Earl Radmacher, *You and Your Thoughts*

OCTOBER 30

Seizing the Day!

Now to him who is able to do immeasurably more than all we ask or imagine, according to his power that is at work within us . . .

EPHESIANS 3:20

We must seize the moment!

As I have talked with Christian leaders across the country, I keep hearing the same refrain: *Carpe Diem!* Seize the day! Seize the God-given opportunity. The Scripture says God will "do immeasurably more than all we ask or imagine, according to his power that is at work within us" (Eph 3:20). For that to happen, however, we must be men of action, men who are ready to respond by faith to what God has initiated.

As Paul said, we must "be very careful, then, how [we] live—not as unwise but as wise, making the most of every *opportunity*, because the days are evil" (Eph. 5:15–16, emphasis added). Millions of women—wives, mothers, sisters and daughters—have been praying that the men of the world would respond to the Lord.

I strongly believe those prayers are now being answered. God's Spirit is calling men to rise up! And they are! They're growing into a new and deeper intimacy with Jesus, and through His power they are seizing the spiritual initiative in their homes, churches, friendships, and communities. The responsibilities men have abandoned for too long are once again being vigorously addressed. Men are rising up to become all God originally intended them to be: men of integrity, men who keep their promises.

Randy Phillips, *Seven Promises of a Promise Keeper—Promise*

October 31

Spiritual Muscles

We ought always to thank God for you, brothers, and rightly so, because your faith is growing more and more, and the love every one of you has for each other is increasing.

II Thessalonians 1:3

Living in the spiritual realm is much like preparing for a race in the physical realm. At one point I'm working on speed, then endurance, then on muscle tone. When not actually running I'm conscious of diet, of rest, and other factors. There are strategies and goals to be considered.

Spiritual growth progresses according to much the same pattern. Every incident I face throughout the day is intended to "train" my spiritual muscles of patience or kindness or reliance on the Lord. The difficulties and trials I continue to encounter teach me endurance in much the same way a ten-mile run every morning does for my body.

Therefore, once my competitive running days were behind me, I found myself training still, but in a much a different way. Now I was developing my mental and emotional and spiritual impulses and reactions, always with the goal of modeling myself after Jesus. We were making headway—ridding ourselves of old attitudes, letting Christ put in His way of thinking and acting.

And that, of course, is the essence of growth, the essence of life itself. That is where the abundant and fulfilling life originates—by living according to the example of Jesus. It is a life outside of one's self, a life founded in a loving and intimate relationship with God the Father.

Jim Ryun, *In Quest of Gold*

November

Surrender

I will praise you as long as I live,
  and in your name I will lift up my hands.

PSALM 63:4

David lifted his hands to God. The lifted hand is symbolic of surrender or submission. If someone put a gun in your back, by lifting up your hands you indicate you have surrendered to them. David stated that his life was surrendered to God. What is it to surrender to someone? It means we become their captive. They own us. We are subject to their whims. To become captive to mere man could be quite devastating. However, you always dwell in places of safety when you are a captive of God.

David was a bondservant of God. A bondservant places himself in a position wherein the Lord has complete mastery over him. A bondservant is one who has the freedom of choice but chooses to continue to serve out of love. In Luke 2:29 we read of Simeon who said, "Sovereign Lord, as you have promised, you now dismiss your servant in peace." The word Lord in this verse is not the typical word for Lord. It literally means authoritarian or dictator. Simeon looked upon himself as the servant of the Lord under His absolute mastery. The Lord was his complete master. Simeon was a mastered, subdued, and subjugated man.

To think of the Lord as a dictator becomes negative only when we do not want to be controlled. David loved his God. He did not view being a bondservant as a negative thing because his desire was to be controlled by God. He submitted himself to God. He lifted his hands in surrender to his

God. This is what separated David from most others. Today we don't often understand such devotion. We tend to live for ourselves and to use God to get our way. We don't see Him as the One who has complete mastery over us, yet we are quick to call Him Lord. Luke 6:46 says, "Why do you call me, 'Lord, Lord,' and do not do what I say?"

Ron Auch, *The Heart of the King*

NOVEMBER 2

Marital Oneness

In this same way, husbands ought to love their wives as their own bodies. He who loves his wife loves himself. After all, no one ever hated his own body, but he feeds and cares for it, just as Christ does the church . . .

EPHESIANS 5:28–29

Husband, take positive steps to meet your partner's emotional needs. Your wife longs to be encouraged, built up, and praised. She wants to feel close to you emotionally. This will come as you love her in the way the Bible describes. A husband can always meet his wife's deepest needs by loving her as Christ loves us, and as a wife begins to respond to that love, she is ready to respond sexually.

The husband's love has been compared to a warm coat he wraps around his wife. As long as she feels encircled and sheltered in his love, she can give herself completely to him. In this safety, she can accept herself as a woman and value her femininity. Then she will be able to entrust herself to her husband in the sexual relationship as the bird gives itself to the air or the fish to water.

We husbands may not be able to fully appreciate the deep longings that influence our wives, but if we love them with the sheltering love that is described in Ephesians 5:28–29 we will see results! Our wives reflect the love or lack of love we have provided.

As you move toward each other physically and emotionally, you should also move closer in the spiritual dimension of marriage. Sharing in warm personal Bible study and prayer together will help prepare the way for sexual fulfillment as a natural result of the spiritual union that is occurring daily. Then you will find that your sexual union can bring you still closer to

God, so that you often want to pray together after making love. Love produces love in all directions!

Ed Wheat, *Love Life for Every Married Couple*

NOVEMBER 3
A Spiritual Father

*For this reason I remind you to fan into flame the gift of God, which is in you
through the laying on of my hands.*

II TIMOTHY 1:6

Timothy was a man of God who received his faith and knowledge of God
through his maternal lineage: his grandmother Lois and his mother, Eunice
(see 2 Tim. 1:5). In fact, the book of Acts explains that Timothy's father was
a Greek, not a Hebrew, and therefore was probably not equipped in any
spiritual way to teach Timothy what he would need to know about manhood in a Jewish community . . . Therefore, in his role of spiritual leadership
and responsibility, Timothy had what the Bible identifies as a "spirit of
timidity" (2 Tim. 1:7). Although this "spirit of timidity" is not clearly understood, the apostle Paul may be trying to shed some light on the subject by
intimating that perhaps Timothy was struggling with a lack of a male role
model in his life and the great insecurity it produced. Therefore, Paul
"adopted" Timothy as his son, becoming his spiritual father and mentor.

Paul reminds him to "fan into flame the gift of God," which was in Timothy through the laying on of Paul's hands (2 Tim. 1:6). In doing so, Paul
provided Timothy with a blessing passed from father to son—something
Timothy did not receive from his own earthly dad.

Why was that blessing so important? So that Timothy, who was a gifted
leader of the early church, would not have to go before the masculine community of his day feeling as though something were lacking in his life . . . or
that somehow he was not manly enough . . . or even that he was not "old
enough" to be called to such an important role within Christendom.

Paul's instructions to Timothy often sound like a father's instructions to
his son—to enable him, to empower him, and to pass on the mantle of
manhood. This becomes more obvious in 2 Tim. 2:2, when Paul tells Timothy: "Flee the evil desires of youth, and pursue righteousness, faith, love
and peace, along with those who call on the Lord out of a pure heart." In 1

Cor. 13:11, Paul uses somewhat parallel language about young faith versus mature faith: "When I was a child, I talked like a child, I thought like a child, I reasoned like a child. When I became a man, I put childish ways behind me."

By adopting Timothy as his son in a spiritual sense, Paul is calling for him to become a man—to become a viable member of the masculine community!

Michael O'Donnell, Home from Oz

NOVEMBER 4
Victory Over Impure Thoughts

We demolish arguments and every pretension that sets itself up against the knowledge of God, and we take captive every thought to make it obedient to Christ.

II CORINTHIANS 10:5

Probably no other problem afflicts so many men as the problem of unclean thoughts in the minds of those who have come to Christ. In the cesspool of their vain imaginings, the enemy torments and oppresses the adopted sons of God with frustration over the seeming evidence that God does not have the power to cleanse their thought life and provide them with true freedom. The more mature they become in their walk of discipleship, the more acute and frustrating this problem becomes. Men of Christ want to be free, but seem to be unable to gain victory for more than a few hours or days at a time. The problem is more widespread now than ever before because of the spreading filth of our society and the dramatic spread of sexual corruption throughout the families of America. It is an awful stench that has fouled our lives for too long, now erupting in our society in the most heinous of crimes against women and children . . .

We have seen too many pictures, too many films, too much TV and been involved in too much immorality and filthiness to simply close down the pictures of our minds. There are huge caves of residence established in our minds in which the enemy was once entertained; he secured legitimate access. Now it seems impossible to close the doors to him. Demonic spirits leap across magazine pages, city streets, restaurants and everyday work places to pursue the stimulation of old evil thought habits. They seem to be everywhere. How does one resist them? Is there any hope of gaining permanent victory over them?

Yes there is, in Christ Jesus.

But we must first learn to stay with our Lord and Shepherd. Having hearts of sheep, we tend constantly to go astray, wandering off on our own. Each victory tends to take us away from the Source of our victory.

It is the incorrect and powerful thought habit of the "old man" that tells us we experience freedom when we are independent. This is not true at all. We find our freedom by becoming bond-slaves to Jesus Christ. It is when our thoughts become *captive* to Christ that we bring down the strongholds and (destroy) speculations and every lofty thing raised up against the knowledge of God. . . .

But when we find a temporary solution to being unoppressed, we tend naturally to revert to going our own way, only to fall into the same trap all over again. Both the independent behavior and the weakness are symptomatic of the natural man. It is this weakness that delivers us to Christ again and again, teaching us to stay with Him.

Remember Paul's lesson in his attempts to get free of the thorn of his flesh. He was finally given specific instructions by the Lord. "My grace is sufficient for you, for power is perfected in weakness." Paul's response was that he would most gladly boast in his weaknesses, that the power of Christ could dwell in him (2 Cor. 12:9).

This is spiritual warfare. It is actual and demanding combat. Praise God that Jesus has secured the victory in our weakness! You will share in this victory as you practice (as any warrior) until you become so skilled in the wielding of your weapons that the enemy sees only the prospects of defeat and a net loss every time he attempts to breach your defenses. As the swing of your sword, the Word of God (Eph. 6:17), becomes more consistent, you will experience freedom. You will come to rejoice at each opportunity to see time-proven principles of warfare do more than provide you with victory. You will see the hand of God gaining new territory for Christ.

Karl Duff, *Restoration of Men*

NOVEMBER 5

A Loving Father

These commandments that I give you today are to be upon your hearts. Impress them on your children. Talk about them when you sit at home and when you walk along the road, when you lie down and when you get up.

DEUTERONOMY 6:6–7

Children are a gift from the Lord. They are to be reared with love and firmness. The Christian parental hope and prayer is that they may be the kind of example which will cause their children to reverence the Lord.

Christian parents are responsible not only for the physical needs of their children—which even nature teaches—but also for spiritual growth (Deuteronomy 6:4–9; 32:45–47). Verbal instruction should be accompanied by example. If they see you do something that is contrary to your preaching or testimony, they will lose confidence in your Gospel. I met a businessman several years ago whose father was one of the best-known pastor/evangelists in North America. He had five sons. Not only did his sons fail to follow in their father's footsteps, but they had all gone away from the Lord. I can imagine the grief and suffering of that father's heart through the years. Whether he and his wife were at fault, I do not know. But the businessman son who sat by my side said, "My father preached wonderful messages, but he did not live them out at home."

If our children hear us talking about honesty and yet fail to see it in our lives, this inconsistency will do great harm. If we talk about God as a loving heavenly Father, and yet we are stern, unloving, or insensitive to our children, should we be surprised if they grow up doubting that God loves them?

A teenager once complained, "The problem with parents is that by the time you get them, they're too old to change!"

No parents are perfect. There will be problems, but the important thing is to build mutual understanding with our children. Love must be evident when correction is necessary. It is a happy husband-wife relationship and their evident oneness in Christ that leads children toward faith in Him and makes for a happy, wholesome family life.

Paul, writing to Timothy, gives the strongest possible admonition and warning to husbands and fathers, "If any provide not for his own and specially for those of his own house, he hath denied the faith, and is worse than an infidel" (I Timothy 5:8). The provision referred to need not be confined to material things, but also to time and energy and concern.

One evangelist was made aware of this when he was thumbing through his diary one evening. His young son, seeing the small book by which his father's life was ordered and controlled, said, "Daddy, could you put my name in there?"

Billy Graham, A Biblical Standard for Evangelists

NOVEMBER 6
Self-Control

Everything is permissible for me—but not everything is beneficial. Everything is permissible for me—but I will not be mastered by anything.

I CORINTHIANS 6:12

Men, is there a hobby or entertainment . . . [that's] in danger of crowding out the best in your life?

One recreational hindrance can be television. Personally, I have made the choice not to hook our house up to cable television. My kids think we are the Beverly Hillbillies. Before they discovered oil.

I have made this "radical" decision for two reasons. First, because I do not want many of those cable programs available to my children. But second, because I know I would become addicted to ESPN (the all-sports network). If I had access to ESPN, it would ruin my life. I know it would. I would be tempted to watch it every night. No, I *would* watch it every night. To the neglect of my family. To the disregard for time in God's Word. For me, it would become an encumbrance, slowing me down in the best things.

You ought to see us on family vacations. The moment we check into a hotel, we immediately flip on ESPN. I tell my wife that I am spending personal time with my boys.

Men, what is your pastime passion? Working on your car? Grooming your yard? Building something in your workshop? Being mesmerized by your PC?

Now, these are not sins. They are innocent things. Legitimate. Good things. But they can become encumbrances. And detract us from the goal.

Steven Lawson, Men Who Win

NOVEMBER 7

A Work to Do

For we are God's workmanship, created in Christ Jesus to do good works, which God prepared in advance for us to do.

EPHESIANS 2:10

Every man has work laid out for him to do; every man's life is a plan of the Almighty, and way back in the councils of eternity God laid out a work for each one of us. There is no man living that can do the work that God has got for me to do. No one can do it but myself. And if the work ain't done, we will have to answer for it when we stand before God's bar. For it says: "Every man shall be brought unto judgement, and every one shall give an account of the deeds done in the body." And it seems to me that every one of us ought to take this question home tonight: "Well am I doing the work that God has for me to do?" God has got a work for every one of us to do. Now in the parable the man who had two talents had the same reward as the man who had five talents. He heard the same words as the man who had five talents. "Well done, thou good and faithful servant, enter thou into the joy of thy Lord." The men that take good care of the talents that God has loaned them, he always gives them more. But if we take the talent that God has given us, and lay it away carefully in a napkin and bury it away, God will take even that from us. God don't want a man that has got one talent to do the work of a man who has got ten. All a man has got to answer for is the one that God has given him. If we were all of us doing the work that God has got for us to do, don't you see how the work of the Lord would advance?

But some men are not satisfied with the talents they have, but are always wishing for some one else's talent. Now, that is all wrong. It is contrary to the spirit of Christ. Instead of wishing for some one else's talent, let us make the best use of the talents God has given us.

Let us do all the business we can. If we can't be a lighthouse, let us be a tallow candle. There used to be a period when the people came up to meeting bringing their candles with them. The first one perhaps wouldn't make a great illumination, but when two or three got there there would be more light. If the people of this city should do this now, if each one should come here with his candle, don't you think there would be a good deal of light?

Let all the gas be put out in this hall, and one solitary candle would give a little light here. If we can't be a lighthouse, let us be a tallow candle. Some one said, "I can't be anything more than a farthing rushlight." Well if you can't be more than that, that is well enough. Be all you can. What makes the Dead Sea dead? Because it is all the time receiving, never giving out anything. Why is it that many Christians are cold? Because they are all the time receiving, never giving out anything. You go out every Sunday and hear good sermons, and think that is enough. You are all the time receiving these grand truths, but never give them out. When you hear it, go and scatter the sacred truth abroad. Instead of having one minister to preach to a thousand people, this thousand ought to take a sermon and spread it till it reaches those who never go to church or chapel. Instead of having a few, we ought to have thousands using the precious talents that God has given them.

Dwight L. Moody, *The Gospel Awakening*

NOVEMBER 8

Ending Sexual Harassment

You shall not commit adultery.

EXODUS 20:14

A word familiar to ... people today is *machismo*. To them it signifies a man who is virile and masculine, sparkling with charisma and sex appeal. I discovered in Venezuela that the word has a less distinguished meaning than our youth suspected. In Spanish-speaking countries, it stems from the word *macho*, which means "animal." Thus, machismo really means "the sexual superiority and animal appeal of men." It is supposed to give the man sexual license to use the woman, obligating her to care for the children while he lives to the satisfaction of the flesh. Down there one encounters a male-dominated world. In fact, a man may marry one woman but maintain four or five others on the side. Not only do men fulfill this role, but women expect it! In actuality, a man's machismo seems related to how many women he keeps on his string—children and all. In Mexico, a man automatically gains control of the children in a divorce unless he is caught in the act of adultery. Machismo, then, serves as the current term for "Don Juan" or "Casanova," but it distinctly does not correspond with *masculinity*.

A truly masculine man has a streak of chivalry in him that causes him to control his sex drive and, instead of using a woman, protect her. In days of old, knights actually fought to defend a woman's virtue, honor, and life. Such actions should characterize our society today—but they are becoming rare. *Redbook* magazine published an article describing the shocking things some married men do to working women (against their will but under threat of job loss). The article reported that nine out of ten working women surveyed claimed that they had been molested, humiliated, or subjected to lurid or insulting remarks against their will by male employers. Rather than genteel masculinity, such deplorable treatment seems more like barbarity or misogyny.

The age of chivalry is not dead. In fact, an engineer recently jeopardized his job in a spontaneous show of it to a superior. He had watched his attractive secretary repeatedly being embarrassed and humiliated by their lecherous department superintendent until he could stand it no longer. He went into the boss's office, closed the door, very calmly objected to these unprovoked advances, and warned that if they didn't stop, he would meet the superintendent outside and teach him "some respect for womanhood." Now that's masculinity!

You may say, "What if he's bigger than I?" Organize a task force! You will find others who agree with you, but don't shirk your responsibility. Something inside you will begin to die if you do.

Tim LaHaye, *Understanding the Male Temperament*

NOVEMBER 9
Godliness with Contentment

*A faithful man will be richly blessed,
but one eager to get rich will not go unpunished.*

PROVERBS 28:20

If you're either participating in state-sanctioned gambling or you want to, my question is, why do you want to play it? For instance, do you want to play the lottery because you want to contribute to the educational program of your state? Is your motivation to help put more police on the street, or whatever the lottery people say will happen with the money?

Or, do you want to play the lottery because the government has come up with a way for you to get rich quickly? If that is your motivation, then you have forfeited God's biblical means to wealth, because He says that those who participate in get-rich-quick schemes will not go unpunished.

Don't misunderstand. The problem is not being rich. The problem is the greed mentality you used to get there. Now let me ask you something else. Let's say you win twenty million dollars in the lottery. Do you think that winning represents God's plan for your life? Can you honestly say you took that step in obedience to God's leading?

Well, I suppose it is possible. But if you'll pardon the pun, I'll have to say the odds are against it. What I mean is that most people who play the lottery simply grab for the pot of gold because it's there. God's leading or His plan doesn't enter the picture at that particular moment.

What's the problem with that? It means winning the lottery is not tied to anything but a thirst for wealth. It is not tied to God's leading or plan for you. It's not even tied to your needs. So what you are doing is asking God to bless nothingness. You are asking Him to bless getting money for money's sake. That's greed and God won't bless it. . . .

If you are not content then you are driven by greed. I don't mean that you shouldn't want to move forward, but God wants you to be content where you are until He decides to give you more. And even when it becomes obvious that God does not want you to have more, He still wants you to be content.

Tony Evans, Gambling

NOVEMBER 10
Developing Character

Not only so, but we also rejoice in our sufferings, because we know that suffering produces perseverance; perseverance, character; and character, hope.

ROMANS 5:3–4

How do we develop character?

I believe most of a person's character is developed as a child. It's the result of values learned from family and other significant people early in life—which is what makes our role as parents and the role of those who coach kids so important.

We also develop character by going through adversity. Coaches sometimes talk about a losing year being a "character-building season." There's truth to that as I've seen from experience. That strength of character so crucial to the 1970 Cowboys who rallied from almost certain failure to go on to the Super Bowl was forged through those difficult years when we couldn't win the big one. . . .

Yet the truth remains, most of our character is established early in life. Adversity can help build it. Coaches can help mold it. But in our adult years, the only thing I've seen that can radically change a person's basic character is a relationship with Jesus Christ.

Just what does that mean?

I think there's a lot of confusion in the world today about what it means to be a Christian. Unfortunately, a lot of well-meaning Christian athletes contribute to that confusion.

Since the time I committed my own life to God, I've tried to be very open about that fact. . . . It's the most important thing in my life. And I think it's important for Christians to speak out and explain what they believe.

But I have to admit that I'm troubled a little and have very mixed reactions when I see a football player kneel down in the end zone and thank God after a touchdown. I have the same feeling of misgiving when I hear from winning locker rooms the excited testimonies of happy players who say, "I just want to thank the Lord because without him this victory wouldn't have been possible!"

Don't get me wrong. I think an athlete should feel gratitude for his God-given abilities. I think we all ought to regularly give thanks to our Creator for our blessings, our opportunities, for life itself. But I'm afraid these little "God helped me score a touchdown" and "God helps me be a winner" testimonials mislead people and belittle God.

I don't believe God plays favorites like that. Neither do I believe God cares who wins a football game, despite the old joke in Dallas that the reason Texas Stadium was designed with a hole in the roof was so God could watch his favorite team play every Sunday afternoon.

While I don't believe God helps Christian athletes run faster, jump higher, or hit harder, I do believe a personal faith in Christ can be a very real advantage in life—as a football player, a surgeon, a business executive, a teacher, a student, or even a parent. Because personal faith in God can change and improve anyone's character.

Tom Landry, *Tom Landry: An Autobiography*

NOVEMBER 11

Majestic Praise

Then I heard every creature in heaven and on earth and under the earth and on the sea, and all that is in them, singing:
  "To him who sits on the throne and to the Lamb
  be praise and honor and glory and power,
  for ever and ever!"

REVELATION 5:13

Today, we glorify the artist who works completely alone. But before the Renaissance no artist even signed his work. Art was not individual expression; it served a corporate purpose, such as worship. Yet the unsigned artists were great artists, with an obvious love for their work, who created (for instance) the great cathedrals of Europe. To be a cog in a machine is not necessarily depersonalizing. It depends on whether you love your place in the machine, and whether you love the work the machine does. Thus, an IBM employee may be known not so much through his personal contribution to IBM as through an understanding of IBM and his place in it. He is part of something bigger than himself, and it is part of him.

I love choral singing for the very reason that my individual effort is deliberately immersed and lost in a vast sea of sound. When I was in college I had the opportunity to sing with the chorus in several concerts with the San Francisco Symphony. I have only an ordinary amateur voice, but I love good music. Those concerts made the greatest musical expression I ever hope to attain. Not because of my efforts—I do not even know whether I sang well or badly. But I was part of beautiful music made by a first-rate orchestra. I was a part so small as to be unidentifiable, but nonetheless an active part. My "work" was an enterprise I cared for, but which surpassed and surrounded me. If you want to understand my musical soul, don't listen to me, listen to the "Missa Solemnis."

This is why, I believe, our activity in heaven is described as choral singing in praise to God. Praise is our eternal work, and the joy of it lies not in our individual contribution but in our participation in a vast, beautiful, collective praise. If you want to understand a believer's ultimate meaning, listen to that praise.

Tim Stafford, *Knowing the Face of God*

NOVEMBER 12
A Way Through the Flood

For the LORD your God dried up the Jordan before you until you had crossed over. The LORD your God did to the Jordan just what he had done to the Red Sea when he dried it up before us until we had crossed over. He did this so that all the peoples of the earth might know that the hand of the LORD is powerful and so that you might always fear the LORD your God.

JOSHUA 4:23–24

Have you come to a place in your life where you are faced with a seemingly insurmountable difficulty? You do not know where to turn or where to go or what to do, and you are looking for a way out.

Don't try to think your way out, because that will only get you into more complexities and difficulties. You need Jesus Christ Himself to operate in the conditions of your life and to change them. God wants you to believe Him, to boldly confess His Word in such a situation and then act upon it.

When you do, this impossible circumstance will become "a way," so you can march right through them to victory. This happened for Joshua and the Children of Israel, when God split the waters of the Jordan, and caused them to stand up in a heap, so that the people could cross over on dry ground. . . .

This seemingly impossible circumstance blocked the Children of Israel from entering the Promised Land, just as there are hindrances that obstruct you from entering into the very promises of God that our Heavenly Father wants to give you.

But because Joshua [believed and boldly confessed] the Word of the Lord he knew that the Children of Israel could cross the River Jordan, even though it was flooding. He understood what God said to him, just as you can read something in the Bible today and know it is the complete revelation of God.

Jim Durkin, *The Bold Confession*

NOVEMBER 13
Friends As Brothers

A friend loves at all times,
  and a brother is born for adversity.

PROVERBS 17:17

At age thirteen, I was required to take metal shop in junior high school. I shall never forget one particular project. The teacher asked us to make a metal box from a sheet of metal. It could only be eight inches square. After we were finished, the shop teacher had the entire class line up with box in hand in front of his desk.

He then took each box in turn from us as we moved through the line, looked at it, graded it, and handed it back.

My box had some problems. Though the right length (eight inches square), solder had clumped in a couple corners, and the sides didn't fully align. Still, it looked acceptable, if less than perfect. When the teacher saw my box, he took one look at it, threw it into the trash, and wrote an F in his grade book. To a young teenager, in front of his peers, that was devastating. From that point onward, I never thought I could make anything, or work with my hands.

Years later, at age twenty-eight, I bought an old house. The place was basically uninhabitable, but my wife and I knew we could make it charming. Unfortunately, we didn't have enough money to finish fixing the place up. And I was forced to do many things myself.

I can still remember friends coming into that house to admire my work. "You're doing a good job, Jim, Keep at it." As my friends sincerely admired what I was doing, my whole perspective on myself as an incompetent builder changed. Now I realized that I could work with my hands.

Friendships are like that. Once we have friends as part of our lives, we are no longer the same.

James Osterhaus, *Bonds of Iron*

November 14

Daily Courage

Be on your guard; stand firm in the faith; be men of courage; be strong. Do everything in love.

I CORINTHIANS 16:13–14

I have a close friend whose father, Jim, didn't set out to be a success. He didn't plan on being a hero either. He turned out to be both. He did it with courage.

The world was at war. Red flags with swastikas and white flags with a red sun in the middle flapped in the breeze over lands they had no prior claim to. German soldiers were entrenched throughout Europe and Japanese soldiers were entrenched on islands in the South Pacific. The United States joined the other countries of the world to do something about it.

That's how Jim found himself on the inside of amphibious landing equipment—four times. The battles to liberate the islands of the South Pacific started offshore as terrified young men climbed down into the insides of these attack vessels. Some went once, and a few went twice, but seldom did anyone hit the beach four times. They usually didn't live long enough to have the privilege.

Jim joined thousands of men like him in facing a common enemy. he shared their fears and anxieties.

He wanted to succeed in overcoming the enemy, but knew that the outcome of the battle was not under his control. He could neither manipulate the enemy nor wield a great deal of control over his fellow marines.

But he did have control over himself.

So he brought to the battle the vital necessity for personal calm and ultimate victory. He brought courage. . . . When I think of men like Jim, I realize that they were successful because they were courageous—not courageous because they were successful. It took courage to run into the exploding guns of the enemy, and it took courage to keep your mind on your mission when all you had to do was sit around cleaning your gun and counting your ammunition. A soldier's inner calm came, therefore, not from the outcome of the battle, but from his ability to maintain courage.

Calm in the workplace requires the same factor as calm on the battlefield. Those who choose to be courageous are those who are going to enjoy inner rest at their jobs. Courageous people are those who subordinate their fears to the task before them. They don't let the heat and anger of the battle distract them from their ultimate purpose.

With this in mind, let me ask a crucial question: Is it possible to be a success at home *and* at work? I believe it is. But I believe it will only happen if we are willing to be courageous enough to make some daring decisions about our work. Men . . . who take these steps of courage can enjoy confidence in the middle of the boredom and calm in the middle of the battle.

Tim Kimmel, *Little House on the Freeway*

NOVEMBER 15

A Dream

. . . we were like men who dreamed.
Our mouths were filled with laughter,
—our tongues with songs of joy.

PSALMS 126:1B–2A

I had a dream. It was a simple dream, more feeling than detail, but it seemed to last a long while.

Simply, a friend of mine was coming to see me, and I was excited by the prospect. I didn't know who the friend was. That didn't seem odd. I suppose I didn't occupy myself with the question *Who*. Just with the anticipation and with the certainty that he would come.

As the time for his arrival drew nearer and nearer, my excitement increased. I felt more and more like a child, beaming with my pleasure, distracted from all other pursuits, thinking of this one thing only. I found that laughter fell from me as easily as rain. I wanted to stand on the porch and bellow to the neighborhood, *My friend is coming!* Joy became a sort of swelling in my chest, and all my flesh began to tingle.

Well, it was clear that I hadn't seen this friend for years. Even in the intensity of excitement, I didn't picture him to myself. Perhaps I didn't know what he looked like. Is that possible? Yet I had no doubt that he was dear to me, and I to him; that he satisfied the fathomless need in me; and that it was me in particular whom he chose to visit. I could scarcely stand the waiting. Strangely, I think I expected to recognize him by his scent, by a certain smell I remembered, rich and steadfast, fleshly, warm, enveloping—

like the strong declaration of a stallion's flank after galloping. It wasn't so much my eyes I strained, then, but my nostrils and the fullness of my mouth.

A wild kind of music attended my waiting. And the closer he came, the more exquisite grew this music—high violins rising higher by the sweetest, tightest, most piercing dissonance, reaching for, weeping for, the final resolve of his appearing.

And when the music had ascended to nearly impossible chords of wailing little notes, and when the familiar scent was a bounty around me, and when excitement had squeezed the breath from my lungs, I started to cry.

And he came.

Then I put my hands to my cheeks and cried and laughed at once.

He was looking directly at me, with mortal affection—and I grew so strong within his gaze. And I knew at once who he was. I was a perfect flame of the knowledge of his name. It was Jesus. He had come exactly as he said he would.

I cherish this dream and think of it often. I was a full grown man when I dreamt it.

Walter Wangerin, Jr., *The Manger is Empty*

NOVEMBER 16

God's Timing

Those who sow in tears
  will reap with songs of joy.

PSALM 126:5

Like sands cascading down in an hourglass, time silently slips away, without the chance of retrieval, from almost everyone everyday. The misuse of anything as precious as time should be a crime. If someone steals your car, it would be an inconvenience but not a tragedy because you can easily acquire another. If someone snatches your wallet, it would be an annoyance but a few phone calls would salvage the majority of your concerns. But who can you call if you suffer the loss of time—and not just time, but *your time*? Who can afford to miss their time? I can't, can you?

Ask God to give you the patience you need to become empowered to perform. You may feel like a child waiting in line at a carnival. There will always be times when other people receive their dues and you are forced to wait your turn. This is not injustice; it is order. There is nothing unjust about order. But after I have waited my turn and paid my dues, there comes a time when it is all mine. The most frightening thing I can think of is the possibility of missing my time. Generally, somewhere on the other side of a tremendous test is the harvest of your dream. If you have planted the seeds of a promise and watered them thoroughly with the tears of struggle, then this is your time. Woe unto the person who has seeds without water. The tears of struggle become the irrigation of the Holy Spirit. It is through your own tear-filled struggles that God directs the waters of life to the field of your dreams.

They that sow in tears shall reap in joy. Psalm 126:5

Greatness has a tremendous thirst. This thirst is quenched in the tear-stained struggle toward destiny. One thing I learned about life is neither fellowship nor friendship can lower the price of personal sacrifice. What I mean is, no one can water your dreams but you. No matter how many people hold your hand, you still must shed your own tears. Others can cry with you, but they can't cry for you! That's the bad news. The good news is there will be a harvest at the end of your tears!

On the other hand, you must know when you have shed enough tears. It is important that you don't get stuck in a state of lamentation. In short, don't overwater the promise! A certain amount of tears is necessary during the time of sowing. But when you have come into harvest, don't let the devil keep you weeping. Tears are for the sower, but joy is for the harvester. Harvest your field with joy. You've paid your dues and shed your tears— now reap your benefits. It's your turn. Reap in knee-slapping, teeth-baring, hand-clapping, foot-stomping *joy*!

T. D. Jakes, *Can You Stand to Be Blessed?*

November 17

Self-Discipline

The plans of the diligent lead to profit
as surely as haste leads to poverty.

Proverbs 21:5

The only way one can develop character is through self-discipline. When a child is young, he is disciplined externally by his parents. As the child develops into maturity, the external discipline of his parents is internalized. By a mechanism of conscience and willpower, he imposes discipline on himself. This internal mechanism is called self-discipline.

The word discipline is related to the word disciple. How can we be a disciple if we are not going to be disciplined by Jesus? How can we be a disciple if we are not going to exercise the self-discipline needed to follow Him? Self-discipline involves an effort to control the will to do what one knows is right. Self-discipline is not allowing the lazy and lustful tendencies of our flesh to guide us. Without self-discipline, our conscience is incapable of taking command over our being. Self-discipline is the demand of the will for our bodies and minds to obey the leading of the Spirit.

Self-discipline will lead toward a productive lifestyle. Proverbs 21:5 states: *The plans of the diligent surely lead to plenty, but those of everyone who is hasty surely to poverty.*

A self-disciplined mind can begin to plan and dream of positive solutions. Self-discipline produces diligence and patience. One who is not self-disciplined will sink into laziness. He will not be able to exercise the self-control to be patient. An undisciplined person will be over-hasty and make mistakes. Diligence, patience and self-discipline work together.

Keith Intrater, *Covenant Relationships*

NOVEMBER 18

Godly Passion

For Christ's love compels us, because we are convinced that one died for all, and therefore all died. And he died for all, that those who live should no longer live for themselves, but for him who died for them and was raised again.

II CORINTHIANS 5:14–15

It takes God to love God. It takes a progressive revelation of God's infinitely satisfying love, His exuberant affections and His indescribable beauty to awaken the church and compel her to give herself wholly back to Him. Like Paul, believers will be compelled by this knowledge of God's love. . . .

Some believers look at the others who have high-energy personalities and say, "If I were wired with 220 volts like you, I'd be filled with zeal and passion for God, too. But I have a totally different temperament. I'm one of those 110-volt folks." Passion for Jesus is not a personality trait. You can have the gentlest human makeup possible and still be consumed with the fire of God. You may not express your passion in the same way a "220-volt" type personality does, but that fiery devotion will be there, and it will be just as real.

It doesn't matter how much human energy or natural zeal we possess. Passion for Jesus is the fruit of recognizing His dedication to us—not the fruit of our dedication to Him. We will walk in a life of commitment to Him because He is committed to us. When we stand before God, not a person on earth will be able to say, "I gave more to You than You gave to me."

Mike Bickle, *Passion for Jesus*

NOVEMBER 19

Refusing Adultery

Why be captivated, my son, by an adulteress?
Why embrace the bosom of another man's wife?
For a man's ways are in full view of the LORD,
and he examines all his paths.

PROVERBS 5:20–21

An epidemic of staggering proportions is taking place in America. I'm not thinking of AIDS. I'm thinking of adultery. It's an epidemic that for the most part used to afflict only those outside the body of Christ. No longer. This epidemic has not only found its way inside the church, but has wormed its way to the highest echelons of church leadership.

There's something strange about this epidemic other than its rolling virtually unchecked through the body of Christ. What is strange is that we don't *call* it "adultery."

Let's cut the double-talk. Let's put the cards on the table. Let's call adultery what it is. In the war on the family, adultery is treason. But we don't call it treason. We have developed a more refined and sophisticated term. Adultery has become an "affair."

When a man leaves his wife and children for another woman and acts as impulsively as an aroused junior high kid on his first date, it's not an "affair." It's adultery . . . an affair . . .

That word has sort of a nice, light, airy ring to it. Like quiche. It certainly isn't a judgmental term like adultery. The word affair is fluffy and nonthreatening. Affair is to adultery what quiche is to pot roast.

When I was a kid, I used to go to a fair. We would have a great time eating cotton candy, riding the Ferris wheel, and playing games on the arcade. When you went to a fair, you left all the responsibilities of normal life behind, at least for a few hours. Life was a lot of fun at a fair.

Maybe that's why we call adultery an affair. It's leaving behind your responsibilities. But let me say something about real men that I failed to mention earlier. Real men don't have affairs because real men are responsible. Real men keep their commitments. Even when their personal needs are not being met the way that they would hope. Even when they are disappointed in their wives for some reason. And that is precisely the time when we need to be on our guard more than ever. . . .

We have seen too many in recent years who have preached righteousness in the pulpit while practicing unrighteousness in some hotel room. We have seen too many who have publicly advocated righteousness with tremendous fervor but have privately practiced immorality with even greater intensity.

Righteousness must not only be found in our pulpits, but in our homes. The home is the church in miniature, and every Christian father has been appointed pastor of his own home. Christian men, whether they are leading in the church or in their home, must seek after righteousness.

Steve Farrar, *Point Man*

NOVEMBER 20

Being Drawn

Draw me, we will run after thee. . . .

SONG OF SONGS 1:4A (KJV)

Even though believers have fervent desires and are stirred to seek the Lord, yet they cannot but become conscious at the same time of an inadequate measure of strength for such arduous pursuit. The power to pursue is not just the power given by the Holy Spirit and deposited within us to enable us to seek Him. It is not that alone. Rather, it is a revelation of the Lord Jesus given by the Holy Spirit as outside and way beyond us, and thus drawing us to Himself by His own beauty and magnificent glory. The drawing power of the Person of the Lord Jesus Himself generates the pursuing power in us. If the Lord draws us by the revelation of Himself through His Spirit, then the seeking after Him is relatively easy.

If the Lord draws, then "we will run after thee." To *run after* means a continuous desire. It is the attracting power of the Lord Himself which alone creates the continuous power to so seek and so run. This is something we must learn and understand. No man of his own volition is able to seek out and come into the realized presence of the Lord of glory. When we were yet sinners we needed the leading of the Holy Spirit, and only by His help were we able to come to the Lord. Likewise, after we have become believers, we still need that same help in order to run after the Lord with continuous desire.

Here also we see a believer's relationship to all other believers. It is *I* who am drawn ("draw me"), but it is *we* who run after Him. It is *I* who am being led into the inner chambers, but it is *we* who will "be glad and rejoice." Whenever the individual believer receives grace from the presence of the Lord, then other believers cannot but receive favorable impressions.

Watchman Nee, *Song of Songs*

NOVEMBER 21
Covenant Friendship

And Jonathan had David reaffirm his oath out of love for him, because he loved him as he loved himself.

I SAMUEL 20:17

The relationship between Jonathan and David was no casual acquaintance. It was a deep, committed love relationship between powerful men. In fact Scripture says more than once that Jonathan loved David as he loved himself (see 1 Samuel 18:1–3, 20:17).

The depth of their commitment to each other was dramatically illustrated by Jonathan's gifts to David, which symbolized the deep level of respect, humility, trust, and loyalty inherent in their relationship. Jonathan took off the items of clothing that symbolized his royal status as son of the king of Israel and gave them to David. He literally handed over the outward evidence of his status in the world to his friend. This is not something a man does lightly. It is even more amazing that Jonathan also gave David his weapons, his means of defense.

Even today men have a strong attachment to their weapons. Men who own guns seem to have no shortage of stories and praises to relate about their favorite pistols, rifles, or shotguns. Boys rarely forget the first knife or .22 rifle they receive. When a boy receives such a gift, he feels as if he has gained recognition that he is more than just a boy. When he carries a knife around in his pocket or walks through the woods or fields with his rifle, he feels as if he belongs in the world of men. He imagines himself as a man, fighting off bears, mountain lions, and bad guys with the weapons in his hands. Can you imagine how much stronger a great warrior's attachment to his weapons would be?

This interaction between Jonathan and David is beautiful. Jonathan's gifts not only communicate his deep commitment to David, but David accepts these symbols of commitment without protest. He does not say, "Oh, Jonathan, you shouldn't do this. This sword is too valuable to give to me." It is not easy for a man to accept a gift of such depth from another man; yet the gift of covenant friendship is a gift all men need in their lives.

Earl Henslin, Man to Man

NOVEMBER 22

His Love to a Hurting Generation

My dear children, for whom I am again in the pains of childbirth until Christ is formed in you. . . .

GALATIANS 4:19

When we are single we long for the intimacy of marriage—just to have somebody of "my own." We fantasize about moments of emotional and physical intimacy. Eventually we may get married and face the reality of actually dividing our time, money and space with another person. That's when we discover how much we really need Jesus.

And then come children. Tiny, poopy, little creatures that demand constant attention. Ah, but what love fills our hearts at first sight of Junior.

Our selfish focus on personal rights is swept away the moment those big baby eyes look into ours.

When a baby is born into a family, the parents virtually become its slaves. We clean them, feed them, warm them, protect them, and sometimes we do it all night long.

During the years of their early childhood, our major concern is for the physical safety of our children. That is often the focus of our prayer life, but then they reach their teens. The day my oldest son entered junior high school, I knew that my prayer life would have to change. Now I can truly identify with Paul's statement in Galatians 4:19. . . .

God, our Father, uses the experience of parenting to help us to identify with Him. The Holy Spirit speaks to us about sharing our faith with others; but most Christians approach evangelism with a heavy heart and a fear of rejection, even though a twinge of guilt reminds them that their obligation is plain.

Why do we share Jesus with others? Why do we pray for people? Because people need Him? Because we look at strangers and just love them so much? Because of duty and obligation?

If you love someone, you will seek to comfort that person and help him or her at the point of greatest hurt. We have a brokenhearted Father who has entrusted us with an awesome responsibility and privilege: the expression of His love to a hurting generation.

John Dawson, *Taking Our Cities for God*

NOVEMBER 23

A Fortified Unit

. . . make my joy complete by being like-minded, having the same love, being one in spirit and purpose.

PHILIPPIANS 2:2

Redwood trees are the giants of the forest. They tower above the earth at heights of over three hundred feet. Unlike most trees, which send their roots to a depth equaling their height, redwoods send their roots outward, intermingling their roots with one another. Together they form a fortified unit, a secure stronghold that allows these giants to withstand high winds.

That is how strength is achieved among men as well, by working together as a unified whole. Men working together brings strength, whether dealing in the workplace, leading families at home, or serving in churches. Unfortunately, individualism among men prevails in the church. In fact, the individual approach has produced a generation of isolated church men.

The individualism among men at church imitates the independence and surface relationships among men in American society. . . .

We weren't created to live in isolation. But we often act as if we were! . . . Men, we need each other!

Pete Richardson, Why Christian Men Need Each Other

NOVEMBER 24
Sexual Boundaries

But a man who commits adultery lacks judgment;
   whoever does so destroys himself.

PROVERBS 6:32

Men play fantasy games in their heads about women; some act out these head games. We fantasize about how they feel toward us. This comes from our insecurity and sometimes the desire to stimulate our bored impulses out of depression. Sometimes, to handle our fear, we try to entice a woman to indicate her interest in us. Her hints of interest might satisfy us enough to leave her alone.

Other men don't know how to back off. They just want sexual conquests. They use women to satisfy selfish needs. Many American men are in denial about this.

Many women who work with men feel incredibly vulnerable. They have already had to overcome discrimination against women to attain their level of success in the business world; now they must fend off sexual advances and harassment. A woman can feel vulnerable to the whims of her bosses. When a man is in a position of authority over a woman, he sometimes feels he has rights with her. Some men have no sense of the limits of power, boundaries of respect and decency, not to mention simple appropriateness. They are users.

Treat *all* persons with dignity and respect. *Always.*

If you are struggling with sexual obsessions or addictions, my heart goes out to you. If you have been sexually traumatized, please seek help. Many men need such help. I have only presented an outline of male sexual dilemmas to help you clarify your issues and pains.

Problems with sexual boundaries are profound because they are shame-based behaviors and attitudes. The perpetrator is a wounded soul.

The antidote to a conscience overburdened with guilt is confession and restitution. Tell God. Tell a confidant. Then try to go back and make things right.

The antidote to shame-based behaviors, however, is conversion and reconstruction. First, you must admit your wrongs. Do what you can to make things right, but do not force reconciliation. Do not force the victim in any way. Second, submit these things to God and submit to reconstruction through competent therapy.

Please remember: You deserve the best possible life. Be responsible with your behavior and feelings! May you find genuine pleasure in a healthy sexual life.

Dick Brian Klaver, *Men at Peace*

November 25
Simplicity

He has showed you, O man, what is good.
And what does the LORD require of you?
To act justly and to love mercy
and to walk humbly with your God.

MICAH 6:8

Have you noticed that some people just see things in a complicated fashion! A few years ago, I made plans to travel to Mexico with a group of men for a hunting retreat. We would spend the morning in fellowship and Bible study, and in the afternoon we would go on a hunting expedition.

One of the young men on this trip had assumed the responsibility of keeping the expedition of our group organized. He was one of those people who thought in such detail that his life was always complicated.

I remember one afternoon he was all in a dither over our schedule. Remember, we were in Mexico, where everything is laid-back and nobody is in a hurry for anything. And all we were going to do was get some ice, put it in a cooler, put in some water and cold drinks, drive out to a field, hunt for a little while, and come back. Our schedule couldn't be complicated. And yet Jack made it an issue of monumental proportion.

He gathered the whole group of men around and said, "Men, we have to make a decision now. It's two o'clock in the afternoon, and we have to know what kind of schedule we are going to operate on. Now, there are several options. We can either go get the ice now and bring it back and put the drinks on it and then go hunting, or we can take the drinks with us and stop by and pick up the ice on the way and go hunting then. Now, which way do you think would be the most advantageous?"

All the men sat around in stunned silence. Nobody could believe what he was hearing. Finally, we all broke into laughter. "Who cares?" someone said. "Let's just do it."

Some people just seem to see life through complex glasses. Life to them is a matrix of decisions, agendas, and schedules. Everything must be figured out, and every decision is major. To fail in a small decision causes as much disruption as failure in the big ones.

Other people seem to have found simplified glasses. They can look at the most complicated situation, see through all the complexities, and cut to the heart of the situation. They seem to have internalized the advice given by a friend: "Don't sweat the small stuff . . . and remember, it's *all* small stuff."

That second perspective, I'm convinced, is the key to inner serenity.

Dudley Hall, *Grace Works*

NOVEMBER 26
The Straight Way

But small is the gate and narrow the road that leads to life, and only a few find it.

MATTHEW 7:14

Jesus said: "Straight is the gate and narrow is the way that leads to life. Broad is the gate and wide is the way that leads to destruction." Many interpret this as meaning that the gate into heaven is narrow and few get in— disconcertingly few, according to some. But this verse isn't talking about heaven; it is talking about "life" here and now. The way that leads to life here and now is narrow and disciplined. It is true physically, mentally, and spiritually—corporately. Here are two young men who have two different ideas of their physical life. One is free to do as he likes with his body, completely undisciplined; the other isn't. he wants to be an athlete, so he disciplines his body, goes through a strict regimen of training. Which of these has found physical freedom? Life will decide: they enter a race together. The first one at the end of a couple hundred yards is falling behind, puffing badly, beating the air, tied in knots. The other goes through rhythmically, masterfully, pulls out ahead of the rest, an easy winner. The first young man thought he could enter life by a broad road of undisciplined physical living and found he couldn't; "destruction" set in: he was eliminated. The other was free—free to excel, free to win because he entered life by a narrow gate of disciplined living. Take two young men mentally: One is undisciplined, listens to the teacher when he wants to, daydreams when he wants; he is free. The other knows what I learned in a course on memory training: the only thing I can remember about that course in memory training is that it is not a matter of memory, but a matter of attention. You don't remember because you don't pay attention when the matter is presented. So don't say, "I have a bad memory," but say, "I have bad attention." This second boy knows that, so he pays attention, and therefore remembers. The examination day comes and render its verdict: The first boy starts bravely, but soon runs out of facts, gets muddled, perspiration on his brow; "destruction" sets in, and he fails. The other boy looks at the questions, smiles—old friends. All the sages of all the ages stand before him and are at his service; he writes confidently, easily, stands at the top of his class. He entered by a very narrow gate of discipline and was free, at home, in the realm of knowledge. A master violinist touches his violin and can make you feel anything; he makes you march with him to martial music, makes you turn and sit with him by the seashore with the moonlight upon the quiet waters. He does it easily, masterfully. Why? I ask him. His reply: "This way was narrow. I've practiced and practiced for years to do that. I entered this freedom through the narrow gate of disciplined practice." But suppose I should say: "This is bondage. I believe in being free." So I bang on any note on the piano I want to bang on. I might be free to do that, but you wouldn't be free to listen. You would ask, "What are you doing?" My reply:

"I'm practicing musical self-expression." Your reply: "You have no musical self to express." A man said, "I'm in harmony with chaos." That's what I would be in harmony with—chaos.

The modern man is trying to be free through the broad road of self-expression, regardless of morality. It is ending exactly as Jesus said: in "destruction." The modern man is in harmony with chaos, a problem to himself and others. He is problem-centered, and he is a problem.

The deepest conviction of my life is this: Self-surrender is the way to self-expression. You realize yourself only as you renounce yourself. You find God when you renounce yourself as God. The self is trying to play God, trying to organize life around itself as God, and it simply doesn't work. The universe doesn't back it. None of your sums add up, except to nonsense. You have to lose your life to find it. You have to lose your life in a higher will and work out that will, and then you find your life again.

E. Stanley Jones, *A Song of Ascents*

November 27
Giving Pleasure

The wife's body does not belong to her alone but also to her husband. In the same way, the husband's body does not belong to him alone but also to his wife. Do not deprive each other except by mutual consent and for a time, so that you may devote yourselves to prayer. Then come together again so that Satan will not tempt you because of your lack of self-control.

I Corinthians 7:4–5

Sex is a joint dimension in which both husbands and wives give pleasure to each other, thereby communicating their love in a largely nonverbal way. It is an experience in giving. It is another situation for being the servants of our wives. In fact, it may be one of the more difficult situations in which we are called upon to serve, given our Western macho traditions of sexual conquest. From boyhood on, we men have been programmed in a thousand different ways to view sex as an area where we *get*, where we *take*, where we *use*. The culture is thoroughly saturated with the image of Don Juan.

But in recent years, a curious thing has happened. Women have decided to follow our example; they've realized there are some rather nice sensations for *them* to get as well. The bookstores are filled with manuals on the female orgasm. The result is that many marriages are now composed of two takers, two seekers of the ultimate personal high, who may or may not happen to provide what the other person wants and needs during the process of their own quest. The traditional setup of one taker and one willing or reluctant giver is indeed a form of rape. The newer setup of two takers is not much better, is it?

When, in contrast, we apply the model of servanthood to this area, all the dynamics change. The goal becomes the provision of her needs rather than our own. And we find, as we've noticed before, that our own needs are met along the way rather automatically. We husbands need to understand the ways and means of female orgasm. We also need to learn more about the psychological, nonphysical aspects of a women's participation in intercourse. Especially since anatomy has given us the role it has, it is all the more our responsibility to set the pattern of true sexual union, not rape.

Dean Merrill, *The Husband Book*

NOVEMBER 28
Strength out of Weakness

For the foolishness of God is wiser than man's wisdom, and the weakness of God is stronger than man's strength.

I CORINTHIANS 1:25

You're probably too young to remember the Charles Atlas ads in the old comic books. They are where we get the phrase "ninety-seven-pound weakling." Here's this droopy little skinny guy at the beach with a fairly neat girl. Along comes a guy built like a professional wrestler on steroids. He deliberately kicks sand in the skinny guy's face. The girl hops up and walks off into the sunset on the bully's arm. Don't let this happen to you, the ad says.

Charles Atlas sold body-building. His philosophy was the stronger you were, the less sand you would have to wash out of your eyes.

Weakness is unacceptable.

Few, if any of us, enjoy being weak. Actually, we hate it. When it comes right down to it, most of us will do anything we can to avoid appearing weak. "Be strong," "Look confident," and "Never let them see you sweat," are just a few of the things we tell ourselves and others most days. Underneath it all is the horribly mistaken notion that to acknowledge weakness is a sin.

In our culture there is such a tremendous emphasis on being strong that we have become a culture of cover-up artists who put on the makeup of "I'm strong" when the real truth underneath is "I'm weak but I'm just too afraid to admit it."

When was the last time you honestly let someone know how weak you were in a given area of your life? Was there ever such an occasion? Most of the time, weren't you trying to put your best foot forward with others so that you could impress them? The best foot forward includes eliminating any hint that you have a weakness or soft spot. Maybe, like me, you expend a lot of effort trying to appear to be something you are really not—strong. . . .

My moments of greatest personal weakness came when I was trying to pretend I was self-sufficient and strong, and my moments of greatest personal strength were when I was able to admit to being needy and weak. Maybe that has been true for you as well. Christ wants to use those experiences to teach us to depend on Him rather than ourselves for the power to do what we do. When Paul depended on Him, the lives of thousands were changed. That can be true for us as well. We can have that kind of influence on others if we let Christ do it through us.

Are you a weak person trying to pretend you are strong, or are you a strong person because you know how weak you are?

Chris Thurman, *If Christ Were Your Counselor*

NOVEMBER 29
Your Own Story

You yourselves are our letter, written on our hearts, known and read by everybody. You show that you are a letter from Christ, the result of our ministry, written not with ink but with the Spirit of the living God, not on tablets of stone but on tablets of human hearts.

II CORINTHIANS 3:2–3

Think of yourself as someone who is writing a story out of the bits and pieces of your life. You are both the author and the main character. And you are here on earth to try to write an honest story, a continuing story—not an unconnected collection of episodes, but a real story about a real person who somehow stays in one piece, inside and out, all the way to the end.

To write a real story, the first thing we have to do is to own the one we are given to write. To own anything involves at least two things. First, we identify ourselves with what we own and say, "This is my story. If you want to know me, you must know my story; and if you know my story, you really know me. I *am* my story." Second, we take responsibility for what we own and say, "What comes of my story is up to me. This is my plot to take credit for, mine to take blame for, mine to own up to."

We own our stories when we are willing to accept the parts we cannot control and then do whatever we can with the rest. We own our stories when we can admit to their ugly sides, their stupid and crazy sides. We own our stories, too, when we celebrate their beautiful aspects, their smart sides and their good sides. We own our stories when we keep holding on to them, even when we feel as if the story we are writing is a bore or gets so confusing we don't know what to make of it.

Nodody writes a simple story. We weave them with threads of our maniacally selfish streaks, our ugly impulses, our lust and our hate; but we also sew them together with the thread of love and courage and a simple ambition to make something of ourselves. We take ownership of one chapter and then another, each in its own time, each in its own way, until we round our story off, whole, in one piece.

Lewis Smedes, *A Pretty Good Person*

NOVEMBER 30
Quality and Quantity Time

Children's children are a crown to the aged,
  and parents are the pride of their children.

PROVERBS 17:6

You cannot give quality time unless you give a quantity of time. You just have to hang around. You need to be there. Be alert for those priceless irreplaceable moments when your child needs to belt down a strong gulp of Dad.

To be honest, most of the time you spend with your child will be wasted. Not much of it will be productive. They won't sit there and lap you up for two straight hours. What they do is suddenly—no one can predict when—spin around, open up, and take a long swig of Dad. The little hole in the window opens up and lets you in. Then they shut it, go back to their preoccupation and put you in a holding mode again. This means you have to waste a quantity of time to get the quality time. You have to hang around.

Another common excuse is "I don't have control over my schedule so I can't spend a quantity of time with my children."

In a national men's survey, I asked the question, "What is the number one obstacle keeping you from being the family shepherd you really want to be?" What do you think their answer was? Ninety-five percent of the men answered: "Time." Men claim they are too busy. They are dramatically overscheduled.

It may be true that they are overscheduled and exhausted. But this reason is still a cop-out. It's not a question of time. A man does what he wants to do. His busy schedule reveals his priorities, not his unavailability. It's a decision problem, not a chronology problem. A man decides what goes into his schedule. He chooses his top priorities and makes sure they get scheduled. . . .

Is any career worth the life of your child? Are any career goals or sales quotas worth your child? When I put it this way, of course not. The problem, however, is that men don't see their choice in such stark black-and-white terms. The see a light gray choice, "For a while, don't you see; just until . . ." They never notice that light gray always darkens gradually until they have slipped into black and can no longer see the child.

Neglect happens. Passive indifference is a creeper. Only intense vigilance keeps job chauvinism at bay. No father says, "Well, today I decide! Is it gonna be my job or my kid?" The subtle lie is, "I don't have to choose, I can have it all if I play my cards right. I can double up here and cut short there and juggle the rest."

By the way, don't think your job really cares. It is not a sentient being with interest in and compassion for you. You fill a box on some chart somewhere, and you are extremely replaceable. After my dad died, I went to his office and gathered his belongings in a small box from another man already sitting at his desk. My mother's personal effects fit into a cigar box, and they didn't miss her a single day after she died.

After I die, I want my personal effects to be found in the hearts of my children, not in a cigar box. I want to clock out in my kids. I am not an organizational box to them. No one on the face of the earth can fill my shoes as the father of Helen and Brandon. Why remove myself from a job fit only for me to fill a job anyone can fit into?

My advice, men, is save your children. The world is full of fathers who will sell out their family for bucks and booty. Well, let them. Let the dead bury the dead. But, not you. A holy calling and ordination summons you to practice the profession of fatherhood.

Dave Simmons, Dad the Family Counselor

December

DECEMBER 1 WORLD AIDS AWARENESS DAY

Compassion

I needed clothes and you clothed me, I was sick and you looked after me, I was in prison and you came to visit me.

MATTHEW 25:36

Not long ago, I attended a play based on stories from a support group comprising people with AIDS. The theater director said he decided to stage the play after hearing a local minister state that he celebrated each time he read an obituary of a young single man, believing each death to be yet another sign of God's disapproval. Increasingly, I fear, the church is viewed as an enemy of sinners.

How does one hold to high standards of moral purity while at the same time showing grace to those who fail those standards? Christian history offers few facsimiles of the pattern Jesus laid down. We give lip service to "hate the sin while loving the sinner," but how well do we practice this principle? All too often, sinners feel unloved by a church that, in turn, keeps altering its definition of sin—precisely the opposite of Jesus' pattern.

The early church began well, placing a high premium on moral purity. Baptismal candidates had to undergo long periods of instruction, and church discipline was rigorously enforced. Yet even pagan observers were attracted to the way Christians cared for each other and devoted themselves to the sick and the poor.

I realize, as I reflect on the life of Jesus, how far we have come from the divine balance he set out for us. Listening to the sermons and reading the writings of the contemporary church in the U.S., I sometimes detect more of Constantine than of Jesus. The man from Nazareth was a sinless friend of sinners, a pattern that should convict us on both counts.

Phillip Yancey, *Finding God in Unexpected Places*

DECEMBER 2

His Life in Us

I have been crucified with Christ and I no longer live, but Christ lives in me. The life I live in the body, I live by faith in the Son of God, who loved me and gave himself for me.

GALATIANS 2:20

Here is a cup of water and by it a tea bag. The water is not the tea and the tea is not the water. They are two separate items. The water is heated and the tea bag is placed in the water. A strange thing takes place . . . the water changes color and nature. It becomes indwelt by a new and dominant nature. The rich tea-color swirls around in the cup until the fluid is tea, not water. For the water to exist now is for tea to exist. The water could say, "It is no longer I that lives, but tea that lives in me." Not many people I know drink hot water. There isn't much demand for it. But if that water, heated in preparation, can be made to become a wholesome and stimulating drink, then it is worthwhile.

So the Christian is just a cup of water, which, when heated with faith and entered by the Savior, becomes something else. The Christ nature comes into him and with his consent dominates. He becomes more and more like Christ and less and less like himself. Just as the "tea in the water is the hope of taste," Christ in the Christian is the hope of glory!

And thus we have discovered the key to triumphant living . . . CHRIST IN YOU THE HOPE OF GLORY!

Jack Taylor, *The Key to Triumphant Living*

DECEMBER 3

Balance

Instead, speaking the truth in love, we will in all things grow up into him who is the head, that is, Christ.

EPHESIANS 4:15

The Bible . . . commends a life of balance. We are to speak the truth, but we are to speak it in love. . . . We are to desire neither poverty nor riches, we're to embrace neither fullness nor want (Proverbs 30:7–9). We are to bear one another's burdens, we are to bear our own (Galatians 6:2–5). Salvation is a free gift; good deeds must necessarily accompany it (Ephesians 2: 8–10). The eternal Gospel is good news; but it is news of fear and judgment (Revelation 14:6–7). We are to hate the sin; we are to love the sinner (Jude 21–23). We are in the world; we are not of the world (John 17:15–16). Faith is not of works, but without works, faith is dead (James 2:26) . . .

Biblical balance is a happy melding of devotion and action, being and doing, patience and passion. It manifests word and deed, faith and works, forgiveness and discipline. It carefully integrates the inner life and the outer life. It makes quiet conviction the natural companion of strident confession. It enables the head to coincide with the heart. Without compromising God's grace it reveres God's decrees. Without suppressing spiritual liberty, it upholds spiritual responsibility.

In other words, it is mature. . . .

Biblical balance is more practical than pragmatism. It is more thoughtful than rationalism. It is more experienced than existentialism and more romantic than sentimentalism. It is more stable than conservatism and more progressive than liberalism . . .

A faithful return to that kind of balance could very well be the announcement of hope, the clarion cry for revival, that we so desperately long for today.

George Grant, *The Micah Mandate*

DECEMBER 4
Time for Our Children

I know that there is nothing better for men than to be happy and do good while they live.

ECCLESIASTES 3:12

Every man lives in two very different worlds: a positional world and a personal world. Most of the mistakes males make in fathering are due to a lack of balance between the two.

In the *positional* world, men develop clout. They flex their authority, title, or buying power and crave respect, particularly among a group of men. This explains why many men drive a certain car, sign their name with a special pen, join certain clubs, or carry prestige plastic. Establishing status symbols is instinctive in the world of men and is part of their competitive nature. Most men thrive in the positional arena—it's what they're wired for, and they typically enjoy the game. That's why they get up early for work and put in overtime at the office. That's also why they buy things they don't need with money they don't have to impress people they don't like. All those actions reflect a man's bent toward success and peer approval.

The *personal* world is where a man develops meaningful relationships and has the potential to become a good friend, an adored husband, and a hero to the kids. But it's also in this world that men struggle the most. Unlike the positional world, the personal world doesn't come naturally. . . .

Because the personal world doesn't come naturally to men, it's easy to see why it often gets neglected. Years ago, a little boy got a new plastic ball and bat from his aunt. He ran out to the garage where his dad was working on the car. "Daddy, Daddy, I got a bat and ball! Would you come out and play ball with me?" The father straightened up, gave the boy a piercing look, and said, "Let's get something straight. I'm your father, not your friend." Forty years later, that incident is still the son's most vivid childhood memory. How tragic. Men need to wake up to the unthinkable damage they are doing by failing to develop their personal skills. Every day, thousands of children are exasperated by their fathers' insensitivity to, or abandonment of, their personal world.

It all comes down to this: What's in the positional world doesn't ultimately matter; what's in the personal world is what really counts. Lee Iacocca was absolutely right when he said, "No one on their death bed wishes they spent more time at the office." Even so, millions of men just keep right on pushing themselves in positional pursuits. Cheered on by ego, success literature, and seminars, men are driven. . . .

When *Industry Week* surveyed managers across the country and asked what they worried most about, the answers revealed a twisted agenda. The number one worry was personal health; second was a lack of time. Number five was personal investments; number six, estate planning. Number seven on the list was their relationship with their children, and number ten was their marriage. Only two of the top ten worries related to a man's personal world—and they ranked number seven and ten. No wonder our children are in crisis.

The myth of youthful resilience is nonsense. The heart of every little boy and girl lies within a father's hands. Every broken promise and abusive word tears a hole that may never be mended.

David Moore, *Five Lies of the Century*

DECEMBER 5
Male Companionship

A man that hath friends must show himself friendly: and there is a friend that sticketh closer than a brother.

PROVERBS 18:24, KJV

Throughout history, men have always come together to "say" or "do" things common to the male gender. That kind of comradeship is healthy for men, and it goes a long way in teaching and reminding men about who they are. I have personally found that having a "night out with the boys" is the most relaxing time for me. In fact, sometimes when I am getting grumpy around the house, my wife will say, "Why don't you go out with some of the guys tonight?" It benefits the whole family for me to share in male companionship.

My wife has learned that my time with other men has not hindered our marriage; rather, it has helped it! It is in that context that men can let go a bit and not have to carry the responsibility required of them in all the other areas of their lives. That time lets them regroup and refresh their vision to be the men they need to be.

What about rounding up some of the guys for a night out at the ballpark? Or a relaxing conversation over a big steak? Or a double-elimination round of bowling? Men need to commit themselves to making a place for male companionship.

Weldon Hardenbrook, *Missing from Action*

December 6

Enjoying Life

Be happy young man, while you are young,
  and let your heart give you joy in the days of your youth.

Ecclesiastes 11:9

Last week I took a noon run in the December sunshine of Southern California. The grass was a rich green. I could see the San Gabriel Mountains, stark and blue and faintly snowcapped, against the northern sky. I could smell the orange blossoms. I could feel the perspiration trickle down my back. My lungs were full and bursting. It was so sensual and exuberant and inexplicable and mysterious and utterly good that I wept with joy. This beauty was not my right, it was a gift.

Last night I sat with my wife in a restaurant. I ate rigatoni paesano: little ridged casings of pasta, cooked in a sauce of sausage, fresh tomatoes and bell peppers. God, it was delicious! That's right—God, it was good. Thank you! I have watched my children wrestle and play and cry and draw spaceships. I have read them stories and tried to answer their questions about God and good and evil. What business do I have in doing all of these remarkable things? What right do I have to them? No business. No right. They are all gifts. I pray that if ever in his infinite wisdom and love God chooses to take them away from me, I will not forget that they were gifts and still be thankful, even though my heart may break with grief.

It takes a radical kind of humility to be set free to wait in the midst of suffering. It is the humility of one who knows that all he or she has ever had or ever will have is a gift from God, and that we have no right to any of the good things in life.

Ben Patterson, Waiting

December 7

Peace

Nation will not take up sword against nation,
  nor will they train for war anymore

Isaiah 2:4c

Whenever I thought of my past, I could not help but think of the mystery of my survival. Why was I still alive, when men all around me had died like flies in the four years of conflict? Gradually I came to believe that I had been supported by some great, unseen power. My sullenness began to be diffused and dispelled by a sense of gratitude.

Moreover, as I continued to live in closer relation to the earth, through the plants and the cattle, and the other aspects of farm life, I was gradually led to think in terms of a Creator of all these things. With the increasing sense of the fact of a Creator-God I came to feel ashamed of my former godless idea that man's own power and ability were his only trustworthy guides.

I had never been an atheist, in the extreme sense of the word, but religion had had little place in my thinking. In my early life there was very little religious atmosphere. Consequently, I grew up to manhood without any formal religion. After I enlisted in the Navy, the former "War Catechism" became the sum total of my ideology. . . .

In [the] editorial column [of a newspaper] there was a commentary which stated that the Bible was the world's best-seller, that it had been translated into the languages of all civilized countries. The writer of the column stated that if Christians were banished to some island and only allowed one book, without exception they would choose the Bible. The writer ended with a call to the Japanese people: "Oh people of Japan, if there is any one of you who has not yet read the Bible, please read the first thirty pages with an open mind. Surely there is something there that will touch your heart."

For me, without a doubt, this was a voice from Heaven. I started to read the Bible. I became absorbed in it. Presently I came to the Gospel of Luke.

There I faced the scene of the crucifixion of Christ. I read the words of Luke 23:34, "Father, forgive them for they know not what they do." Jesus prayed for the very soldiers who were about to thrust his side with the spear. . . .

I am not ashamed to say that my eyes filled with tears. Immediately I accepted Jesus as my personal Savior. . . .

I am positive of my conversion. There was a time when my back was turned to Christ, but now I look to Him in faith. I firmly believe that Christ is the only answer and the only hope of this world.

Eleven years after Pearl Harbor! Little did I dream that eventful morning that my view of life would be so revolutionized. Today I am a Christian! I say it over and over again. This is the message I send to all mankind with a fervent prayer that there will be "No More Pearl Harbor."

Mitsuo Fuchida, lead pilot in the raid on Pearl Harbor,
From Pearl Harbor to Golgotha

DECEMBER 8

The Perfect Investment

Since everything will be destroyed in this way, what kind of people ought you to be? You ought to live holy and godly lives . . .

II PETER 3:11

Devotion to God is not only the central magnetic pull to God, it is also our commitment. Christians are convinced that God is great and good. It's not that God is overpowering us and we are being dragged along, kicking and screaming against His pull. We want our lives centered on Him; we enjoy having our lives centered on Him. We are committed to God.

You might compare this to a soldier during wartime. When the United States entered World War I and World War II, the government drafted young men to fight. On the one hand, it could be argued that those soldiers were on the front lines because the government was like a giant magnet pulling them there. They had no choice. It was almost impossible to resist. But the records from the past and the testimonials of survivors report that they wanted to be there. They were fiercely patriotic and welcomed military service. They were even willing to die for their country. To these veterans "patriotism" is one of the most wonderful and emotional words in their vocabulary. They believed wholeheartedly in the cause and the country. They were committed.

That's the way it is with Christians who value godliness. Our lives are centered on God and we are committed to Him. We would die for Him because we believe God is worth our lives. It's far more than submitting to the power of God, although it is that. Godliness is like patriotism only more so—an enthusiastic and wholehearted allegiance to God. Committed Christians are convinced nothing else really matters or lasts. God is the only permanent value to be committed to. . . .

We could also compare this to investments. If you were convinced that every other investment would fail except gold, you would commit everything you had to gold. Christians who value godliness are convinced that God is the only investment that will last, so we commit everything we have to Him. We are fully invested in God.

Leith Anderson, *Winning the Values War in a Changing Culture*

DECEMBER 9

Thankfulness in All Situations

. . . give thanks in all circumstances, for this is God's will for you in Christ Jesus.

I THESSALONIANS 5:18

I know an inspiring man of great faith who owned a lumber mill. Two summers ago, it was my privilege to be given a personal tour of this fascinating operation by the head man himself. Afterward he shared his tremendous faith in God with me as he related this experience:

In 1965, his mill was completely wiped out by fire. Only twenty percent of it was insured. From all appearances everything he and his family had worked a lifetime to build was wiped out.

Just before the fire, another small mill he owned, which had not been doing very well, had been put up for sale. A few days after the fire in the large mill, the small mill was sold. He took the money from the sale and the insurance money, worked with his crews day and night for eighty straight days, and completely rebuilt the mill. Before the fire, lumber prices were a minimum of $48.00 per 1,000 to break even. However, in building the new plant, with many innovations and the best up-to-date machinery, the cost of the operation was reduced greatly. Just as the mill was completed, the price of lumber dipped to an all-time low and stayed there for the next year. If he had been operating the old mill, he would have lost $120,000 a month. But since the new mill was in operation, he was able to weather the storm. The next year, lumber rose to an all-time high. With tears in his eyes, he praised God and testified to the fact his Heavenly Father was taking care of him all the time.

My friend believes Romans 8:28, "And we know that all things work together for good to them that love God, to them who are called according to his purpose." Here is the secret of true optimism—no matter what happens, God reigns, and he is at work to bring out good from bad. For the Christian, the best is yet to come.

Dale Galloway, Rebuild Your Life

DECEMBER 10

The Goal of Our Faith

. . . for you are receiving the goal of your faith, the salvation of your souls.

I PETER 1:9

The great trouble with the majority of us is that we do not expect anything to happen. We are not looking for results. We are content to go on in the same old humdrum way, and if a soul in anguish should cry out: "What must I do to be saved?" we should be dumbfounded.

I have never yet been content to see things go on in the usual quiet way. Unless something happened I felt I had failed. I have always expected the extraordinary, nor have I been disappointed.

You remember that young preacher who came to Mr. Spurgeon discouraged because he was not seeing results.

"Why, you don't mean to tell me," exclaimed Spurgeon, "that you expect results every time *you* preach, do you?"

"Well, no," responded the young man, somewhat taken back.

"Then that is why you don't get them," was the pointed reply.

I notice that when men play football they do not kick the ball at random, but they endeavour to drive it into the goal, and so with hockey. And, thank God, we too can have a goal.

I never saw a race where men ran this way and that, all over the field. They had an object in view, and they ran toward a certain point. And we too are in a race, but a race, thank God, for souls.

When a lawyer pleads a case he does not merely entertain. He is there for a verdict. And, praise God, we are out for a verdict. Nor should we be satisfied without one.

In a shooting match every man fires at a mark. Have we a mark, and do we take aim?

In the days of the Great War recruiting meetings were held, not to entertain, but to secure recruits. Apart from this result the meeting was in vain.

Are we looking for recruits for our King, and do we expect some to respond? Let us have faith for definite results.

Oswald Smith, *The Man God Uses*

DECEMBER 11
A Personal Mission Statement

Commit to the Lord whatever you do, and your plans will succeed.

PROVERBS 16:3

What is your mission in life? Have you thought about it? Have you taken all of your talents and experiences along with the desires of your heart and boiled them down into a concise understanding of the mission you are on? Would any friend or family member be able to accurately tell what mission you are on? Does anyone know your goals and how you are trying to accomplish them? Do you?

If you responded with a lot of noes, it is time that you lay the cornerstone to the foundation of everything you are doing professionally and personally. That cornerstone is a personal mission statement that reflects who you are, what you are doing, and the way in which you are doing it. You may be caught up in the momentum of earning a living, fulfilling your roles as a spouse and a parent, nurturing friendships, and meeting obligations without having a conscious awareness of where you're headed. You've never stopped to analyze what your life's purpose is all about. You function, do your best, and hope and pray that everything comes out all right.

A mission statement provides you with a compass. It states in black and white what you want to be, what you want to accomplish, and what your governing values are. It becomes both an anchor and a rudder. It is an anchor because it allows you to stay steadfastly in place while you decline offers and temptations that would distract you from your mission. It is a rudder because it helps you stay the course while you are moving toward your goals. A good mission statement can prevent a thousand failures and wasted effort. When you are confused by outside influences or internal emotional turmoil, the mission statement can be the solid rock that grounds your decisions in reality. . . .

Writing a personal mission statement is, in a sense, the ultimate goal-setting exercise. Actually, it is the distillation of multiple goals into a central theme. If you haven't thought concretely about the goals you can and would like to accomplish, now is the time to do it, especially before you compose your first draft of a mission statement. When goals of a mission are balanced and healthy, they include family priorities, not just business concerns. They incorporate values, not just ambitions. Goals on the way to a mission involve relationships, not just productivity . . .

Words, especially written ones, have power. Writing a mission statement does not guarantee compliance with it, but the act of writing it out is almost like making a commitment to yourself and others. When you have composed yours, I think you will be surprised at just how much power is there to help you make good, solid decisions about today that will lead you to the tomorrows of your dreams.

Steve Arterburn, *Winning at Work*

DECEMBER 12
Daily Dependence on God
You then, my son, be strong in the grace that is in Christ Jesus.

II TIMOTHY 2:1

I once saw a boxing movie in which one fighter was hopelessly outmatched by the other. Yet, courageously, he kept approaching his opponent, time after time, round after round, taking tremendous physical punishment. After each round, his manager would say to him, "Why don't we stop the fight?"

"I can lick him," the boxer would say. "Give me another round."

The fight went on for fifteen rounds, and predictably, the weaker fighter was knocked out in the final few seconds. Carried off in defeat, he could be heard saying to his manager through puffed and bleeding lips, "Give me one more round . . . I can lick this guy." The defeated fighter did his level best, but his best wasn't good enough to win. He couldn't accept his limitations in the match.

I often encounter Christians like this boxer. They try to eliminate their shameful parts by various omnipotent methods: willpower; discipline; self-denial; trying harder; looking at the "bright side."

All of these aspects are helpful traits. However, without acceptance of our limitations and recognition of our need for grace, all of our efforts are doomed to failure: "They are of no value against fleshly indulgence" (Colossians 2:23).

Most of us can identify with the experience of having a compulsive or addictive behavior or thought. We'll promise ourselves or God, "I'll never do this again" (it can be an unacceptable thought, sexual behavior, a drug problem, or money impulsivity, to name a few). Then, after a period of hours to months, the behavior reemerges, causing us to fall into despair.

The problem is the *omnipotent promise*. The Fall guaranteed us that we are all capable of incredible destructiveness at any given moment. And there is no guarantee that we will abstain from destructiveness. Instead, we are to depend daily on the grace of God and His people to help us accept and mature through our badnesses. That's the biblical way.

John Townsend, *Hiding from Love*

DECEMBER 13
A Firm Decision

Elijah went before the people and said, "How long will you waver between two opinions? If the Lord is God, follow him; but if Baal is God, follow him."

1 KINGS 18:21

Decisions never get easier "tomorrow." Although when facing them, it always looks as though such will be the case. It takes courage to make hard-nosed decisions between thorny options, to be decisive in the face of opposition. It takes courage to stand firm under pressure. It takes courage not to buckle under stress and adversity. It takes courage to chart an unfamiliar course. But in all situations, whether of everyday or crisis proportions, indecision leads to aimless wandering.

This does not mean you egotistically assume that every decision you make is a wise one, but that you simply have confidence in yourself and in what you are trying to accomplish. You must acknowledge that sometimes making a wrong decision and then moving on in the Lord's grace is better than to have made no decision and allow the work to grind to a standstill.

While the average man or woman shies away from stressful situations and knotty decisions, the determined individual seeks them out. He tackles them head-on.

A coach I once had instructed us, "When you're in a race and you come to a hill, pick up the pace. All the other runners will be slowing down to take it easy—that's the time for you to pour it on."

That's wise advice. Approach decisions like hills. When they confront you, *pour it on.*

There will always be repercussions from the decisions you make. Pressure will exist both before and after. It is always easy to entertain doubts and think, *Did I make the wrong choice?*

But you must not allow such thoughts to push you back into indecisiveness. You must keep moving ahead. Except in unusual circumstances, once you have made a decision, don't vacillate and harbor second thoughts about what you have done. If you are living in daily obedience to God and have made the choice thoughtfully and prayerfully, then you can know that God will oversee your progress.

In the spiritual realm, *adversity signifies advance.* If there are no problems, no tensions, no uncertainties, things are not functioning according to the biblical norm. The more you try to accomplish things and the higher you set your goals, the greater the pressure you'll experience.

This constant battle builds a fighting spirit. Such a wholeheartedness will keep you from being thrown off target, especially when you must make decisions. You must learn to slough off tension, failure, and doubts. You must be confident enough to tackle the most difficult problems with a sense of challenge.

Sometimes a roadblock will require a period of reflection and reevaluation; there you will stop long enough to weigh various alternatives before you proceed. Such periodic slowdowns can be a healthy investment of time. But when the assessment is complete, you must pick up the pieces, stand tall once again, and move out, confident that God's faithfulness and the job He assigned you are still intact.

Mike Phillips, *Getting More Done In Less Time and Having More Fun Doing It!*

December 14

Patience During Trials

A man's wisdom gives him patience;
it is to his glory to overlook an offense.

Todd was the president of his high-school class. He played first team on the basketball squad, and his dream was to play college ball.

After the Christmas break during Todd's senior year, the coach never played him again. No explanation was given. The Lord gave Todd the grace to sit on the bench. He never complained. He never even asked the coach why, though many parents of other players were asking.

Week after week, sitting in the stands, the father of another player gained a profound respect for Todd as he quietly observed Todd's character. Two years later, when this high-powered businessman needed a key executive assistant, the first call he placed was to Todd. Today Todd attends college full-time and pays his tuition by working for this man part-time in a career field he loves.

Todd didn't get to play college basketball—the basketball scouts never saw him play. Yet, Todd did find a rewarding career field. That's because a different kind of "scout" saw the character with which he *didn't* play. In a way, Todd did get a scholarship after all.

Every man must decide whether or not he will take the blows. This is the issue of suffering and hard times. They are defining moments.

To suffer is to be in God's school. The hard blow is a hammer that shapes our character on God's anvil.

Sometimes God's agenda is *correction*. We suffer for doing *wrong*. We experience discipline and punishment. God wants us to know that, yes, He does love us but, no, we can't have our own way.

Other times we suffer *persecution*. We suffer for doing *right*. We experience confusion, and we don't know why. But we do know that God is good. We can trust Jesus. As Mother Teresa said, "Your sufferings are the kisses of Jesus."

Have you settled the issue of whether or not you will accept God's gracious blows? You can try to ward off life's blows if you want, or you can decide to stop chafing against the wisdom of God. Get in touch with the

Father, not in resignation, but in submission. Know that His love is a Father's love.

Patrick Morley, The Seven Seasons of a Man's Life

December 15

A Ready Witness

A wise son brings joy to his father.

Proverbs 10:1a

In a visit prior to [my father's] death, I prayed and planned some clever ways of talking with him about the gospel. Since he would not talk about his faith, I planned to audiotape an interview with him about his early life experience in order to ask about the development of his core convictions. The hook was the likely reality that his three-year-old grandson would never be able to ask him those questions directly. He agreed. Before we taped our talk, I sat with him on our front porch step and asked him what he had been thinking about. He answered, "Death. I've been thinking a lot about what will happen after I die. I think I'll be in heaven, but I'm not sure. Frankly, I am scared I've not done enough."

No door could have been more widely opened to the good news that he had not done enough, nor could ever do enough, to erase the failure to love. We talked about the futility of earning love, using our relationship as an example. During the period of my adolescence, I failed him terribly in many shameful and tragic ways. I broke his heart so many times that he should have refused to let me matter, but instead he continued to love me. The comparison was not hard to draw to his relationship with God. I asked him directly if he had put his trust in the finished work of Jesus Christ as the only remedy for sin, or if he believed that his efforts were sufficient to make a claim on God's love and forgiveness. He said, "It is clear. I cannot earn a spot in heaven." The next day, a close friend of my father, a trusted pastor, and I prayed for him and anointed him with oil. My father glowed with the joy of a man who could smell heaven was near. Few moments in my life are as poignant or wonderful as seeing him embrace faith in the living Christ.

In the days to follow, we talked about the things of life that were off limits. Many topics, sadly, still remained closed or answerable in a way that left me empty. Our relationship was never close to ideal. We had some painful and healing talks about our failure of one another. Even days before he died, I still fought with him to get him to see another physician. I believe God honored my unrelenting persistence with a closeness that was tangible and tasty to the soul.

Dr. Dan Allender, *Bold Love*

December 16

Pleasing the Lord

When a man's ways are pleasing to the LORD,
  he makes even his enemies live at peace with him.

PROVERBS 16:7

When I was a boy I tried to do what my parents wished—most of the time! I loved them, but I also knew there would be consequences if I disobeyed. Later in life when I joined the Royal Marines, I tried hard to do what my commanding officer ordered for rather obvious reasons—I had no desire to become acquainted with the "brig," and also for the less obvious reason that I respected him. When I married Jill, I wanted to do what she wanted me to do because I loved her and wanted to make her happy. So for a variety of reasons throughout my life I have tried to do what I ought. But I have to admit that the greatest joy in doing what I ought has always been in bringing pleasure to the one for whom I was doing it. . . .

We cannot quote [Proverbs 16:7] without commenting on the remarkable assertion that the result of pleasing the Lord is a peace pact with the opposition, even though our emphasis is on the first half of the proverb! Remember that this proverb is generally true, but even so, practical experience may leave us a little skeptical of its truthfulness. Look at it this way: If I do things God's way, there is no doubt that my attitudes even toward my enemies will be extraordinary, and that being the case, it is very likely that the opposition will eventually respond with more of a spirit of cooperation than competition. But whatever the consequences may be, we should aim to please the Lord. And he is pleased when we desire what he desires and do what he wishes.

Stuart Briscoe, *Choices for a Lifetime*

December 17
Finding Our Life in Him

We do not want you to become lazy, but to imitate those who through faith and patience inherit what has been promised.

HEBREWS 6:12

It is the highest stage of manhood to have no wish, no thought, no desire, but Christ—to feel that to die were bliss, if it were for Christ—that to live in penury, and woe, and scorn, and contempt, and misery, were sweet for Christ—to feel that it matters nothing what becomes of one's self, so that our Master is but exalted—to feel that though, like a mere leaf, we are blown in the blast, we are quite careless whither we are going, so long as we feel that the Master's hand is guiding us according to his will; or, rather, to feel that though, like the diamond, we must be exercised with sharp tools, yet we care not how sharply we may be cut; so that we may be made fit brilliants to adorn his crown. . . .

I do think that one of the worst sins a man can be guilty of in this world is to be idle. I can almost forgive a drunkard, but a lazy man I do think there is very little pardon for. I think a man who is idle has as good a reason to be a penitent before God as David had when he was an adulterer, for the most abominable thing in the world is for a man to let the grass grow up to his ankles and do nothing. God never sent a man into the world to be idle. And there are some who make a tolerably fair profession, but who do nothing from one year's end to the other.

Charles Haddon Spurgeon

December 18
The Potter's Sure Hand

Woe to him who quarrels with his Maker,
    to him who is but a potsherd among the potsherds on the ground.
Does the clay say to the potter,
    "What are you making?"
Does your work say,
    "He has no hands"?

ISAIAH 45:9

The potter sets the clay where he will. Repent of wishing to be something other than what God made you to be. Male, female, rich, poor, black, or white; don't ever want to be anything different because God, the potter, chose how the clay was going to be formed, and you are wonderfully and beautifully made. You do not have the prerogative to make such wishes because it assumes you know what is better for you than your creator, the potter. Your journey is to find out what God wants to do with you as His clay and to realize that you are greatly valued. God never creates objects that have no value.

The potter can set you where He wants to set you. He can allow circumstances to happen in your life or prevent them. It makes no difference, you are His vessel for honor or dishonor. Get out of your mind the thought that greatness deals with the size of a ministry. Greatness deals with the ability that God gives you to handle trouble. Do not reproach His nature in your assessment of what you have gone through. Greatness does not consist in reducing others to your service, but reducing yourself to theirs.

Wellington Boone, Breaking Through

DECEMBER 19

Truth As a Sure Foundation

Test me, O LORD, and try me,
examine my heart and my mind;
for your love is ever before me,
and I walk continually in your truth.

PSALM 26:2–3

There is a sense in which the Christian should be the most passionate scientist of all because he should be rigorously open to truth wherever it is found. He should not be afraid that a new discovery of something that is true will destroy his foundation for truth. If our foundation for truth is true, all other truth can only support it and enhance it. It can't destroy it. Therefore, Christians ought not to be afraid of scientific inquiry. This does not mean that we should uncritically accept all pronouncements and pontifications of scientists. Scientists are fallible and may occasionally make arrogant statements that go far beyond the realm of their own expertise. . . .

Occasionally, we read an article about why a certain scientist believes in God or why some other scientist does not. I am delighted when a scientist says that he has studied his area of science and is driven to the awesome majesty of God. But he is no more an expert on the existence of God than you are. Why? Because that is a theological question, not a scientific one. Today when somebody steps outside of his area of expertise, people tend to follow and believe him. That is the basis of much advertising. For example, a baseball star may appear on television and promote a particular brand of razors. If that star were to tell me how to hit a baseball, he would be speaking with authority. But when he tells me the best razor blade to buy is a certain brand, then he is speaking outside of his area of expertise. Advertisers understand that most people will easily transfer a person's authority in one sphere to other spheres. Scientists may be guilty of this fallacy too. We must be wary of scientists who make theological statements outside the boundaries of their discipline.

R. C. Sproul, *Lifeviews*

DECEMBER 20
Life at the Center

. . . that we may live peaceful and quiet lives in all godliness and holiness.

I TIMOTHY 2:2

Within all of us is a whole conglomerate of selves. There is the timid self, the courageous self, the business self, the parental self, the religious self, the literary self, the energetic self. And all of these selves are rugged individualists. No bargaining or compromise for them. Each one screams to protect his or her vested interests. If a decision is made to spend a relaxed evening listening to Chopin, the business self and the civic self rise up in protest at the loss of precious time. The energetic self paces back and forth impatient and frustrated, and the religious self reminds us of the lost opportunities for study or evangelistic contact. If the decision is to accept an appointment on the human services board, the civic self smiles with satisfaction, but all the excluded selves filibuster. No wonder we feel distracted and torn. No wonder we overcommit our schedules and live lives of frantic faithfulness. But when we experience life at the Center, all is changed. Our many selves come under the unifying control of the divine Arbitrator. No longer are we forced to live by an inner majority rule which always leaves a disgruntled minority. The divine Yes or No settles all minority reports. Everything becomes oriented to this new Center of reference. The quiet evening can be enjoyed to the fullest because our many selves have been stilled by the Holy Within. The business self, the religious self, the energetic self, all are at peace because they know we are living in obedience. There is no need to wave the flag of self interest, since all things good and needful will be given their proper attention at the appropriate time. We enter a refreshing balance and equilibrium in life.

Richard Foster, *Freedom of Simplicity*

DECEMBER 21
Forgiving Others

For if you forgive men when they sin against you, your heavenly Father will also forgive you. But if you do not forgive men their sins, your Father will not forgive your sins.

MATTHEW 6:14–15

After speaking to a men's group about forgiving others, I was approached by two brothers. One had brought the other who had not gone to church for many years. His opening line was, "Neil, my problem is canonicity. I've read seven books on the subject, and I just can't accept it."

At first I wasn't sure what he meant. All I could picture in my mind was an old rusty cannon! I finally realized he was talking about the determination of which books could accurately and authoritatively be included in the Bible. "Oh, you mean the closing of the canon!"

Do you really believe that was his problem? I couldn't believe his faith had been thwarted because he didn't agree with the rationale behind the collection of the books of the Bible. I pressed him further and discovered what was really the issue.

Both brothers related their story, which centered around their stepfather who never accepted them. He wasn't a bad person, but they never connected with him. There was never a bonding relationship, not even with their mother. Consequently, their relationship with God was only theological, as their relationship with their parents was only functional.

When I started to explain the nature of a bonding relationship, one of them looked at his watch and said, "It's getting late.

"See," I responded, "anytime someone gets too close personally, you change the subject." That night the backslidden brother forgave his stepfather, and the following morning he asked to sing a song of testimony for the gathering of men. There wasn't a dry eye in the house.

Many people are like these brothers. When you get too close, they look for a way out. We will never connect with God until we confront the personal issues in our lives. Some people hid behind their theology. It is not uncommon at a conference to have someone, usually a man, approach me with his Bible and want to argue with me. If the situation warrants it, I will say, "That's a legitimate question, but can I ask what you are personally struggling with? Is it your marriage or family? Is it your sense of purpose in life?" Some are touched that I care enough to ask, while others continue arguing, creating a smoke screen to keep me from getting too close.

Neil Anderson, *Living Free in Christ*

DECEMBER 22

A Precious Cornerstone

So this is what the Sovereign LORD says:
"See, I lay a stone in Zion,
a tested stone,
a precious cornerstone for a sure foundation;
the one who trusts will never be dismayed."

ISAIAH 28:16

I live in earthquake country. And the church I serve in Berkeley, California, is next to the campus of the University of California, which sits astride the Hayward fault, itself connected to the gigantic San Andreas Fault that stretches from Mexico to Alaska, and directly under the city of San Francisco.

Earthquake specialists have pointed up several important facts about home construction in earthquake terrain: A wood structure is ideally suited for the stresses of horizontal land movement, which is the terror of an earthquake, provided that the wood structure is bolted to its foundation. Another discovery is that 3/4-inch plywood corner reinforcements that extend the side walls of a house to the foundation will also greatly strengthen a house against the horizontal land movement. What has been found in recent quakes is that the nonbolted home moves a few inches away from its foundation, and that move away from the foundation causes the collapse of the structure. In other words, a safe house is that house which relates as much of the house as possible to its foundation. It not only rests upon a rock; it is built into the rock.

I have often thought of the Golden Gate Bridge in San Francisco as our city's boldest structure in that its great south pier rests directly upon the fault zone of the San Andreas Fault. That bridge is an amazing structure of both flexibility and strength. It is built to sway some twenty feet at the center of its one-mile suspension span. The secret to its durability is its flexibility, which enables this sway, but that is not all. By design, every part of the bridge—its concrete roadway, its steel railings, its cross beams—is inevitably related from one welded joint to the other up through the vast cable system to two great towers and two great land anchor piers. The towers bear most of the weight, and they are deeply imbedded into the rock foundation beneath the sea. In other words, the bridge is totally preoccupied with its foundation. This is its secret! Flexibility and foundation. In the Christian life, it is the forgiveness of the gospel that grants us our flexibility; and it is the Lord of the gospel who is our foundation. There is no other.

Earl Palmer, *The Enormous Exception*

DECEMBER 23
Unto Us a Son Is Born

For to us a child is born,
*   to us a son is given,*
*   and the government will be on his shoulders.*
And he will be called
*   Wonderful Counselor, Mighty God,*
*   Everlasting Father, Prince of Peace.*

ISAIAH 9:6

While I was driving home the other day, I saw the ugliest car I have ever seen. This car wasn't just ugly—it was ugly on top of ugly. It had a large gash on its side; one of the doors was held together with baling wire; and several other body parts were almost completely rusted out. The car's muffler was so loose that with every bump, it hit the street, sending sparks in every direction. I couldn't tell the original color of the car. The rust had eaten away much of the paint, and so much of the car had been painted over with so many different colors that any one of them (or none of them) could have been the first coat. The most interesting thing about the car was the bumper sticker: "THIS IS NOT AN ABANDONED CAR."

We live in a fallen world, and sometimes it looks as ugly as that car. Almost everywhere you turn, you can see tragedy and heartache. Only a fool misses the point from the morning headlines that we are sitting on the edge of disaster.

But it isn't just the world. It's us. Sometimes the effort to keep on keeping on doesn't seem worth it. Guilt, loneliness, hurt, and fear become constant companions. One wonders sometimes if any of life makes any difference. One wonders about things such as home and meaning.

A long time ago, in a manger, a baby was born. He was a sign to us. His presence read, "THIS IS NOT AN ABANDONED WORLD."

During every Christmas season, there's a break in the bleakness; a bit of beauty in the middle of the ugliness shines through. People will laugh and make merry. Most won't understand why they laugh. Many of them will make merry because that is what one is supposed to do during the holiday season. But there are some who will pause and remember, "For unto us a child is born."

We have not been abandoned. Someday the Owner will return, then all the ugliness will be remedied. There won't be any more pain, and all the tears will be dried.

May you live merrily because He came. Make your life merry because He keeps coming. Keep it merry because He is coming again to set all things right.

Steve Brown, *Jumping Hurdles, Hitting Glitches and Overcoming Setbacks*

DECEMBER 24

A Savior

So Joseph also went up from the town of Nazareth in Galilee to Judea, to Bethlehem the town of David, because he belonged to the house and line of David. He went there to register with Mary, who was pledged to be married to him and was expecting a child. While they were there, the time came for the baby to be born, and she gave birth to her firstborn, a son. She wrapped him in cloths and placed him in a manger, because there was no room for them in the inn.

LUKE 2:4–7

I'll not forget that first Christmas Eve in captivity. It was terribly cold, and though I knew of at least one other American nearby, I was still alone. My body still ached, and my wounds were only beginning to heal. As I lay there in my ice-cold misery, somewhere in my cell a Christmas carol began to play. It was an incredible surprise; I sat up and searched the cell. For a moment I thought my mind was playing treacherous tricks—"Silent Night, Holy Night." The fidelity was awful, but it was the first song I had heard since bailing out more than a month ago. Scratches and all, that carol was beautiful beyond describing.

Then the carol ended, and the voice of Hanoi Hanna came on with a barrage of propaganda. Later I learned that in the walls every cell had a speaker that broadcast bizarre programming for the prisoners. Many of the programs were recorded in the United States, and were designed to agitate homesick Americans. "Radio Stateside" may have been a tool to break us down, but the snatches of American music, especially that carol on Christmas Eve, with Hanoi Hanna ranting in the background, I recalled at least eight or ten carols, verse by verse. It was like discovering hidden treasure, and I reveled in it.

Howard E. Rutledge, *In the Presence of Mine Enemies*

DECEMBER 25 Christmas Day

Good News

But the angel said to them, "Do not be afraid, I bring you good news of great joy that will be for all the people. Today in the town of David a Savior has been born to you; he is Christ the Lord."

LUKE 2:10–11

Each December in the days when I was young, the congregation of the Presbyterian church down the road built a manger, spread real straw on the floor, and arranged in the new construction life-size figures of the Holy Family, two sheep, a donkey, shepherds, and three kings. It was part of our family's tradition in the Christmas season to visit this crèche.

Early one December when I was nine years old, my father announced that we were going to walk downtown and pay our respects to the baby Jesus. This visit was unique because we walked to the church after dark. In the past we had always driven to the manger scene because it was too cold to walk, and there was always a baby in our family that prevented us from pursuing much adventure. When I was nine, the baby was four, could walk on her own, and wanted to carry the flashlight.

"Everyone—take a hat and gloves. It's very cold," my mother announced as she reached into the closet for our coats.

We walked out of the house and proceeded to follow my four-year-old sister in single file down the sidewalk. Now that I look back it was like following a star, in a way, the star of Bethlehem in the hands of my little sister leading us to the newborn King.

By the time we arrived at the manger, my father was carrying my sister in his arms and the flashlight batteries had died, but the church had erected soft lights that illuminated the ancient scene that stood before us. My mother reminded us that we celebrate Christmas as a reminder of Christ's birthday. She retold the story of Mary and Joseph, how they were searching for a vacant inn. While my mother spoke about the manger, I leaned over and touched the robe of one of the three kings. To my surprise, a small yellow piece of the robe broke off and fell into my hand. I didn't know what to do with it. I didn't want to tell my parents because I was afraid that they might be angry that I had ripped the robe of one of the three kings. I didn't want to drop the piece of cloth because I felt it was sacrilegious, like dropping the American flag to the ground, so I quickly stuck the yellow bit of cloth into my pocket just as my mother finished telling us about the angels and the arrival of the three kings.

"Time to go home," my father announced as he rearranged my sleeping sister on his shoulder.

That night my sisters and brothers, my mother and father, and I walked home in the dark. As we entered the house, my father flicked on a single lamp in the living room so that we could find our way upstairs and to our beds.

After brushing our teeth, after slipping into our pajamas, and after kissing my parents good-night, I pulled the yellow piece of cloth out of my pants pocket and slipped it under my pillow.

Three wise men also followed a light many years ago. What they found at the end of their journey was a Child who filled them with immense joy. They kneeled down before the Child. Perhaps they smiled, nodded their heads in approval, praised Mary and Joseph. These three kings stepped back and unwrapped the gifts they brought: gold, frankincense, and myrrh. This is what my mother told me.

I kept the yellow piece of cloth from the robe of the wise man for many years. Perhaps it was a gift. I believed for a time that the cloth had magical powers, perhaps the power to keep my hands warm, or the power to illuminate a dark room.

Today I understand the true gift of the Magi: the Christmas faith, the image of Mary and Joseph protecting the Baby, my father carrying my sister home on his back.

We all have bits of the wise man's cloth in our hands. It is our responsibility to use this gift, to believe in its power, to be humble in the reality that something significant happened a little over two thousand years ago in the small town of Bethlehem. It is our faith. It is our salvation.

"I bring you good news of great joy that will be for all the people," the angels said to the shepherds. "Today in the town of David a Savior has been born to you; he is Christ the Lord" (Luke 2:10–11).

Today, and every day, enjoy the simple wonders of the Lord. Glory to God in the highest, and peace on earth and goodwill to all. Today let's go to Bethlehem.

Christopher de Vinck, *Simple Wonders*

The Discipline of Reading

When you come, bring the cloak that I left with Carpus at Troas, and my scrolls, especially the parchments.

II TIMOTHY 4:13

In our age of mass media, the younger generation is finding it harder and harder to acquire the discipline of reading, and that may be one of the greatest losses of our time. Nothing substitutes for what can be found when we master books.

Paul gave evidence of his own hunger for reading when he wrote to Timothy asking for parchments and books. Even at that older age, he was anxious to grow. Some of us are not naturally given to reading, and it is hard for us. But to whatever extent we can press ourselves in this direction, we should acquire the habit of reading systematically.

My wife and I are students of biography, and there is hardly a time in our home when the two of us are not making our way through two or three biographical accounts. These books have poured priceless insights into our minds.

Others will be drawn to psychology, theology, history, or good fiction. But all of us need to have at least one good book going at all times, more if possible. When I visit with pastors who are struggling with their own effectiveness, I often ask, "What are you reading lately?" It is almost predictable that if a pastor is struggling with failure in his ministry, he will be unable to name a title or an author that he has been reading in recent days. If he is not reading, the chances are strong that he is not growing. And if he is not growing, then he may rapidly slip into ineffectiveness. . . .

In my own disciplines, I have tried to set aside a minimum of an hour each day for the purpose of reading. I have found that one should never read without a pencil in hand to mark salient passages, and I have developed a simple series of codes that will remind me of impressive thoughts or quotes worth clipping and filing for future use.

Gordon MacDonald, *Ordering Your Private World*

DECEMBER 27
A Blameless Walk

Better a poor man whose walk is blameless
than a rich man whose ways are perverse.

PROVERBS 28:6

No man can be happy unless he is living out his calling to be a man. Exciting but shallow pleasures, the kind that do not require us to worry about some deep call to manhood, may disguise themselves as true happiness. Power, influence, money, status, connections, achievement, success, possessions, food, sex, recreation: lots of things, many of them good in their place, get defined as the source of happiness. And the tricky thing is that they do keep their promise—or at least seem to—for varying periods of time, occasionally for years. They make us feel good; they do something for us.

But they don't really do the job. They do not produce a contentment that survives loss, a joy that deepens through suffering, a humble confidence that persists through failure and setback.

By going after these sources of pleasure, we reduce ourselves to puppets, supported by strings that—if cut—leave us in a heap on the ground.

No man can be happy without living out the call to make visible that which is hard to see about God. Happiness comes for a man when he shows, by his life, that God is always moving, is never stopped by darkness, and is continually up to something good, no matter how bad things may appear.

Larry Crabb, The Silence of Adam

DECEMBER 28
A High Standard

Whoever claims to live in him must walk as Jesus did.

I JOHN 2:6

As Christians, I challenge you. Have a great aim—have a high standard—make Jesus your ideal. Be like him in character. Be like him in outlook and attitude toward God and others. Be like him in the home—thoughtful, patient, loving. Be like him in your work—honest, reliable, always willing to go the second mile. Be like him in your social life—approachable, unselfish, considerate. Make him an ideal not merely to be admired but also to be followed.

The life of Jesus illustrates nearly every variety of true character. Humility, gentleness, patience, sympathy, charity, courage—all are blended together in that one personality.

Crowds gathered round him, for he spoke with authority, and not like the scribes, who merely parroted what they had studied. The people wondered at the gracious words that proceeded out of his mouth. Here is that unity of gentleness and power that stamps a really great character.

He entered the homes of the social outcasts without any snobbishness or pretension. He was known as the friend of publicans and sinners.

Courage and love, perfectly blended, were characteristic of his whole life. *He sought God's will and fearlessly followed it, no matter what the cost.* In his outlook toward people and his treatment of them, sympathy and love found expression in a practical way.

Allow the beauty of this character to absorb your thoughts so that whenever you deviate from his ideal, your conscience will convict you. When that happens, do not try to excuse yourself. Face your fault. Own it to be yours and yours alone. Ask God's forgiveness and where it affects others, ask their forgiveness too. Ask God's Spirit to stand by you and help you till that part of your character, outlook, or attitude comes into line with the ideal you have in Jesus.

Eric Liddell, *Disciplines of the Christian Life*

DECEMBER 29
Honoring One Another

Be devoted to one another in brotherly love. Honor one another above yourselves.

ROMANS 12:10

Our little church at Carville includes one devout Christian named Lou, a Hawaiian by birth, who is marked with visible deformities caused by leprosy. With eyebrows and eyelashes missing, his face has a naked, unbalanced appearance, and paralyzed eyelids cause tears to overflow as if he is crying. He has become almost totally blind because of the failure of a few nerve cells on the surface of his eyes.

Lou struggles constantly with his growing sense of isolation from the world. His sense of touch has faded now, and that, combined with his near-blindness, makes him afraid and withdrawn. He most fears that his sense of hearing may also leave him, for Lou's main love in life is music. He can contribute only one "gift" to our church, other than his physical presence: singing hymns to God while he accompanies himself on an autoharp. Our therapists designed a glove that permits Lou to continue playing his auto-harp without damaging his insensitive hand.

But here is the truth about the Body of Christ: not one person in Carville contributes more to the spiritual life of our church than Lou play-ing his autoharp. He has as much impact on us as does any member there by offering as praise to God the limited, frail tribute of his music. When Lou leaves, he will create a void in our church that no one else can fill—not even a professional harpist with nimble fingers and a degree from the Jul-liard School of Music. Everyone in the church knows that Lou is a vital, contributing member, as important as any other member—and that is the secret of Christ's Body. If each of us can learn to glory in the fact that we matter little except in relation to the Body, and if each will acknowledge the worth in every other member, then perhaps the cells of Christ's Body will begin acting as He intended.

Paul Brand and Philip Yancey, *Fearfully and Wonderfully Made*

December 30

One Day at a Time

. . . do not worry about tomorrow, for tomorrow will worry about itself. Each day has enough trouble of its own.

MATTHEW 6:34

Persons who are anxious spend much of their time worrying about the future and playing "what if" games. On the other hand, people who suffer depression are stalled in the past and waste much of their present playing "if only" games. For these reasons, the suggestion to take one day at a time may seem impossible to follow.

An average person gets up in the morning and may have three items to accomplish in the course of the day. He may complete two of the three, doing one right and the second wrong. Still, he shrugs it off as "no big deal." The perfectionist gets up in the morning with a list of twenty tasks to complete. If he achieves nineteen of the twenty, he is dissatisfied with himself. He's guilt ridden because he feels he's fallen short, He doesn't stop to realize that his goals were unrealistic and had him programmed for failure. If he had managed to accomplish all twenty items, he probably would have felt his objectives weren't challenging enough. The next day's list might have included twenty-one tasks. In both cases, anxiety is the result, either from his failure to set tough goals or his failure to meet the goals he set.

In the hit Broadway play and the film *Annie,* the little red-haired, orphaned heroine looks forward to tomorrow with the words, "You're only a day away." The idea is that everything will be better, brighter, more secure, and less harried in the future. But constant anticipation breeds constant anxiety. The future never measures up to its expectations.

What about today? Jesus advises us, "Therefore do not worry about tomorrow, for tomorrow will worry about its own things. Sufficient for the day is its own trouble."

Frank Minirth, et al., Worry-Free Living

DECEMBER 31
Redeeming the Time

Redeeming the time, because the days are evil.

EPHESIANS 5:16 KJV

Many believers in the West are too busy either climbing the ladder of material success or reclining in the easy chair of home entertainment. We must be disturbed enough by the Holy Spirit to move out of our comfort zones, We must awaken if we are to reach this generation for Christ.

Two realities will arouse us: the threat of death and the imminent return of Christ. Most of us feel that we have plenty of time left. We have surrounded ourselves with a false sense of security.

None of us can presuppose that we have even one more day to live. And we will have to give an account of our lives when we die. Many of us will be embarrassed to say, "Well, I watched countless hours of TV." Others will say, "Lord, I made hundreds of thousands of dollars." God will say, "What did you do of eternal value?"

Ken Leeburg . . . was the best friend I ever had. He was not only my jogging partner, but he also dreamed with me of reaching the world for Christ. We spent hours praying and talking together.

Ken was a picture of health. He was thirty-six years old and had a beautiful family. I was shocked when he was killed in a freak automobile accident. Questions ran through my mind. Here was a man who loved God. He had a vision for the world. He was an outstanding Christian, a great husband and father. Why did he have to die?

It doesn't matter if we live to be thirty-six or 100, life is short. We will all die and give an account of our lives. After Ken's death, I determined that the sum total of my life would be given to things of eternal value.

The Scripture exhorts us to redeem "the time, because the days are evil" (Ephesians 5:16). There is an urgency about the gospel. The eternal destiny of mankind hangs in the balance.

Many Christian acts I do on earth I will also do in heaven. I pray. I will pray in heaven. I sing. I will sing in heaven. I serve God. I will serve God in heaven. There is one thing I will not be able to do in heaven: bring the lost to Jesus. It will be too late. My heart must be set aflame for the lost now. We must all be about our Father's business.

The other truth that should drive us out of our easy chairs is that Jesus is coming again. . . .

We need to learn to long for the coming of Jesus. Anticipate His coming, not by debate but by practice. We need to be on the streets, in the workplace, and throughout the neighborhoods calling people to Jesus. We need to live as though Jesus would come today.

Some may argue that Paul and the early Christians anticipated the coming of Christ, and He didn't come in their generation.

Yet Paul and other early Christians shook the Roman Empire for the glory of God. Perhaps if we anticipated the imminent return of Christ, we would shake Western civilization for His glory.

Awake, Christian! Life is short! Christ is coming! Redeem the time!

Samuel Tippit, *Fire in Your Heart*

Afterword

This year has ended. I hope you can count it as among the best in your life.

This book, too, draws to a reluctant close with the hope that it's brought you a little closer to your Christian manhood, to the source of that manhood, the Lord Jesus Christ, and to your Christian brothers walking the same path.

If the book has been meaningful to you and you'd care to write and let me hear about your successes, failures, joys, losses, and hopes; please do so. You can reach me in care of the address below.

As tomorrow begins a new year, I hope you'll resolve to continue having a special time alone with a good devotional book, in addition to your time alone with God. There are many good devotionals to choose from—*My Utmost for His Highest*, for instance, is a book everyone should spend at least one year with. Or, you might want to go through *Promises to Keep* again. You'll be amazed at how a second reading can illuminate a truth only barely understood the first time around.

Remember—keep your focus on Jesus Christ in your quest to be fully a man. Don't allow the world's misperceptions of masculinity to entice you to seek after a mirage.

Finally, when, in the course of your busy days you come across a non-Christian man who seems to be adrift, befriend him. Encourage him to consider Christ and the brotherhood of believers who await him.

Keep looking forward! And God bless!

Nick Harrison
c/o HarperSanFrancisco
1160 Battery Street
San Francisco, California 94111–1213

Biographical Appendix

The editor would like to acknowledge two excellent reference books consulted in the compiling of some of the following biographies: *Who's Who In Christian History* and *America's God and Country*, two fine volumes that belong in the library of any Christian interested in his or her spiritual predecessors.

Joseph Aldrich has served as president of Multnomah School of the Bible in Portland, Oregon, and is the author of *Gentle Persuasion*.

Dr. Dan Allender teaches in the Biblical Counseling Department at Colorado Christian University. He's the author of *The Wounded Heart* and *Bold Love*.

Aubrey C. Andelin is the author of the classic men's book *Man of Steel and Velvet*. He resides in Arizona.

James Anderson was a popular nineteenth-century clergyman with the Methodist Episcopal Church and the author of *Thoughts That Breathe*.

Leith Anderson is the senior pastor of Wooddale Church in Eden Prairie, Minnesota, and the author of *Winning the Values War in a Changing Culture*.

Neil Anderson is the founder and president of Freedom in Christ Ministries and the author of such bestselling books as *The Bondage Breaker*, *Victory Over the Darkness*, and *Living Free in Christ*.

Steve Arterburn is the founder of New Life Treatment Centers, a program that treats emotional problems and addictive disorders. He is the author of more than fifteen books, including *Winning at Work*.

Ron Auch is the founder of Pray-Tell Ministries, dedicated to challenging the Body of Christ to pray. He is also the author of *Taught by the Spirit* and *The Heart of the King*, published by New Leaf Press.

Augustine (354–430) was one of the Christian Church's most influential fathers. His *City of God* and *Confessions* are still widely read and respected today.

Bob Beltz is a speaker, author, and pastor of Cherry Hills Community Church in Denver, Colorado.

Mike Bickle is the senior pastor of Metro Vineyard Fellowship in Kansas City, Missouri, which he founded in 1982. He's the author of *Passion for Jesus*.

Henry Blackaby is director of the Office of Prayer and Spiritual Awakening at the Home Mission Board of the Southern Baptist Convention. He, along with co-writer Claude King, developed the highly popular *Experiencing God* study, which has been used extensively across America.

Ken Blue is pastor of Foothills Christian Fellowship in San Diego. He is also the author of *Authority to Heal* and, with John White, *Healing the Wounded.*

James Montgomery Boice is pastor of Philadelphia's Tenth Presbyterian Church and is the author of nearly forty books on the Bible and related subjects.

Dietrich Bonhoeffer (1906–1945) was a German pastor during Hitler's oppressive dictatorship. His resistance against the Fuhrer led to his imprisonment and eventual hanging. His writings have remained popular since his death. His best known works are *The Cost of Discipleship, Life Together,* and *Ethics.*

Wellington Boone is founder and president of New Generation Campus Ministries and is senior pastor of Manna Christian Fellowship in Richmond, Virginia. He's a contributor to the bestselling book *The Seven Promises of a Promise Keeper* and the author of *Breaking Through.*

William Booth (1829–1912) was a British evangelist and, with his wife, Catherine, founder of the Salvation Army.

Frank Boreham (1871–1959) pastored in New Zealand, Tasmania, and Australia. In his later ministry, he became one of the twentieth century's most well-known religious writers, authoring more than fifty books.

Dr. Paul Brand has been honored for his pioneering research on leprosy in India and is highly regarded in his role as an eminent hand surgeon. He is a Commander of the Order of the British Empire. His best-known books include *Fearfully and Wonderfully Made* and *In His Image,* both co-written with Philip Yancey.

Bill Bright is the founder of the influential ministry Campus Crusade for Christ, largely known for their successful evangelistic work with Dr. Bright's "Four Spiritual Laws" tract. He's also the author of several books on both witnessing and living the Christian life.

Stuart Briscoe has served, since 1970, as senior pastor at Elmbrook Church in Brookfield, Wisconsin, with a congregation of more than 6,000. He is also the author of many books, including *Choices for a Lifetime.*

Steve Brown ministers as president of KeyLife Network in Maitland, Florida, and is the author of *Jumping Hurdles, Hitting Glitches and Overcoming Setbacks.*

Alexander Balmain Bruce (1831–1899) was an influential Scottish theologian and the author of the classic book *The Training of the Twelve.*

Bob Buford is president of a successful cable television company and the founder of Leadership Network, a support service to leaders of large churches.

Tim Burke, former major league baseball pitcher, gave up his career to devote more time to his wife and children. He's the author of *Major League Dad,* which tells the story of the trials that almost destroyed his marriage and of his retirement decision.

Larry Burkett is a popular Christian writer on financial issues. His many books include *The Coming Economic Earthquake, Debt Free Living,* and *Business by the Book.*

Dennis Byrd played four seasons of professional football for the New York Jets. Currently he lives in Owasso, Oklahoma, where he is establishing the Dennis Byrd Foundation, which will send children with disabilities to summer camp. He is the author, with Michael D'Orso, of *Rise and Walk.*

Dr. Ross Campbell is the author of two bestselling parenting books, *How to Really Love Your Child* and *How to Really Love Your Teenager,* both published by Scripture Press.

Tony Campolo is professor of sociology at East College in St. Davids, Pennsylvania. His many books include *The Kingdom of God Is a Party* and *How to Rescue the Earth.*

Ken Canfield is the director of the National Center for Fathering, based in Manhattan, Kansas. He's the author of *The Seven Secrets of Effective Fathers.*

Michael Card is a popular musician and poet and author of the book *Immanuel.*

Jim Carlson is the president of Spring Arbor, one of the largest book distributors in the United States, and the author of *Choosing to Be Fully Alive.*

Carman is one of the most popular contemporary gospel performers in America today. He's also the author of the book *Raising the Standard.*

Merlin Carothers is a former Army Chaplain Lieutenant Colonel with the 82nd Airborne Division and the author of several bestselling books, including *Prison to Praise, Power in Praise,* and *What's on Your Mind.*

Dr. Ben Carson was raised in inner-city Detroit by a mother with a third-grade education. Through hard work, faith, and determination, Ben won a full scholarship to Yale and graduated from the University of Michigan Medical School. At the age of thirty-three he became director of pediatric neurosurgery at Johns Hopkins Hospital in Baltimore. He's the author of *Gifted Hands* and *Think Big.*

Les Carter is a psychotherapist with the Minirth-Meier Clinic and the author of *Putting the Past Behind.*

George Washington Carver (1864–1943) was an agricultural chemist whose many accomplishments include discovering more than 300 uses for the peanut. He also helped develop a cure for infantile paralysis and was asked by both Henry Ford and Thomas Edison to join them in their respective works. Carver's laboratory was named "God's Little Workshop" because he never took scientific texts as his source, but rather simply asked God how to perform his experiments.

Paul Yonggi Cho is the pastor of one of Full Gospel Central's Church in Seoul, Korea, one of the world's largest churches. He's the author of several books, including *The Fourth Dimension* and *Solving Life's Problems*.

Chap Clark is chairman of the Youth Ministry Department at Denver Seminary, and author of several books, including *Next Time I Fall In Love*, and co-author, with Steve Lee, of *Boys to Men*.

Dr. Henry Cloud is a co-director (with Dr. John Townsend) of the Minirth-Meier Clinic West, a group of treatment centers headquartered in Newport Beach, California. He's the author of *Changes That Heal* and, with Dr. Townsend, *Boundaries*.

Edwin Lewis Cole is the founder of Christian Men's Network amd the author of several books, including *Maximized Manhood* and *Real Man*.

Charles Colson served as an aide for president Richard Nixon and served time in prison as a result of his involvement in the Watergate scandal. While in prison he became a Christian and later founded Prison Fellowship, a ministry to those behind bars. Since then he has written several bestselling and award-winning books, including *Born Again, The Body*, and *Who Speaks for God?*

Christopher Columbus (1451–1506), in an effort to find a shortcut to the Indies, sailed to a land that would later be named "America." A strongly devout man, on his deathbed Columbus uttered as his last words the same final words of Christ, "Into your hands, Father, I commend my soul."

Jim Conway is the author of several books, including the best-selling *Men in Midlife Crisis*.

Jon Courson is the pastor of the 4000-member Applegate Christian Fellowship in the Applegate Valley of Southern Oregon, and the author of the "Tree of Life" Bible Commentary series.

Larry Crabb, Jr., is the founder and director of the Institute of Biblical Counseling. He also is professor of biblical counseling at Colorado Christian University in Morrison, Colorado. He has authored many books, including *Inside Out* and *The Silence of Adam*.

Russ Crossan is a certified financial planner and has been a partner with the nationally recognized financial and investment advisory firm of Ronald Blue and Co. for more than ten years.

Nicky Cruz's story was widely told in the books *The Cross and the Switchblade* and *Run Baby Run*. He now heads "Nicky Cruz Outreach," based in Colorado Springs, and has written several books, including *The Magnificent Three*.

Gordon Dalbey is a United Church of Christ minister and a graduate of Harvard Divinity School. He's the author of *Healing the Masculine Soul*, one of the first books to take on the issues of manhood with a Christian perspective and, his more recent title, *Fight Like a Man*.

J. N. Darby (1800–1882) was one of the leaders of the Plymouth Brethren movement. He wrote and preached widely and his influence is still felt in evangelical churches today.

John Dawson works with Youth with a Mission and is respected internationally as a teacher at conferences and leadership workshops. He's the author of *Taking Our Cities for God*.

Dick Day is a licensed marriage, family, and child counselor and is the co-founder and director of the Julian Center in Julian, California. He lectures internationally and is a co-author with Josh McDowell and appears in numerous films, videos, and video series with Josh.

Edward Dayton has been an aerospace executive, a midlife seminary graduate, and a popular teacher of management practices. He has written more than a dozen books, including *The Art of Management for Christian Leaders*, *Strategy for Leadership*, and *Succeeding in Business*.

Max DePree is chairman and CEO of Herman Miller, Inc., the furniture maker that was named one of *Fortune* magazine's ten "best managed" and "most innovative" companies. It was also chosen as one of the hundred best companies to work for in America. DePree is the author of *Leadership Jazz* and *Leadership is an Art*.

Christopher de Vinck is the author of several books, including *The Power of the Powerless*, *Only the Heart Knows How To Find Them*, and *Simple Wonders*. He lives with his family in Pompton Plains, New Jersey.

Dr. David De Witt is the president of Relational Concepts, an organization with an emphasis on discipling men, and the author of *The Mature Man*, published by Vision House.

Dion DiMucci is remembered as a pop idol of the 1950s when as "Dion and the Belmonts" he had such hits as "Lonely Teenager" and "Teenager in Love." As a solo artist his big hits included "Runaround Sue" and "Abraham, Martin, and John." His autobiography is *The Wanderer*.

Dr. James Dobson is founder and president of "Focus on the Family," a major Christian publisher and radio ministry. His many bestselling books include *Dare to Discipline*, *The Strong-Willed Child*, *What Wives Wish Their Husbands Knew About Women*, and *Straight Talk to Men and Their Wives*.

Dave Dravecky is a former pitcher with the San Francisco Giants. At the height of his career he was sidelined by an operation to remove a cancerous tumor from his pitching arm. Told his chances of ever pitching again were near zero, he nevertheless returned to pitch two games before breaking his arm during a game. His story is told in two books, *Comeback* and *When You Can't Come Back.*

Henry Drummond (1851–1897) was a popular Scottish writer and evangelist, best known for his popular book on I Corinthians 13, *The Greatest Thing in the World.*

Karl Duff retired in 1989 as a captain in the U.S. Navy. He holds a Doctor of Science degree in mechanical engineering from M.I.T., and has spent twenty-seven years scoutmastering Boy Scout groups. He is the author of *Restoration of Men.*

Jim Durkin (1925–1996) was for many years the pastor of Gospel Outreach in Eureka, California. From his church, numerous evangelistic teams established churches in many countries throughout the world.

Jonathan Edwards (1703–1758) was one of America's legendary men of faith. His preaching ushered in "The Great Awakening" revival. He and his wife, the former Sarah Pierrepont, committed themselves to raising their eleven children in the respect of God. A study done in 1900 revealed that their descendants included thirteen college presidents, sixty-five professors, thirty judges, 100 lawyers, nearly 100 missionaries, three governors, three United States Senators, and one vice president of the United States.

Ted Engstrom has served the Body of Christ for many years, including as president of World Vision International, a Christian relief agency. He is also the author of more than thirty books, including *The Fine Art of Friendship.*

Gayle Erwin has spent thirty years as a pastor, college teacher, and magazine editor. He is the author of *The Jesus Style,* a popular book on personal evangelism.

Tony Evans is the president of The Urban Alternative, a ministry devoted to promoting a clear understanding and relevant application of Scripture to bring about changes in urban communities. He's the author of several books, including *Our God Is Awesome.*

Steve Farrar is the president of Point Man Leadership Ministries in Dallas, Texas, and is the author of several books, including *Standing Tall: How a Man Can Protect His Family* and *Point Man.*

Francois Fenelon (1651–1715) was an influential French writer, preacher, and the Archbishop of Cambrai, whose writings are still popular today.

Charles Finney (1792–1875) was converted in 1821 and became one of the most influential preachers and leaders of evangelical revivalism of the nineteenth century. His autobiography and revival lectures are still widely read today.

Richard Foster is the author of several bestselling books, including *Celebration of Discipline* and *Freedom of Simplicity.*

Francis de Sales (1567–1622) was a French bishop whose *Introduction to the Devout Life* is a classic book, still widely read by both Catholics and Protestants.

Francis of Assisi (1182–1226) is remembered today for his emphasis on the use of nature as a means of communing with God and his insistence on vows of poverty. He died at age forty-four and was canonized by the Catholic Church two years later.

Francis Frangipane is the senior pastor of River of Life Church in Cedar Rapids, Iowa, and author of *The Three Battlegrounds* and *The House of the Lord*.

Mitsuo Fuchida led the Japanese attack on Pearl Harbor. Several years later he became a Christian and worked for a world where there would be no more Pearl Harbors. His story is told in the book *From Pearl Harbor to Golgotha*.

Bill Gaither is one of the most successful and honored artists in the history of contemporary Christian music. In more than thirty years as a pianist, composer, and producer, he has received three Grammy Awards, twenty Dove Awards and the first Gold Record ever awarded to an inspirational album.

Dale Galloway is affiliated with Asbury Theological Seminary in Wilmore, Kentucky, and is the author of *Rebuild Your Life*.

Bob George is the founder and president of Discipleship Training Services and the author of *Classic Christianity* and *Growing in Grace*, both published by Harvest House.

Gene Getz has served as director for the Center for Church Renewal and pastor of Fellowship Bible Church, Plano, Texas. He's the author of many books, including the bestselling *Measure of a Man*.

Joseph Girzone is a retired Catholic priest whose book *Joshua* was a surprise best-seller. He went on to write several other popular books, including *Joshua in the City*, *The Shepherd*, and *Never Alone*.

Bill Glass, former all-pro defensive end for the Cleveland Browns is the author of several books on the Christian life, and ministers through his Bill Glass Ministries based in Cedar Hill, Texas.

S. D. Gordon (1859–1936) was the author of the popular "Quiet Talks" books, including *Quiet Talks on Prayer* and *Quiet Talks on Power*.

Geoff Gorsuch has served for fourteen years with Navigators. Currently he is working with Promise Keepers.

Colonel Archibald Gracie, U.S. Army, retired, is generally considered the last man to have left the sinking Titanic. He told the tale of his incredible escape in his book *The Truth About the Titanic*. He died eight months after the Titanic went down.

Billy Graham has been the church's pre-eminent evangelist of the twentieth century, leading tens of thousands to Christ. His many books include *Peace with God*, *How to Be Born Again*, and *The Holy Spirit*.

William Franklin Graham III is president of Samaritan's Purse, a Christian relief organization spreading the gospel by meeting the physical and spiritual needs of victims of war, famine, disease, and natural disasters. Graham is the author of a children's book *Miracle in a Shoe Box* and his autobiograhy, *Rebel with a Cause.*

George Grant is the executive director of Legacy Communications and vice president of Coral Ridge Ministries. He's the author of several books, including *Third Time Around* and *The Micah Candidate.*

A. C. Green currently plays basketball for the Phoenix Suns, after eight seasons with the Los Angeles Lakers. For six of those seasons Green led the team in rebounds and was named an NBA All-Star in 1990. He is also the founder of the A. C. Green Programs for Youth. He also works with Athletes for Abstinence and is the author of *Victory.*

Keith Green was a popular contemporary Christian singer, modern-day prophet, and founder, with his wife, Melody, of Last Days Ministries. The story of his life is told in *No Compromise: The Keith Green Story,* and some of his messages are included in a posthumous collection, *A Cry in the Wilderness.*

John Grisham is one of American's bestselling novelists, author of books such as *The Client, The Pelican Brief,* and *The Chamber.* Mr. Grisham recalls his conversion at age eight, "I came under conviction. . . . I told [my mother], 'I don't understand this, but I need to talk to you.' We talked and she led me to Jesus."

Dudley Hall is the president of Successful Christian Living Ministries and the author of numerous books, including *Out of the Comfort Zone* and *Grace Works.* He lives in Euless, Texas.

Tim Hansel was raised in Seattle, educated at Stanford University, and is the author of several books, including the best-selling, *You Gotta Keep Dancin'.* He also heads Summit Expedition, a wilderness ministry that has a profound impact on its participants.

Weldon Hardenbrook is the author of one of the pioneering books addressing men and Christianity, *Missing in Action: Vanishing Manhood in America.*

Willard Harley has been a psychologist and marriage counselor for more than thirty years. His books include *Love Busters* and the bestselling *His Needs, Her Needs.*

Will J. Harney was a successful preacher and evangelist, and author of *Praying Clear Through.*

Doyle "Buddy" Harrison is the founder of Harrison House Publishers and the author several books, including *Man, Husband, Father,* a companion to his wife Pat's book, *Woman, Wife, Mother.*

Archibald Hart is dean of the Graduate School of Psychology and professor of theology at Fuller Theological Seminary. His many books include *Unlocking the Secrets of Your Emotions* and *Healing for Hidden Addictions.*

Fred Hartley is the senior pastor of Lilburn Alliance Church in Atlanta and the author of *Men and Marriage.*

Jack Hayford is the pastor of The Church on the Way in Van Nuys, California, and the author of several books, including *A Man's Starting Place*.

Howard Hendricks is a professor and lecturer at Dallas Theological Seminary. He's written several books, including *Heaven Help the Home* and, with his son, William, *As Iron Sharpens Iron*.

William Hendricks is the president of the Hendricks Group, a communications development group in Dallas, Texas. He has written or co-written seven books, including *Exit Interviews* and, with his father, Howard, *As Iron Sharpens Iron*.

Earl Henslin is a counselor who conducts relationship seminars and is the author of *Forgiven and Free* and *Man to Man*.

Orel Hershiser is a World Series–winning major league baseball pitcher. His story is told in his book, *Out of the Blue*, with co-writer, Jerry Jenkins.

Roy Hession is the author of several books, including the classic *The Calvary Road* and *Forgotten Factors: An Aid to Deeper Repentance*.

Robert Hicks is a counselor and frequent speaker on men's issues and is Professor of Pastoral Theology at Seminary of the East in Drescher, Pennsylvania. His books include *Uneasy Manhood* and *The Masculine Journey*.

R. Kent Hughes is senior pastor of College Church in Wheaton, Illinois, and the author of several books.

John Hus (1373–1415) was a Bohemian priest whose sometimes Protestant-like beliefs caused him controversy with his superiors. He eventually was burned at the stake for his views. He died with the words from a Greek liturgical prayer on his lips, "Lord, have mercy."

Bill Hybels is pastor of the innovative Willow Creek Community Church in South Barrington, Illinois. He's served as chaplin to the Chicago Bears and has written several books, including *Honest to God?* and *Laws of the Heart*.

Jack Hyles has served as pastor of the First Baptist Church of Hammond, Indiana for many years; a church widely respected for its effective Sunday School programs and bus ministry. Dr. Hyles is also the author of several books.

Keith Intrater is pastor of El Shaddai, a Messianic Jewish congregation. He and his wife, Betty, live with their three children in Frederick, Maryland. He's the author of *Covenant Relationships*, published by Destiny Image.

Harry Ironside was one of the most influential clergymen of the early twentieth century and the author of many books, including his still widely used commentaries.

Jim Irwin (1930–1991) was an astronaut with NASA. He later founded High Flight, a missionary organization through which he was able to share his Christian witness with others. His autobiography is *To Rule the Night*.

T. D. Jakes is the senior pastor and founder of Temple of Faith Ministries in Charleston, West Virginia. His television ministry on Trinity Broadcasting Network

(TBN) is watched by millions of viewers. He's the author of such bestselling books as *Can You Stand to Be Blessed?* and *Loose That Man and Let Him Go!*

Ron Jenson is an author, speaker, and executive consultant. He also is the chairman of MaxLife, a company providing educational programs, products, and services for personal development. Jenson lives with his wife Mary and their two children in San Diego, California.

Jerry Jenkins is a noted novelist, biographer, and magazine writer, whose books include *Hedges* and *Out of the Blue.*

E. Stanley Jones (1884–1973) became a Christian at age seventeen. Educated in law, he became a missionary to India where he established Christian *ashrams*, centers for meditation and worship. He authored twenty-nine books and was twice nominated for the Nobel Peace Prize.

Dino Kartsonakis is a talented pianist with many bestselling albums to his credit. He performs regularly in Branson, Missouri, and told his life story in his autobiography, *Dino.*

Bil Keane's popular "Family Circus" comic strip is read by millions daily. He's an active Christian and many of his humorous strips have been collected in *Count Your Blessings,* published by Focus on the Family.

W. Phillip Keller is a Canadian citizen, agrologist, lecturer, photographer, rancher, and the author of several bestselling books, including *A Shepherd Looks at the Twenty-Third Psalm* and *Taming Tension.*

Ron Kenoly is a popular worshiper and leader with several bestselling albums to his credit. He is the author of *Lift Him Up.*

William Kirk Kilpatrick is a frequent lecturer on religious and psychological topics at colleges and universities. He is the author of *Identity and Intimacy* and *Psychological Seduction.*

Tim Kimmel travels throughout the United States and Canada speaking to young people and their parents on behalf of Generation Ministries, of which Tim is director. He lives in Scottsdale, Arizona, and is the author of *Little House on the Freeway.*

Ben Kinchlow is the co-host of The 700 Club television program and author of *Plain Bread* and *You Don't Have to If You Don't Want To.*

Jerry Kirk is a retired pastor and is active in the crusade against pornography, working with the National Alliance for the Protection of Children and Families. He is a contributor to the bestselling book *Seven Promises of a Promise Keeper.*

Dick Brian Klaver is the pastor of First Reformed Church, West Glenville, New York. Previously he was a marriage and family therapist and domestic violence counselor. He's the author of *Men at Peace.*

Larry Kreider is the president of The Gathering U.S.A., Inc., and has served with Youth for Christ for twenty-five years. He is the author of *Bottom Line Faith*.

Tim LaHaye has, for many years, been an active Christian speaker, pastor, and activist. He is the author of many bestselling books, most notably *The Act of Marriage*, *Spirit-Controlled Temperament*, and *Understanding the Male Temperament*.

Tom Landry is a legend among football fans. For many years he was head football coach of Superbowl champions, The Dallas Cowboys. *Tom Landry: An Autobiography*, written with Gregg Lewis, was published by HarperCollins.

Greg Laurie has served the Body of Christ as a pastor, evangelist, and author. His books include *Life: Any Questions?*

Brother Lawrence (1611–1691) worked as a cook in a Christian community for thirty years. It was there that he discovered that God must be experienced in the everyday tasks of life. His writings were edited into a small book, *The Practice of The Presence of God*, which is still widely circulated more than 300 years later.

Dr. Steven Lawson is a former sportswriter for the Texas Rangers and the Dallas Cowboys. He now pastors The Bible Church of Little Rock, Arkansas, where he lives with his wife, Anne, and their four children. He is the author of *Men Who Win*.

Steve Lee is professor and chair of the psychology department at Huntington College. He and his wife, Twyla, are partners in leading marriage and family workshops.

Leonard LeSourd edited hundreds of books and was chairman of the board of directors of "Breakthrough," an intercessory prayer ministry. He was the author of *Strong Men, Weak Men*.

R. G. LeTourneau was a farmhand, foundry apprentice, master molder, garage mechanic, laborer, inventor, manufacturer, industialist, Christian businessman, and lay evangelist whose book *Mover of Men and Mountains* has inspired many. His motto was, "Not how much of my money do I give to God, but how much of God's money do I keep for myself?"

C. S. Lewis (1898–1963) was a tutor and lecturer at Cambridge and Oxford Universities for many years. His Christian writings have influenced young (*The Chronicles of Narnia*) and old (*Mere Christianity*) alike. The story of his love for Joy Davidman was recounted in the popular movie, *Shadowlands*.

Paul Lewis is the editor of *Smart Dads* newsletter. He teaches fathering courses and seminars for Dads University, which he founded. He's the author of *Five Key Habits of Smart Dads*.

Eric Liddell (1902–1945) won the 400-meter dash in the 1924 Olympics. The story of his refusal to race on Sunday during those games was depicted in the Academy Award–winning film *Chariots of Fire*. He went on to serve as a Christian missionary in war-torn China, where he died in a Japanese concentration camp near the end of World War II.

Abraham Lincoln (1809–1865) was the sixteenth president of the United States and, though not a member of any specific church, consistently voiced his opinion on the truth of Scripture.

Fred Littauer has been a businessman for most of his life. Now he is a full-time speaker and writer and managing director for CLASS Speakers, Inc. His books include *The Promise of Restoraton* and *Wake Up, Men!*

Max Lucado is one of today's most popular Christian authors. His many best-sellers include *No Wonder They Call Him Saviour, In the Eye of the Storm,* and *When God Whispers Your Name.*

Martin Luther (1483–1546) was the father of the German Reformation and one of Christendom's most influential leaders. His many writings, including his popular commentaries on Romans and Galatians, continue to be read today.

John MacArthur, Jr., is pastor-teacher at Grace Community Church in the San Fernando Valley of southern California. He has written many books, including *The Gospel According to Jesus* and *The Family.*

Bill McCartney is the former head coach of the University of Colorado Buffaloes, one of the founders of Promise Keepers, and the author of *From Ashes to Glory* and *What Makes a Man?*

George MacDonald (1824–1905) was a Scottish writer whose books of the late nineteenth century rivaled those of Charles Dickens in popularity. The recent reissue of many of his books in edited editions have spawned renewed interest in MacDonald.

Gordon MacDonald formerly pastored Grace Chapel in Lexington, Massachusetts, the largest congregation in New England. He served as president of Inter-Varsity Christian Fellowship and is the author of numerous books, including *Ordering Your Private World.*

Josh McDowell is the author of several bestselling books, including *More Than a Carpenter,* considered by many to be the best modern evangelistic book available. He also wrote, with Dick Day, *How to Be a Hero to Your Kids.*

Robert McGee is the founder and president of Rapha, a Christ-centered health care organization specializing in adults and adolescents suffering from psychiatric and substance abuse problems. He is the author of *The Search for Significance,* among others.

Alan McGinis is co-director of Valley Counseling Service in Glendale, California. He's the author of several books, including *The Friendship Factor* and *Confidence.*

Mike Mason is a Canadian writer, active in Anglican lay ministry. His short stories have appeared in several of Canada's literary magazines. His books include *The Mystery of Marriage.*

Martin Mawyer is the president and founder of the Christian Action Network, a nonprofit lobbying organization dedicated to the protection of the American family. He is the author of *Pathways to Success.*

Ron Mehl is the pastor of a large church in Beaverton, Oregon. He's a frequent speaker at leadership conferences and retreats and is the author of *Surprise Endings* and *God Works the Night Shift.*

Dean Merrill has served as editor of *Christian Herald* magazine and currently works with Focus on the Family in Colorado Springs. He's the author of several books, including *The Husband Book.*

In 1911 William P. Merrill, former minister of the Fifth Avenue Brick Church of New York City, was asked to write a brotherhood hymn. The result was the popular "Rise Up O Men of God," which he later recalled "seemed just to come of itself."

J. C. Metcalfe was a popular minister and teacher, and the author of *If There Be Heresies.*

Calvin Miller has been a successful pastor and writer with many books to his credit including *The Singer Trilogy, The Taste of Joy,* and *A Hunger for Meaning.*

Dr. Frank Minirth is a member of the American Board of Psychiatry and Neurology and a founder (along with Dr. Paul Meier) of the renowned Minirth-Meier Clinics. He's the author of or contributor to many books, including *The Workaholic and His Family* and *How to Beat Burnout.*

Dwight L. Moody (1837–1899) was one of America's premiere evangelists, wielding a wide influence that continues today. His story is recounted in *The Gospel Awakening.*

David Moore is the senior pastor of Southwest Community Church in Palm Desert, California. He's also the president of Paradigm Ministries, host of a radio program, "Moore on Life," and author of *Five Lies of the Century.*

Patrick Morley resides in Orlando, Florida, where he leads a ministry for men. He has authored many bestselling books, including *The Man in the Mirror, Walking with Christ in the Details of Life,* and *The Seven Seasons of a Man's Life.*

Tom Morton is an award-winning reporter with ten years of experience in religious, investigative, and environmental journalism. He's the author of *The Survivor's Guide to Unemployment.*

Andrew Murray (1828–1917) was a South African clergyman who strongly influenced the missionary movement to South Africa. Today he is largely remembered for his many devotional books, still in print and still strong sellers.

Charles Mylander is the author of several books, including *Running the Red Lights, Secrets for Growing Churches*, and *Supernatural Energy for Your Race*.

Watchman Nee was a prominent Christian worker in China during the first half of the twentieth century. He spent his last years in a Communist prison. His many oral messages have been transcribed into books, some of which have already attained classic status. Such books include *The Normal Christian Life, Sit, Walk, Stand* and *Changed into His Likeness*.

Alan Nelson is the founder and pastor of the West Coast Wesleyan Church in Mission Viejo, California, where he lives with his wife, Nancy, and their three sons. He is also the author of *Five Minute Ministry*.

David Nowell received his Ph.D. in historical theology from Baylor University, where he is an officer in university relations. He lives with his wife and two step-daughters in Waco, Texas. He's also the author of *Stepparent Is Not a Bad Word* and *A Man's Work Is Never Done*.

Michael O'Donnell is the director of the Southwest Center for Fathering and an associate professor at Abilene Christian University in Abilene, Texas. He is the author of *Home from Oz*.

Lloyd John Ogilvie is the author of many books and served for many years as pastor of First Presbyterian Church in Hollywood, California. He is currently Chaplain for the United States Senate.

Gary Oliver is a psychologist at Southwest Counseling Associates and the author of *Real Men Have Feelings Too*.

Juan Carlos Ortiz is a popular Argentine pastor and writer with several books to his credit, including *Disciple, Call to Discipleship*, and *Cry of the Human Heart*.

Dr. James Osterhaus is a practicing psychologist in Fairfax Station, Virginia, a former director with Campus Life, and the author of *Bonds of Iron*.

Jesse Owens impressed the world when he won three gold medals in the 1936 Olympic games. A chagrined Adolf Hitler left the stands rather than watch the American athlete. Owens told the story of his life and faith in his autobiography, *Jesse*.

Luis Palau is an international evangelist who has preached the gospel to more than nine million people on six continents and to millions more through radio and television broadcasts in ninety-four countries. He is the author of twenty-nine books and booklets.

Dr. Earl Palmer has served as pastor of the First Presbyterian Church in Berkeley, California, for many years. He's written several books, including *The Enormous Exception*.

Patrick (c.390-c.461) was a missionary to Ireland whose popularity spawned many legends, such as his expelling snakes from that country. Though never formally canonized, today he is popularly thought of as "St." Patrick.

Ben Patterson is pastor of Irvine Presbyterian Church in Irvine, California and author of *Waiting.*

J. C. Penney (1875–1971) was a noted businessman, founding the Golden Rule Stores, which eventually became the chain of department stores bearing his name. He was a devout Christian and wrote of his experiences in books such as *Lines of a Layman* and *Fifty Years with the Golden Rule.*

Bill Perkins is the senior pastor of South Hills Community Church in Portland, Oregon, and the author of *Fatal Attractions,* published by Harvest House.

Eugene Peterson has been a pastor and is a popular author of several books, including *A Long Obedience in the Same Direction* and *Traveling Light.* He's also the editor of the highly acclaimed *The Message* Bible.

Mike Phillips is the author of many bestselling books, both fiction and nonfiction. He's an authority on writer George MacDonald and has edited many of the Scottish author's books for the modern reader. He lives with his family in Eureka, California.

Randy Phillips is the president of Promise Keepers and a contributor to the bestseller *Seven Promises of a Promise Keeper.*

John Piper is the senior pastor of Bethlehem Baptist Church in Minneapolis, and the author of *Desiring God* and *The Pleasures of God.*

Earl Radmacher is President Emeritus of Western Seminary and now lives in Scottsdale, Arizona.

Dennis Rainey has worked extensively with families while serving as national director of the Family Ministry of Campus Crusade for Christ. He has authored several books, including *The Tribute.*

Ron Rand is co-pastor of Congregational Life and Leadership at College Hill Presbyterian Church in Cincinnati, Ohio, and is the founder of HELPER Ministries, dedicated to helping lay people to evangelize regularly as well as of FATHERS Ministry, dedicated to assisting men as fathers accountable to healthy enduring relationships and spirituality. He's the author of *For Fathers Who Aren't in Heaven.*

Pete Richardson is Editorial Advisor for Promise Keepers and the author of *Why Christian Men Need Each Other.*

Tim Riter, a pastor for eighteen years, is a popular conference speaker and author of *Deep Down.* He and his wife, Sheila, spend their free time motorcycling through their home area of southern California.

Haddon Robinson has served as president of Denver Seminary in Denver, Colorado, since 1979 and has written extensively on preaching. His book *Biblical Preaching* is used as a text in nearly 100 seminaries and Bible colleges in North America.

James Robison is a popular evangelist based in Fort Worth, Texas. He's the author of more than a dozen books, including *Winning the Real War.*

Gary Rosberg is a marriage and family counselor and the president of CrossTrainer Ministries, a weekly study for 500 men in central Iowa. He's also the author of *Guard Your Heart*.

Ken Ruettgers is a former offensive tackle for the Green Bay Packers and is the author of *Home Field Advantage*, which was co-authored by Dave Brannon.

Howard Rutledge spent seven years in a Vietnam prison camp. The story of those years is told in his book, *In the Presence of Mine Enemies*.

Jim Ryun was the first high schooler to break the four-minute mile and was a member of the 1964, 1968, and 1972 U.S. Olympic teams, winning a silver medal in the 1968 Mexico City Olympics. He lives in Lawrence, Kansas, with his wife, Anne, and their four children, where he ministers through Jim Ryun Running Camps.

Jerry S. and Friends in Recovery are anonymous contributors to the book *Meditations for the Twelve Steps—A Spiritual Journey*, a companion for the book *The Twelves Steps for Christians*. Jerry S. is an ordained pastor in personal recovery who, along with a group of other men, has chosen to remain anonymous as part of the tradition of twelve step recovery.

John Sandford, along with his wife, Paula, has authored several books, including *Transformation of the Inner Man, Healing the Wounded Spirit, The Elijah Task*, and *Restoring the Christian Family*.

Loren Sandford is a minister and author of *Wounded Warriors*, which recounts his struggle to come back from bitter disappointment.

Francis Schaeffer (1912–1984) was a Presbyterian minister who in 1955 founded L'Abri, an international study and ministry community in the Swiss Alps. In the following years many young adults found Christ through the ministry of Schaffer and his wife, Edith. He wrote many books, still widely read, including *Escape from Reason, He Is There and He Is Not Silent*, and *The God Who Is There*.

Dale Schlafer is vice president of Church Relations with Promise Keepers and a contributor to the bestselling book, *Seven Promises of a Promise Keeper*.

Charlie Shedd is a well-loved author of many books, including the perennial best-sellers, *Letters to Phillip* and *Letters to Karen*.

Dave Simmons, former NFL linebacker with the St. Louis Cardinals, New Orleans Saints, and Dallas Cowboys, is the founder and director of Dad the Family Shepherd, a ministry that assists the local church to equip their men to be better fathers. He's the author of a trilogy of fathering books, *Dad the Family Coach, Dad the Family Counselor*, and *Dad the Family Mentor*.

A. B. Simpson (1844–1919) was the founder of the Christian and Missionary Alliance Church and author of more than seventy books.

Gary Smalley is the author of several bestselling books, including *If Only He Knew, For Better or for Best, Joy That Lasts* and, with co-author John Trent, *The Blessing* and *The Hidden Value of a Man.*

Lewis Smedes is professor of philosophy at Fuller Graduate School of Psychology in Pasadena, California, and the author of several books, including *Forgive and Forget* and *A Pretty Good Person.*

David Smith is the British author of the book *Fasting: A Neglected Discipline.*

Oswald Smith was pastor of The People's Church in Toronto, Ontario, for many years and is the author of many books on the Christian life, including *The Man God Uses.*

Jim Smoke is the founder of Growing Free and the Center for Divorce Recovery in Tempe, Arizona. He's the author of eight books, including the bestselling *Growing Through Divorce* and *Facing Fifty.*

Chuck Snyder owns and operates an advertising agency, writing and appearing in ads for clients such as Sears and Safeway. He and his wife, Barb, have written several books.

Aleksandr Solzhenitsyn is a Nobel Prize–winning author and champion of the Russian people. He was expelled from the former Soviet Union and lived for many years in New England before his return to his native land, after the collapse of the Soviet Empire. His many works include *The Cancer Ward, The Gulag Archipelago,* and *One Day in the Life of Ivan Denisovich.*

R. C. Sproul is a popular Bible teacher and writer, with an especially vital ministry to college students. He is chairman of the board of Ligonier Ministries and professor of systematic theology and apologetics at Reformed Theological Seminary, Orlando, Florida. He's the author of many books, including *Lifeviews.*

Charles Haddon Spurgeon (1834–1892) was a highly influential preacher of the nineteenth century and a prolific writer. Many ministers consider his *Treasury of David* a must for their library.

Tim Stafford is a frequent contributor to *Christianity Today* and the author of several books, including *Knowing the Face of God* and *A Thorn in the Heart.* He also was the co-author, with Dave Dravecky, of *Comeback.*

Charles Stanley is pastor of the historic First Baptist Church in downtown Atlanta and the author of many bestselling books, including *How to Handle Adversity* and *A Man's Touch.*

Roger Staubach is a former star quarterback for the Dallas Cowboys, a popular motivational speaker, and the author of *First Down, Lifetime to Go.*

David Stoop is director of the Minirth-Meier-Stoop Clinic in southern California and the author of several books, including *Making Peace with Your Father.*

Joseph Stowell is the president of Moody Bible Institute in Chicago, Illinois and the author of several books.

Doug Stringer is the founder of Turning Point Ministries International, a ministry that has worked in more than twenty-seven nations. He's the author of *The Fatherless Generation*.

Charles Swindoll serves as president of Dallas Theological Seminary. He's also the Bible teacher on "Insight for Living," a radio broadcast ministry aired daily worldwide, and the author of many bestselling books, including *Growing Strong in the Seasons of Life*.

Jack Taylor is the president of Dimensions in Christian Living and the author of several books, including *God's New Creation* and *The Key to Triumphant Living*.

Jeremy Taylor (1613–1667) was an Anglican churchman who wrote widely. His books include *Holy Living* and *Holy Dying*.

Ken Taylor is a man of many accomplishments, including translating *The Living Bible*, founding Tyndale House Publishers, and authoring twenty-four books, including his autobiography, *My Life: A Guided Tour*.

Keith Thibodeaux is known to television viewers worldwide as "Little Ricky" Ricardo, which he played for several years on the classic sitcom "I Love Lucy." After his conversion he traveled with his Christian rock group, David and the Giants.

Brock Thoene is the manager of one of the largest Prudential Insurance agencies in central California. He's also been a financial planner for more than ten years and with his wife, Bodie, has written both historical fiction and nonfiction books. The Thoenes make their home on a ranch in California.

Thomas à Kempis (1380–1471) was the author of many devotional works, including the classic *Imitation of Christ*.

Dr. Chris Thurman is a licensed psychologist at the Minirth-Meier, Tunnel, and Wilson clinics in Austin, Texas. He's the author of *The Lies We Believe* and *If Christ Were Your Counselor*.

Lewis Timberlake is a Christian motivator and seminar speaker for Timberlake and Associates in Austin, Texas, and is the author of *Born to Win* and *It's Always Too Soon to Quit*.

Dr. Sammy Tippit is the founder and president of God's Love in Action, an international evangelistic ministry. He has written several books, including *Fire in Your Heart*.

Dr. John Townsend is co-director (with Dr. Henry Cloud) of the Minirth Meier Clinic West in Newport Beach, California. He's the author of *Hiding from Love* and, with Dr. Cloud, *Boundaries*.

Casey Treat is a pastor and author and can be seen on his Trinity Broadcasting Network (TBN) television program. He's the author of *Renewing Your Mind*, published by Harrison House.

John Trent is vice president of Today's Family and author or co-author of many bestselling books, including *The Blessing* and *The Hidden Value of a Man*.

Elton Trueblood (1900–1994) was a popular author, philosopher, and lecturer for many years. His books include *Alternative to Futility*, *The Humor of Christ*, and *The Life We Prize*.

Jeff VanVonderen is pastor at the Christian and Missionary Alliance Church of the Open Door in Minneapolis. He's the author of *Tired of Trying to Measure Up*.

Bob Vernon, Assistant Chief of Police (Ret), Los Angeles Police Department, is the author of *The Married Man* and *L.A. Justice*. He now works with Hume Lake Christian Conference Grounds at Hume Lake, California.

E. Glenn Wagner is Promise Keepers vice president of Ministry Advancement. Dr. Wagner has pastored churches in Pennsylvania, New Jersey, and Colorado. He's the author of *Strategies for a Successful Marriage* and a contributing author of *Seven Promises of a Promise Keeper*.

Walter Wangerin, Jr., is the author of several popular books such as *Ragman* and *Book of the Dun Cow*, which won an American Book Award.

George Washington (1732–1799) was a surveyor, planter, soldier, and the first president of the United States. Active in the Episcopal Church, Washington kept a personal prayer book in his field notebook from which the entry on February 22 was taken.

Dolphus Weary is president of Mendenhall Ministries, an outreach arm of Mendenhall Bible Church in Mendenhall, Mississippi, and the author of *I Ain't Comin' Back*.

Leslie Weatherhead (1893–1976) was a popular British minister in the Methodist Church during the first half of the twentieth century. He authored many books.

Stu Weber is the founding pastor of Good Shepherd Community Church in Oregon, author of a popular men's book, *Tender Warrior*, and the recipient of three bronze stars for his service as a Green Beret with the U.S. Army in Vietnam.

Daniel Webster (1782–1852), one of America's greatest orators, served as a congressman, senator, and secretary of state for three presidents.

Doug Webster is executive director of the National Instutition of Youth Ministry, a popular conference speaker, and the author of *Dear Dad: If I Could Tell You Anything*.

Noah Webster (1758–1843) is largely remembered today for his dictionary. However, Webster was also a statesman and advocate of public education, the goal of which he said was to "discipline our youth in early life in sound maxims of moral, political, and religious duties."

John Wesley (1703–1791), one of the giants of the Christian faith was the fifteenth child of Samuel and Susanna Wesley. He, along with his brother Charles and evangelist George Whitefield was instrumental in the founding of Methodism.

Ed Wheat is a physician and certified sex therapist whose books, *Intended for Pleasure* and *Love Life for Every Married Couple,* have been longtime bestsellers.

John White is a writer and speaker with a worldwide ministry. He has served as associate professor of psychiatry at the University of Manitoba. His many books include *Eros Defiled, The Fight,* and, with co-author Ken Blue, *Healing the Wounded.*

Thomas Whiteman is a licensed psychologist who speaks on relational issues around the country. He is the founder and president of Life Counseling Services in Paoli, Pennsylvania and the president of Fresh Start Seminars, a divorce recovery program for adults and children. He has worked with freelance writer Randy Petersen on several projects including, *Love Gone Wrong* and *Becoming Your Own Best Friend.*

Warren Wiersbe has served as pastor of Moody Church in Chicago, Bible teacher for "Back to the Bible" radio ministry, and is the author of more than 100 books.

David Wilkerson is a well-known evangelist and pastor. The story of his work with gangs in New York City was told in the popular book and movie *The Cross and the Switchblade.* He's the author of many books including, *The Vision, Racing Towards Judgement,* and *Set the Trumpet to Thy Mouth.*

Jim Wilson has combined military strategy with Christian living since he became a Christian during his student days at the Naval Academy in Annapolis. Now based in Idaho, Jim directs Community Christian Ministries, an organization of evangelism and social concern. He is the author of *Principles of War: A Handbook on Strategic Evangelism* from which his devotion was taken.

John Wimber has long been associated with the growing Vineyard Church movement and is the author of *Power Healing, Power Evangelism,* and *Power Points.*

Norman Wright is a licensed marriage, family, and child therapist. He has taught graduate school for more than twenty-five years and is the founder and director of Family Counseling and Enrichment and Christian Marriage Enrichment. He's the author of more than fifty books on the Christian life, including *Recovering from the Losses of Life* and *Seasons of a Marriage.*

Philip Yancey is the bestselling author of many books including *Disappointment with God* and *Finding God in Unexpected Places,* and is a regular contributor to *Christianity Today* magazine.

Ravi Zacharias is the president of Ravi Zacharias International Ministries based in Norcross, Georgia, and the author of books such as *Can Man Live Without God* and *A Shattered Visage: The Real Face of Atheism.*

Title Index

Author Index

Luther, Martin, February 15
MacArthur, Jr., John, June 1
McCartney, Bill, January 25; September 6
MacDonald, George, April 21
MacDonald, Gordon, July 5;
    December 26
McDowell, Josh, May 5
McGee, Robert, June 20
McGinnis, Alan, April 9
Mason, Mike, May 4
Mawyer, Martin, April 29
Mehl, Ron, February 10; July 20;
    October 22
Merrill, Dean, January 13; November 27
Merrill, William P., March 4
Metcalfe, J. C., September 16
Miller, Calvin, August 4
Minirth, Frank, April 22; June 12;
    June 29; July 31; December 30
Moody, Dwight L., November 7
Moore, David, March 3; December 4
Morley, Patrick, January 23; February 19;
    July 14; September 12; December 14
Morton, Tom, May 24
Murray, Andrew, September 20
Mylander, Charles, March 19
Nee, Watchman, November 20
Nelson, Alan, September 10
Nowell, David, March 23; April 24
O'Donnell, Michael, November 3
Ogilvie, Lloyd John, May 25
Oliver, Gary, August 20; October 27
Ortiz, Juan Carlos, March 22
Osterhaus, James, November 13
Owens, Jesse, August 3
Palau, Luis, February 6
Palmer, Earl, December 22
Patrick, St., March 17
Patterson, Ben, December 6
Penney, J. C., August 2
Perkins, Bill, August 9
Peterson, Eugene, March 29; June 13

Phillips, Mike, August 27; December 13
Phillips, Randy, October 30
Piper, John, January 20; June 3
Radmacher, Earl, June 10; October 29
Rainey, Dennis, September 11
Rand, Ron, March 5
Richardson, Pete, November 23
Riter, Tim, August 19
Robinson, Haddon, October 3
Robison, James, July 24
Rosberg, Gary, February 13; August 12
Ruettgers, Ken, January 5; May 7
Rutledge, Howard E., December 24
Ryun, Jim, May 31; October 31
S., Jerry, May 22
Sandford, John, April 30; June 26
Sandford, Loren, May 11
Schaeffer, Francis, March 13
Schlafer, Dale, September 13
Shedd, Charlie, October 18
Simmons, Dave, November 30
Simpson, A. B., October 20
Smalley, Gary, January 26; September 3;
    October 14
Smedes, Lewis, May 28; November 29
Smith, David, July 15
Smith, Oswald, December 10
Smoke, Jim, June 27
Snyder, Chuck, January 18
Solzhenitsyn, Aleksandr, March 1
Sproul, R. C., September 4; December 19
Spurgeon, Charles Haddon, December 17
Stafford, Tim, July 7; November 11
Stanley, Charles, June 17; July 16
Staubach, Roger, April 5; September 18
Stoop, David, February 18
Stowell, Joseph, May 15
Stringer, Doug, February 11; September
    26; October 13
Swindoll, Charles, February 17
Taylor, Jack, December 2
Taylor, Jeremy, April 20

Permissions

The editor and publisher of *Promises to Keep: Daily Devotions for Men of Integrity* wish to thank the following publishers and individuals for permission to use materials from their books:

ABINGDON

E. Stanley Jones, *A Song of Ascents;* Copyright © 1968 by Abingdon Press. Reprinted by permission.

Eric Liddell, *Disciplines of the Christian Life;* Copyright © 1985 by the estate of Florence Liddell Hall. Reprinted by permission, Abingdon Press.

Leslie Weatherhead, *The Transforming Friendship;* Copyright © 1977. Reprinted by permission, Abingdon Press.

ALBURY PUBLISHING

T. D. Jakes, *Loose That Man and Let Him Go!* Copyright © 1995 Albury Publishing. Used by permission.

AUGSBURG

Alan McGinnis, *Confidence;* Copyright © 1987 Augsburg Publishing House. Used by permission of Augsburg Fortress.

BAKER BOOK HOUSE

Bob Beltz, *The Solomon Syndrome;* Copyright © Baker Book House, 1995.

James Montgomery Boice, *Mind Renewal in a Mindless Age* by James Montgomery Boice; copyright 1993. Baker Book House.

Edward Dayton, *Succeeding in Business;* Copyright © 1992, Baker Book House.

Willard Harley, *His Needs, Her Needs;* Copyright © 1986, Baker Book House.

Dino Kartsonakis, *Dino;* Copyright © 1975, Baker Book House.

W. Phillip Keller, *Taming Tension;* Copyright © 1979, Baker Book House.

Tim LaHaye, *Understanding the Male Temperament;* Copyright © 1977, Baker Book House.

Leonard LeSourd, *Strong Men, Weak Men*; Copyright © 1990, Baker Book House.

Frank Minirth, Paul Meier, Frank Wichern, Bill Brewer, States Skipper; *The Workaholic and His Family*; Copyright © 1981, Baker Book House.

Howard Rutledge, *In the Presence of Mine Enemies*; Copyright © 1973, Baker Book House.

R. C. Sproul, *Lifeviews*; Copyright © 1986, Baker Book House.

Lewis Timberlake, *It's Always too Soon to Quit*; Copyright © 1988, Baker Book House.

David Wilkerson, *Man, Have I Got Problems*; Copyright © Baker Book House, 1969. Used by permission.

Norman Wright, *Recovering from the Losses of Life*; Copyright © 1991, Baker Book House.

BANTAM DOUBLEDAY DELL

Max DePree, from *Leadership is an Art* by Max DePree. Copyright © 1987 by Max DePree. Used by permission of Doubleday, a division of Bantam Doubleday Dell Publishing Group, Inc.

Joseph Girzone, *Never Alone: A Personal Way to God* by Joseph F. Girzone. Copyright © 1994 by Joseph F. Girzone. Used by permission of Doubleday, a division of Bantam Doubleday Dell Publishing Group, Inc.

BETHANY HOUSE

Leith Anderson, *Winning the Values War in a Changing Culture*; Bethany House; Copyright © 1994 Leith Anderson. Used by permission.

Fred Hartley, *Men and Marriage*; Bethany House; Copyright © 1994 Fred Hartley. Used by permission.

Mike Phillips, *Getting More Done in Less Time and Having More Fun Doing It*; Copyright © 1982. Used by permission.

Brock Thoene, *Protecting Your Income and Your Family's Future*; Bethany House; Copyright © 1989, William Brock Thoene. Used by permission.

Jeff VanVonderen, *Tired of Trying to Measure Up*; Bethany House; Copyright © 1989, Jeff VanVonderen. Used by permission.

BRIDGE/LOGOS

Paul Yonggi Cho, *Solving Life's Problems*; Published by Bridge/Logos. Used by permission.

Jesse Owens, *Jesse*; Published by Bridge/Logos. Used by permission.

BROADMAN AND HOLMAN

Henry Blackaby and Claude King, *Experiencing God*; Nashville: Broadman and Holman Publishers, 1990. All rights reserved. Used by permission.

Wellington Boone, *Breaking Through;* Nashville: Broadman and Holman Publishers, 1996. All rights reserved. Used by permission.

James Irwin, *To Rule the Night;* Nashville: Broadman and Holman Publishers, 1973. All rights reserved. Used by permission.

Jack Taylor, *The Key to Triumphant Living;* Nashville: Broadman and Holman Publishers, 1971. All rights reserved. Used by permission.

CHARIOT FAMILY PUBLISHING

Jim Conway, Materials from *Men In Midlife Crisis*, copyright © 1978. Used by permission of Chariot Family Publishing.

Tim Hansel, Materials from *When I Relax I Feel Guilty* by Tim Hansel, copyright © 1979. Used by permission of Chariot Family Publishing.

CHRISTIAN LITERATURE CRUSADE

Roy Hession, *Forgotten Factors*; Copyright © 1976, Used by permission.

Watchman Nee, *Song of Songs*; Copyright © 1965, Used by permission.

David Smith, *Fasting, A Neglected Discipline*; Copyright © 1954, Used by permission.

CREATION HOUSE

Mike Bickle, *Passion for Jesus* (Lake Mary, FL: Creation House, 1993. Pp. 54, 72, 102). Used by permission.

John Dawson, *Taking Our Cities for God* (Lake Mary, FL: Creation House, 1989). Used by permission.

Francis Frangipane, *The House of the Lord* (Lake Mary, FL: Creation House, 1991. Pp. 88, 105). Used by permission.

A. C. Green, *Victory* (Lake Mary, FL: Creation House, 1994). Used by permission.

Ron Kenoly, *Lift Him Up* (Lake Mary, FL: Creation House, 1995, p. 21). Used by permission.

Juan Carlos Ortiz, *Disciple* (Lake Mary, FL: Creation House, 1975, pp. 75–76). Used by permission.

James Robison, *Winning the Real War* (Lake Mary, FL: Creation House, 1991, pp. 25–26). Used by permission.

CROSSWAY BOOKS

Charles Colson, *Who Speaks for God?* by Charles Colson, copyright 1985, pp. 121–23, Used by permission of Good News Publishers, Crossway Books, Wheaton, 129–31. IL 60187.

R. Kent Hughes, *Vital Signs* by George Barna and William Paul McKay, copyright © 1984 page 51, as used in *Disciplines of a Godly Man* by R. Kent Hughes, copyright © 1991, pages 76 & 77. Used by permission of Good News/Crossway Books, Wheaton, IL 60187.

Francis Schaeffer, *Pollution and the Death of Man* by Francis Schaeffer, Copyright © 1970; pp. 74–77. Used by permission of Good News Publishers, Crossway Books, Wheaton, IL 60187.

DESTINY IMAGE

Karl Duff, *Restoration of Men*; Used by permission, Destiny Image Publishers; P.O. Box 310, Shippensburg, PA. 17257.

Keith Intrater, *Covenant Relationships*; Used by permission, Destiny Image Publishers; P.O. Box 310, Shippensburg, PA. 17257.

T. D. Jakes, *Can You Stand to be Blessed?*; Used by permission, Destiny Image Publishers; P.O. Box 310, Shippensburg, PA. 17257.

Doug Stringer, *The Fatherless Generation*; Used by permission, Destiny Image Publishers; P.O. Box 310, Shippensburg, PA. 17257.

FOCUS ON THE FAMILY

Tim Burke, *Major League Dad* by Tim and Christine Burke. Copyright © 1994, Tim and Christine Burke. Used by permission of Focus on the Family.

Gary Smalley and John Trent, *Hidden Value of a Man* by Gary Smalley and John Trent, Ph.D. Copyright © 1992 Gary Smalley and John Trent, Ph.D. Used by permission of Focus on the Family.

Seven Promises of a Promise Keeper, edited and published by Focus on the Family. Copyright © 1994, Promise Keepers. Used by permission of Focus on the Family.

John Wimber, *Power Points* by John Wimber and Kevin Springer. Copyright © 1991 by HarperSanFrancisco. Reprinted by permission of Harper-Collins.

HARRISON HOUSE
Buddy Harrison, *Man, Husband, Father* (Tulsa: Harrison House, Inc. Copyright © 1995).

Casey Treat, *Renewing the Mind* (Tulsa: Harrison House, Inc. Copyright © 1994).

HARVEST HOUSE
Bob George, *Classic Christianity* by Bob George. Copyright © 1989 by Harvest House Publishers, Eugene, OR. Used by permission.

Bob George, *Growing in Grace*, by Bob George. Copyright © 1991 by Harvest House Publishers, Eugene, OR. Used by permission.

Bill Perkins, *Fatal Attractions* by Bill Perkins. Copyright © 1991 by Harvest House Publishers, Eugene, OR. Used by permission.

INTER-VARSITY
Ben Patterson, Reprinted from *Waiting* by Ben Patterson. Copyright © 1989 by Ben Patterson. Used by permission of InterVarsity Press. P.O. Box 1400, Downers Grove, IL 60515.

Eugene Peterson, Reprinted from *Run with the Horses* by Eugene H. Peterson. Copyright © 1983 by InterVarsity Christian Fellowship of the USA. Used by permission of InterVarsity Press, P.O. Box 1400, Downers Grove, IL 60515.

KING FEATURES SYNDICATE
Bil Keane, reprinted with special permission of King Features Syndicate.

LEADER ENTERPRISES
Orel Hershiser, *Out of the Blue* by Orel Hershiser and Jerry Jenkins. Copyright © 1989. Used by permission.

MOODY
Les Carter, *Putting the Past Behind* by Les Carter. Copyright © 1989, Moody Bible Institute of Chicago. Moody Press. Used by permission.

Tony Evans, *Our God Is Awesome* by Tony Evans. Copyright © 1994, Moody Bible Institute of Chicago. Moody Press. Used by permission.

Tony Evans, *Tony Evans Speaks Out on Gambling* by Tony Evans. Copyright © 1995. Moody Bible Institute of Chicago. Moody Press. Used by permission.

George Grant, *The Micah Mandate* by George Grant. Copyright © 1994 Moody Bible Institute of Chicago. Moody Press. Used by permission.

Howard and William Hendricks, *As Iron Sharpens Iron* by Howard Hendricks and William Hendricks. Copyright © 1995, Moody Bible Institute of Chicago. Moody Press. Used by permission.

Harry Ironside, *Full Assurance* by Harry Ironside. Copyright © 1937, Moody Bible Institute of Chicago. Moody Press. Used by permission.

Jerry Jenkins, *Twelve Things I Want My Kids to Remember Forever.* Copyright © 1991. Moody Bible Institute of Chicago. Moody Press. Used by permission.

Steve Lee and Chap Clark, taken from *Boys to Men* by Steve Lee and Chap Clark. Copyright © 1995, Moody Bible Institute of Chicago. Moody Press. Used by permission.

John MacArthur, *The Family* by John MacArthur. Copyright © 1982. Moody Bible Institute of Chicago. Moody Press. Used by permission.

Frank Minirth, *How to Beat Burnout* by Frank Minirth. Copyright © 1986. Moody Bible Institute of Chicago. Moody Press. Used by permission.

Gary Oliver, *Real Men Have Feelings Too* by Gary Oliver. Copyright © 1993, Moody Bible Institute of Chicago. Moody Press. Used by permission.

James Osterhaus, *Bonds of Iron* by James Osterhaus. Copyright © 1994 Moody Bible Institute of Chicago. Moody Press. Used by permission.

Pete Richardson, *Why Christian Men Need Each Other* by Pete Richardson. Copyright © 1994, Pete Richardson. Moody Bible Institute of Chicago. Moody Press. Used by permission.

Sammy Tippit, *Fire in Your Heart* by Sammy Tippit. Copyright © 1987, Moody Bible Institute of Chicago. Moody Press. Used by permission.

E. Glenn Wagner, *We Stand Together* by Rodney Cooper. Copyright © 1995, Moody Bible Institute of Chicago. Moody Press. Used by permission.

MOORINGS

Philip Yancey, *Finding God in Unexpected Places* by Philip Yancey. Reprinted with permission of Moorings. Copyright © 1995.

Ed Cole, *Real Man*; Thomas Nelson Publishers, Copyright © 1990. Used by permission.

Russ Crosson, *A Life Well Spent*; Thomas Nelson Publishers; Copyright © 1994. Used by permission.

Ted Engstrom, with Robert C. Larson; *The Fine Art of Friendship*; Thomas Nelson Publishers; Copyright © 1985. Used by permission.

Bill Gaither; *I Nearly Missed the Sunset*; Thomas Nelson Publishers, copyright © 1992. Used by permission.

Franklin Graham, *Rebel with a Cause*; Thomas Nelson Publishers, copyright © 1995. Used by permission.

Weldon Hardenbrook, *Missing from Action: Vanishing Manhood in America*; Thomas Nelson Publishers; Copyright © 1987. Used by permission.

Jack Hayford, *A Man's Starting Place*; Thomas Nelson Publishers; Copyright © 1995. Used by permission.

Earl Henslin, *Man to Man*; Thomas Nelson Publishers; Copyright © 1993. Used by permission.

Ron Jenson, *Make a Life, Not Just a Living*; Thomas Nelson Publishers, copyright © 1995. Used by permission.

William Kirk Kilpatrick, *Psychological Seduction*; Thomas Nelson Publishers; Copyright © 1983. Used by permission.

Ben Kinchlow, *You Don't Have to if You Don't Want to*; Thomas Nelson Publishers; Copyright © 1995. Used by permission.

Dick Brian Klaver, *Men at Peace*; Thomas Nelson Publishers; Copyright © 1993. Used by permission.

Bill McCartney, *From Ashes to Glory*; Thomas Nelson Publishers; Copyright © 1995. Used by permission.

Gordon MacDonald, *Ordering Your Private World*; Thomas Nelson Publishers; Copyright © 1984. Used by permission.

Frank Minirth, Paul Meier, Don Hawkins; *Worry Free Living*; Thomas Nelson Publishers; Copyright 1989. Used by permission.

Patrick Morley, *The Seven Seasons of a Man's Life*; Thomas Nelson Publishers; Copyright © 1995. Used by permission.

Alan Nelson, *Broken in the Right Places*; Thomas Nelson Publishers; Copyright © 1994. Used by permission.

David Nowell, *A Man's Work Is Never Done*; Thomas Nelson Publishers; Copyright © 1995. Used by permission.

Dennis Rainey, *The Tribute*; Thomas Nelson Publishers; Copyright © 1994. Used by permission.

Jim Smoke, *Facing Fifty*; Thomas Nelson Publishers; Copyright © 1994. Used by permission.

Chris Thurman, *If Christ Were Your Counselor*; Thomas Nelson Publishers; Copyright © 1993. Used by permission.

Doug Webster, *Dear Dad: If I Could Tell You Anything*; Thomas Nelson Publishers, copyright © 1995. Used by permission.

Thomas Whiteman and Randy Petersen, *Becoming Your Own Best Friend*; Thomas Nelson Publishers; Copyright © 1994. Used by permission.

Warren Wiersbe, *On Being a Servant of God*; Thomas Nelson Publishers; Copyright © 1993. Used by permission.

New Leaf Press

Ron Auch, *The Heart of the King*, New Leaf Press; Copyright © 1995. Used by permission.

Ron Auch, *Taught By the Spirit*, New Leaf Press; Copyright © 1991. Used by permission.

Martin Mawyer, *Pathways to Success*, New Leaf Press; Copyright © 1994. Used by permission.

Keith Thibodeaux with Audrey T. Hingley, *Life After Lucy*; New Leaf Press; Copyright © 1994. Used by permission.

Questar

Joseph Aldrich, Excerpted from the book *Gentle Persuasion* by Joseph Aldrich; Multnomah Books, Questar Publishers; Copyright © 1988 by Joseph Aldrich.

Steve Farrar, Excerpted from the book *Point Man* by Steve Farrar; Multnomah Books, Questar Publishers; Copyright © 1990 by Steve Farrar.

Tim Kimmel, Excerpted from the book *Little House on the Freeway* by Tim Kimmel; Multnomah Books, Questar Publishers; copyright © 1987 by Tim Kimmel.

Max Lucado, Excerpted from the book *God Came Near* by Max Lucado; Multnomah Books, Questar Publishers; Copyright © 1987 by Max Lucado.

Mike Mason, Excerpted from the book *The Mystery of Marriage* by Mike Mason; Multnomah Books, Questar Publishers; Copyright © 1985 by Mike Mason.

Ron Mehl, Excerted from the book *God Works the Night Shift* by Ron Mehl; Multnomah Books, Questar Publishers; Copyright © 1994.

Luis Palau, excerpted from the book *Say Yes!* by Luis Palau; Multnomah Books, Questar Publishers; copyright 1991 by Luis Palau.

John Piper, Excerpted from the book *The Pleasures of God* by John Piper; Multnomah Books, Questar Publishers; Copyright © 1991 by John Piper.

Gary Rosberg, Excerpted from the book *Guard Your Heart* by Gary Rosberg; Multnomah Books, Questar Publishers; Copyright © 1994 by Gary Rosberg.

Ken Ruettgers, with Dave Brannon. Excerpted from the book *Home Field Advantage* by Ken Ruettgers; Multnomah Books, Questar Publishers; Copyright © 1995 by Ken Ruettgers.

Chuck Snyder, Excerpted from the book *I Prayed for Patience* by Chuck Snyder; Multnomah books, Questar Publishers; Copyright © 1989 by Chuck Snyder.

Stu Weber, Excerpted from the book *Locking Arms* by Stu Weber; Multnomah Books, Questar Publishers; copyright © 1995 by Stu Weber.

Stu Weber, Excerpted from the book *Tender Warrior* by Stu Weber. Multnomah Books, Questar Publishers; Copyright © 1993 by Stu Weber.

REGAL BOOKS

Neil Anderson, *Living Free in Christ* by Neil T. Anderson; Copyright © 1993; Regal Books, Ventura, CA 93003. Used by permission.

Gene Getz, *The Measure of a Man* by Gene Getz; Copyright © 1985; Regal Books, Ventura, CA 93003. Used by permission.

Charles Mylander, *Supernatural Living for Your Daily Race* by Charles Mylander; Copyright © 1990; Regal Books, Ventura, CA 93003. Used by permission.

Ron Rand, *For Fathers Who Aren't in Heaven* by Ron Rand; Copyright © 1987; Regal Books, Ventura, CA 93003. Used by permission.

RPI PUBLICATIONS

Jerry S. and Friends in Recovery, *Meditations for the Twelve Steps: A Spiritual Journey.* Used by permission.

SERVANT PUBLICATIONS

Dudley Hall, *Grace Works*; Servant Publications, Copyright © 1992.

Archibald Hart, *Healing for Hidden Addictions*; Servant Publications; Copyright © 1992.

VICTOR BOOKS

Ross Campbell, *How to Really Love Your Child* by Ross Campbell, published by Victor Books; Copyright © 1977, SP Publications, Inc., Wheaton, IL 60187.

Bill Hybels, *Laws of the Heart* by Bill Hybels, published by Victor Books; Copyright © 1985, SP Publications, Inc., Wheaton, IL 60187.

Haddon Robinson, *Decision Making By the Book* by Haddon Robinson, published by Victor Books; Copyright © 1991, SP Publications, Inc., Wheaton, IL 60187.

Dave Simmons, *Dad the Family Counselor* by Dave Simmons, published by Victor Books; Copyright © 1991, SP Publications, Inc., Wheaton, IL 60187.

Charles Stanley, *A Man's Touch* by Charles Stanley, published by Victor Books; Copyright © 1977, SP Publications, Inc., Wheaton, IL 60187.

Joseph Stowell, Reprinted from *Tongue in Check* by Joseph Stowell, published by Victor Books, 1983, SP Publications, Inc., Wheaton, IL 60187.

VICTORY HOUSE

John (and Paula) Sandford, *Restoring the Christian Family*, Copyright © 1979. Used by permission; Victory House Publishers, Victory House, Inc., Tulsa, OK.

Loren Sandford, *Wounded Warriors;* Copyright © 1987, used by permission; Victory House Publishers, Victory House, Inc., Tulsa, OK.

VISION HOUSE

David De Witt, *The Mature Man*; Vision House Publishers; Copyright © 1994. Used by permission.

WORLDWIDE PUBLICATIONS

Billy Graham, *A Biblical Standard for Evangelists*, by Billy Graham, copyright © 1984, Billy Graham Evangelistic Association. Used by permission.

WORD, INC.

Gordon Dalbey, *Healing the Masculine Soul*, Gordon Dalbey; Copyright © 1988 Word, Inc., Dallas, TX. All rights reserved.

Gayle Erwin, *The Jesus Style,* Copyright © 1988, Word, Inc., Dallas, TX. All rights reserved.

Greg Laurie, *Life: Any Questions?* Copyright © 1995, Word, Inc. Dallas, TX. All rights reserved.

Fred Littauer, *Wake Up Men*, Copyright © 1994, Word, Inc., Dallas, TX. All rights reserved.

Max Lucado, *When God Whispers Your Name*, Copyright © 1995, Word, Inc., Dallas, TX. All rights reserved.

Josh McDowell and Dick Day, *How to be a Hero to Your Kids*, Copyright © 1993, Word, Inc., Dallas, TX. All rights reserved.

Robert McGee, *The Search for Significance*, Copyright © 1990, Word, Inc., Dallas, TX. All rights reserved.

Michael O'Donnell, *Home from Oz*, Copyright © 1994, Word, Inc., Dallas, TX. All rights reserved.

Lloyd John Ogilvie, *If God Cares, Why Do I Still Have Problems?* Copyright © 1985, Word, Inc., Dallas, TX. All rights reserved.

Earl Palmer, *The Enormous Exception*; Copyright © 1986 Word Inc., Dallas, TX. All rights reserved.

Roger Staubach, *First Down, Lifetime to Go*, Copyright © 1974, Word, Inc., Dallas, TX. All rights reserved.

Norman Wright, *Understanding the Man in Your Life*, Copyright © 1987, Word, Inc., Dallas, TX. All rights reserved.

Ravi Zacharias, *Can Man Live without God?*, Ravi Zacharias, copyright © 1994, Word, Inc., Dallas, TX. All rights reserved.

ZONDERVAN

Paul Brand and Philip Yancey, *Fearfully and Wonderfully Made* by Paul Brand and Philip Yancey. Copyright © 1980 by Paul Brand and Philip Yancey. Used by permission of Zondervan Publishing House.

Bob Buford, Taken from *Half-Time* by Bob Buford. Copyright © 1994 by Robert P. Buford. Used by permission of Zondervan Publishing House.

Ben Carson, *Think Big* by Ben Carson. Copyright © 1992 by Ben Carson, M.D. Used by permission of Zondervan Publishing House.

Henry Cloud and John Townsend, *Boundaries;* Copyright © 1992 by Henry Cloud and John Townsend. Used by permission of Zondervan Publishing House.

Larry Crabb, *The Silence of Adam;* Copyright © 1995 by Lawrence J. Crabb, Jr., Ph.D., P.A. dba Institute of Biblical Counseling. Used by permission of Zondervan Publishing House.

Christopher de Vinck, *Simple Wonders;* Copyright © 1995 by Christopher de Vinck. Used by permission of Zondervan Publishing House.

Dave Dravecky, Taken from *When You Can't Come Back* by Dave and Jan Dravecky. Copyright © 1992 by Dave and Jan Dravecky. Used by permission of Zondervan Publishing House.

Tom Landry, taken from *Tom Landry: An Autobiography* by Tom Landry with Gregg Lewis. Copyright © 1990 by Tom Landry. Used by permission of Zondervan Publishing House.

Paul Lewis, *Five Key Habits of Smart Dads*; Copyright © 1994 by Paul Lewis. Used by permission of Zondervan Publishing House.

Dean Merrill, *The Husband Book;* Copyright © 1977 by the Zondervan Corporation. Used by permission of Zondervan Publishing House.

Charles Swindoll, *Growing Strong in the Seasons of Life;* Copyright © 1983 by Charles Swindoll, Used by Permission of Zondervan Publishing House.

Ed Wheat, *Love Life for Every Married Couple* by Ed Wheat and Gloria Okes Perkins. Copyright © 1980, 1987 by Ed Wheat, M.D. Used by permission of Zondervan Publishing House.

INDIVIDUALS

Aubrey C. Andelin, *Man of Steel and Velvet*. Published by Pacific Santa Barbara. Used by permission.

Steve Brown, *Jumping Hurdles, Hitting Glitches, and Overcoming Setbacks*. Steve Brown, KeyLife Network, P.O. Box 945000, Maitland, FL 32794. Used by permission.

Jim Carlson, *Choosing to Be Fully Alive*; Used by permission.

Nicky Cruz, *The Magnificent Three*; Nicky Cruz Outreach, P.O. Box 25070 Colorado Springs, CO 80936. Used by permission.

Jim Durkin, *The Bold Confession*; Gospel Outreach, P.O. Box 1022, Eureka, CA 95502. Used by permission.

Dale Galloway, *Rebuild Your Life*; Scott Publishing, P.O. Box 407, West Linn, OR 97068. Used by permission.

Bill Glass, *Expect to Win*; Bill Glass Ministries, Used by permission.

John Grisham, Interview in *Christianity Today* by Will Norton, Dean of the College of Journalism and Mass Communications, University of Nebraska; Lincoln. Used by permission.

Jack Hyles, *How to Rear Children*; First Baptist Church of Hammond (Indiana) P.O. Box 6448, Hammond, IN 46325. Used by permission.

Calvin Miller, *A Hunger for Meaning*; Used by permission.

Eugene Peterson, *Traveling Light*; Helmers and Howard, Colorado Springs, CO.

Earl Radmacher, *You and Your Thoughts*. Used by permission.

Jim Ryun, with Mike Phillips, *In Quest of Gold*. Used by permission.

Charlie Shedd, *A Dad Is for Spending Time With*. Used by permission.

Tim Stafford, *Knowing the Face of God*. Used by permission.

Bob Vernon, *The Married Man*. Used by permission.

Dolphus Weary, *I Ain't Comin' Back*. Used by permission.

John White and Ken Blue, *Healing the Wounded*. Used by permission.

Jim Wilson, *Principles of War*. Jim Wilson, Community Christian Ministries, P.O. Box 9754, Moscow, ID 83843.